'Gary Christopher has produced a comprehensive, informative and accessible text to understand dementia and its treatment. He combines research, academic evidence and translates theory into a highly readable book, useful for a variety of disciplinary areas and which makes essential reading for professionals and anyone studying dementia and ageing.'

Judith Phillips, *OBE, Deputy Principal (Research)*
at the University of Stirling, Professor of Gerontology,
and Research Director for the Healthy Ageing Challenge
delivered by UK Research and Innovation (UKRI)

'Although research on the dementias continues to be the poor relation of medical and psychosocial research, it covers a wide range of areas, from the biological to the sociological, and is expanding continually. Gary Christopher has bravely tackled the challenge of providing a primer that covers the breadth of research and treatment and has succeeded in producing a work that is accessible to the non-specialist and personal in its tone. By offering a research-informed context, the book serves as a useful companion to the now widely available accounts written by people living with dementia, who provide an invaluable "insider" view of the condition.'

Bob Woods, *Professor Emeritus at Bangor University*

Dementia

This book explores how our conception of dementia has changed since its initial discovery, taking in advancements in knowledge that translate into better ways to manage the condition.

Providing detailed reports of the latest research, the book explores the myriad forms of dementia. Written in accessible language, it looks at current methods of assessing and diagnosing the condition before turning to contemporary approaches to treatment. Chapters dedicated to often overlooked issues include raising awareness about how dementia affects the lives of those with an intellectual developmental disorder, the fundamental need to consider cultural differences, and the need to fully acknowledge and support informal carers. The final section of the text examines how COVID-19 has spotlighted serious gaps in healthcare for those living with dementia.

Fortified with straightforward explanations and references to clinical material throughout, the book is essential reading not only for clinical psychologists in training and those in practice seeking an overview of the field and latest developments, but for a broader audience as well.

Gary Christopher, PhD, is a gerontologist working in the Centre for Innovative Ageing at Swansea University. His research focuses on memory and emotion regulation within the context of older adult mental health. He is particularly interested in dementia as an existential threat and ways to mitigate its impact.

Dementia

Current Perspectives in Research and Treatment

Gary Christopher

Routledge
Taylor & Francis Group

LONDON AND NEW YORK

Designed cover image: Getty Image

First published 2023
by Routledge
4 Park Square, Milton Park, Abingdon, Oxon OX14 4RN

and by Routledge
605 Third Avenue, New York, NY 10158

Routledge is an imprint of the Taylor & Francis Group, an informa business

British Library Cataloguing-in-Publication Data
A catalogue record for this book is available from the British Library

Library of Congress Cataloging-in-Publication Data
Names: Christopher, Gary (Lecturer in psychology), author.
Title: Dementia: current perspectives in research and treatment / Gary Christopher.
Description: Abingdon, Oxon; New York, NY: Routledge, 2023. | Includes bibliographical references and index.
Identifiers: LCCN 2022045807 (print) | LCCN 2022045808 (ebook) | ISBN 9781138904101 (hardback) | ISBN 9781138904118 (paperback) | ISBN 9781315681580 (ebook)
Subjects: LCSH: Dementia. | Dementia—Treatment.
Classification: LCC RC521 .C4975 2023 (print) | LCC RC521 (ebook) | DDC 616.8/31—dc23/eng/20221223
LC record available at https://lccn.loc.gov/2022045807
LC ebook record available at https://lccn.loc.gov/2022045808

ISBN: 9781138904101 (hbk)
ISBN; 9781138904110 (pbk)
ISBN: 9781315681580 (ebk)

DOI: 10.4324/9781315681580

Typeset in Times New Roman
by Apex CoVantage, LLC

Contents

Acknowledgements

I have so many people to thank for their guidance and support throughout my career that I will not be able to capture them all here. My work as an academic has always been grounded in the experiences of those whose lives have been touched by dementia in so many ways. I have gained so much personally and profession-ally from working with them. It is impossible to put it into words. I continue to work with some fantastic people whose dedication to making the world a better place for people with dementia is truly astounding. This book was beset with many a setback, but Marie has always been there to motivate me. I dedicate this book to my mother, who sadly passed away in September 2020, days before her 80th birthday.

Chapter 1

What is dementia?

The context

This first chapter then asks the question, what is dementia? A simple enough question, surely. We all know what dementia is. We hear it or read about it every day in the news. I would argue, however, that what people generally refer to when talking about dementia is, in fact, a mish-mash of many things.

Dementia is a syndrome where the principal symptom is severe cognitive impairment that encompasses myriad domains, including memory, language, reasoning, and visuospatial processing, among other things (1). These are essentially the result of disease processes. We often hear people talk about Alzheimer's disease synonymously with dementia. However, this is not really accurate. Dementia is not a disease. Instead, dementia refers to symptoms of the disease process itself. As a case in point, dementia may also be caused by other conditions, such as cerebrovascular disease, as in vascular dementia. In the majority of cases, deterioration is progressive. The rate of decline varies with each person affected. In each case, while the problems may first appear relatively isolated and distinct, affecting only one or two areas of cognitive functioning, with time, impairment spreads to all aspects of a person's life.

If we wish to turn the clock back further, pre-DSM[1] even, the word *dementia* derives from the Greek, *de-mentis*, literally "out of" "mind." This verbatim translation then probably more accurately reflects the concept of dementia that many have in their head. People use the word dementia and its variants often in pejorative ways. Someone who absent-mindedly forgets where they placed their keys is not experiencing dementia. Well, at least, not in the majority of cases—and that is one of the things with dementia; it is hard to draw a line where it starts to some extent. A great deal of research money is targeted at diagnosing dementia early on so that treatments can start sooner rather than later to maximize their effectiveness. There are also conditions such as mild cognitive impairment that may or may not presage the onset of dementia. Indeed, misplacing keys is one of many indicators of something more insidious. When most of us use the term, we are merely cataloguing an instance of a slip of action, an everyday memory failing that we all experience from time to time. We must be careful about how we

DOI:10.4324/9781315681580-1

use these terms. A diagnosis of dementia is now seen as the most feared condition (2). There is even greater dread here than cancer. Cancer, in many cases, can be successfully treated; not so dementia.

After defining what we mean by dementia, we will look at how dementia has been studied throughout the centuries. I shall pay particular attention to the pivotal work of the man after which the most common form of dementia is named: Alois Alzheimer. His accurate and insightful work still holds up to close scrutiny today. Such early accounts of diseases generally make a fascinating read. After this, we will look at the spread of dementia, the costs associated with it, and the stigma accompanying the diagnosis. The final section will examine what is being done to overcome people's misconceptions around dementia.

Defining dementia

Dementia is a term much used in all walks of life today. Its adoption into ordinary parlance means it suffers the same fate as other readily accepted terms such as migraine or depression. Each refers to a severe clinical condition, yet the way it is used in everyday language to a greater extent strips it of this severity. Much in the same way people complain of a migraine when they are merely experiencing a mild headache or the fact that they say they feel depressed when they are experiencing a slightly lowered mood, people talk of dementia when referring to normal everyday lapses of memory. The term dementia has a specific meaning. As stated earlier, dementia is not a disease but rather relates to symptoms of the underlying disease process. Symptoms are severe and progressive, with cognitive decline the main symptom. Importantly, we need to be reminded that each individual is affected uniquely, depending on the location and extent of brain tissue damage.

In Chapter 3, we shall explore the various diagnoses in detail. For the time being, to more fully expand what we mean by dementia in general, one of the main overriding symptoms is difficulties with everyday memory, particularly remembering information or events that happened in the recent past. It is not just issues with memory, however. Global cognitive problems occur, with individuals experiencing difficulty concentrating, making plans, solving problems, and making decisions. Planned, sequential activity, such as cooking, becomes problematic. Visual and spatial processes are impaired, which has several significant knock-on effects in terms of being able to lead an everyday life, particularly issues around safety, especially where one considers problems judging changes in depth or distance, and general lack of orientation. Communication becomes affected with increasing problems both contributing to and following conversation. The underlying disease process targets areas of the brain that impair higher-level cognitive processes. However, it is essential to note that some more basic-level functions are also affected. These are needed so that more advanced operations can be carried out.

Of course, cognitive impairment does not happen in isolation. Several other psychological and behavioural problems occur in dementia, often bringing with them many challenges for carers, family, and friends. Emotional turmoil underpins these conditions from the initial stages, where someone feels something is not right, through to the more advanced stages of disease progression, a period often marked by severe changes in mood and heightened irritability and aggression. Many experience rather disturbing delusions and hallucinations; in other words, holding beliefs that are not based on reality and perceiving things that are not present. As expected with diseases of this nature, the severity of symptoms goes hand in hand with neurological degeneration, resulting in patients becoming increasingly restless and agitated. Alongside these more advanced stages of the condition, patients grow increasingly fragile due to the combined effect of factors, including general weakness and noticeable weight loss.

Having set out what is meant by the term dementia, the following section focuses on the early pioneering work of Alois Alzheimer. Before that, though, let us first see how earlier physicians understood the condition and what the implications were in terms of care for these vulnerable individuals.

Historical perspective

Over the centuries, there have been various words to describe conditions that we would now refer to as a form of dementia. Many conflated terms could be bes described as either organic or functional, developmental or acquired (3, 4). The included alienation, dotage, fatuitas, foolishness, idiocy, imbecility, insanity, p' e-nesis, senility, simplicity, and stupidity. It is clear that, although we have a better understanding of the causes of dementia symptoms and that such terms fell out of the medical lexicon a long time ago, one might argue that these terms still resonate somewhere in the collective consciousness. It is perhaps not rare for members of the public to still use such words to describe people with profound cognitive impairment. Not out of malice or intentional derogation, but purely because these are terms that are familiar and, to them, best describe what they are seeing. In this sense, it is no wonder the stigma around dementia is still rife.

Before we consider the pivotal work of a certain Dr Alzheimer, I would like to take a step further back in time to look at how dementia was conceptualized in very early accounts. An awareness of a severe disorder that affected memory was remarked by the ancient Egyptians more than 4,000 years ago (5). The link between ageing and poor memory was written about by Solon in the sixth century BC (6). The classical Greek scholar, Plato, suggested that dementia and growing old were synonymous, a link many still believe exists today. This claim likely prompted Cicero to argue that this was not necessarily the case (7).

Aretheus, in the second century AD, made the distinction between acute and chronic mental health disorders. Much as we define it today, acute conditions that impair thinking were seen as being reversible. Aretheus termed such states delirium. Chronic conditions of a similar nature were instead irreversible. To these, he assigned the term dementia (3). Of course, the actual term *dementia* was not coined until many centuries later. In fact, there is evidence that the word *dementia* was first used in this context in 1381 in France (8).

Skipping through the centuries to the Middle Ages, evidence of dementia in various writings was scarce. When disturbances of the mind were referred to, the explanation was invariably couched in terms of mysticism. Indeed, Bacon suggested that the origin of such disorders could be found in the original sin (9).

Fast forward another 500 years, and we start to see much more straightforward accounts of dementia, ones that resonate more closely with those we are familiar with nowadays. Pinel, the founding father of modern psychiatry, presented a detailed description of the condition.

Boller and Forbes (10) present a case for Jean Etienne Esquirol, who in his book, *Des Maladies Mentales*, lists causes of dementia (11). They argue that his thinking is often taken out of context and subsequently reviled. Instead, they propose that we consider his work within the context of the medical writers of the day. Some of the causes he listed—progression of age, paralysis, apoplexy, syphilis, mercury abuse, fears, unfulfilled ambitions, head injury—accurately reflect thinking at this time. In fact, some are far from being flights of fantasy even to modern eyes.

Quite apart from this, Esquirol penned some wonderfully descriptive accounts of dementia. One particularly poignant phrase is " 'l'homme en démence est privé des biens dont il jouissait autrefois; c'est un riche devenu pauvre." In translation, "a demented man has lost the goods he used to enjoy; he is a wealthy person turned poor." Apart from a handful of modern writers, such beautifully poetic accounts of disorders no longer grace academic texts. In no sense am I suggesting that we should romanticize mental disorders. Absolutely not. Many writers have been accused of this in the past. I am saying that, through such eloquent phrases, we often obtain a deeper understanding of the true nature of a condition. The pathos of such lines hammers home the existential challenge[2] these conditions bring to bear on the individual (12). More of that in Chapter 7.

In a pivotal work on the codification of mental illness, Griesinger proposed that all forms of mental illness are the result of a disease process (13). These conditions were seen as being progressive in nature. The climactic effect of such deterioration was the fragmentation of the self, a state that we now associate with dementia.

Alois Alzheimer

Aloysius Alzheimer (1864–1915), or Alois Alzheimer as he is more commonly referred, will always be remembered by his association with a disease we are now all too familiar with, Alzheimer's disease. Unlike many other leading lights in the early days of neurology and psychiatry, he will not be remembered as a major personality of the time. Freud and Kraepelin steal the limelight from him. However, his zeal and determination more than made up for his lack of celebrity status. His appointment in Frankfurt-am-Main at the Institute for Lunatics and Epileptic—referred to as the Irrenschloss, the castle of the lunatics—is now seen as a significant turning point in his life. It was here that he first encountered Auguste Deter, a lady who plays a vital part in this unfolding story.

The original medical records of Auguste Deter were discovered in 1995 lying untouched in the archives of Goethe University Hospital, Frankfurt (14). This unearthing by Professor Maurer has allowed us to read the original observations made by Alzheimer. They make for insightful reading. Perhaps the most haunting statement to emanate from Frau Deter's lips was the statement, "Ich habe mich verloren." I have lost myself.

Dr Alzheimer's career was forging ahead. He later moved to Munich to take up a post there. While heading a laboratory in Munich, he received a parcel from a colleague in Frankfurt. It contained the brain of Auguste Deter. She had died, aged 56, on 28 April 1906. The cause of death was likely sepsis—an inflammatory response to infection that can damage organs if allowed to advance unchecked, followed by septic shock, then death—resulting from a bedsore (15).

Along with the brain were her medical notes. Alzheimer examined her brain, assigning it Case Number 181 (16). It was clear that merely on an inspection with the naked eye, that something catastrophic had occurred. Her brain had significantly withered away. Alzheimer went on to describe the pathological changes at the neuronal level. He described the presence and thickening of fibrils, noting in particular that they formed bundles on the surface of the cells, what we now call neurofibrillary tangles. He was able to do so by using the Bielschowsky silver stain, one of the many significant advancements in histology during the latter half of the nineteenth century (17). The Bielschowsky stain helps delineate the cytoskeleton of individual neurons. In many cases, the fibrils are all that remain of the cell itself, the nucleus being completely disintegrated. He also noted deposits of a "metabolic substance" (18) inside the neuron, although he indicated that further elucidation was needed. When looking at the top layer of the cortex, Alzheimer observed the mass destruction of neurons, what we refer to now as neuritic plaques.[3]

Dr Alzheimer was the first to provide an account of what is now heralded as the three critical pathological indicators of Alzheimer's disease. From the many signs and symptoms, Alzheimer concluded that what he was seeing constituted a "special illness" (18), examples of which had been seen in increasing numbers around that time.

Alzheimer's findings were eventually reported in his paper of 1907, "Über eine eigenartige Erlranliung der Hirnrinde"[4] (English translation; 18). In this paper, Alzheimer made the observation that, although postmortem examination of Frau Deter's brain did show signs comparable to senile dementia—a term no longer used but once referred to dementia of old age—the sheer density of the plaques and tangles, in combination with the relative young age of the patient, perhaps was indicative of an as-of-yet unidentified disease. At the time, little was made of this paper.

I have always relished reading the originals of pivotal documents in the development of psychology and psychiatry, such as the original paper, "An Essay on the Shaking Palsy" by James Parkinson (19). There is an absolute joy in reading scientific papers in the style of the day. So much more entrancing than the formulaic manner of modern journal articles that we all now must adopt. Of course, there is a clear rationale why we need this in our modern age. The original paper by Alois Alzheimer is another excellent example and well worth reading to obtain a truly historical context in which to embed our understanding of this condition (20). It is presented in an excellent English translation by Stelzmann, Schnitzlein, and Reed Murtagh (18).

In his 1907 paper, aside from setting down the structural changes, Alzheimer sets out by describing the case of Frau Deter from a psychological perspective. The behaviour that first set off the chain of events was her profound jealousy of her husband. Following this, it became increasingly apparent that memory problems were becoming more dramatic. She also became increasingly disoriented in terms of time and space. She expressed fears that someone was trying to kill her. Her comprehension and understanding of what was unfolding around her were severely affected too. It was also apparent that Frau Deter experienced auditory hallucinations. Those working in the institution reported that she would often scream for hours on end. Her confusion about what was going on around her made physical examination extremely challenging. On many occasions, her initial response was to scream uncontrollably at the perceived invasion.

For me, this hammers home why we all must try to appreciate what might be at the root of certain behaviours. Faced with this situation, the carer might be surprised why the person is screaming when they are only performing a routine task. It is so irrational. However, from the perspective of someone with dementia, someone is invading their privacy for no apparent reason. So, they do what any rational person would do and protest against such perceived violation.

In terms of memory, Alzheimer observed that she could name objects but failed to retain the memory of them immediately afterwards. Reading text was chaotic in the sense that she would flit all over the place, often spelling out the words rather than reading them. The act of writing was severely affected, as was comprehension and speech. In terms of physical functioning, walking was unaffected; indeed, motor coordination, in general, was reported to be okay. Alzheimer noted a progressive increase in symptom severity over time. During the final stages, she was unresponsive and incontinent. Frau Deter died four and a half years later.

From this original paper by Alzheimer, it is clear that Frau Deter was in the throes of "progressive presenile dementia with general cortical atrophy," one that closely resembles Pick's disease (18).

The short paper setting out the case of Frau Deter is, without doubt, a pivotal moment and one that is frequently referred to. However, his 1911 article, while being more comprehensive, is less often referenced (21). The 1998 commentary by Moller and Graeber proves interesting reading (22). In this paper, Alzheimer provides an in-depth analysis of another patient, Johann F. Histological sections uncovered in the archives of the University of Munich meant that Johann's case could be analysed with all the techniques and methods available to modern researchers.

Johann F. was a male aged 56 when admitted to the hospital in 1907. He was initially diagnosed with vascular dementia, although the autopsy record designates Alzheimer's disease. The case history records that the patient had become increasingly forgetful, poor at navigating, and experienced problems with everyday tasks. He was unable to care for himself. Language production was slow, and comprehension was impaired. His ability to perform simple arithmetic was also severely affected. He showed profound disturbance in the conceptual representation of objects. Response to instructions was delayed and prone to difficulties. Again, as the weeks and months go by, Alzheimer studiously notes the increasing severity and escalation of symptoms. As with Frau D, although given the profound impairment in mental function, there was no objective evidence of physical impairment. During the final stages of his illness, JF became incontinent and increasingly experienced seizures. He became emaciated, with death occurring at the end of 1910, three years after initially being hospitalized. Pneumonia was recorded as implicated in the death.

Alzheimer noted that although plaques were present in the cortex, there was a total absence of neurofibrillary tangles. Indeed, this version of the disease, referred to as plaque dementia, may be a subgroup (23). What is remarkable, but not surprising, maybe given his reputation, is the overall accuracy and insight of Alzheimer's original clinical observations even when considered alongside the analytic paraphernalia the modern laboratory has to offer.

The condition was given the name Alzheimer's disease in 1910, appearing in Kraepelin's *Compendium der Psychiatrie*.[5] Alzheimer's work on senile dementia resulted in the field of psychogeriatrics (24). Aside from the disease with which his name will forever be synonymous, Alzheimer was responsible for advancements in our understanding of epilepsy and what was then called Huntington's chorea, among other conditions. His final post was at the University of Breslau. He died at the age of 51 in 1915 (25).

Having now an understanding of the history behind the diagnoses of dementia, the next thing to consider is how dementia presents in our modern society. We shall first look at the extent to which dementia is a concern worldwide and reflect on this in terms of the various costs associated with the condition.

Prevalence

In the UK alone, 850,000 people are living with dementia (26), and this figure rises to almost 25 million people when considered worldwide (26). Although commonly seen as a disease of old age, and indeed it is true that it is more common among those over the age of 65, dementia can hit people a great deal younger; roughly 40,000 people aged under 65 are diagnosed with dementia in the UK alone. The emotional impact on an individual and their family of a diagnosis of this nature is enormous, as is the cost associated with healthcare.

It is now recognized that dementia is a significant public health concern (27). By 2021, the prediction is that there will be over one million people with dementia in the UK alone (28). On top of this, there is still no cure, and interventions vary in how effective they are. Despite this, we should focus on helping people to "live well with dementia." The former British Prime Minister David Cameron called for "high quality, compassionate care from diagnosis through to end of life care" (29).

Costs

Although difficult to assess accurately, one estimate of the economic cost of dementia is £23 billion per annum. This figure is likely to be three times higher by 2040. The cost of dementia far outweighs that incurred by cancer, heart disease, and stroke (30). Looking at a breakdown of these costs, around £4 billion each goes to healthcare and state social care, £6 billion to individual social care, and a staggering £12 billion spent on unpaid care (31). Increasingly, more people with dementia are being admitted to hospital. A reasonable proportion of these admissions could have been prevented as they consist of acute complaints such as urinary tract infection, among other things.

As we can see, one of the most considerable costs associated with dementia is associated with informal care. There are roughly 540,000 carers in England (30). Half of them are still in employment, although many are forced to cut back on the number of hours they work to better care for their family member. Others still find themselves having to cease employment altogether in order for them to take on the role of carer full-time. On a purely monetary level, this means their standard of living is significantly lower.

Having seen the true extent of the issue worldwide, we shall focus on the impact of the stigma surrounding dementia and how it still pervades society today. After doing so, we will look at what is being done to help reduce or eliminate stigma through the various initiatives to raise awareness of dementia and develop a dementia-friendly environment.

Stigma

Although we would generally like to consign stigma to a bygone era, given that we are now living in the enlightened twenty-first century, sadly, we must admit that it still manifests in all too many places. Indeed, the pairing of the word enlightened and all it promises with our century might be seen as ill-judged, to say the least. Recent national and international events would support this. I am using the word here to refer to the vast advancements in medical science and continued growth in education across societies. However, again, we are only too aware that many fall through the gaps of progress. What is truly concerning is that stigma surrounding mental health issues is still prevalent, specifically stigma around dementia. In the ensuing sections, I shall look at what is being done to alleviate this. Still, first, it is important to examine why such feelings exist.

Probably the most recognized description of what we mean by stigma was penned by the American sociologist Erving Goffman:

> While the stranger is present before us, evidence can arise for his possessing an attribute that makes him different from others in the category of persons available, for him to be, and of a less desirable kind—in the extreme a person who is quite thoroughly bad or dangerous, or weak. He is thus reduced in our minds from a whole, and usual person to a tainted discounted one. Such an attribute is a stigma.
>
> (32)

Different cultures have their own ideas about what makes someone different: the colour of a person's skin, their accent, their beliefs, a diagnosis of dementia. Not only is stigma damaging at a societal level, from a personal level, but it also causes significant physical and emotional stress. People feel isolated, ashamed of who they are. They will likely be excluded, feel disempowered (33).

It is fair to say that a news item appears that has dementia as the focal point almost daily. Terry Jones, who died in 2020, was diagnosed with primary progressive aphasia (see Chapter 3 for more details on this condition). He is the latest in a string of icons who have been thus diagnosed. Ronald Reagan and Iris Murdoch are but two prominent figures who are forever linked to the condition. More recently, along with Terry Jones, personal heroes of mine diagnosed with dementia include the late Terry Pratchett, wordsmith extraordinaire. The singer-songwriter Glen Campbell lately penned a poignant song, *Adiós*, laying bare his awareness of what is in store. Of course, there are plenty of accounts by those who never achieved celebrity status. This evidences the determination and dignity that I believe can be found in each of us when faced with such crushing adversity.

However, having just written this, I am falling into the trap of implying that the person with dementia is suffering from the condition. It could also smack of being patronizing. For many with this diagnosis, the intention is to lead their lives in a meaningful way and be treated like anyone else. Yes, they have received a diagnosis of dementia, but they are not an embodiment of the diagnosis. They are the same person they have always been and will continue to be so. They only need others to act in accordance.

Even though the condition continues to demand high levels of media attention, understanding of dementia among the general population is still reasonably poor. A lack of knowledge of what is behind often disturbing symptoms acts as a fertile hotbed for misunderstanding and misconception. With stigma, it is never entirely clear whether a lack of understanding leads to stigma or if stigma prevents people from enquiring about a condition.

Apart from the emotional cost that stigma brings, there is a concern that it significantly affects making an early diagnosis (34). Because of the widespread stigma, people are often loath to raise concerns or seek support. Matters of this nature were reported by the International Longevity Centre UK (ILC-UK). The report identified fear—fear of loss of identity and being a burden to others—as the main reason for stigma (35). Fear of the "other" also occurs as a reaction to being faced with something unknown and different. The report also raised the concern that a more systemic problem exists, where dementia is just another aspect of the "problem" of an ageing society. So, it is not just dementia that is stigmatized but ageing in general. This is compounded by media stereotypes of dementia, depicting someone who is old and in the later stages of the condition.

Aside from encouraging people to keep quiet about their worsening problems, societal discrimination of this nature will inevitably push the person into withdrawing. With time, they become increasingly isolated and depressed. The person with dementia is seen merely as that: someone with dementia. They are the diagnosis manifest, an embodied host of dementia symptoms. They are no longer an individual. They have lost their personhood in the eyes of others (42). Of course, let us not forget that it is not just the person with the diagnosis that experiences such isolation, but also those caring for them.

Dementia awareness

We are now moving into an age that is more dementia aware, although there is much work left to do. From the perspective of the UK—although I hesitate to use this term given our current predicament surrounding Brexit—the most important political statement regarding the future of dementia care comes from the Prime Minister's challenge on dementia 2020 (29). This document makes several bold claims about its vision of the future, although underpinning much of the report is the desire to provide people with dementia, along with their carers and families, "high quality, compassionate care from diagnosis through to end of life care" (29). Other aspirations set out in this document include a plan to double research funding for dementia, to reduce waiting times for initial assessments, for all healthcare staff to have appropriate training, and most ambitious of all, for cures or disease-modifying therapies to be in place by 2025.

Dementia-friendly communities

There is a strong drive now to develop dementia-friendly communities. This is a community where people better understand the condition and know how to support someone with the diagnosis. Such initiatives are central to the notion of living well with dementia, ensuring that those with dementia remain central to community life (36). In the previous section, we talked about stigma, and how for a number of reasons, both the person with dementia and their carer tend to withdraw, becoming isolated and shut-off from others around them. The concept of dementia-friendly communities is just one way to combat this. Reinforcing that a person still remains a valuable member of a community regardless of their dementia diagnosis needs to be strengthened. Being able to retain that sense that one's life has meaning and feeling connected to others is vital to a person's well-being. This is described in more detail in a book I co-authored with my colleague, *Confronting the Existential Threat of Dementia: An Exploration into Emotion Regulation*.

The problem of dementia?

I think it essential to address the thorny issue of dementia as a problem early on. We need to view the situation through the eyes of the person with dementia rather than seeing dementia as merely a set of symptoms. In much the same way, Julian Hughes, in his excellent text, *Alzheimer's and Other Dementias* (37), questions whether the problems experienced, not only by those with dementia but also with normal ageing, should, in fact, be labelled problems. Indeed, neither age nor dementia precludes someone from experiencing a high quality of life. Even given my natural inclination as a psychologist—we who love to immerse ourselves in the disordered workings of the mind and construct ever-expanding nosology of abnormal behaviour—I hope to highlight this crucial point throughout this book.

Summary

My intent in writing this chapter was to set out what we mean by the word dementia. In doing so, we have looked at definitions of dementia from a historical perspective. We focused mainly on the groundbreaking work of Alois Alzheimer and how his careful study and efforts led us to our current understanding of Alzheimer's disease and other related dementias. We all know that dementia is now a global concern and that dementia has now superseded cancer as the most feared diagnosis. However, stigma still surrounds this condition, in part feeding the fear. There is a constant battle to eliminate stigma, as evidenced by local, national, and international initiatives to raise public awareness of dementia and create dementia-friendly spaces. I shall come back to the concept of future-proofing in the final chapter. Let me end this chapter by echoing something that I said in the previous paragraph, and that is, regardless of our knowledge of dementia, we must endeavour to keep in full sight at all times the person, not the symptoms. Only by doing so can we hope to act compassionately and afford the individuals affected with this devastating disease the dignity they deserve.

Notes

1 DSM refers to the *Diagnostic and Statistical Manual of Mental Disorders* that is published by the American Psychiatric Association (APA). In its current guise, the Fifth Edition, it is one of the main ways clinicians classify mental health conditions. It provides a common language for the codification of disorders. It is not without its critics. More of this later.

2 A book co-written with a colleague explores the concept of dementia as an existential threat. In *Confronting the Existential Threat of Dementia: An Exploration into Emotion Regulation*, we examine in depth the emotional turmoil that develops in the wake of a

diagnosis, and look at some of the psychological mechanisms that come into play to help protect an individual from distress.
3 It is important to note that such plaques had been identified previously by other physicians when examining a case other than dementia.
4 "On an Unusual Illness of the Cerebral Cortex."
5 Textbook of Psychiatry.

References

1 Kaszniak AW, Kaszniak AW. Dementia. In: Ramachandran VS, editor. Encyclopedia of the human brain, four-volume set. London: Academic Press; 2002.
2 YouGov. Alzheimer's the greatest concern for over-60s 2015. Available from: https://yougov.co.uk/topics/lifestyle/articles-reports/2015/07/26/alzheimers-greatest-concern-over-60s.
3 Donnet A, Foncin J, Habib M. Démence et vieillissement cérébral: évolution des concepts de lAntiquité à nos jours. Démences et syndromes démentiels Paris: Masson. 1991;1991:1–13.
4 Berrios GE. Dementia during the seventeenth and eighteenth centuries: A conceptual history. Psychol Med. 1987;17(4):829–837.
5 Signoret J-L, Hauw J-J. Maladie d'Alzheimer et autres démences: Flammarion médecine-sciences. France: Flammarion; 1991.
6 Freeman KJ. The work and life of Solon. Cardiff: University of Wales Press Board; 1927.
7 Cicero M. De Senectute (44 BC). Loeb Classical Library. Cambridge, MA: Harvard University Press; 1923.
8 Lanteri Laura G. Le concept opératoire de démence en médecine. Perspect Psychiatr. 1984;22(95):17–24.
9 Albert ML, Mildworf B. The concept of dementia. J Neurolinguistics. 1989;4(3–4): 301–308.
10 Boller F, Forbes MM. History of dementia and dementia in history: An overview. J Neurol Sci. 1998;158(2):125–133.
11 Esquirol E. Des maladies mentales. Chez J B Bailliere. 1838;678.
12 Cheston R, Christopher G. Confronting the existential threat of dementia: An exploration into emotion regulation. Cham: Palgrave Pivot; 2019.
13 Griesinger W. Mental pathology and therapeutics. London: New Sydenham Society; 1867.
14 BBC News. The world's forgotten first Alzheimer's patient. BBC; 2016. Available from: www.bbc.co.uk/news/av/magazine-35279750/the-world-s-forgotten-first-alzheimer-s-patient.
15 Mayo Clinic. Sepsis: Mayo Clinic; 2018. Available from: www.mayoclinic.org/diseases-conditions/sepsis/symptoms-causes/syc-20351214.
16 Lees AA. Alzheimer's: The silent plague. London: Penguin; 2012.
17 Ryan NS, Rossor MN, Fox NC. Alzheimer's disease in the 100 years since Alzheimer's death. Brain. 2015;138(12):3816–3821.
18 Stelzmann RA, Norman Schnitzlein H, Reed Murtagh F. An English translation of Alzheimer's 1907 paper, "Über eine eigenartige Erkankung der Hirnrinde". Clin Anat. 1995;8(6):429–431.

19 Parkinson J. An essay on the shaking palsy. London: American Psychiatric Publishing, Inc.;1817. Available from: https://neuro.psychiatryonline.org/doi/full/10.1176/jnp.14.2.223.

20 Alzheimer A. Ueber eine eigenartige Erkrankung der Hirnrinde. Allgem Zeit Psychiatrie Psychisch-Gerichtliche Med. 1907;64:146–148.

21 Alzheimer A. Über eigenartige Krankheitsfälle des späteren Alters. Zeitschrift für die gesamte Neurologie und Psychiatrie. 1911;4(1):356–385.

22 Möller H-J, Graeber M. The case described by Alois Alzheimer in 1911. Eur Arch Psychiatry Clin Neurosci. 1998;248(3):111–122.

23 Terry RD, Hansen LA, DeTeresa R, Davies P, Tobias H, Katzman R. Senile dementia of the Alzheimer type without neocortical neurofibrillary tangles. J Neuropathol Exp Neurol. 1987;46(3):262–268.

24 Porter R. Madness: A brief history. Oxford: Oxford University Press; 2002.

25 Roy Porter, editor. The Hutchinson dictionary of scientific biography. Abington: Helicon. Alzheimer, Alois (1864–1915).

26 Who gets dementia? Alzheimer's Society; 2017. Available from: www.alzheimers.org.uk/info/20007/types_of_dementia/1/what_is_dementia/4.

27 Alzheimer's Society's view on public health, prevention and dementia: Alzheimer's Society; 2014. Available from: www.alzheimers.org.uk/about-us/policy-and-influencing/what-we-think/public-health-prevention-dementia?documentID=2766.

28 Dementia UK. London: Alzheimer's Society; 2014. Available from: https://www.alzheimers.org.uk/about-us/policy-and-influencing/dementia-uk-report.

29 Prime Minister's challenge on dementia 2020. In: Office PMs, editor. London: Cabinet Office; 2015.

30 Dementia: NHS England; 2018. Available from: www.england.nhs.uk/mental-health/dementia/.

31 Public Health England. Dementia: Applying all our health. Gov.UK; 2018. Available from: www.gov.uk/government/publications/dementia-applying-all-our-health/dementia-applying-all-our-health.

32 Goffman E. Stigma: Notes on the management of spoiled identity. London: Simon and Schuster; 2009.

33 Mason-Whitehead E. Stigma. In: SAGE key concepts: Key concepts in palliative care [Internet]. London: SAGE; 2010. Available from: https://search.credoreference.com/content/entry/sageukjlcz/stigma/0.

34 Alzheimer's Research UK. Report highlights social stigma surrounding dementia 2014. Available from: www.alzheimersresearchuk.org/report-highlights-social-stigma-surrounding-dementia/.

35 Bamford S, Holley-Moore G, Watson J. New perspectives and approaches to understanding dementia and stigma. International Longevity Centre; 2014. Available from: https://ilcuk.org.uk/wp-content/uploads/2018/10/Compendium-Dementia.pdf.

36 Alzheimer's Society. What is a dementia-friendly community? Alzheimer's Society; 2019. Available from: www.alzheimers.org.uk/get-involved/dementia-friendly-communities/what-dementia-friendly-community.

37 Hughes JC. Alzheimer's and other dementias. Oxford: Oxford University Press; 2011.

Chapter 2

Is dementia part of the normal ageing process?

Is it inevitable?

In no way is dementia part of normal or typical ageing. It is not a given that you will develop one of these conditions once you reach a certain age. The symptoms experienced by those with dementia far exceed in severity the types of difficulties faced by those who experience cognitive problems associated with age. Having said that, age is a significant risk factor. By the very fact that a person ages, the likelihood of developing dementia increases with each successive year. This is because our destiny is primarily the result of the admixture of genetic predisposition and environmental effects. This is something we cannot escape. However, the point is, dementia is not an inevitability.

When you examine the ageing brain, several changes occur across the board. The most important given the current context of dementia is the presence of plaques and tangles in the brains of typically ageing adults (1). Given that this pathology is a vital component for a positive diagnosis of Alzheimer's disease, one might see this as evidence that dementia is unavoidable. Fortunately, this is not the case. Although such pathological changes are present in the ageing brain, they do not herald the onset of Alzheimer's disease. The majority remain symptom-free for the duration of their lives. This does, however, pose a significant problem for researchers as there does not seem to be a clear-cut distinction between the brain of a healthy older adult and one who will later develop a neurodegenerative disease (2).

Having now taught classes on memory impairment for many years, I often find solace in the knowledge that young, healthy undergraduates experience the same foibles of memory that we all complain about from time to time. The classic is entering a specific room for a particular reason, then experiencing confusion about why you are there. Such everyday memory failures can occur for many reasons. For most of us, because our minds are full of things that we need to do, we often find our focus of attention being enticed away from our current train of thought. When this happens, we become confused. Take the example just mentioned. You need to go upstairs to retrieve your reading specs when a beep informs you that you have a reminder on your phone. You immediately turn your attention

DOI:10.4324/9781315681580-2

to the prompt, as you do. The reminder has prompted your memory to remember to do something, but the thing you need to do now has been lost in that very act. You might not be aware of that until you find yourself in a room in another part of the house without the foggiest reason why you are there. The irony of the situation is lost on you because you are miffed, quite rightly, that you have sauntered upstairs without knowing why. So, you head back downstairs to continue reading that remarkable book that you have been engrossed in. That one by Christopher: *The Psychology of Ageing: From Mind to Society*, or something like that. You are foiled in this activity. Well, you need your reading spectacles, don't you? And where are your reading spectacles? Upstairs, of course. You ease out of your chair with a huff and head towards the stairs. A beep from your phone announces a reminder. Ah, yes, I need to read that joyful book. You have time. Excellent. You sit down to read it at last, but, nooooooo, you need your reading glasses. The only thing to benefit from all this is the step-counter thing that you have on your wrist.

It is only human nature that our own explanations for such cognitive failures differ at each stage of our life. These lapses can be seen as merely symptomatic of our busy lives as young adults. Inevitably, as we age, we start to experience concern that there is something more insidious going on. The occasional error is likely due to age, but what then if it occurs more frequently? Is it presaging the onset of dementia? If we start doubting our own memory, worry ensues, and worry competes for our attention, taking away vital resources that we need, thus leading to more problems. This can quite quickly turn into a vicious cycle of burgeoning self-doubt.

Sometimes, the extent to which problems with memory occur warrants further investigation. For some, this might result in receiving a diagnosis of mild cognitive impairment (MCI). Diagnosis of MCI does not mean that dementia will naturally follow. With MCI, people tend to forget things more frequently than others of their age. They may find it difficult sometimes to follow what someone is saying and may, on occasion, find difficulties navigating around a familiar environment. However, overall independence is not affected. On the contrary, age often brings with it myriad ways to offset such challenges. We are great at compensating for lapses in behaviour and thought. Older adults have a lifetime's worth of experience to draw upon.

Subjective cognitive decline is increasingly seen as an early indicator of accelerated deterioration in mental functioning (3). As the name implies, reports are entirely personal. Although potentially significant when considering early detection of dementia, there needs to be a note of caution. This is because the types of impairment reported could be due to a host of other factors affecting the individual. These could include depression, anxiety, general health problems, and chronic conditions (4, 5). At the moment, there is inadequate consensus on what constitutes subjective cognitive decline and which measures are most appropriate to use (3).

Now that we have seen that dementia is not inevitable, we shall spend some time identifying some of the significant risk factors that alone or in combination act to increase the risk that someone might actually develop dementia. Such risk factors are wide-ranging, and this is by no means an exhaustive list. It should be pointed out that these may, in fact, be risk factors for some but not for others. Individual susceptibilities have a role to play alongside this. With this knowledge, we can help put into place strategies and interventions to reduce risk, be it at the global or individual level.

Risk factors

It is clear then that dementia is not an inevitable part of ageing. Having said that, we cannot escape the fact that age is a significant risk factor for dementia. Our knowledge about what we can do to reduce the likelihood of developing dementia grow almost daily. As with many conditions, some relatively simple changes to one's lifestyle can lead to marked improvements in health-related outcomes. It is important to note that not all factors are amenable to change. We cannot prevent ourselves from ageing, for example, much to our chagrin. We have yet to identify the elixir of life.

First off, a couple of definitions. Risk refers to the likelihood of a specific event happening. A risk factor by its presence increases the probability of someone developing a particular condition. As with most things, avoiding or reducing risk factors does not necessarily mean a person will not develop a disease, much in the same way that having certain risk factors does not mean it is inevitable that a person will develop the condition. The interplay between biological predisposition and the environment is central in determining who develops (or does not develop) what disease when. Given the range of potential risk factors, no two individuals will be alike in terms of whether or not they develop dementia and what factors played a crucial role in this outcome.

Before looking at the individual risk factors, we need to consider the issue of causality here. Large-scale epidemiological studies provide evidence about risk factors. Being linked to a condition is not the same as causing it. Indeed, the direction of the effect is also uncertain to some extent. In other words, is it the case that a particular risk factor increases the likelihood of dementia or is it that dementia increases the chances of developing that risk factor, or maybe both. Therefore, it is crucial to identify the possible mechanism underlying these changes. Clinical trials are effective at helping garner insight into such what-if scenarios. Much of the evidence so far gathered has focused on the three most common diagnoses of dementia, namely Alzheimer's disease, vascular dementia, and mixed dementia (see Chapter 3 for more information about these), not surprising given their prevalence.

Age

We have already indicated that dementia is not inevitable once we reach a certain age. However, we cannot get away from the fact that the older we are, the more likely becomes our chance of developing dementia. The risk of developing either Alzheimer's disease or vascular dementia doubles every five years once one has reached the age of 65. That is 1 in 14 over 65, 1 in 6 over 80 (6). Innumerable changes occur as we age, many of which influence health outcomes. I provide a more detailed account of this in my book on ageing (1) that I may have mentioned previously.

Aside from the visible changes that occur with age, the efficiency with which our internal systems functions are also affected. Age changes the functioning of the endocrine system—which controls a range of bodily functions—by altering levels of various hormones. There is evidence to show that levels of cortisol rise as we age. Cortisol prepares the body to respond to stress. Such elevated levels have been linked to neuronal depletion within the hippocampus, leading to increasing deficits in cognitive function (7, 8). Control of the sleep–wake cycle is affected by changing melatonin levels (9). Disturbances to our sleep pattern have several knock-on effects, including lower overall levels of alertness and concentration.

The brain itself alters with age, both physically and functionally. Take, for example, the cerebral cortex. The cortex consists of two hemispheres connected by the corpus callosum. Each region is associated with different functions. The left hemisphere is associated with language, the right with visuospatial activities (10). Efficiency of processing declines with age. As a result, such hemispheric specialization decreases. This is because comparable structures in contralateral hemispheres are recruited to support activities to compensate for deficits in function.

The frontal lobe theory of ageing argues that activity within the prefrontal and medial-temporal regions is reduced (11). This has important implications for cognition, as the frontal lobes underpin much of what we describe as cognitive function. Among other things, the encoding of new information is less efficient. It is important to note that, although this is the case, the explanation seems to be that older adults tend not to use effective strategies when processing new material. When instructed to do so, deficits disappear. It is not the case that they cannot do it; it is merely that they choose less effective ways of doing things as default (12). Again, this might be a way of compensating for age-related changes. In other words, they reduce the level of cognitive load.

Contrary to the argument that activation within the frontal lobes reduces with age, evidence suggests the opposite. It seems to be the case that over-recruitment of related sites occurs when performing specific tasks. Again, the explanation here seems likely to be one of compensation (13).

Changes in the operation of various neurotransmitter pathways seem to be at the root of many diseases of old age. Levels of acetylcholine decline with age. Because of its centrality to a range of cognitive operations, reduced levels are linked to increasing deterioration in function (14).

Neurofibrillary tangles are essential for a positive diagnosis of Alzheimer's disease. Strands of cytoplasm—neurofibrils—cluster together within neurons. Their presence destabilizes communication between cells and the transportation of vital nutrients. Proteins also aggregate to form neuritic plaques. At their heart is the protein fragment β-amyloid. These disrupt neural transmission and result in localized cell death.

Sex and gender

For the majority of dementia, there does seem to be a sex bias (15). Both age and sex are major risk factors for dementia. Unlike other risk factors, such as diet, which are modifiable, neither age nor sex is (16). It is important to briefly define what we mean by the terms "sex" and "gender" before exploring this further. Sex refers to the chromosomal make-up of the individual. Females are XX, males XY. Gender, on the other hand, reflects a person's social identity, traditionally separated into male and female. However, this fails to consider transsexualism and androgyny (17).

A good summary of the sex differences in the different dementias is presented by Podcasy and Epperson (16). Women are twice as likely to develop Alzheimer's disease as men. However, men tend not to live as long following diagnosis. Although risk factors for vascular dementia are more common in men, the impact of these risk factors is more severe in women. Mixed dementia is more common in men. Dementia with Lewy bodies is more prevalent in men, and deterioration in cognitive function is more rapid in men. Parkinson's disease dementia is higher in men with more severe cognitive impairment. Frontotemporal dementia is more common in men, although there are no sex differences in terms of survival. In the case of Creutzfeldt–Jakob disease, no sex differences have been reported.

In the case of Alzheimer's disease, there is a higher prevalence in women than in men. The reverse pattern is shown for men and vascular dementia. The presence of the ε4 alleles of the apolipoprotein ε4 gene (APOE ε4) in women is linked to them being at a higher risk of developing Alzheimer's disease compared to men with the same allele (18). Also, the same study showed higher levels of disinhibited behaviour for women with this allele. It might also be the case that women suffer hippocampal atrophy faster than men (19).

There are apparent sex differences generally in how different dementia diagnoses manifest. In the case of men, there is more evidence of overt aggression, higher levels of comorbidity, and higher mortality rates. For women, emotional disturbances are more prominent, as are levels of disability. Still, they tend to live longer than men (20).

Ethnicity

There is much-needed work looking at the role of ethnicity in dementia, be it in terms of risk or how the condition is conceptualized and supported. I have dedicated Chapter 10 to exploring some of these cross-cultural differences.

Genetics

Much as I love genetics and bioscience in general, I am a cognitive psychologist. Geneticists may wish to look away now.

Evidence from many studies has isolated more than 20 genes that impact the risk of developing dementia. However, with conditions like dementia, having this, that, or other genes will not mean that dementia is inevitable for us. Conditions develop through complex interactions between our age, the way we have led our life, our health, as well as our genetic heritage.

Genes are the fundamental components of heredity, the transmission of genetic material from parents to offspring (21). We each possess about 30,000 genes. Genes occur on chromosomes, of which we have 23 pairs, one of which determines our biological sex. Genes exert their influence by controlling the production of proteins. Genetic variation is the norm. We all share the same genes, but there are slight variations in the coding across individuals.

Most of this variation in DNA coding has little if any real consequence on our lives. However, sometimes, it does. It may make us at a higher risk for developing certain conditions. Genes can mutate and thereby cause a range of genetic disorders (22). Genetics may work differently. It might be the case that a person inherits a faulty gene. This is rare. Such genetic mutations have dramatic effects, even to the point of directly causing a specific disease to develop. This is rare in dementia, but it does happen (23).

Apolipoprotein E

Apolipoprotein E, or ApoE, is the best-known genetic risk factor, specifically risk gene, for dementia. ApoE is concerned with synthesizing a protein involved in ensuring neurons are healthy. ApoE is one of the proteins that convey cholesterol through the blood, controlling the uptake of cholesterol and lipids into cells. It exists in three forms. ApoE4 is linked to higher levels of low-density lipoprotein (LDL) cholesterol. Because of this, the risk of coronary heart disease is doubled (24). Those who receive one copy of ApoE4 are faced with a threefold risk of developing Alzheimer's disease at a much younger age. A small minority obtain two copies of this gene. The chances of this group developing the condition are increased eight times (23).

Presenilin

On rare occasions, people can develop Alzheimer's disease at a much earlier age, sometimes in their 50s. The pathology of early-onset Alzheimer's disease is not entirely clear at this stage. Some cases are due to the presence of a faulty gene that has been passed down. At the moment, three such abnormal genes have been implicated here: amyloid precursor protein (APP), presenilin 1 (PSEN1), presenilin 2 (PSEN2). All three are linked to the generation of amyloid, insoluble proteins that stick together to form fibrils. The faulty gene results in an accumulation of this substance in the brain. A build-up of this nature is a defining feature of Alzheimer's disease (23).

Tau and progranulin

Frontotemporal dementia is a less common form of dementia. This condition has several distinct forms (see Chapter 3 for more detail). For some, there is evidence of heritability. This is particularly the case for the behavioural variant of this condition. Three genes have been linked explicitly to the inheritance of this form of dementia: tau (MAPT), progranulin (GRN), C90RF72. Tau is increasingly linked to dementia. A mutated tau gene causes the tau protein to clump. Where this occurs, neurons and their connections are damaged. It is less clear what the mechanisms are for progranulin and C90RF72. However, the latter gene is implicated in motor neuron disease and frontotemporal dementia (23).

CADASIL

Vascular dementia, on the whole, is influenced by the presence of genes that increase a person's risk of stroke and heart disease. Numerous lifestyle factors impact here. However, there are rare genetic disorders that result in vascular dementia. Cerebral autosomal dominant arteriopathy with subcortical infarcts and leukoencephalopathy—CADASIL for short—is one such mutation that damages blood vessels in the brain (23).

Amyloid precursor protein

Down's syndrome is intimately linked to dementia. People with this condition are born with an additional stretch of DNA. This includes an extra copy of the amyloid precursor protein (APP) gene. As seen earlier, this results in an abnormal level of amyloid building up in the brain.

Medical conditions

A balanced, healthy life is essential for reducing various risk factors that have been linked to dementia. It will also help reduce the likelihood of developing other acute or chronic health conditions (25). Here we will explore some of the medical conditions associated with dementia in some way.

Blood pressure

Hypertension is a condition where a person's blood pressure is chronically raised above the norm. It is a significant contributor to stroke and heart attack. Sustained high blood pressure induces strain on arteries and leads to arteriosclerosis.

Arteriosclerosis describes the wide-scale thickening of arteries and a loss in elasticity. Fats in the blood lead to them forming deposits on the wall of the arteries, the net result of which is they become narrower. Arteries can become blocked, in which case a person experiences an ischaemic stroke. Arteries may burst, a condition described as a haemorrhagic stroke. Less dramatic events may also occur, but with the outcome being comparable. Smaller blood vessels may become either blocked, or microbleeds occur. The person to whom this is happening may be unaware of this. However, with time, the steady accrual of damage resulting from these small bleeds do eventually manifest in noticeable impairment. This is described as small vessel disease. Much of the evidence suggests that high blood pressure during middle-adulthood increases the likelihood that a person will develop dementia, particularly vascular dementia, later on (26, 27). After Alzheimer's disease, vascular dementia is the most common form of dementia. It occurs following areas of the brain being starved of oxygen due to a lack of blood flow to that region. Just as a matter of balance, hypotension—low blood pressure—has also been implicated in dementia. The evidence for this tends to be among the old-old.

Cardiovascular disease

Cardiovascular disease is an umbrella term for conditions that affect the circulatory system (28). In general, where there is a build-up of tau and Aβ proteins, a reduction in cerebral blood flow will accentuate any cognitive deficits that are present. Coronary artery disease—narrowing of arteries—is strongly associated with dementia, particularly small vessel disease (29).

Atrial fibrillation is a condition where a person's heart beats irregularly and rapidly. It is a risk factor for ischaemic stroke. Atrial fibrillation does contribute to the onset of dementia, even when stroke is absent (30). Atrial fibrillation increases a person's likelihood of experiencing cerebral infarction and transient ischaemic attacks; in other words, brief stroke-like events (31).

Aortic and mitral valve disease appears to be also linked. This is a condition where the heart valves separating the atrium and ventricle do not close particularly tightly, resulting in a backflow of blood into the atrium during heart contractions. Pressure increases, raising blood pressure. The resultant effect is an increase in fluid build-up in the lungs. The presence of such valvular calcification increases the risk of infarcts, thereby leading to an increased risk of stroke and cognitive decline (32).

Heart failure occurs when the heart cannot supply the body with enough blood and oxygen to meet its demands. The mechanism linking this with dementia is unclear at the moment (33). Heart failure increases the risk of cerebral emboli—blood clots in the brain—and so is linked to greater cognitive impairment (34).

Diabetes mellitus

Diabetes mellitus is one of the most potent risk factors for dementia (35). It is a common condition. With diabetes, the body is no longer able to regulate glucose levels in the blood. Because of this, high levels of blood glucose ensue. This occurs because the body can no longer respond appropriately to the presence of insulin. Insulin is a hormone that controls blood sugar levels. It might be the case that the pancreas cannot produce sufficient quantities of insulin, thus providing another mechanism whereby diabetes develops. Diabetes has been linked to cortical brain atrophy (36). The insulin-degrading enzyme (IDE) results in reduced levels of insulin. There is also evidence showing that it degrades Aβ (37). In people with Alzheimer's disease, levels of IDE are significantly reduced (38). This would link to the accumulation of Aβ seen in this condition.

Cholesterol

Hypercholesterolemia refers to an accumulation of fats in the blood. There is a debate still over the potential link between cholesterol levels and dementia. Because of that, little advice can be given concerning possible treatment options (39).

Obesity

Obesity is an ever-increasing global concern. We know that a person's body mass index (BMI)—a ratio of weight and height used to assess whether or not a person scores within the healthy range—is linked to heart disease and that heart disease is linked to dementia. There is some evidence to suggest high BMI during mid-life may increase the risk of dementia later on (40).

Sleep apnoea

There is a suggestion that sleep apnoea might be a risk factor for dementia. Sleep apnoea is a condition where a person's airways are obstructed during sleep. Breathing and, as a result, sleep are interrupted. It often goes undetected. The only indication is excessive tiredness throughout the day. A recent study offering evidence for a link is fraught with problems (41), thereby making it impossible at this stage to draw any firm conclusion (42).

Hearing loss

Evidence surfaced recently that indicated that those who experienced hearing loss tended to be at higher risk of developing dementia (43, 44). However, it was not clear why this might be the case. Arguments abound and include explanations based on cognitive load, among others (45). In terms of the cognitive load hypothesis, the idea is that as hearing becomes poorer, a higher proportion of the finite mental resources is reallocated to processing auditory information. Because of this, other activities are adversely affected, and that with time, this will lead to dementia (46). There is another argument based on a psychosocial explanation.

With hearing loss, communication becomes increasingly difficult. This has a negative impact on relationships. It may even lead to social isolation (47). Some argue that this loss of social interaction leads to dementia. We shall return to the issue of social isolation shortly.

Oral hygiene

Several claims have been made that gum disease increases the risk of developing dementia later on (48). Chronic periodontitis refers to inflammation of the tissues supporting teeth. If not treated, it can lead to gum damage and tooth loss. The mechanism is unclear. It is unknown how microbes in the gums affect an inflammatory response in the brain, increasing the risk of dementia. However, given the potential for a link here, it is imperative that oral hygiene is maintained throughout life and effectively monitored and reinforced after a diagnosis of dementia. We need to remember to brush our teeth regularly to keep this up. In someone with severe cognitive impairment, this is unlikely.

Psychological conditions

Depression

There is a complicated relationship between pseudodementia, vascular dementia, and apathy (49). The overlap of symptoms across depression and the early stages of dementia is significant. This makes accurate diagnosis extremely difficult. Pseudodementia refers to a condition with no organic basis for the observed impairment. The impairment is reversible once a person receives the appropriate treatment. Subjective memory deficits may help differentiate depression from dementia. Although present in both conditions, subjective memory complaints in those with dementia tend to be associated with better objective function (50).

Due to the nature and severity of the cognitive deficits seen in people with depression, it is better to associate the impairment with depression rather than seeing them as a form of pseudodementia. In fact, it might be the case that these symptoms presage the onset of dementia later on in life (51).

Cerebrovascular disease appears to play an important role in all this. It seems to cause and sustain depression in some cases (52), although the relationship is unclear again.

Apathy is present in both depression and dementia. It is defined as a lack of feeling, a general indifference. Apathy increases as symptoms of dementia become more severe. However, depression, as we have seen, decreases. Because of this, from a clinical standpoint, it is crucial to consider apathy in isolation from the other symptoms of depression in such cases (53). This is vital as apathy seems important for cases where someone with mild cognitive impairment later develops dementia. These are referred to as conversions. Apathy is present to a higher degree in those who undergo this conversion (54).

Loneliness and social isolation

It has been suggested that loneliness and social isolation can lead to dementia (55). The problem with this and similar types of research is that it is challenging to tease out whether loneliness is a risk factor for dementia or whether social withdrawal is a reaction to increasing cognitive impairment.

Neurological conditions

Parkinson's disease

Parkinson's disease is a progressive neurological condition characterized by people exhibiting a tremor at rest, slowed movement, difficulty initiating action, and muscle rigidity (56). Those with this condition are at a higher risk of developing dementia during the later stages of the illness. When this does occur, a person shows marked memory impairment and an inability to carry out most everyday tasks. They may be prone to emotional outbursts and obsessional behaviour (57). Visual hallucinations may occur. Parkinson's disease dementia accounts for 2 per cent of dementia diagnoses (57).

Multiple sclerosis

Multiple sclerosis (MS) is a chronic inflammatory condition that attacks the central nervous system. Sometimes called disseminated sclerosis, it is a disease that damages the myelin sheath that protects cells in the brain and spinal cord. It also strikes cells that produce the myelin in the first instance (58). Myelin is a fatty substance. The sheath is interrupted regularly by the presence of nodes of Ranvier. It is at these points neural impulses speed down the nerve axon. Speed of transmission is higher in myelinated fibres. As such, myelinated fibres are said to propagate neural impulses (59). People with MS experience problems with memory and concentration, but not to the same extent as seen in dementia. Emerging evidence might suggest a link between MS and dementia (60). The association at this stage is far from robust.

HIV

For some with HIV or AIDS, cognitive impairments may occur at more advanced stages of the condition. HIV, or human immunodeficiency virus, weakens a person's immune system. It is described as a retrovirus (61). AIDS stands for acquired immune deficiency syndrome. It is caused by HIV (61). The infection can affect brain functions, known as HIV-associated neurocognitive disorder (HAND). Symptoms tend to be milder than those seen in dementia. Before effective antiretroviral drugs were available, about a third of those with HIV developed dementia. The figure now stands around 2 per cent (62).

Learning disabilities

In Chapter 8, we shall explore this in more detail. An important thing to note at this stage is that specific learning disabilities increase the likelihood that someone will also develop dementia later on (63). This is especially the case for those diagnosed with Down's syndrome.

Education

Numerous studies have been conducted to explore the relationship between educational attainment and dementia. One review of this literature indicated that poorer education attainment was linked to dementia for many of the studies. However, this was not so in all cases (64). One problem with these studies is how the researchers define and operationalize education. The main explanation behind the link between education and dementia is that those who have attained higher levels of education will have more cognitive reserve. Cognitive reserve is the mental equivalent of functional reserve seen in organs of the body. For example, someone who has exercised regularly and eaten a balanced diet will have a higher cardiac reserve than someone who has led a sedentary life eating junk food. As a result, they will be more able to bounce back from a heart attack. A similar case is made for cognitive reserve. If one has had a strong record of education, compared to someone who has not, they will be able to better compensate for the declines one generally associates with age. It will also mean they will be better able to offset some of the more advanced cognitive impairments associated with dementia, at least for a more extended period. However, as one might expect, the relationship between education and dementia is not simple, and many confounds need to be considered before making confident claims here. I shall come back to this in Chapter 10 when I consider the literature on bilingualism.

Lifestyle

In a subsequent chapter, we shall explore how lifestyle changes can improve the chances of living well with dementia (see Chapter 11). However, here, we shall focus on the evidence for the role of poor lifestyle choices in the development of dementia. Notably, those who adopt healthy behavioural routines during mid-life have a lower risk of dementia later. The usual suspects make up this group: regular physical exercise, a nutritious diet, drinking in moderation, and not smoking.

Physical exercise

We shall explore physical activity later in Chapter 11. Certainly, more evidence suggests physical exercise is superior in its effectiveness than the various brain training programmes that abound (65). Physical exercise helps cognitive function on several levels (66). There is a general disagreement around what type of exercise is best and how long and how regularly we should all aim to engage in it. However, not all evidence is positive. Some argue against the neuroprotective effects of exercise (67). However, findings have been confounded by a reduction in physical activity years before the diagnosis of dementia occurred (68).

Diet

As we shall see in later sections when we explore the different forms of dementia, various deficiencies in diet can have severe long-term consequences (see Chapter 3). A balanced diet is linked to better overall health. We all know the effects of not eating well. Weight loss is prevalent in dementia. This can be for several reasons, including a general lack of appetite, problems recognizing hunger, and difficulties chewing and swallowing (69).

Aside from food, there is an issue with drinking. Ensuring that people with dementia do not become dehydrated is essential. This is because they may not recognize they are thirsty, or they may not be able to communicate their thirst to others. They may indeed forget to drink regularly (69). Not maintaining a sufficient level of hydration will lead to headaches, mental confusion, urinary tract infection, and constipation. All these will accentuate some of the dementia symptoms. Ensuring this does not happen will also reduce the likelihood that a person with dementia will require emergency care, which is incredibly distressing for someone who experiences problems with confusion and orientation and is, in many cases, entirely preventable.

Alcohol intake

In much the same way as nutrition can affect mental health, alcohol misuse over time can increase a person's likelihood of developing dementia. Chronic excess of alcohol can result in vascular damage occurring within the brain. However, as with many risk factors, the actual relationship between it and dementia is unclear. It is likely, as always, to be a combination of factors all interacting with each other. In the case of people who drink heavily, there is the added likelihood that they are also smokers, experiencing depression, and leading less than healthy lifestyles (70).

Although there is much made of the negative role of alcohol, quite rightly so, there is also some evidence that alcohol may help reduce risks (see Chapter 11).

The issue of alcohol and whether it is good or bad is a prime example of how media reporting of study results can lead to wholesale confusion either through sensationalized reporting of less than conclusive findings or intentional misrepresentation. Some days, a whiff of alcohol is bad; others that alcohol is to be embraced at all cost. The toing-and-froing of advice is more nausea-inducing than having that one sherry too many. People need to be presented with a considered, consistent message; otherwise, they are likely to lose faith in medical science.

Smoking

Smoking increases the risk of developing dementia (71). However, as with most if not all risk factors, just because you smoke does not mean you will definitely develop the condition. The primary mechanism involved here is the cerebrovascular system. We know smoking increases the risk of heart disease and stroke, which itself is a risk factor for Alzheimer's disease and vascular dementia in particular (see section "Medical conditions"). On top of this is the effect of various toxins that appear in cigarette smoke. These toxins have been linked to increased oxidative stress and inflammation, both of which are linked to Alzheimer's disease. Oxidative stress results from ineffective neutralization by antioxidants of the impact of free radicals. Free radicals are released when bonds in stable molecules are broken (72). Free radicals cause localized damage by affecting the oxygen level of cells (73). However, findings from studies exploring this are not without problems. For one, there are lifestyle issues to consider. In a similar argument to what has already been stated for alcohol, people who smoke tend to consume more alcohol, and alcohol is itself a risk factor (74).

Head injury

In a recent paper reporting findings from a cohort study, evidence pointed to brain injury being associated with an increased risk of dementia (75). This is an important piece of research. Evidence suggests that the absolute increase in risk is relatively small at this stage. Research of this nature has sparked off much debate, such as concern about which games are acceptable to be played at school.

While dementia cannot be cured, we now realize there is a chance that the onset of some forms of dementia may be either prevented or postponed. This is because the risk of developing dementia results from a range of highly individual and complex interactions between our genes, the environment, and our lifestyle. From a disease prevention point of view, it has been estimated that about one-third of cases of Alzheimer's disease can be explained as being due to factors that could be modifiable (76); in other words, elements that we have some control over. Aside from depression, known potentially modifiable factors include diabetes, hypertension, obesity, inactivity, and, of course, smoking.

Making changes relatively early on in a person's life could have dramatic effects later. Even relatively simple alterations in behaviour could drastically reduce a person's risk of developing dementia. Changes that reduce risk early on can profoundly affect the overall number of people who develop dementia (76). For instance, one consistent public health message is that "What is good for your heart is good for your brain" (77–79). Thus, simple steps like reducing levels of obesity, changing one's diet, and taking more exercise can all play a role in reducing the risk of developing dementia in years to come. If steps such as these mean that it proves possible to delay the onset of dementia by five years, then by 2030, the number of predicted cases of dementia in the UK would be reduced by over a third, and that equates to almost half a million people who do not develop dementia.

Summary

Hopefully, by now, you feel that the popular misconception that dementia is an inevitable part of ageing has been put to rest if it was even there in the first place. A great deal of the chapter has focused on identifying risk factors for dementia; in other words, what increases the chances that we might develop the condition. One thinks immediately of genetics, specifically hereditary predisposition. We have seen that, although genetics does indeed play a role, as with most conditions, it is more complicated than whether we have a specific gene or a combination of genes. Instead, whether a person develops dementia depends on a host of factors all interacting with one another. One might be genetically predisposed to a condition, but it is only when exposed to other elements that the disease will develop. Age itself, however, is a significant risk factor for dementia. We explored various medical, psychological, and neurological conditions that play a role in dementia in some detail. Lifestyle and education were also considered. The impact of these last two is probably somewhat familiar to all who read this. This is because we cannot seem to escape the almost daily barrage of news headlines that proclaim the danger or protective value—usually danger—of some food item, diet, exercise routine, or alcoholic beverage in relation to developing dementia. Much of this should be taken with a pinch of salt, although salt is also bad for you, so not too much. You could confidently predict that today's terror-inducing headline that Foodstuff A causes dementia will be declared tomorrow as a significant way to defend against the disease. As always, it is essential to go behind the headlines. This is why websites such as the NHS's *Behind the Headlines*[1] are so valuable in revealing the scientific truth hidden behind the media gloss.

Note

1 www.nhs.uk/news/

References

1 Christopher G. The psychology of ageing: From mind to society. Basingstoke, Hampshire: Palgrave Macmillan; 2014.
2 Hughes JC. Alzheimer's and other dementias. Oxford: Oxford University Press; 2011.
3 Rabin LA, Smart CM, Crane PK, Amariglio RE, Berman LM, Boada M, et al. Subjective cognitive decline in older adults: An overview of self-report measures used across 19 international research studies. J Alzheimers Dis. 2015;48(s1):S63–S86.
4 Comijs HC, Deeg DJ, Dik MG, Twisk JW, Jonker C. Memory complaints; the association with psycho-affective and health problems and the role of personality characteristics. A 6-year follow-up study. J Affect Disord. 2002;72(2):157–165.
5 Boone KB. Fixed belief in cognitive dysfunction despite normal neuropsychological scores: Neurocognitive hypochondriasis? Clin Neuropsychol. 2009;23(6):1016–1036.
6 Alzheimer's Society. Concerned about someone else's memory problems? 2017. Available from: www.alzheimers.org.uk/site/scripts/documents_info.php?documentID=102.

7 Angelucci L. The glucocorticoid hormone: From pedestal to dust and back. Eur J Pharmacol. 2000;405(1–3):139–147.

8 Comijs HC, Gerritsen L, Penninx BW, Bremmer MA, Deeg DJ, Geerlings MI. The association between serum cortisol and cognitive decline in older persons. Am J Geriatr Psychiatry. 2010;18(1):42–50.

9 Mahlberg R, Tilmann A, Salewski L, Kunz D. Normative data on the daily profile of urinary 6-sulfatoxymelatonin in healthy subjects between the ages of 20 and 84. Psychoneuroendocrinology. 2006;31(5):634–641.

10 FilleyCM.Neuroanatomy[cited26July2012].In:Encyclopediaofthehumanbrain[Internet]. Elsevier Science [cited 26 July 2012]; 2002. Available from: www.credoreference. com/entry/esthumanbrain/neuroanatomy.

11 Grady CL, McIntosh AR, Horwitz B, Maisog JM, Ungerleider LG, Mentis MJ, et al. Age-related reductions in human recognition memory due to impaired encoding. Science. 1995;269(5221):218–221.

12 Logan JM, Sanders AL, Snyder AZ, Morris JC, Buckner RL. Under-recruitment and nonselective recruitment: Dissociable neural mechanisms associated with aging. Neuron. 2002;33(5):827–840.

13 Park DC, Reuter-Lorenz P. The adaptive brain: Aging and neurocognitive scaffolding. Annu Rev Psychol. 2009;60:173–196.

14 Katz S, Peters KR. Enhancing the mind? Memory medicine, dementia, and the aging brain. J Aging Stud. 2008;22(4):348–355.

15 Mazure CM, Swendsen J. Sex differences in Alzheimer's disease and other dementias. Lancet Neurol. 2016;15(5):451–452.

16 Podcasy JL, Epperson CN. Considering sex and gender in Alzheimer disease and other dementias. Dialogues Clin Neurosci. 2016;18(4):437–446.

17 Abbey A, Saenz C, Parkhill M, Parkhill M, Jr. Gender. In: Loue S, Sajatovic M, editors. Encyclopedia of women's health. Springer Science & Business Media; 2004.

18 Altmann A, Tian L, Henderson VW, Greicius MD. Alzheimer's disease neuroimaging initiative I. Sex modifies the APOE-related risk of developing Alzheimer disease. Ann Neurol. 2014;75(4):563–573.

19 Ardekani BA, Convit A, Bachman AH. Analysis of the MIRIAD data shows sex differences in hippocampal atrophy progression. J Alzheimers Dis. 2016;50(3):847–857.

20 Sinforiani E, Citterio A, Zucchella C, Bono G, Corbetta S, Merlo P, et al. Impact of gender differences on the outcome of Alzheimer's disease. 2010;30(2):147–154.

21 The Penguin dictionary of psychology. London: Penguin Press; 1995.

22 Marcovitch H. Black's medical dictionary. 43rd/edited by Harvey Marcovitch. London: Bloomsbury Information; 2017.

23 Alzheimer's Research UK. Genes and dementia. Alzheimer's Research UK; 2018. Available from: www.alzheimersresearchuk.org/about-dementia/helpful-information/ genes-and-dementia/.

24 Wilson PW, Myers RH, Larson MG, Ordovas JM, Wolf PA, Schaefer EJ. Apolipoprotein E alleles, dyslipidemia, and coronary heart disease. The Framingham Offspring Study. JAMA. 1994;272(21):1666–1671.

25 Calder PC, Carding SR, Christopher G, Kuh D, Langley-Evans SC, McNulty H. A holistic approach to healthy ageing: How can people live longer, healthier lives? J Hum Nutr. 2018;31(4):439–450.

26 Kennelly SP, Lawlor BA, Kenny RA. Blood pressure and dementia—a comprehensive review. Ther Adv Neurol Disord. 2009;2(4):241–260.

27 Kennelly SP, Lawlor BA, Kenny RA. Blood pressure and the risk for dementia: A double edged sword. Ageing Res Rev. 2009;8(2):61–70.

28 Dictionary of medical terms. London: Bloomsbury; 2015.

29 Newman AB, Fitzpatrick AL, Lopez O, Jackson S, Lyketsos C, Jagust W, et al. Dementia and Alzheimer's disease incidence in relationship to cardiovascular disease in the Cardiovascular Health Study cohort. J Am Geriatr Soc. 2005;53(7):1101–1107.

30 Sabatini T, Frisoni GB, Barbisoni P, Bellelli G, Rozzini R, Trabucchi M. Atrial fibrillation and cognitive disorders in older people. J Am Geriatr Soc. 2000;48(4):387–390.

31 Vermeer SE, Prins ND, den Heijer T, Hofman A, Koudstaal PJ, Breteler MM. Silent brain infarcts and the risk of dementia and cognitive decline. N Engl J Med. 2003;348(13):1215–1222.

32 Oliveira-Filho J, Massaro AR, Yamamoto F, Bustamante L, Scaff M. Stroke as the first manifestation of calcific aortic stenosis. Cerebrovasc Dis. 2000;10(5):413–416.

33 Justin BN, Turek M, Hakim AM. Heart disease as a risk factor for dementia. Clin Epidemiol. 2013;5:135–145.

34 Pullicino PM, Hart J. Cognitive impairment in congestive heart failure? Embolism vs hypoperfusion. Neurology. 2001;57(11):1945–1946.

35 Ott A, Stolk RP, van Harskamp F, Pols HA, Hofman A, Breteler MM. Diabetes mellitus and the risk of dementia: The Rotterdam Study. Neurology. 1999;53(9):1937–1942.

36 Schmidt R, Launer LJ, Nilsson LG, Pajak A, Sans S, Berger K, et al. Magnetic resonance imaging of the brain in diabetes: The Cardiovascular Determinants of Dementia (CASCADE) Study. Diabetes. 2004;53(3):687–692.

37 Farris W, Mansourian S, Chang Y, Lindsley L, Eckman EA, Frosch MP, et al. Insulin-degrading enzyme regulates the levels of insulin, amyloid beta-protein, and the beta-amyloid precursor protein intracellular domain in vivo. Proc Natl Acad Sci U S A. 2003;100(7):4162–4167.

38 Qiu WQ, Folstein MF. Insulin, insulin-degrading enzyme and amyloid-β peptide in Alzheimer's disease: Review and hypothesis. Neurobiol Aging. 2006;27(2):190–198.

39 Vance JE. Dysregulation of cholesterol balance in the brain: Contribution to neurodegenerative diseases. Dis Model Mech. 2012;5(6):746–755.

40 Fitzpatrick AL, Kuller LH, Lopez OL, Diehr P, O'Meara ES, Longstreth WT, et al. Midlife and late-life obesity and the risk of dementia: Cardiovascular health study. Arch Neurol. 2009;66(3):336–342.

41 Cross NE, Memarian N, Duffy SL, Paquola C, LaMonica H, D'Rozario A, et al. Structural brain correlates of obstructive sleep apnoea in older adults at risk for dementia. Eur Respir J. 2018;52(1).

42 NHS. Is sleep apnoea a risk factor for dementia? NHS; 2018. Available from: www.nhs.uk/news/neurology/sleep-apnoea-risk-factor-dementia/.

43 Lin FR, Metter EJ, O'Brien RJ, Resnick SM, Zonderman AB, Ferrucci L. Hearing loss and incident dementia. Arch Neurol. 2011;68(2):214–220.

44 Amieva H, Ouvrard C, Giulioli C, Meillon C, Rullier L, Dartigues JF. Self-reported hearing loss, hearing aids, and cognitive decline in elderly adults: A 25-year study. J Am Geriatr Soc. 2015;63(10):2099–2104.

45 Thomson RS, Auduong P, Miller AT, Gurgel RK. Hearing loss as a risk factor for dementia: A systematic review. Laryngoscope Investig Otolaryngol. 2017;2(2):69–79.

46 Pichora-Fuller MK, Schneider BA, Daneman M. How young and old adults listen to and remember speech in noise. J Acoust Soc Am. 1995;97(1):593–608.

47   Weinstein BE, Ventry IM. Hearing impairment and social isolation in the elderly. J Speech Lang Hear Res. 1982;25(4):593–599.
48   Chen CK, Wu YT, Chang YC. Association between chronic periodontitis and the risk of Alzheimer's disease: A retrospective, population-based, matched-cohort study. Alzheimers Res Ther. 2017;9(1):56.
49   Muliyala KP, Varghese M. The complex relationship between depression and dementia. Ann Indian Acad Neurol. 2010;13(Suppl 2):S69–S73.
50   Dementia Research Group. Subjective memory deficits in people with and without dementia: Findings from the 10/66 Dementia Research Group Pilot Studies in low-and middle-income countries. J Am Geriatr Soc. 2009;57(11):2118–2124.
51   Ganguli M. Depression, cognitive impairment and dementia: Why should clinicians care about the web of causation? Indian J Psychiatry. 2009;51(Suppl 1):S29.
52   Alexopoulos GS, Meyers BS, Young RC, Campbell S, Silbersweig D, Charlson M. 'Vascular depression' hypothesis. Arch Gen Psychiatry. 1997;54(10):915–922.
53   Panza F, Frisardi V, Capurso C, D'Introno A, Colacicco AM, Imbimbo BP, et al. Late-life depression, mild cognitive impairment, and dementia: Possible continuum? Am J Geriatr Psychiatry. 2010;18(2):98–116.
54   Vicini Chilovi B, Conti M, Zanetti M, Mazzù I, Rozzini L, Padovani A. Differential impact of apathy and depression in the development of dementia in mild cognitive impairment patients. Dement Geriatr Cogn Disord. 2009;27(4):390–398.
55   Holwerda TJ, Deeg DJ, Beekman AT, van Tilburg TG, Stek ML, Jonker C, et al. Feelings of loneliness, but not social isolation, predict dementia onset: Results from the Amsterdam Study of the Elderly (AMSTEL). J Neurol Neurosurg Psychiatry. 2014;85(2):135–142.
56   Jahanshahi M. Parkinson's disease. In: Ayers S, Wallston KA, editors. Cambridge handbook of psychology, health and medicine. Cambridge: Cambridge University Press; 2007.
57   Alzheimer's Society. Parkinson's disease: Alzheimer's Society. Available from: www.alzheimers.org.uk/about-dementia/types-dementia/parkinsons-disease?gclid=Cj0K CQjw6fvdBRCbARIsABGZ-vQcUry7GxkY31AeTqmkU_mIeqqCndJT4UOOEF-AZ-PQRkmk9PSOuzIaAqxhEALw_wcB.
58   Alzheimer's Society. Multiple sclerosis: Alzheimer's Society; 2019. Available from: www.alzheimers.org.uk/about-dementia/types-dementia/multiple-sclerosis.
59   The Penguin dictionary of psychology. London: Penguin Press; 1995.
60   MS Society. MS and dementia. MS Society; 2017. Available from: www.mssociety. org.uk/research/latest-research/latest-research-news-and-blogs/ms-and-dementia-whats-the-evidence#.
61   Saunders VA, Margham JP, Hale WGCdb. Collins dictionary of biology. Rev. and updated 3rd ed. London: Collins; 2005.
62   Alzheimer's Society. HIV-related cognitive impairment. Alzheimer's Society; 2019. Available from: www.alzheimers.org.uk/about-dementia/types-dementia/hiv-cognitive-impairment.
63   Alzheimer's Society. Learning disabilities and dementia. Alzheimer's Society; 2019. Available from: www.alzheimers.org.uk/about-dementia/types-dementia/learning-disabilities-dementia.
64   Sharp ES, Gatz M. Relationship between education and dementia: An updated systematic review. Alzheimer Dis Assoc Disord. 2011;25(4):289–304.

65   Ahlskog JE, Geda YE, Graff-Radford NR, Petersen RC, editors. Physical exercise as a preventive or disease-modifying treatment of dementia and brain aging. Mayo Clinic Proceedings. 2011;86(9):876–884.
66   Erickson KI, Hillman CH, Kramer AF. Physical activity, brain, and cognition. Curr Opin Behav Sci. 2015;4:27–32.
67   Sabia S, Dugravot A, Dartigues JF, Abell J, Elbaz A, Kivimäki M, et al. Physical activity, cognitive decline, and risk of dementia: 28 year follow-up of Whitehall II cohort study. BMJ. 2017;357:j2709.
68   Alibrahim A. Effects of physical activity in dementia: Is it neuroprotective? Response to physical activity, cognitive decline, and risk of dementia: 28 year follow-up of Whitehall II cohort study. BMJ; 2017;357:j2709.
69   Alzheimer's Society. Eating and drinking. Alzheimer's Society; 2019. Available from: www.alzheimers.org.uk/get-support/daily-living/eating-drinking.
70   BBC. Alcohol and dementia: What's the truth? BBC; 2018. Available from: www.bbc.co.uk/news/health-43141457.
71   World Health Organization. Tobacco and dementia. World Health Organization; 2014. Available from: https://www.who.int/publications/i/item/WHO-NMH-PND-CIC-TKS-14.1.
72   Cristofalo VJ, Tresini M, Francis MK, Volker C. Biological theories of senescence. In: Bengtson VL, Schaie KW, editors. Handbook of theories of aging. New York: Springer; 1999, pp. 98–112.
73   Lu T, Finkel T. Free radicals and senescence. Exp Cell Res. 2008;314(9):1918–1922.
74   Alzheimer's Society. Smoking and dementia. Alzheimer's Society; 2019. Available from: www.alzheimers.org.uk/about-dementia/risk-factors-and-prevention/smoking-and-dementia.
75   Fann JR, Ribe AR, Pedersen HS, Fenger-Grøn M, Christensen J, Benros ME, et al. Long-term risk of dementia among people with traumatic brain injury in Denmark: A population-based observational cohort study. Lancet Psychiatry. 2018;5(5):424–431.
76   British Psychological Society Dementia Advisory Group. Psychological dimensions of dementia: Putting the person at the centre of care. Leicester: The British Psychological Society; 2016.
77   Alzheimer's Society's view on public health, prevention and dementia. Alzheimer's Society; 2014. Available from: www.alzheimers.org.uk/about-us/policy-and-influencing/what-we-think/public-health-prevention-dementia?documentID=2766.
78   Lincoln P, Fenton K, Alessi C, Prince M, Brayne C, Wortmann M, Patel K, Deanfield J, Mwatsama M. Blackfriars Consensus on promoting brain health: Reducing risks for dementia in the population. London: UK Health Forum; 2014.
79   Dementia: Applying all our health. Public Health England; 2018. Available from: https://www.gov.uk/government/publications/dementia-applying-all-our-health/dementia-applying-all-our-health

Chapter 3

Forms of dementia

Disease or symptom?

The use of the term 'dementia' can be misleading. Instead, it is best to conceive dementia as a syndrome with myriad symptoms of disparate origins (1). Common across all diagnoses of dementia is a sense of overarching cognitive decline that affects all aspects of a person's behaviour (2). That is the dementia being described. Dementia is the symptom, not the cause; it is a disease that causes dementia. Even within diagnostic categories, there is heterogeneity. The variety and severity of symptoms vary significantly from patient to patient. Then, of course, there is the issue of mixed dementia. This makes the dementias very difficult to diagnose with any accuracy.

DSM-5

Dementia is classified in the DSM-5 (3) under neurocognitive disorders (NCDs). The principal area of impairment is cognitive function. Importantly, cognitive impairment occurs later in life rather than being present at birth. In other words, the dysfunction is acquired rather than developmental. To this extent, one can observe a marked decline in function from the usual. Unlike different DSM categories, those appearing under NCDs have a specified disease pathology and aetiology. With NCDs, dementia is under the sub-classification of major neurocognitive disorder. The term *dementia* is still used as it is something with which both clinicians and patients are familiar. The term *neurocognitive disorder* is the term generally used for conditions affecting younger adults, referring to conditions linked to traumatic brain injury, among other things. In this chapter, I shall continue to use the more familiar terms while at the same time making a clear link between these and current DSM-5 terminology. Before looking in detail at each diagnosis, I shall describe some of the key aspects of the DSM-5 structure used to define and explain each condition. I shall start by examining what is meant by neurocognitive domains.

Neurocognitive domains

There are several cognitive domains of operation affected to varying extents by the different diagnoses within NCDs. These include complex attention (e.g., divided

DOI:10.4324/9781315681580-3

attention), executive function (e.g., planning), learning and memory (e.g., immediate memory), language (e.g., fluency), perceptual-motor (e.g., visual perception), and social cognition (e.g., emotion regulation). Each of these will be described in more detail in the following sections. The DSM-5 refers to mild or major instances of each diagnosis.

Complex attention refers to a range of activities that we all carry out non-stop throughout our lives. It covers actions where we need to (1) keep our attention on something for extended periods (sustained attention), (2) focus down on something to the exclusion of everything else (selective attention), and (3) keep track of more than one thing at a time (divided attention). Those who experience mild problems with such activity tend to take longer to perform routine tasks and to make more errors. More severe impairment makes one prone to distractions in the environment, less able to keep information in one's mind, and generally slower in performing mental tasks.

Executive function is fundamental to adaptive living. It is a set of higher-order cognitive processes. Executive function lies behind our ability to (1) carry out related activities in the proper order to achieve a particular goal (planning), (2) choose an appropriate course of action from various alternatives (decision-making), (3) generate a solution and utilize feedback in an attempt to resolve an issue (problem-solving), and (4) stop ourselves from being distracted by information that is not relevant to the task at hand (inhibition). Executive function enables us to be flexible and adaptive in all situations. Those manifesting mild impairment in executive function experience greater difficulty working through tasks that require several discrete stages to be completed. They tend to experience fatigue as a result of such activity. For those who have severely impaired executive function, it is necessary to merely focus on one action at a time. Distractibility is a significant problem. Planning ahead is next to impossible. As a result, people with severe executive impairment become increasingly reliant on others to help them through their daily existence.

It is important to note that semantic (general knowledge), autobiographical (life experiences), and implicit (outside of conscious awareness) memory are mostly unaffected in all but the most severe forms of NCDs. It is memory for recent events that are most obviously disrupted. Mild symptoms concern problems recalling things that happened recently. There is an increasing reliance on *aide-memoire*. When issues become more severe, people often find themselves repeating what they have just said in a conversation. There is a constant need to use prompts to make sure they remain on-task. The ability to lay down new memories is much affected.

When a person starts to experience problems with language, it becomes pretty evident to those around them. Experiencing increasing difficulty remembering peoples' names is an example of the milder end of symptom spectrum. When the problems become more severe, the person suffers from global language impairment. Echolalia and embolalia (automatic speech)—repetition of what someone has said and overuse of filler words and phrases respectively—often occur, frequently as a prelude to mutism, characterized by an inability to speak.

When people start to find themselves lost in familiar environments, it is evidence of mild impairment in perceptual-motor functioning. Evidence for more severe impairment comes from a person's increasing inability to drive, for example. Praxis—a person's ability to sequence a series of related activities—and gnosis—one's ability to recognize objects through their senses such as touch—are increasingly affected as the disease progresses.

Social cognition is also affected. In other words, the individual's ability to this time navigate a range of social situations successfully. Initially, others might detect a subtle change in someone's personality. They increasingly become less empathic, less inhibited, and less able to read the subtle visual cues we all rely on. As the illness progresses and symptoms intensify, people start to behave in socially unacceptable ways, and decisions are made without recourse to concerns with safety.

Having looked at the various domains of cognitive functioning, we shall look at the specific diagnoses that make up this category.

Specific diagnoses

It is not the aim of this section to cover all diagnoses under NCDs. I shall refer to the more familiar names for each of these conditions, but also make explicit links to the current terminology adopted by the DSM-5. Before doing so, let us look at how the DSM-5 presents each diagnosis.

Major or mild neurocognitive disorders

As indicated earlier, the main characteristic of all these conditions is a decline in function from what would be expected in one or more of the domains of cognitive functioning listed previously. At the less severe end of the scale, a person's ability to perform everyday tasks is not affected significantly. When symptoms are more severe, all aspects of a person's life are affected. People may experience behavioural disturbance, such as symptoms of psychosis or agitation.

The DSM-5 refers to subtypes in its classification. Many NCDs are subtyped in accord with the underlying pathology, such as the presence of Parkinson's disease. In other words, there is a known cause for the condition. Alternatively, for other NCDs, diagnosis is based entirely on the cognitive, behavioural, and functional symptoms that occur. Such NCDs include frontotemporal lobar degeneration.

Some NCDs are associated with specific behavioural symptoms, referred to as specifiers, the most obvious being psychotic symptoms and depression. Psychotic symptoms are present in several NCDs, especially in Alzheimer's disease, Lewy body disease, and frontotemporal lobar degeneration. In such instances, people experience a combination of delusions and hallucinations. Delusions are often persecutory in nature, with paranoia being particularly dominant in some cases. Hallucinations can occur, with visual hallucination being most common, although hallucination can occur in other modalities. Unlike conditions such as schizophrenia, there is no evidence of disorganized speech or behaviour.

Mood might also be affected in this condition, specifically elation, anxiety, and depression. As might be expected with a diagnosis of NCD, depression often occurs at the early stages of the condition, primarily due to the presence of Alzheimer's disease or Parkinson's disease. Elation is associated mainly with fronto-temporal lobar degeneration.

Agitation—movement or utterances deemed troublesome—is present in many cases of NCDs. This is particularly the case when symptoms are more severe, a response, in many cases, to increased feelings of confusion and frustration, or indeed some unmet need. Also, problems with sleep often accompany NCDs, such as insomnia—the inability to sleep—or hypersomnia—general drowsiness that is not due to a lack of sleep. The person might also show apathy—a general lack of motivation—a condition common in Alzheimer's disease.

A range of other behavioural symptoms also occurs in NCDs. Wandering is seen as being a particular problem. More about this and other symptoms in later chapters. The person may become more disinhibited as the disease progresses. They might demonstrate hyperphagia—increased appetite—as well as hoarding behaviour.

Diagnostic features

Major NCD is the equivalent to the DSM-IV diagnosis of dementia. Cognitive deficits seen in this condition are acquired and so are not present at birth. One should not use objective tests in isolation when making diagnoses in this area. This is because the findings can be misleading for many reasons. It might very well be the case that a person, on performing such measures, does not appear cognitively impaired. This might not be an accurate reflection of their situation. Indeed, if one had access to and were able to consider their prior level of performance, that person's current functioning might be markedly below that seen previously. Because of their earlier level of high functioning, they were able to perform at an adequate level on various assessments, thereby not raising any concern in the clinician. Conversely, if one is unaware of the person's premorbid level of functioning, which is the usual state of affairs, a person performing poorly on such tests of cognitive functioning might be misdiagnosed as exhibiting NCD when, in fact, it might be the case that such poor performance is usual for them and that the snapshot seen in clinic does not represent a significant decline in function.

Likewise, one should not rely solely on subjective ratings. These, too, can mislead the clinician. A person may report high symptomology but may be functioning adequately. They may be one of the "worried well" (3). This is a term used to describe people who are in good health yet express concern over a particular issue (4). That is not to say that worrying is bad in this context. Worry can be advantageous if it is channelled and used constructively. Being concerned about one's health often means one can reduce risks for developing certain conditions. However, in all too many cases, people tend to worry about things that do not apply to them.

Alternatively, a person may be showing a marked decline in their ability to function on a daily basis yet be completely unaware of these difficulties. In such cases, the person shows no insight into their condition and so cannot report problems even though they are occurring. Linked to this is a condition, anosognosia. This describes a position where a person is unaware of neurological impairment.

As we have seen, there are several limitations to both subjective and objective assessments of functioning. Therefore, it is crucial to elicit information from spouses and/or family. They are often better placed to identify patterns of behaviour that indicate a change in the person's ability to function in routine tasks. However, this is not always the case, especially in the milder forms of the condition. Slight changes in how a person behaves might be explained as mere symptoms of growing older rather than indications of something more serious. Also, we are all excellent at masking or hiding our failings. Where changes from the norm are evident, the clinician should then determine whether these indicate changes in cognitive functioning itself or whether the symptoms are due instead to increasing impairments in either sensory processing or motor function.

In the case of major neurocognitive disorder, the impairments here are sufficiently severe to lead to a marked reduction in independence, with the person becoming increasingly reliant on the support of others to achieve what they could once accomplish on their own. For minor neurocognitive disorder, independence is retained, although more effort is needed to successfully complete routine tasks.

The premise behind the current DSM diagnosis of major or mild neurocognitive disorder is that there is no real clear distinction between the two diagnoses. Rather, NCDs should be seen as existing along a continuum.

Development

How a particular NCD develops depends on the cause of the condition. In the case of stroke, the stroke itself leads to the impairment, and there is no further escalation unless the person were to experience additional cerebrovascular accidents. With Alzheimer's disease, one characteristic is that its onset is described as insidious. In this sense, there is no obvious single point where one can denote a clear connection between an event and a subsequent cognitive decline. Instead, the progress of the disease is gradual, with initial symptoms being relatively subtle. The types of symptom clustering that occur distinguish between the different subtypes of these conditions.

In cases where the diagnosis of NCD occurs at a later age, in many circumstances, existing medical conditions are implicated in the picture, as is increasing frailty and deficits in sensory perception. These factors make it increasingly difficult for the clinician to perform an accurate diagnosis.

Age at onset is important here. This is because changes in cognitive function are more easily pinpointed in younger adults. The changes are more noticeable. This may be because they are in mid-career and have to deal with the daily pressures of holding down a job and supporting a family. The opposite is the case in older adults, where escalating cognitive impairment may not be a cause of any particular concern. At the mild end of the neurocognitive disorders, change in functioning might easily be explained as merely symptomatic of growing older. Indeed, it is difficult to distinguish what is undoubtedly the effects of typical ageing from symptoms that might indicate the prodromal phase—the initial manifestation of a problem before the sheer enormity is fully realized—of a more severe NCD.

Having looked in some detail at how the DSM-5 presents the various diagnoses under the auspices of NCD, we shall now turn our attention to these specific diagnoses. For the diagnoses included under NCD, I will follow the format laid out in the DSM-5, presenting information about specific diagnostic features, how the condition develops over time, diagnostic markers, prevalence, and risk factors.

Alzheimer's disease

Alzheimer's disease, referred to in the DSM-5 as major or mild neurocognitive disorder due to Alzheimer's disease, is the most prevalent dementia. An important diagnostic feature of this condition is that the onset is gradual. As such, there is no obvious starting point. In this sense, Alzheimer's disease is described as being of insidious onset. However, the decline in function is progressive once the disease process has started. For those who had initially been diagnosed with the milder form of this diagnosis, due to the nature of the disease process, functioning deteriorates over time, with symptoms increasing in severity, such that they eventually meet the requirement for a diagnosis of Alzheimer's disease.

The types of cognitive impairment experienced here include severe problems with learning and memory. These are described as amnestic in nature. One of the defining features of Alzheimer's disease is a gradual and progressive deterioration in episodic memory. We shall explore methods to assess such impairment in more detail in the next chapter. However, in brief, episodic memory refers to memories of specific events in our lives. These memories are tethered within space and time. In other words, our memories of particular events are tagged in terms of where they occurred and when. A prominent feature in the development of Alzheimer's disease is a poor memory for recent events but apparently intact recall of events experienced earlier in that person's life. However, with time, erosion of these distant memories occurs as well. Memory problems profoundly affect a person's ability to function effectively in everyday life. Other forms of memory, such as procedural memory—our ability to perform actions automatically—are relatively intact.

Problems with visuospatial processing and language are key here also. Deficits in executive function are evident in those with mild NCD. Those with major NCD will show severe impairment in language ability, visual construction, and perceptual-motor activity.

The majority of those meeting a diagnosis for Alzheimer's disease experience a combination of behavioural and psychological symptoms, although some of these may also be present to a lesser extent in those with milder forms of this condition. These symptoms are often distressing. Depression or apathy is evident in the milder form of this diagnosis. With increasing severity, symptoms such as agitation, wandering, increased aggression, and psychotic features begin to appear. The late stages of the condition are characterized by disturbances in gait, difficulty swallowing (dysphagia), incontinence, involuntary muscle contractions (myoclonus), and seizures.

As already described, onset is insidious, and the disease's progress is defined as gradual. Although highly variable, generally, individuals live with the disease for around ten years post-diagnosis. However, this largely depends on how advanced the pathology was before a definite diagnosis was made. During the late stages of the condition, individuals are entirely dependent on others for even the most straightforward task, many being bed-bound and mute throughout the final stage of the disease. The cause of death, in many cases, is pulmonary aspiration. This is when food or drink enters the lower respiratory tract. This can lead to pneumonia, an inflammation of the alveoli in the lungs. However, there is growing evidence that coroners are increasingly ascribing dementia as the cause of death. However, deaths ascribed to Alzheimer's disease and other causes of dementia are still under-reported.[1, 2] Things are changing. In the UK, the Office of National Statistics (ONS) followed guidance from the World Health Organization (WHO), making it more acceptable to report dementia as the leading cause of death.

With ever-increasing advancements in our understanding of the neuropathology involved, our knowledge of the biochemical underpinnings of dementia is improving year on year, although, clearly, we are a long way from building a fully realized picture. The research to date has highlighted the importance of isolating biomarkers to help assess the condition. A biomarker is a substance that is associated with a specific condition when it occurs at abnormal levels. Proposed biomarkers include, among other things, marked atrophy in the medial temporal lobe—a region of the brain central to episodic memory—the presence of amyloid or tau in the cerebral spinal fluid, and presence of a specific gene mutation in a member of that person's immediate family that increases the likelihood of developing the condition in siblings (5).

A great deal of change occurs in the brains of those with Alzheimer's disease, both in terms of global changes in size and also at the microscopic level with the formation of plaques and tangles. Amyloid plaques comprise a combination of damaged cellular tissue and extracellular deposits of β-amyloid. Their presence interferes with communication between neurons and also result in cell death. They also trigger an inflammatory response leading to additional cellular damage (6). Neurofibrillary tangles form inside neurons. These intracellular deposits consist of insoluble tau proteins due to their atypically hyperphosphorylated state. Neurofibrils within nerve cells transport chemicals essential to the creation of neurotransmitters. However, their usual functioning is disrupted by the presence of these tangles, therefore, impacting further down the line (7).

An examination of the brain following death is needed to provide conclusive evidence for a positive diagnosis of Alzheimer's disease (8). It is only through close inspection of the brain tissue that sufficient evidence can be obtained to the degree of damage inflicted by amyloid plaques and neurofibrillary tangles. Although plaques and tangles do appear in the brains of healthy older adults, the density of such formations in some with Alzheimer's disease considerably exceed that seen in such brains. The critical aspect then is the extent to which plaques, and to some degree tangles, occur and also whereabouts in the brain they develop. Such histology is confirmed during *post-mortem* examination. Loss of neural connections and cell death abound. Holes—termed vacuoles—are apparent in the brain tissue.

Structurally the brain shrinks. Atrophy also occurs. The hippocampus is one of the first regions of the brain to be affected by such change. Changes here manifest as marked impairment in laying down new memories. The nucleus basalis is similarly affected. This brain area, part of the ventral forebrain, is home to a significant proportion of cholinergic neurons. The neurotransmitter acetylcholine is vital for efficient cognitive functioning. A decrease in the cholinergic pathway results in problems with awareness and overall alertness (9). As we shall see in Chapter 6, many drugs used to treat Alzheimer's disease work by raising levels of acetylcholine.

As the disease progresses, ventricles in the brain expand, and the grooves in the surface of the cortex—the sulci—become wider. The march of the disease extends into the temporal and parietal cortices, thereby affecting the processing and integration of information from the senses before enveloping the entire brain.

The heritable form of Alzheimer's disease is rare, accounting for only around 5 per cent of cases. This figure rises when one looks at early-onset Alzheimer's disease or early-onset autosomal dominant familial Alzheimer's disease. This is down to mutations in three separate genes, specifically the APP gene (chromosome 21), PS1 (chromosome 14), and PS2 (chromosome 1). The mutation on the APP gene results in an increase in β-amyloid. In contrast, mutations on the presenilin (PS) genes leads to the disease process beginning at an earlier stage.

When looking at instances of Alzheimer's disease in older adults, there is less evidence of heritability. However, studies indicate genetics still plays a significant role (5). The main risk factor here appears to be related to the gene for the protein apolipoprotein E (ApoE; chromosome 19). ApoE is involved in repairing neurons following damage. There are three different variants of this gene: ε2, ε3, ε4. Each variant differs in terms of its effectiveness in the repair process. The ε4 variant is the least effective and is implicated in the development of Alzheimer's disease. We all have two genes for ApoE. In each case, we might carry two of the same variant (homozygous) or two different variants (heterozygous). The risk for this disease is highest for those who are homozygous for ε4. The presence of the ε4 allele[3]—one of a pair of genes located on the corresponding chromosome—increases the risk of Alzheimer's disease following stroke and head injury (5).

Prevalence rises considerably with advancing age. Just under 10 per cent of such diagnoses occur among those aged 65–74, whereas this figure increases to over half in those 75–84. Depending on the source, up to 90 per cent of all NCDs in this category is attributable to Alzheimer's disease. Alzheimer's disease is likely behind a high proportion of those who show evidence of mild cognitive impairment (MCI).

One of the leading environmental risk factors for Alzheimer's disease is a traumatic brain injury. In terms of genetics, age is the leading risk factor. Apolipoprotein ε4 also increases risk and is associated with an earlier age of onset. It has become apparent that trisomy 21, or Down's syndrome as it is more commonly referred to, is also linked to this condition. Now that people live longer with Down's syndrome, there are increasing numbers of cases who develop Alzheimer's disease purely as a consequence of this increased longevity. Cerebrovascular pathology is also intimately linked with other dementias, such that vascular events increase the risk.

Many cultures see poor memory as merely indicative of the ageing process. Because of this, some of the early symptoms that might otherwise presage the onset of something more menacing tend to be overlooked. Such signs might also not be evident in situations where individuals operate within low-demand parameters or where educational attainment is low and is therefore associated with everyday difficulties itself.

Frontotemporal dementia

Much like Alzheimer's disease, frontotemporal dementia, or major or mild frontotemporal neurocognitive disorder, is characterized by insidious onset and a gradual progression over time of symptom severity. There are distinct behavioural symptoms associated with this condition. The main elements are disinhibition, apathy, a lack of empathy, perseveration or ritualistic behaviour, hyperorality—a compulsion to explore objects with the mouth—and marked changes in diet. The ability to behave appropriately in social situations deteriorates, linked mainly to marked impairment in executive functions. Because of the impairment in executive functions, the person with this diagnosis finds it increasingly challenging to plan and organize, become highly distractible, and make a series of poor judgements. The person will display repetitions in both speech and behaviour. Incontinence is also an issue. There is also blunting of affect where the person can no longer express emotion. These symptoms are associated with the behavioural variant of this diagnosis. Unlike some of the other conditions discussed, the person with this behavioural variant of frontotemporal lobar degeneration (FTLD) loses insight into their decline early on.

There is also another variant where language impairment is a prevalent feature. There are three subtypes: semantic, agrammatic/non-fluent, and logopenic variants. The onset is gradual. In this diagnosis, several crucial cognitive functioning domains are relatively unaffected, including perceptual-motor function and memory, at least in the condition's early stages.

All aspects of language function are affected, including the production of speech and comprehension. A person gradually loses all sense of words so that they can no longer understand what people are saying and what objects surround them (10). This is a manifestation of a gradual loss of conceptual knowledge. In some instances, face recognition is lost, a condition referred to as prosopagnosia.[4] They are likely to become preoccupied with specific activities, engaging in repetitive motor behaviours. Semantic dementia is sometimes referred to as fluent aphasia. Aphasia is an acquired language disorder affecting language production rather than just articulation. Using the term fluent aphasia acknowledges speech can be articulate and grammatical even though semantic knowledge is lost (11).

The initial symptoms of progressive non-fluent aphasia reflect speech problems, particularly expressive language. Words are difficult to find, thinking becomes disorganized, speech output is slow, with problems articulating—verbal apraxia—and many experience stuttering. There are problems both expressing and understanding speech. When the symptoms become more severe, the person is often rendered mute. Other cognitive operations appear reasonably intact, including memory and visuospatial processing. As such, there is not a pronounced drop in a person's ability to function in everyday life that is observed in other forms of dementia.

Although there are behavioural and language variants of this condition, and some individuals may present with one or the other, many do, in fact, present with features of both variants.

For some, there may be the presence of extrapyramidal features to contend with. These refer to the presence of tremor, muscle rigidity, restlessness, and problems initiating movement. There may also be an overlap with other conditions, such as progressive supranuclear palsy—characterized by cognitive slowing and diminished verbal fluency—and corticobasal degeneration—a prominent feature being an inability to use tools and experiencing visuospatial impairment. Symptoms generally associated with motor neuron disease—deterioration of the motor neurons—such as muscle atrophy and muscle weakness may also occur. Others also experience visual hallucinations.

This condition is associated with significant disturbances in work life and family life. This is due primarily to the fact that the condition can occur at such a young age and because of the severe language and/or behavioural impairments. The manifestation of socially inappropriate behaviour is particularly disruptive.

For most, diagnosis is made around the age of 60, although the age of onset can be as early as 30. The disease is progressive in nature. People can live up to a decade following the initial onset of symptoms. The decline is quicker in this condition compared to that seen in Alzheimer's disease. As a result, people tend not to live as long following the inception of the disease.

Brain imaging techniques can identify a pattern of atrophy characteristic of this diagnosis. In the case of the behavioural variant, the frontal lobes and the anterior temporal lobes are particularly affected. In the case of the semantic variant, atrophy occurs bilaterally in the middle, inferior, and anterior temporal lobes. Atrophy in the left posterior frontal-insular is associated with non-fluent language-variant frontotemporal NCD. The left posterior perisylvian or parietal regions are most affected by the logopenic variant. Hypoperfusion—decreased blood flow—and cortical hypometabolism—reduced functioning—are seen in these regions and may occur before atrophy begins. Differential diagnosis is difficult given the overlap with Alzheimer's disease.

The onset of this condition often occurs earlier than other NCDs. Prevalence ranges up to 10 individuals in every 100,000 being diagnosed with major or mild frontotemporal neurocognitive disorder. Both behavioural and semantic variants are more prevalent in males.

Just under half of those diagnosed with frontotemporal dementia have someone in their family who had early-onset NCD. However, this increased risk is not associated with any known genetic mutation for the majority. Deterioration tends to be quicker in those who also have motor neuron disease.

Dementia with Lewy bodies

As with some of the conditions mentioned earlier, the onset of dementia with Lewy bodies (major or mild neurocognitive disorder with Lewy bodies) is insidious, and the progress of the disease itself is gradual. Core features of this diagnosis are disturbances in attention and alertness, visual hallucinations, and Parkinsonian symptoms. The hallucinations are vivid and persistent. Also, the presence of rapid eye movement sleep behaviour disorder—a condition where dreams are physically acted out while asleep—and heightened sensitivity to neuroleptic medication is indicative of this diagnosis. Diagnosis is made difficult because various symptoms may present at different time points. The severity of cognitive impairment changes, often quite dramatically from moment to moment, in particular levels of alertness. There is less of an obvious memory problem here, although executive dysfunction is prominent. As already mentioned, visual disturbances are associated with this condition, and visuospatial processing is particularly affected, more so than some other cognitive domains. Because of this, to be sure, reports of how the individual behaves should be obtained from either spouse or carer. Cognitive impairments begin to appear about a year before the onset of noticeable symptoms of parkinsonism.

In some cases, there is evidence of problems with autonomic functions. Many experience orthostatic hypotension—a rapid drop in blood pressure on rising—as well as problems with both bladder and bowel. Problems experienced when changing posture has implications when considering risk from falls. They also experience occasional loss of consciousness without an obvious explanation. It might not be surprising to learn that falls and syncope—fainting, in other words—are common among those who receive a diagnosis of Lewy body dementia.

The severity of functional impairment here seems to go above and beyond the cognitive difficulties experienced by this group such that they initially exceed those of some of the other NCDs. This is because of the disruptions in motor and autonomic functioning. Such disturbances result in the person experiencing difficulties using the bathroom and eating for themselves, among other things. Problems are exacerbated in many cases by poor sleep and other comorbid psychopathology.

In many cases, there are episodes of delirium that are, by their nature, acute in onset. This phase is often linked to illness or having undergone an operation. Lewy bodies—abnormal protein deposits—are involved both here and in Parkinson's disease. However, in both instances, the pathology is distinct, as are the patterns of symptoms. The main site of pathology in Parkinson's disease is the basal ganglia. In contrast, the area of damage is primarily cortical in Lewy body dementia. Evidence of marked cognitive impairment occurs early in dementia with Lewy bodies, preceding motor problems by around 12 months. Onset is seen in people in their 70s, and people live for up to 7 years on average.

The pathology of dementia with Lewy bodies is distinct. In addition to the presence of Lewy bodies, changes in the brain also resemble Alzheimer's disease in many cases, notably higher levels of amyloid plaques and vascular disease. Levels of both acetylcholine and dopamine are particularly affected in this condition. Reductions in acetylcholine are even greater than that seen in Alzheimer's disease, whereas reductions in dopamine are comparable to those seen in Parkinson's disease patients. PET[5] and SPECT[6] scans can detect low striatal dopamine transporter uptake—the dopamine transporter leads to the reuptake of dopamine—a factor that indicates dementia with Lewy bodies, as are several other neurological and psychophysiological changes too numerous to mention here.

In-depth cognitive testing is required to clearly delineate the types of impairment the person is experiencing. REM sleep behaviour disorder is also co-occurring in many cases. As mentioned previously, this is where a person carries out a range of behaviours during REM sleep. These behaviours can be distressing and also dangerous to self and others. In normal REM sleep, our bodies are paralysed. This is not the case with REM sleep behaviour disorder (12).

Prevalence rates in the general population are estimated as high as 5 per cent. In contrast, when expressed as a proportion of all cases of dementia, the estimate can be up to 30 per cent. There is a slightly higher prevalence among males.

Although there is some evidence of potential genetic risk factors, there is no suggestion of family history for this diagnosis for the majority of cases.

Vascular dementia

With vascular dementia or major or mild vascular neurocognitive disorder, the appearance of cognitive impairment coincides with a cerebrovascular event. This can include a range of possible causes, including stroke. The presenting problem may not necessarily be one of memory. Instead, patients generally exhibit executive function deficits as manifested by poor motivation and carrying out planned behaviour. How the symptoms manifest vary greatly, depending on the type of vascular event, the location of the lesion, and its severity. Stroke can occur throughout the brain and so is not limited to specific sites as in some forms of dementia. There is a further clear distinction here between vascular dementia and Alzheimer's disease. With vascular dementia, there is little evidence of any change in personality despite the decline in cognitive abilities. This is clearly not the case for Alzheimer's disease, where personality changes accompany the progression of cognitive deterioration. Insight into what changes are occurring is often maintained, again in stark contrast to Alzheimer's disease. Additional impairments with daily life are caused by other physical problems that accompany this condition.

Lesions can be described as focal (localized), multifocal (two or more sites), or diffuse (widespread). In the majority of cases, there is more than one event. As a result of these multi-infarcts, the decline in function occurs stepwise, with impairment becoming noticeably worse with each event. The brain is susceptible to even minor fluctuations in blood supply and the resultant drop in oxygen levels. The cause of stroke can be the result of inadequate blood reaching the affected region (ischaemic stroke), extensive furring of the blood vessels (transient ischaemic attack, TIA), or an internal bleed (haemorrhagic stroke). In the case of TIA, a person may experience momentary dizziness or visual disturbance.

Because of the nature of the underlying cause, there is generally no decline in function between infarctions. Some, in fact, show some improvement during these intervals. However, this is by no means the only pattern of impairment. Some may indicate a gradual onset, with the severity of symptoms slowly worsening over time. This latter pattern of impairment is invariably due to small-vessel disease that results in lesions appearing in the white matter, basal ganglia, and the thalamus.

Multi-infarct dementia is the most common of the various forms of vascular dementia. The nature of the decline is progressive, and the outcome tends to be worse for this patient group. Also associated with poorer outcomes are holes in the brain tissue—specifically within the subcortex, although even within the cortex—where blood supply has been lost. These are referred to as lacunar infarcts.

Loss of white matter (leukoencephalopathy) is mainly associated with impairment in executive function. In fact, a specific form of vascular dementia, subcortical ischaemic vascular dementia, reflects damage primarily occurring in the white matter and is characterized by evidence of severe executive dysfunction.

A positive diagnosis here requires evidence of some cerebrovascular event. This can be obtained in several ways, including a combination of neuroimaging and physical examination. In the case of stroke, there is often no need for brain imaging as a direct causal link between the cerebrovascular event and the decline in function is evident.

Neurological assessment will give rise to evidence of stroke, transient ischaemic episodes, and proof of infarctions. There are non-neurological symptoms associated with these changes. These include changes in personality, mood lability, inability to make decisions (abulia), and depression in many cases. Both MRI[7] and CT[8] scans are essential when making a diagnosis here.

This condition may occur at any age, although it generally occurs in those over the age of 65. As we have already seen, the course of this condition varies, being described as stepwise in some cases, in others progressive.

After Alzheimer's disease, vascular dementia is the second commonest. Estimates in the United States indicate 16 per cent of people in their 80s will experience this condition. Rates are higher in certain societies, including African Americans and East Asia. Prevalence is also higher in males.

Many factors influence how someone will recover following a cardiovascular event. Most important is a person's level of education, their level of physical activity, and the degree of mental stimulation they experience. There are also several known risk factors linked to cardiovascular disease. These are numerous but include hypertension, diabetes, smoking, and obesity.

Although very rare, a hereditary form of vascular dementia does exist. CADASIL—cerebral autosomal dominant arteriopathy with subcortical infarcts and leukoencephalopathy—develops in 50 per cent of siblings of parents with the condition. There is also a recessive form of the disease where the figure is reduced to 25 per cent, with a 50 per cent chance the sibling carries the gene for the condition.

Mixed dementia

Having just discussed vascular dementia, this next section focuses on mixed forms. Vascular dementia often occurs alongside other forms of the condition. It has been argued that the presence and severity of vascular damage account for the substantial individual differences seen in those with the various types of dementia. Alzheimer's disease and vascular dementia are most common. Around one in every ten individuals who receive a diagnosis of dementia will show evidence of more than one type. Mixed dementia is more apparent over the age of 75. Because of its nature, it is not possible to describe a discrete clustering of symptoms. This is because it depends entirely on the combinations of dementia present. It is challenging to diagnose, especially given that one form of dementia generally predominates and will cloud any clinical decision. A positive diagnosis cannot be made until death, at which point a postmortem will be performed.

Primary progressive aphasia

Primary progressive aphasia (PPA) is characterized by problems finding words, naming objects, and comprehension (11). These symptoms initially occur in the absence of dementia. Some have argued that PPA is, in fact, one of the frontotemporal dementias. The onset of PPA can be as early as 50 years of age (13). Other cognitive domains become affected with time, although language impairment retains prominence.

Terry Jones, of Monty Python fame, who died in 2020, was diagnosed with this condition. Although tragic regardless of your status, celebrities diagnosed with these conditions bring another level of awareness to the general population. Your neighbour who had received the same diagnosis would not attract the same level of interest. For someone like Terry Jones, who had a fantastic way with words, a disease that predominantly affects language seems particularly cruel. This is something I thought myself on first hearing of his condition. However, we all rely on language. It keeps us connected to others, be it through the written word, hilarious comedy sketch, or brief snatched conversations on the way back from the shop. Celebrity status here has a flipside. While it may help others better understand the various forms of dementia, one thing that is essential for anyone who has been diagnosed with dementia is the maintenance of dignity. A person may, over time, become increasingly frail and dependent on others, but it is the responsibility of their family and friends to ensure the person is treated with the respect they deserve. For a celebrity with a terminal condition, this is so much harder, especially given the ever-increasing ways by which we, the general public, invade the lives of luminaries.

What am I trying to say here? I am trying to say that status should not affect how sympathetic we are to people. A person you may have grown up reading or watching is familiar to you. Their tragedy affects you. That is only understandable. You feel their loss, albeit in a highly attenuated way. Our perceived link to celebrity is at the highest it has ever been with the various forms of social media at our disposal. You may not have that same link to someone you do not know who lives a couple of streets away. It is unlikely you follow them on social media, so you do not have intimate knowledge of their daily lives. However, their needs are the same.

Dementia related to alcohol

A significant risk factor for various forms of dementia is alcohol. Like other readily available and socially accepted substances, alcohol possesses neurotoxic properties. Heavy drinking over prolonged periods can increase a person's risk of developing one of these conditions. Alcohol increases risk in several ways. Extensive misuse of alcohol leads to, among other things, a range of problems concerning nutrition. There is a pronounced lack of vitamin B_3 (niacin) in the diet in such cases. If prolonged, low levels of niacin can result in dementia. Vitamin B_1 (thiamine) deficiency is also linked to severe cognitive problems in the form of Wernicke–Korsakoff syndrome (see subsequent section). As it leads to hypertension, alcohol is linked to vascular forms of dementia. Alcohol damages the liver. With liver functioning reduced, toxins build up, resulting in some cases in dementia-like symptoms of cognitive confusion, such as the condition hepatic encephalopathy, a disease of the liver commonly seen in cirrhosis, which is scarring of the liver tissue. Repeated head injury is also a significant risk factor. The likelihood of sustaining an injury in this way increases exponentially in line with the degree of alcohol intoxication.

Wernicke–Korsakoff syndrome is characterized by two stages: one that is short-lived, the other more long-term. The initial, acute phase is referred to as Wernicke's encephalopathy. It is acute in that it can be treated successfully given the appropriate dietary supplement of vitamin B_1. This stage is associated with extreme confusion, extremely poor coordination of body movement (ataxia), and impairments in eye movement and pupillary response. If not treated, coma followed by death is the outcome. Wernicke's encephalopathy may be succeeded by a condition called Korsakoff's psychosis. This is, again, due to a deficiency in vitamin B_1. Where it does occur, the situation is chronic. The main symptoms seen here include a loss in the ability to lay down new memory (anterograde amnesia) and deficits in the ability to recall past memories (retrograde amnesia). As is often seen in cases of amnesia, the person fills the gaps in memory retrieval usually by making things up, a process referred to as confabulation. Alongside this is a complete lack of insight into the problems they are experiencing. Those with this form of alcohol-related dementia often appear to lack interest in their surroundings, exhibiting extreme apathy.

Intellectual development disorders

In Chapter 8, I shall focus entirely on dementia among those with intellectual development disorders. Of most relevance here is Down's syndrome, with its known genetic cause linked to chromosome 21, a chromosome that happens to also contain the APP gene that is so closely tied with Alzheimer's disease. However, Down's syndrome is not the only condition of concern here. Many other intellectual developmental disorders are affected differently by dementia. The main problem is one of diagnosis. Given the nature of the pre-morbid impairment, differentiating additional issues related to the progression of dementia is even more of a challenge.

HIV-associated neurocognitive disorder (HAND)

We know the human immunodeficiency virus (HIV) as the retrovirus that results in people developing acquired immunodeficiency syndrome (AIDS). The virus lessens the body's ability to fight infection. Since the first major outbreak in the 1980s, fewer AIDS-related deaths have been recorded each year. As in other cases, reduced death rates for a condition have unfortunate consequences in the sense that other illnesses then develop later in life. In other words, the risk for other conditions increases because one is living longer. In the case of AIDS, now that more survive, there is an increased risk of severe, progressive cognitive decline. Diagnosis can be a challenge because the symptoms are very similar to depression. In terms of symptomology, it transcends the classic, albeit artificial, cortical–subcortical divide. HIV-associated dementia presents with both memory and language impairment as well as behavioural and motor functioning problems. More and more research focuses on finding medication for reversible forms of dementia. Indeed, the impairments experienced here can often be reversed by highly active antiretroviral therapy (HAART), a treatment initially developed to treat HIV.

Creutzfeldt–Jakob disease

Abnormal proteins called prions have a noticeable and lasting effect on the brain. Prions are different because they can lie dormant in the body for decades before exerting any influence. Prion disease is transmitted in several ways, although usually due to eating contaminated meat or undergoing surgery. Prion proteins can start to be problematic when an appropriate trigger results in expansive replication. When this occurs, prions begin to accumulate. They form stacks. Their toxic nature means that their presence destroys the cells in which they appear. As a result, the natural process of housekeeping, carried out by astrocytes, means that destroyed cell debris is removed. The resultant effect of this is that there is now a gap in the brain that neurons used to occupy, giving the characteristic sponge-like appearance of this and other related diseases (spongiform disease).

Creutzfeldt–Jakob disease (CJD) is the most well-known of all prion diseases. This condition poses its own set of problems to clinicians. Early symptoms may not be considered signs of illness as they manifest as lowered mood or fatigue. After only a very brief period, there is little doubt that something more serious is going on. Decline is rapid and pervasive, catching all too many unaware. The symptoms are severe and dramatic. The impact on cognitive functioning is brutal. The patient quickly goes on to exhibit disturbing, spasmodic movements, a condition referred to as myoclonus. The person affected soon becomes unable to move or speak, described as akinetic mutism. Death is quick, usually within six months.

A new form, or variant, of this condition appeared in the 1990s. It became a prominent fixture of local news in the UK during this time in connection with controversies surrounding contaminated meat, making it onto supermarket shelves amidst the major mad cow disease scare at the time. New variant CJD (vCJD), as it became known, reflected the fact that humans were becoming infected with bovine spongiform encephalopathy (BSE) via the food chain. Early symptoms include mood disturbances as well as some psychotic behaviour, such as delusions and hallucinations. Pain is common here also. After a few months, evidence of more widespread neurological damage becomes apparent, with severe problems with coordination, memory, and again myoclonus, loss of movement and speech (akinetic mutism), and eventual death. The onset of variant CJD is earlier than for CJD; age 28 rather than 60. However, death is not as rapid, with patients surviving for around 14 months.

The long-term concern here is that we know prion disease can remain dormant in a person for many years. Many would have consumed meat that was contaminated during the initial period of the scare. Because of this, there is fear that more cases of vCJD will appear over the ensuing years. To date, though, numbers are low. However, in terms of gauging the true extent of the impact, all we can do is wait.

Inflammation

As we shall discuss in Chapter 11, much research looks at the role of brain inflammation in dementia. One of the main reasons for this is the hope that treatment with anti-inflammatories or immunosuppressants will stop or reverse any damage. We know that inflammation is how our bodies react to an injury. Inflammation can occur in the brain. The swelling associated with this response is problematic under such conditions. Many related conditions reflect such a response. Cerebral vasculitis describes inflammation of the blood vessels in the brain. If left untreated, dementia occurs swiftly. Symptoms include extreme confusion, and in some cases, seizures. It is, however, preventable through known treatments. Limbic encephalitis occurs when inflammation appears in the limbic part of the brain and may occur as an autoimmune response—this is where the immune system starts to attack a person's own (self) tissue—although more commonly as the result of cancer.

Metabolic disease

Several inherited metabolic diseases exist that can produce dementia-like impairments if they attack the grey matter in the brain. These include Gaucher's disease, metachromatic leukodystrophy, Niemann–Pick disease, and Wilson disease. Most can be treated successfully with either a dietary supplement or an enzyme. Other conditions can occur later in life. These include folic acid deficiency, hypothyroidism (reduced levels of thyroid hormone), hypercalcaemia (raised plasma concentrations of calcium), and vitamin B_{12} deficiency. Although this is the case, very few suspected cases of dementia are due solely to these acquired metabolic diseases. Nonetheless, appropriate screening should take place to ensure such conditions do not exist and potentially account for the symptoms the person is manifesting.

Posterior cortical atrophy

Posterior cortical atrophy (PCA), also called Benson's syndrome, is a relatively rare atypical variant of Alzheimer's disease. The late Sir Terry Pratchett—a high-profile campaigner for dementia—lived with this condition. The condition results from atrophy in the posterior part of the cortex, specifically in the occipital, parietal, and temporal lobes. Its most prominent symptom, as a result, is impairment in visual processing. With time, damage spreads to areas most associated with Alzheimer's disease pathology, such as the hippocampus and prefrontal cortex. This results in severe impairment in memory and language. PCA tends to occur at an earlier age than Alzheimer's disease. PCA is believed to be primarily the resultant effect of mutations in the presenilin 1 gene (PSENI1). PSEN1 is part of the complex that processes amyloid precursor protein which is involved in creating new nerve cells, a process called synaptogenesis. It is also implicated in early-onset Alzheimer's disease.

Young-onset dementia

This refers to people who develop dementia before the age of 65. It is estimated 42,000 people in the UK fall into this category. People who develop the condition at such a young age will naturally experience it differently. They will have distinct needs from older adults and will require different forms of support. Among this group, there is a higher likelihood of problems with movement and balance, with walking being significantly affected. One significant difference between younger people who develop the condition and their older counterparts is that they tend not to have the chronic health complaints of this latter group.

About a third of all early-onset cases are diagnosed with an atypical form of Alzheimer's disease. Memory impairment is not the symptom picked up first. Instead, people first experience difficulty with vision, speech, planning, and decision-making.

A variant of vascular dementia, cerebral autosomal dominant arteriopathy with subcortical infarcts and leukoencephalopathy (CADASIL), also hits people at a younger age, usually between 30 and 50. Typical symptoms include migraine, stroke, lowered mood, and increasing cognitive impairment.

About a sixth of cases will be diagnosed with frontotemporal dementia, higher than the number diagnosed in older adults. It tends to occur around the ages of 45 and 65. Around 5 per cent of cases show evidence for dementia with Lewy bodies. Around one in ten cases are diagnosed with alcohol-related brain damage, usually around 50. Causes include thiamine (vitamin B_1) deficiency and general poor diet, neural loss due to alcohol toxicity, and head injuries often resulting from falls sustained or being injured in fights. Unlike other dementias, positive outcomes can occur through changes in diet and behaviour.

Rarer forms of dementia are more common in younger adults. They account for around a quarter of all diagnoses in this age group. Diagnoses include Huntington's disease, progressive supranuclear palsy, corticobasal degeneration, and Creutzfeldt–Jakob disease. These mainly cause problems with movement on top of issues with memory and general cognitive functioning. In some cases, the progression of the disease is rapid.

As already seen in this book, other diseases can cause dementia-like symptoms. These include inherited conditions, some of which have previously been mentioned in the section on metabolic disorders. Other conditions include problems with a person's thyroid, Addison's disease—an endocrine disorder characterized by low levels of cortisol and aldosterone, vitamin deficiency, inflammatory conditions such as multiple sclerosis, and infection, as in the case of HIV. Impaired cognitive functioning can be also due to sleep apnoea, a condition where people momentarily stop breathing, sometimes for up to 30 seconds, at repeated points throughout the night.

Related conditions

As already mentioned, improved treatment and survival for many conditions inevitably increase the risk of developing dementia later in life. The following section will highlight conditions where this occurs. As already indicated, intellectual development disorders will be tackled separately (see Chapter 8).

Huntington's disease

Huntington's disease is an inherited condition that results in the loss of neurons in the basal ganglia and cerebral cortex. The onset of the disease can be very early indeed, occurring during adolescence, but it can also develop later in life. The majority develop the condition during middle adulthood. The main symptoms are severe motor disturbances. Initially, these may manifest as clumsiness or awkwardness, but chorea—jerky involuntary movement—engulfs the whole body later on. The person is only at rest when asleep. Symptoms include problems with executive function, memory, and language. Mood disorder often accompanies this condition, and there may even be elements of psychosis. In the late stages of Huntington's disease, the patient depends entirely on carers due to the severity and combination of both physical and mental problems. The ability to communicate is lost (14). The severity of the symptoms means the person is at constant risk of injuring themselves. Death is often caused by infection following the inhalation of food—aspiration pneumonia—or heart disease resulting from extreme weight loss and continual movement.

Multiple sclerosis

Multiple sclerosis is a chronic and progressive condition that affects the central nervous system. It is the most common neurological condition in the young. Indeed, depending on location, it accounts for 1 in every 500 individuals in Northern Europe (15). Despite this, causes are unknown, although it is more common among women than among men. Patterns of impairment differ significantly across individuals. Like many of the conditions I have discussed in this book, there is no known cure. In terms of pathology, lesions occur in the central nervous system that attacks the myelin sheath enveloping the axons that transmit nerve impulses. The oligodendrocytes—the cells that form myelin—degenerate. Glial cells, in this case, astrocytes, are activated and produce scarring, hence the name multiple sclerosis, or multiple instances of hardening of the tissue.

Symptoms may appear quite suddenly. The types of symptoms people experience vary dramatically from person to person, reflecting the potential widespread distribution of lesions throughout the brain and spinal cord. At the early stages, symptoms are often focused around vision. Lesions on optic nerves can cause blurred vision and, in some cases, blindness. Others experience weakness and numbness in their limbs. In terms of cognitive impairment, deficits in executive function are prominent and reduced attention and speed of processing information. Fatigue is often the most significant and pervasive symptom a person experiences. Pain also occurs in around a third of patients.

Parkinson's disease

Parkinson's disease takes its name from James Parkinson's original paper of 1817, in which he described the "shaking palsy" (16). The presence of Lewy bodies is the primary pathology associated with this disease. The main site affected is the substantia nigra within the basal ganglia, particularly dopamine-producing cells. Lewy bodies extend into the cortex as the disease progresses, and this is especially the case in those with concomitant dementia (see subsequent section). Although generally seen as a disease of old age, up to around a fifth of cases start before a person reaches the age of 40 (17).

The main symptoms include tremor at rest, slowed movement (bradykinesia), and muscle rigidity. Functioning for many is unpredictable. This is best described as on-off periods where patients are at risk of injury, often due to falls, during off-periods. Fear of falling can escalate such that people fear to leave their homes. Fatigue and apathy are prominent; pain too mainly as the result of muscle rigidity.

A range of cognitive problems is associated with Parkinson's disease and cover attention and executive function, memory, visuospatial processing, and language (18). With the progression of the disease, the likelihood of developing dementia also increases. In such cases, it is referred to as Parkinson's disease dementia (PDD). There is less evidence of language impairment here; rather, there is a predominance of poor memory and slowed thinking. Personality is affected, as is mood.

Progressive supranuclear palsy

Progressive supranuclear palsy is a neurodegenerative disorder that progresses rapidly (19). Presenting symptoms include muscle rigidity, problems with speech, parkinsonism, and marked cognitive impairment. Speed of processing is particularly affected, and there is a general sense of apathy and lowered mood. Falls are frequent, primarily due to postural instability. A key symptom is vertical gaze palsy, a restriction in eye movement. Visuospatial processing is significantly affected. Neuropathology is mainly concentrated subcortically, although cortical damage does occur as well. Dopamine is depleted and results in parkinsonian symptoms.

Head injury and trauma

Trauma to the brain is often severe. Symptoms vary depending on which areas of the brain have been affected by the injury. Not only does head trauma cause direct damage, but it also results in an increase in the amount of β-amyloid deposits occurring in the brain.

Any blow to the head can result in profuse damage depending on the force of impact. Bleeding inside the skull regularly occurs under such conditions. In many instances, effects are instantaneous. A person may quickly lose consciousness as the result of an extradural bleed. However, bleeding may occur between the dura mater—the outer covering of the brain and spinal cord—and the arachnoid—the middle of the three membranes—after relatively mild trauma, especially in older adults. This is referred to as a subdural bleed. A subdural haematoma will develop as blood accumulates and clots in many such cases. Because this progresses gradually, there is no marked onset of obvious symptoms. Instead, the person experiences worsening confusion. If a person with dementia experiences a fall, it is essential that a brain scan is carried out as there may be underlying pathology associated with the fall that might produce symptoms that would otherwise be attributed to advancing dementia and so go untreated.

Dementia pugilistica is a condition forever associated with those who engage in boxing, or pugilism, although increasingly cases among those who play American football develop the same symptoms, again due to the nature of the injuries sustained during the game. This particular form of dementia is the result of repeated blows to the head, and as such, is called chronic traumatic encephalopathy.

Tumour

The growth of tumours within the brain can result in various symptoms due to the location and extent of growth. Pressure within the skull can increase—intracranial pressure—and will result in loss of consciousness and eventual death. Growths most commonly associated with the development of dementia include gliomas—where neural connective tissue becomes malignant—and meningiomas—tumours occurring in the membranes covering the brain.

Having spent some time now expanding upon the various diagnoses of dementia, this final section of the chapter will look at a range of factors linked in multiple ways to the conditions described earlier. We will begin by examining why our ability to see clearly and navigate well is so important. After this, we will focus on subjective cognitive decline and mild cognitive impairment, again examining why they are important in the broader context of dementia research. The chapter will end by considering how we all compensate and, thus, hide our failings in cognition and the implications of this.

Visuospatial functioning

Difficulties in processing and making sense of visual and spatial information are present in many cases of dementia, such as Alzheimer's disease and dementia with Lewy bodies. In what was to be the first account of a patient with Alzheimer's disease, it was noted that "[the patient] could not find her way about her home. . . . She suffered from serious perceptual disorders" (20). In the case of Alzheimer's disease, even at relatively early stages of the condition, posterior areas of the brain are affected, particularly the parietal lobes. This region of the brain is vital for processing visuospatial information (21). Typical age-related changes to sight and the processing of visual-spatial information compound these difficulties.

Such changes include reductions in contrast sensitivity and depth perception due to structural changes in the eye (22).

There is much variation among patients with Alzheimer's disease in terms of visuospatial problems. In some instances, patients experience severe impairment in basic visuospatial functioning, cognitive issues such as associative agnosia—described as "perception stripped of meaning" (23)—and in some cases Balint's syndrome. Balint's syndrome is characterized by the presence of a deficit in the ability to reach for objects guided by vision (optic ataxia), an inability to fixate on things (ocular apraxia), and a lack of ability to make sense of a complex scene (simultanagnosia) (24).

Alzheimer's disease is by no means the only dementia to be plagued by such processing difficulties. Dementia with Lewy bodies is characterized by such impairments. In this condition, patients often experience visual hallucinations, problems recognizing material from the various senses (agnosia), difficulty working with objects (constructional apraxia), and a belief that the identity of a person or place has changed (delusional misidentification).

Posterior cortical atrophy (PCA), a relatively rare form of dementia, is associated with marked visuospatial and perceptual difficulties and impairment with reading and carrying out skilled movement (praxis). The brain areas affected are the parietal, occipital, and occipitotemporal lobes. The process of neurodegeneration seen here is for the majority due to Alzheimer's disease, although other causes are implicated in some cases. Such inconsistency makes it extremely difficult to accurately diagnose and has led to many variations in terminology. PCA tends to develop in people between 50 and 65, but due to the inconsistencies reported earlier, people can experience delays before an accurate diagnosis is made. A helpful review published in *The Lancet* provides a good overview of knowledge about PCA (25).

Impairment in visuospatial processing has serious knock-on effects on a person's ability to function independently. Distortions of reality, in the form of a range of illusions, can lead the person with dementia to see faces in highly patterned materials, among other things. Visual over-stimulation can result in a person becoming restless or confused. A series of misperceptions is also made due to damage to the visual system, such as poor contrast sensitivity making it difficult to position oneself accurately when sitting down. This is compounded by misidentifying items perceived, such as misinterpreting their own reflection in a mirror for someone else, seeing an intruder rather than recognizing themselves. These difficulties result in the person often behaving in an inexplicable and seemingly bizarre manner. Behaviour may appear delusional when, in fact, it is merely due to confused and incomplete information reaching the senses. Of course, as already seen, sometimes such unusual behaviour is fuelled by hallucination.

Some patients may develop Charles Bonnet syndrome. Hallucinations are intense and intricate. They occur abruptly and may last for hours. The person experiencing the visions know that what they are seeing is not actual reality. This syndrome may appear under various conditions, including those who experience a gradual deterioration of vision and in some dementias. Visual hallucinations are common in dementia with Lewy bodies, and they also occur in some with Alzheimer's disease. The eloquent account of this condition is provided by Oliver Sacks in his book *Hallucinations* (26). Indeed, he is, for me, the foremost writer in the field of neurology.

Problems with vision and perception have many consequences for a person's ability to carry out everyday tasks and activities. Having looked at some of the symptoms associated with different conditions, it is worthwhile considering how visuospatial difficulties can be a source of danger.

One of the major problems here is the risk of falls. Falls have ever more severe consequences the older we get. The injury itself may hugely reduce activity levels in people's lives. Some may respond with fear and confine themselves to the relative safety of their own home, a situation referred to as post-fall syndrome (27–29). Dementia is a risk factor for falls, especially those with dementia with Lewy bodies (30). Figures indicate that between 50 and 80 per cent of people living with dementia fall within 12 months (31). There are cognitive factors that have been identified as risk factors here. These include poor performance on the Clock Drawing Test and an inability to copy a line drawing in the Mini-Mental State Examination (MMSE) (32, 33).

A number of these risk factors can be reduced. Essential things to review include medications that affect the cardiovascular system (31). Falls are also more likely in those prescribed hypnotics and anxiolytics (33, 34). Also, antidepressants have been implicated in this, particularly selective serotonin reuptake inhibitors (35), although there is debate about causality (36). This is especially pertinent given the prevalence of prescribed antidepressants among those with dementia.

On a positive note, exercise has been shown to reduce falls in those with dementia (37). We have talked much about the cognitive impairments seen in dementia, and we shall explore the role of emotion later. Still, for now, I shall focus on some of the physical problems people living with dementia face. Gait is affected, as is postural control. This, in combination with cognitive impairments, often result in people becoming less active (38). Several studies have been conducted to see if exercise can reduce the likelihood of falls. On the whole, the findings are positive. The programmes that seem most likely to benefit patients combine strength training, balance, and endurance (37).

One of the major concerns for the carer is the increased compulsion to walk in people with dementia. Such activity is positive from the point of view that it is a form of exercise and might help relieve some of the boredom experienced. However, there are several risks from such activity, the most serious of which is the increased likelihood of falling. Such excessive walking can be seen as troublesome for carers as it may appear to occur for no apparent reason. It is essential to consider what the underlying causes are for this behaviour. In fact, there are several plausible explanations, such as the person has always enjoyed walking, it is a way of using up energy, and it gives the person something to do. More worryingly, increased walking might be symptomatic of the person feeling lost, of being confused. In some instances, people move about to ease the pain they experience (39). The presence of restless leg syndrome might also explain some of this activity.

Restless leg syndrome is where people experience sensations in their calves when sitting or lying prone. People describe crawling, tearing, and grabbing sensations, among others in the limb. The feelings are alleviated with motion.

Gaining a better understanding of when cognitive decline starts and how it progresses is vital in our attempts to identify and treat dementia early on. Mild cognitive impairment is one such condition where a sizeable number convert to dementia further down the line. A more recent concept, that of subjective cognitive decline, is also of potential use, although problems abound in terms of how to assess it at the moment.

Subjective cognitive decline

Having already talked about various dementias in detail, we shall now consider conditions that are subclinical in the sense that, although multiple cognitive impairments are experienced, the symptoms are less severe and pervasive than the conditions defined earlier.

Subjective cognitive decline (SCD) refers to self-reported decline in memory and attention and is something that might, in fact, indicate an atypical drop in function that may eventuate in dementia (40). However, SCD is likely to be important when considered alongside depression, anxiety, and chronic health conditions (41).

A major problem at the moment is that there is no agreement on how one actually assesses this (42, 43). A review by Rabin and colleagues (44) identified essential considerations when looking at the literature on subjective cognitive decline. They concluded that, although the main focus will be on cognitive functioning, it is also necessary to consider mood, personality, and general health as these will likely explain a good deal of the variance in performance observed (45, 46).

The level of education appeared relevant; the reported cognitive decline was more indicative of subsequent dementia in those most highly educated. As such, subjective decline could be the most accurate way of gauging deterioration in this group. This is because they tend to perform at ceiling on many of the standard neuropsychological measures (47). Because they do well on standardized tests, personal concern about drops in performance might offer the best route for understanding what is going on.

Age was identified as another critical factor to consider. Reports of cognitive problems tend to become more accurate the older one is. Those classified as young-old tend to be less reliable, with many of the memory problems reported being better explained by the presence of anxiety, depression, or personality (48).

Mild cognitive impairment

A person may be described as showing mild cognitive impairment (MCI) if they show slight difficulties with both thinking and memory. The important thing here is that the deficits are more significant than expected through healthy ageing, but a great deal less than one would see in dementia.

The symptoms experienced include general problems with concentration and memory, issues with planning and problem-solving, and word-finding difficulties, among other things. There are various forms of MCI. The type where memory is the primary concern is referred to as amnestic MCI. Other forms include MCI—multiple domains—impairment in two or more cognitive areas that include memory—and MCI—single non-memory domain—impairment in one area of functioning that is not memory-related (49). Although help from others can be useful, there is little impact on a person's ability to perform all the activities associated with an independent life.

There are many potential causes of MCI, both biological and psychosocial. These include the presence of the ApoE e4, low levels of vitamin B_{12}, chronic kidney disease, depression, and social isolation (50).

The cognitive deficits described could be linked to anxiety and depression. Physical problems, such as infection or thyroid deficiency, can result in similar symptoms. Age-related decline in the various senses acts to compound these difficulties.

Up to 20 per cent of those aged 65 and over could be classified as showing MCI. This is significant because, even though symptoms are relatively mild, there is much evidence to show that those who do classify as having MCI are more likely to develop dementia later on in life. Because of relatively high rates of conversion from MCI to dementia, there is a real need to diagnose MCI early on so that, as with dementia itself, strategies can be put in place to help the individual and, wherever possible, reduce the risks of developing dementia in the future. At the moment, there are no clear-cut ways to predict those who convert. The presence of MCI symptoms can mean that the person is entering a pre-dementia stage where deterioration is already underway due to disease processes. In such cases, the decline is unlikely to be reversed. However, having received a diagnosis of MCI will likely mean that further deterioration in function will be detected much sooner than in someone where the precursor symptoms have not been identified.

Therefore, monitoring change is essential for the well-being of the individual concerned. At the current point in time, there is no standard practice for tracking the progress of individuals diagnosed with MCI. In some instances, individuals are provided with a follow-up appointment 6–12 months post-diagnosis, whereas in other cases the onus is on the individual to make an appointment should they feel there is any deterioration in their condition. Given the likely mental turmoil a person might be facing, this is far from ideal.

It is also essential to consider at this point the impact of a diagnosis of MCI on someone who may not then go on to develop dementia. As we have seen, the conversion rate is not 100 per cent. This means a fair proportion of those given the diagnosis will not tip over into a more progressive form of illness. However, as with all diagnoses, there is a concern about what the individual believes will happen. Often increasing memory problems are seen as being the warning signs that dementia is on the horizon. If people think this is the case, the concomitant anxiety and fear will be for nothing. How we tackle unnecessary worry is not clear, but it is undoubtedly an aspect that needs addressing (5).

In a later chapter, there will be a focus on treatment for the various dementias. MCI will not be discussed here, so the issue of treating MCI will be briefly discussed now. There is no evidence to indicate that drugs are an effective way of treating the symptoms of MCI. The most effective way of protecting against the condition eventually deteriorating into dementia is by tackling the major health risk factors of chronically raised blood pressure and high cholesterol levels. This can mainly be achieved by adopting a healthier lifestyle, chiefly through diet and exercise, as well as reviewing smoking and alcohol consumption.

What's in a name?

The diagnosis of MCI is, and likely will always be, contentious for many reasons. From a personal point of view, there is much resting on this diagnosis. It indicates that what they are experiencing is something more severe than mere age-related cognitive decline. Behind such a diagnosis, the ever-present spectre of dementia looms. We always hear about the quest to identify measures that will pick up cognitive decline early on, and in doing so, improve the odds that appropriate interventions can be mobilized to either slow or halt further deterioration. However, Corner and Bond (51) argue that, contrary to popular belief among researchers, there is more to diagnosing MCI or dementia than precise measures of cognitive functioning. They say that clinical judgement is vital to accurately make a decision that the types of deficits a person is experiencing are more than what one would expect from merely ageing.

It is not the place here to talk about what we mean by typical ageing. Further discussion on this and other age-related issues can be found in my book, *The Psychology of Ageing: From Mind to Society* (22). What I shall say here is that there is much variation in cognitive function as one ages; the end result of a combination of lifestyle choices, psychological and physical health, the environment, and so on it goes. To fully comprehend healthy ageing, we need to adopt a holistic approach that considers all these factors and more (52).

Having just defined mild cognitive impairment, one might argue that MCI reflects a situation where a person experiences significant memory problems in isolation from other cognitive decline (53). However, there is an issue here. What does it mean to function on par with others of your age, with the sole difference being significantly impaired memory? (54).

A point that needs to be considered here is whether the memory problem identified in MCI is memory in general or, more accurately, poor memory for the explicit recall of material. Sabat uses the example of the MMSE (see Chapter 4 for more information). The MMSE, like various other measures, was initially developed as a screening tool but tends to be frequently used as an outcome measure to gauge either decline in function or efficacy of an intervention. It is purported to provide a quick assessment of global functioning. However, when you examine the individual activities in detail, it is not as clear cut as that. The orientation questions, which account for a third of the overall marks, actually require recall of facts. We know that recall is severely affected in someone with MCI. Less so recognition memory. Would all individuals perform as badly if the orientation questions were rephrased and presented as a recognition memory task? Probably not. There are various other instances that the bias is towards recall, which disadvantages someone with dementia.

In that light, the cut-off for MCI on the MMSE reflects severe impairment in recall memory, not memory per se. However, when people talk about memory problems, we usually mean issues recalling information. It could be argued that MCI is an inaccurate label for a condition where recall is affected, but cognition, in general, remains intact.

This raises some critical questions about terminology and whether it actually reflects the type of symptoms a person is experiencing. Of course, as we saw in the previous section, MCI is not just about memory problems. It can encompass other domains of cognitive functioning. Nonetheless, considering the impact of the MCI diagnosis and all the name implies is highly relevant.

Compensatory strategies

Before leaving this chapter, following the discussion about MCI, we should consider a vital and adaptive aspect of human behaviour: finding ways to deal with and hide any problems we may be experiencing. We find solace in sharing our problems with family and friends in many cases. A little support along the way is a good thing. However, there are instances where we tend to shun this. In a later chapter, we shall be exploring the emotional impact of dementia and talk about it in relation to our sense of self. Dementia clearly chips away at this. However, even milder forms of cognitive impairment make us fearful that we are no longer functioning as of old and that we might be on the precipice of losing a vital aspect of who we are.

The types of problems experienced with MCI might be mild compared to dementia. After all, people can continue to lead an independent existence. Nonetheless, any form of cognitive impairment is a challenge. We do not like to accept that we forget things. Because of that, we use notes or objects left in strategic locations, set reminders on our smartphones, and so on. All of this is great. We are using our initiative. We are compensating for whatever problems we might be experiencing. The downside to all this is that others around us may not be aware of our difficulties. In fact, that is the whole point in many cases. People like to feel they can cope just as well on their own. The problem here is that if the person experiencing MCI is one of those set on a trajectory towards dementia, the advantages afforded by early detection and intervention will be lost for that individual.

Again, how this is tackled is unclear. At one and the same time, we need to protect the individual's rights and yet ensure that their future well-being is supported and protected. Hypervigilance among family and friends might only encourage higher levels of deception by those trying to cope, enforcing even further the barrier between appearance and reality. Over-zealousness on behalf of family and friends can undermine the confidence of the person they care for, fuelling fear instead. Having said that, the opposite case is just as fraught with problems. Only accurate knowledge of the symptoms and expectations around what the future holds can help alleviate some of these issues. The notion of acceptance and understanding is something we shall come back to again in Chapter 5.

Summary

My intention in this chapter was to describe the varying forms dementia takes. To a large extent, this chapter has been arranged around the organizing principles inherent in the current edition of the DSM (3). I have, however, continued using the more familiar names for the various conditions defined here purely because these are terms to which we are more accustomed. As we have seen, although different dementias share many symptoms, each, as we would expect, has its own specific clustering of these, bringing with it its own set of challenges. I then spent some time looking at problems with vision and spatial orientation. This is an oft-overlooked area with significant implications for a person's physical and mental well-being. We ended the chapter by examining subclinical conditions that may or may not presage the onset of dementia at some future point. Given the possibility that future deterioration might occur, there is an obvious need to find better ways of detecting these conditions sooner and offering improved levels of support that are maintained over time. In the final chapter of this book, I shall look at what the future holds for the early detection of dementia. Identifying those experiencing MCI who will then convert to dementia is a vital part of the overall jigsaw.

Notes

1 www.hmpgloballearningnetwork.com/site/altc/blog/completing-death-certificates-patients-alzheimer-disease
2 www.alzheimers.org.uk/blog/research-UK-biggest-killer-high-dementia-deaths
3 Short for allelomorph.
4 This is one of those conditions that seem to hook people's interest. The most well-known account of this is found in Oliver Sack's book, *The Man Who Mistook His Wife for a Hat*, the title of which refers to a specific case of prosopagnosia. It sparked off much debate concerning how faces are processed. Whether, for example, faces have some sort of privileged status. Oliver Sacks is a personal hero of mine, so I would heartily recommend exploring his writings.
5 PET stands for positron emission tomography and is a neuroimaging technique. A radioactive isotope is injected into the patient's blood. Due to the presence of this isotope, X-ray technology can track the flow of blood.
6 SPECT refers to single photon emission computed tomography. This technique measures cerebral blood flow. It is similar to PET in that it uses radioactive isotopes, and so it too comes under the umbrella of a nuclear medicine scan. SPECT is less expensive than PET. Different isotopes allow specific neurotransmitters to be tracked.
7 MRI stands for magnetic resonance imaging. It is a technique that makes use of a magnetic field to provide images of the internal structures of the body. Individual "slices" of the body can be combined to produce a 3D image of the target structure.
8 Computed tomographic (CT) scans are produced by utilizing a 360° X-ray beam. It produces cross-sectional views of the internal organs and structures.

References

1　Ames D, Chiu E, Lindesay J, Shulman KI. Guide to the psychiatry of old age. Cambridge: Cambridge University Press; 2010. Available from: www.dawsonera.com/depp/reader/protected/external/AbstractView/S9780511772863.

2　Corey-Bloom J. Dementia. In: Whitbourne SK, editor. Psychopathology in later adulthood. New York; Chichester: Wiley; 2000, pp. 217–243.

3　American Psychiatric Association. Diagnostic and statistical manual of mental disorders: DSM-5. 5th ed. Arlington, VA: American Psychiatric Association; 2013.

4　Shmerling R. Are you worried well? In: Harvard Health Publications, editor. Harvard Medical School commentaries on health. Boston, MA: Harvard Health Publications; 2014.

5　Hughes JC. Alzheimer's and other dementias. Oxford: Oxford University Press; 2011.

6　Martin LJ. Neurodegenerative disorders. 2002. In: Encyclopedia of the Human Brain [Internet]. Elsevier Science & Technology. Available from: www.credoreference.com/entry/esthumanbrain/neurodegenerative_disorders.

7　Kensinger EA, Corkin S. Alzheimer disease. In: Encyclopedia of Cognitive Science [Internet]. Wiley; 2005. Available from: www.credoreference.com/entry/wileycs/alzheimer_disease.

8　Whitehouse PJ. Dementia: Alzheimer's. In: Birren JE, editor. Encyclopedia of gerontology. 2nd ed. Amsterdam; London: Elsevier; 2007, pp. 374–397.

9　Smythies J. The neurochemistry of consciousness. In: Encyclopedia of Consciousness [Internet]. Elsevier Science & Technology; 2009. Available from: www.credoreference.com/entry/estcon/the_neurochemistry_of_consciousness.

10　Coulthard E, Firbank M, English P, Welch J, Birchall D, O'Brien J, et al. Proton magnetic resonance spectroscopy in frontotemporal dementia. J Neurol. 2006;253(7):861–868.

11　Noggle CA, Dean RS, Horton AM. The encyclopedia of neuropsychological disorders. New York: Springer; 2012.

12　Mayo Clinic. REM sleep behavior disorder. Mayo Clinic; 2018. Available from: www.mayoclinic.org/diseases-conditions/rem-sleep-behavior-disorder/symptoms-causes/syc-20352920.

13　Westbury C, Bub D. Primary progressive aphasia: A review of 112 cases. Brain Lang. 1997;60(3):381–406.

14　Nadel L. Encyclopedia of cognitive science. London: Nature Publishing Group; 2003.

15　Smith KJ, Sharief MK. Multiple sclerosis. In: Nadel L, editor. Encyclopedia of cognitive science. London: Nature Publishing Group; 2003.

16　Parkinson J. An essay on the shaking palsy. London: American Psychiatric Publishing, Inc.;1817. Available from: https://neuro.psychiatryonline.org/doi/full/10.1176/jnp.14.2.223.

17　Jahanshahi M. Parkinson's disease. In: Ayers S, editor. Cambridge handbook of psychology, health and medicine. 2nd ed. Cambridge: Cambridge University Press; 2007.

18　Watson GS, Leverenz JB. Profile of cognitive impairment in Parkinson's disease. Brain Pathol. 2010;20(3):640–645.

19　Sim AH, Hoelzle JB. Progressive supranuclear palsy. In: Noggle C, editor. The encyclopedia of neuropsychological disorders. New York, NY: Springer Publishing Company; 2011.

20 Alzheimer A. Über eigenartige Krankheitsfälle des späteren Alters. Zeitschrift für die gesamte Neurologie und Psychiatrie. 1911;4(1):356–385.

21 Goldberg ME. Parietal lobe. In: Smelser NJ, Baltes PB, editors. International encyclopedia of the social & behavioral sciences. Oxford: Pergamon; 2001, pp. 11051–11054.

22 Christopher G. The psychology of ageing: From mind to society. Basingstoke, Hampshire: Palgrave Macmillan; 2014.

23 VII. Associative Agnosia. Encyclopedia of the human brain. Elsevier Science & Technology; 2002.

24 Balint's syndrome. The penguin dictionary of psychology. Penguin; 2009.

25 Crutch SJ, Lehmann M, Schott JM, Rabinovici GD, Rossor MN, Fox NC. Posterior cortical atrophy. Lancet Neurol. 2012;11(2):170–178.

26 Sacks O. Hallucinations. London: Picador; 2012.

27 Tinetti ME, Richman D, Powell L. Falls efficacy as a measure of fear of falling. J Gerontol. 1990;45(6):P239–P243.

28 Walker JE, Howland J. Falls and fear of falling among elderly persons living in the community: Occupational therapy interventions. Am J Occup Ther. 1991;45(2):119–122.

29 Lord SR, Sherrington C, Menz HB, Close JC. Falls in older people: Risk factors and strategies for prevention. Cambridge: Cambridge University Press; 2007.

30 Olsson RH, Wambold S, Brock B, Waugh D, Sprague H. Visual spatial abilities and fall risk. J Gerontol Nurs. 2005;31(9):45–51.

31 Allan LM, Ballard CG, Rowan EN, Kenny RA. Incidence and prediction of falls in dementia: A prospective study in older people. PLoS One. 2009;4(5):e5521.

32 Folstein MF, Folstein SE, McHugh PR. "Mini-mental state". A practical method for grading the cognitive state of patients for the clinician. J Psychiatr Res. 1975;12(3):189–198.

33 Kudo Y, Imamura T, Sato A, Endo N. Risk factors for falls in community-dwelling patients with Alzheimer's disease and dementia with Lewy bodies: Walking with visuocognitive impairment may cause a fall. Dement Geriatr Cogn Disord. 2009;27(2):139–146.

34 Leipzig RM, Cumming RG, Tinetti ME. Drugs and falls in older people: A systematic review and meta-analysis: I. Psychotropic drugs. J Am Geriatr Soc. 1999;47(1):30–39.

35 Coupland C, Dhiman P, Morriss R, Arthur A, Barton G, Hippisley-Cox J. Antidepressant use and risk of adverse outcomes in older people: Population based cohort study. BMJ. 2011;343:d4551.

36 Gebara MA, Lipsey KL, Karp JF, Nash MC, Iaboni A, Lenze EJ. Cause or effect? Selective serotonin reuptake inhibitors and falls in older adults: A systematic review. Am J Geriatr Psychiatry. 2015;23(10):1016–1028.

37 Burton E, Cavalheri V, Adams R, Browne CO, Bovery-Spencer P, Fenton AM, et al. Effectiveness of exercise programs to reduce falls in older people with dementia living in the community: A systematic review and meta-analysis. Clin Interv Aging. 2015;10:421–434.

38 Suttanon P, Hill K, Said C, Dodd K. Can balance exercise programmes improve balance and related physical performance measures in people with dementia? A systematic review. Eur Rev Aging Phys Act. 2010;7(1):13.

39 Alzheimer's Society. Walking about 2017. Available from: www.alzheimers.org.uk/info/20064/symptoms/262/walking_about.

40 Mitchell A, Beaumont H, Ferguson D, Yadegarfar M, Stubbs B. Risk of dementia and mild cognitive impairment in older people with subjective memory complaints: Meta-analysis. Acta Psychiatr Scand. 2014;130(6):439–451.

41 Caracciolo B, Gatz M, Xu W, Marengoni A, Pedersen NL, Fratiglioni L. Relation of multimorbidity to subjective and objective cognitive impairment: A population-based twin study. J Alzheimers Dis. 2013;36(2):275.

42 Abdulrab K, Heun RJEP. Subjective memory impairment. A review of its definitions indicates the need for a comprehensive set of standardised and validated criteria. Eur Psychiatr. 2008;23(5):321–330.

43 Jessen F, Amariglio RE, Van Boxtel M, Breteler M, Ceccaldi M, Chételat G, et al. A conceptual framework for research on subjective cognitive decline in preclinical Alzheimer's disease. Alzheimers Dement. 2014;10(6):844–852.

44 Rabin LA, Smart CM, Crane PK, Amariglio RE, Berman LM, Boada M, et al. Subjective cognitive decline in older adults: An overview of self-report measures used across 19 international research studies. J Alzheimers Dis. 2015;48(s1):S63–S86.

45 Kliegel M, Zimprich D. Predictors of cognitive complaints in older adults: A mixture regression approach. Eur J Ageing. 2005;2(1):13–23.

46 Slavin MJ, Brodaty H, Kochan NA, Crawford JD, Trollor JN, Draper B, et al. Prevalence and predictors of "subjective cognitive complaints" in the Sydney Memory and Ageing Study. Am J Geriat Psychiatry. 2010;18(8):701–710.

47 Weaver Cargin J, Collie A, Masters C, Maruff P. The nature of cognitive complaints in healthy older adults with and without objective memory decline. J Clin Exp Neuropsychol. 2008;30(2):245–257.

48 Jonker C, Geerlings MI, Schmand B. Are memory complaints predictive for dementia? A review of clinical and population-based studies. Int J Geriatr Psychiatry. 2000;15(11):983–991.

49 Petersen RC, Doody R, Kurz A, Mohs RC, Morris JC, Rabins PV, et al. Current concepts in mild cognitive impairment. Arch Neurol. 2001;58(12):1985–1992.

50 Etgen T, Bickel H, Förstl HJ. Metabolic and endocrine factors in mild cognitive impairment. Ageing Res Rev. 2010;9(3):280–288.

51 Corner L, Bond J. The impact of the label of mild cognitive impairment on the individual's sense of self. Philos Psychiatry Psychol. 2006;13(1):3–12.

52 Calder PC, Carding SR, Christopher G, Kuh D, Langley-Evans SC, McNulty H. A holistic approach to healthy ageing: How can people live longer, healthier lives? J Hum Nutr. 2018;31(4):439–450.

53 Hogan DB, McKeith IG. Of MCI and dementia: Improving diagnosis and treatment. Neurology. 2001;56(9):1131–1132.

54 Sabat SR. Mild cognitive impairment: What's in a name? Philos Psychiatry Psychol. 2006;13(1):13–20.

Chapter 4

Assessment

What is assessment?

As for many conditions, assessment for dementia is a multi-stage process that takes time. In many cases, an evaluation of some description takes place long before clinicians become involved. Either the person themselves or their family and friends feel that something is amiss. For many, it is the sense that day-to-day activities are becoming more of a challenge and that there is an increase in the incidence of mistakes or problems. At this stage, people broach the subject of cognitive decline with their GP. This then starts the formal process of assessment that will eventuate in a diagnosis. This is a process fraught with emotional issues. The role of emotions will be discussed in depth in a subsequent chapter (Chapter 5). For the purpose of this chapter, the focus will be on the various methods of assessment used clinically to make sense of the cluster of symptoms individuals are experiencing.

Pre-diagnostic counselling

A common theme throughout this book is an acknowledgement of the emotional cost to the individual themselves and their family and friends of a diagnosis of dementia. It is a genuinely life-changing diagnosis. But we must remember that those changes take time. They do not happen overnight. To adapt, one must first understand. Having an assessment is an important step. Before embarking on this journey, people should be given time to talk things over with their clinician. They need to be given space to talk about their feelings and voice any fears they may have.

This initial consultation aims to help people better understand why they have been referred to a memory service and some potential outcomes. People are provided with sufficient information to make sense of events that have led up to this initial consultation. This is needed to give consent for the assessment to take place. As we shall see in Chapter 5, part of the process is to take a detailed medical history to feed into the subsequent diagnosis. Also, a range of physical tests and examinations will rule out other potential causes for the symptoms

DOI:10.4324/9781315681580-4

being described. However, this chapter will focus on tests of cognitive functioning and the use of neuroimaging to capture the range of difficulties a person is experiencing.

History taking

Although there is a focus on assessing the person's abilities first-hand, a great deal of helpful information can be obtained from the spouse or significant other. Valuable corroborating evidence is often obtained in this way.

When asking questions about a person's history, the patient and the person accompanying them must be interviewed separately. Indeed, the mere presence of someone else, be it a family member or a friend, often indicates a more profound problem with memory. A great deal of information can be obtained from such an interview, long before the formal cognitive assessment occurs. Relevant here is evidence of a person's ability to comprehend and cooperate, providing understanding into their language abilities and insight into their own difficulties. This is just not possible when someone else is present as family members or friends often offer help or interrupt the flow to correct something. How the person behaves during the interview is extremely useful, especially if any inappropriate behaviour becomes evident. The clinicians can also gauge how alert the individual appears. Problems here might indicate issues with their current prescription, or it might flag concerns that the person is, in fact, experiencing delirium.

Asking individuals to provide concrete examples of some of the problems they experience will also help build a more complete picture and suggest potential underlying causes. Evidence that a person finds it difficult to follow the plots of films or television programmes and loses objects frequently indicates problems with anterograde memory. An inability to find the correct word for an object and the increasing use of the word "thing" highlights issues with semantic memory (1).

Other specific points of interest to focus on in the interview include a description of the first recognized symptoms, how quickly symptoms worsened, the degree to which life has been affected, concerns around safety, as well as details of past medical history and disclosure of a family history of dementia. Generally, the first manifestation of a problem has a great deal of clinical significance when first formulating a diagnosis (2).

The clinician will start by establishing an estimate of pre-morbid capabilities. This is achieved by obtaining as much information as possible about a person's educational background, employment history, and details about the significant relationships in that person's life. A person's hobbies and interests provide valuable insight into their capacities.

Neuropsychological assessment

At the beginning of this chapter, it was stated that the progression of each disease follows a specific pattern. Taking Alzheimer's disease as an example, the initial site of pathology is the perihippocampal region. It then widens out to affect the tempo-roparietal association cortex and, later, the frontal lobes. This pattern of structural damage mirrors the types of functional impairments seen in the patient. Initially, the person experiences problems recalling recent experiences—anterograde episodic memory loss—but soon finds it difficult maintaining their attention on tasks, finding the right words (semantic memory), problems navigating and orientating self (visuoperceptual), and eventually their character changes (personality) (3).

Neuropsychological assessment batteries aim to provide as complete a picture of a person's cognitive functioning as possible. Individual tests focus on specific skills and abilities that include attention and memory. In many cases, they are pencil-and-paper tests. Relatively simple tasks can build up a picture of the unique deficits a person is experiencing. Scores on these tests at the initial screening can then gauge decline over the ensuing months and years. At the end of the assessment, the clinician should be better positioned to firm up a diagnosis or otherwise refer the patient for a more detailed investigation. For a more in-depth account of neuropsychological testing, especially for older adults, please see Chapter 8 of my book on the psychology of ageing (4).

A person's performance on tests of neuropsychological functioning is compared to normative data (5). For every standardized test, there are normative data whereby a clinic assessment score can be compared against healthy control data matched for age, education, and culture, among other things.

To contribute to a diagnosis of major neurocognitive disorder, a person will be performing two or more standard deviations—variability around the mean—below the published norm. Performance is around one to two standard deviations below the norm for mild neurocognitive disorder.

Many factors influence performance on such tests. The conditions under which assessment is taken may be far from ideal. It is essential to consider whether conditions may confound the results obtained, such as sensory impairment or concurrent mental health or health condition. Is poor hearing contributing to low scores on the various measures, for instance?

An alternative to more extensive neuropsychological assessment comes in a range of brief measures that can be administered where more intensive evaluation is not practical.

In all cases of neuropsychological testing, to some extent, one could argue that findings only make sense if a person has performed the same test or tests in the past, and their results are available to compare against current performance. If not, there is no evidence to indicate whether current performance is indicative of a marked decline in function. However, in most cases, such data is not available. One obvious exception here is adults who have registered on participant databases for research purposes. Most such databases include data from a range of assessments. It is, indeed, a requirement of researchers to monitor and identify any changes to how someone is performing when recruited onto studies. Should a person recruited as a healthy control show a decline in functioning, it is the ethical duty of the researcher to inform the participant and encourage consultation with an appropriate specialist.

In the majority of cases, however, current performance must be compared against normative data. Such comparisons also need to consider a person's educational background and occupation. Comparisons with normative data are potentially flawed when applied to individuals at both ends of the education spectrum. Another problem with many normative datasets is that they do not cover all cultures. As a result, such comparisons can again be flawed. Indeed, as we shall see in Chapter 10, the language a person is tested in is of importance. A person tested in their acquired language, as opposed to their native language, may be at a disadvantage, especially in the case of a possible diagnosis of dementia.

Issues with neuropsychological screening

There are, as one might expect, drawbacks to neuropsychological screening tools. What does that score, in fact, say about the person's cognitive capacity? What can it be compared to? Nothing in the vast majority of cases. When running an experiment, we always take what are called baseline measures. This means we can use these scores later to compare against current performance. This allows us, for example, to gauge if an intervention has been effective. It can also inform us if there has been a deterioration in performance. There are no such baseline measures to compare against for people entering a memory clinic. As previously mentioned, the only obvious exception was those who had once signed up to take part in memory research. Healthy control data is essential when studying the effects of the disease. Many join such databases as they fear developing the same illness as a close relative.

Because we do not know a person's baseline level of functioning, a person may enter a memory clinic and score within the acceptable range on memory assessments. However, unknown to the clinicians, if the test had been administered just a few years earlier, that same person would have scored exceptionally well on it. In this case, what is assessed as being acceptable is, in fact, a significant decline in function. To ameliorate this issue, a great deal of emphasis is placed on reported subjective change in memory functioning (6).

Standard neuropsychological measures

There are many measures to choose from. Rather than attempt to list them all or even evidence the main ones, I shall instead explore the major domains of function that are of interest to clinicians to make an accurate diagnosis. Along the way, I shall refer to specific measures as appropriate.

Orientation

It is helpful to gauge how accurately a person is oriented in time and place. This is generally assessed by asking someone the day, date, month, season, and year. Also, a person will be asked where they are at that moment; in other words, the name of the building and the floor they are on. There are concerns about how accurate such assessments of orientation are. Indeed, in the previous chapter, I presented Sabat's (7) argument that perhaps these questions actually measure memory.

However, given the current tools, perhaps the most useful question concerns orientation in time. We are all sometimes a little unsure what the current date is. However, knowing the rough time of day is valuable. We may not know the precise time, but we all know whether it is late morning, lunchtime-ish, or early afternoon. We are also pretty accurate at gauging time intervals, such as the length of time spent somewhere or doing something. This is less accurately monitored in people experiencing delirium or moderate dementia symptoms (2).

There may be many reasons why a person appears to perform poorly on assessments of orientation, ones that do not include dementia as a potential cause. Indeed, it may become increasingly common now that we live in a more technologically advanced age. Before smartphones existed, before the internet consumed our lives, people kept diaries and populated wall calendars. Milk was delivered to the doorstep on particular days. The daily newspaper was delivered. Radio and television schedules dictated what you did at certain times on specific days. News programmes were shown at certain times throughout the day. Now, of course, most have no need for paper diaries. Shopping is conducted online. People read about the news online or receive regular push messages with headlines. There are 24-hour news channels. We are no longer tied to the broadcasters' schedules with catch-up and streaming services. We can choose when we want to watch something. This is all great. I certainly would not listen to or watch anything if not for these services. However, it does come at a cost. We have lost myriad instances throughout our days that anchored us in time. Each loss is minor, but combined, it has a dramatic effect.

A large proportion of our life centres around school and work. We have a daily routine. This is something that keeps us in check. This is lost when we retire or stop work for health reasons. Without this constant reinforcement of orientation, many lose track of time. There are many reasons why keeping active in retirement is so important. One of these is that having plans, goals, taking part in voluntary work, all help retain that vital sense of structure.

In cases where poor health or mobility issues prevent a person from doing any of this, problems can quickly arise. If one does not go out for any significant time, each day merges into the next. This is something we can all relate to, especially during extended lockdowns due to COVID-19. I experience it often. I am hugely fortunate to hold a job where there is a great deal of flexibility regarding how and when I work. If I work from home for several days over the summer, I lose awareness of time. Because I am a poster person for bad working habits—my own making, no one else's, I know—I often do not know what day it is. I have lost the distinct marker of the weekend to identify the close of the working week. I also work irregular hours. Because of this, I am set adrift and have no fixed mark of time. The same happens if a person finds themselves restricted in their mobility or feels too frightened to venture out independently. Even though we relish no longer adhering to the nine-to-five routine when we retire, some structure is essential.

It has also been suggested that we should maintain a fixed sleeping schedule. This is especially important for those who work during the week and lie in at the weekend. Such behaviour might be doing us more harm than good. Recent research shows that we are inducing a state comparable to jetlag—termed social jetlag—by doing this as we are inducing a disconnect between the body's natural circadian rhythm and a socially imposed sleep pattern (8). We are not making up for lost sleep. All we are doing is throwing the body out-of-synch. It has been suggested that we need to stick to a routine regardless of whether it is a workday or not (9).

Memory

Problems with memory are the most common complaints initiating the referral for assessment. Memory, as we know, can be divided into discrete domains of function. We shall look at the most prominent in turn.

Episodic memory

Episodic memory is a first-person account of a situation. You, as an individual, inhabit these memories. They are multifaceted, comprising feelings as well as links to other memories. Such memories are highly contextual in nature (10). The medial temporal lobes, particularly the hippocampus, underpin these memories. The frontal lobes are also involved in controlling and monitoring the retrieval of episodic memories, especially in the context of learning.

Autobiographical memory is derived from episodic memories (11). Such memories constitute our sense of who we are; our sense of self, in other words. In addition to the personal memories we have just been talking about—episodic memory—autobiographical memories also contain details of who we are—autobiographical knowledge—such as where we went to school, where we lived, and so on (12). These memories bind our sense of self to the here-and-now. When this connection is lost, through either brain injury or a mental health problem, profound problems arise. In some extreme cases, such as psychogenic fugue, a person loses all sense of self, personal memories, even their name.

The information we hold about ourselves often manifests as statements or beliefs. Oftentimes visual imagery supplement these assertions. This is referred to as autobiographical knowledge. This package of knowledge becomes bound to specific episodic memories in the formation of autobiographical memory. When such memories are recalled, the person is described as having a recollective experience. This is best described as the person inhabiting a memory of their self in the past and experiencing the feelings associated with that remembrance.

Recollective experience refers to the thoughts, feelings, and sensations experienced in retrieving an autobiographical memory (13). Bringing to mind episodic memories, with its concomitant deluge of contextual information, brings with it a sense that this has already happened; it is in the past. As you dwell on various aspects of these memories, greater detail is brought to mind. There is a real sense of reminiscence.

In contrast, recalling a fact from semantic memory is nothing more than mere retrieval. It is a piece of information held in mind devoid of context. Because of that, one does not experience reminiscence, of the past being once again brought to life. There is only knowing. Asked who wrote La Cenerentola, I would immediately say Rossini. I would have no sense how I came to acquire this piece of information. No specific feelings are activated. It is just a fact. It may have started off as episodic memory, but all the trappings have been stripped away. It has been divested of all context. The original episodic memory may have been my first hearing this opera on the radio. I may then have read a review of a new recording of the same piece. Now I know Rossini wrote this work. There is no hint of that first experience of hearing it anywhere. Remembering refers to episodic memory; knowing is semantic memory. What I am describing here is the distinction between recollection and familiarity.

There is a lifespan element to consider. There are differences in how we recall our previous life experiences with time. This can be plotted as the lifespan retrieval curve (14). There are three sections to this curve reflecting childhood (up to the age of 5), ages 10–30, and then more recent memories.

The period of childhood is shrouded in mystery. It is generally referred to as childhood amnesia. It is not entirely clear why this happens, especially as the child reaches closer to their fifth birthday. Memory is clearly functioning at this time, but why can one not remember anything?

The period of our lives between the age of 10 and 30 is described as the reminiscence bump. We tend to recall more memories during this period than at any other time in our lives. One explanation is that this period is fraught with novel, self-defining experiences, thus offering a reason why these memories are particularly enduring. On closer inspection, on the whole, the types of memories remembered during this period are not necessarily novel. Instead, they reflect memories of events that mirror one's interests and particular settings or situations (11). One might argue that memories are better recalled when there is an overriding connection to one's self; they are self-defining episodes in our lives (15).

There is less debate over the last phase of the curve. This aspect reflects memories after the age of around 30. More recent memories are more accessible because they occurred relatively recently. Older memories are prone to interference or decay. The recency—or regency as my auto-correct would have it—effect has been demonstrated many times in well-controlled laboratory experiments. This is where people can better recall the final few items in a list. The same experiments show that we are also better at remembering the first few items. The bits in the middle tend to disappear.

As mentioned earlier, the integrity of autobiographical memories can be eroded through illness. Damage to the frontal lobes can result in people not recalling detailed memories associated with their past. When damage is more severe, false memories may be created through a process of confabulation. Those who have experienced damage to the temporal lobes, specifically structures in the limbic system, the region containing the hippocampal formation, lose the capacity to lay down new memories, although, depending on the sites affected and the extent of the damage, past memories preceding the injury are retained and are accessible. Damage to the hippocampal formation has long been known to cause anterograde amnesia. One of the most important papers ever written in psychology was a report on the now famous patient, Henry Molaison, or H.M. as he is known. In this paper, Scoville and Milner (16) describe the profound amnesia experienced by Henry as the result of the rogue surgical intervention—bilateral excision (or resection) of the medial temporal lobe—that took place to cure his epilepsy.

Damage to other areas, the occipital lobes, eventuate in an inability to generate mental images of one's past. Again, this compounds the amnesia due entirely to the nature of autobiographical memory, specifically the episodic components. Episodic memory is mainly visual in nature. Because these patients can no longer create mental images, they cannot access other aspects of episodic memory (11).

Mental health conditions also affect autobiographical memory. I mentioned a severe condition, psychogenic fugue, previously. This is a rare condition that is thought to be caused by extreme psychological stress or abuse. It is just one of the conditions described as dissociative disorders. However, the more commonplace condition, depression, affect the recall of these memories. In such states, the entire structure of autobiographical memories change. Rather than being specific, they lack detail and can best be described as schematic. A person experiencing depression would only be able to describe going to see concerts; they would be unable to hone in on a specific memory of a specific performance.

Coming back to dementia, we can talk about anterograde memory loss and retrograde memory loss (2). Anterograde memory loss refers to problems with laying down new memories. Examples of anterograde memory loss include forgetting appointments, losing items, and failing to follow plots of films or television programmes. Retrograde memory loss refers to an inability to recall previously held memories. Examples of this include an inability to remember a job one had in the past or finding oneself lost in what should be a familiar environment.

Both anterograde and retrograde memory loss occurs in Alzheimer's disease. However, this is not always the case. Herpes simplex encephalitis—inflammation of the brain due to the herpes simplex virus—is associated with pure anterograde memory loss due to focal damage to the hippocampus. Korsakoff's syndrome, caused by a severe thiamine deficiency, is related to extensive confabulation. On the whole, this takes the form of confusion among actual memories, with the material being recalled out of context.

Semantic memory

I have already mentioned semantic memory when elaborating upon autobiographical memory. Semantic memory refers to our store of factual knowledge. Because of this, it does not come laden with contextual information. In addition, there is no sense of self embedded in semantic memories as there is in autobiographical memory. Semantic memory is an example of declarative memory. Declarative memory is consciously recalled. It is often referred to as explicit memory. In other words, specific information is brought to mind. Such memories are reflected upon and used to answer questions or solve problems. We can express them verbally to ourselves and others. On the other hand, nondeclarative memories are not open for conscious inspection and only become apparent through action (17).

Semantic memory is involved in language processing as it contains our knowledge about words and categories. It is intrinsic to how we form mental representations. Mental representations are the basis of understanding the world in which we live.

In Chapter 3, we covered semantic dementia. This is where there is a specific impairment in semantic memory. Our store of semantic knowledge is vital here. This is referred to as the semantic network. The semantic memory system accesses this semantic network.

The semantic network is hierarchical, comprising representations of concepts and categories (18). It is a graphical representation of the interconnections between individual elements that together build up our understanding of the world. Take, for example, the category of animals. There are many different types of animals. There are cats, dogs, horses, cows, birds, and so on and so forth. Within each of these, there are differences. The oft used example is birds, so I shall also use it as it perfectly suits the purpose. So, within the category of animals, we have birds. Birds typically fly. We immediately think of swifts or gulls.[1] There are, of course, birds that do not fly: think ostrich, penguin, Orville the Duck (who dreamed of flying, high into the sky, but couldn't). The speed with which we access information from this semantic network depends on many things, including how typical the example is. We access information about typical birds more quickly than we do about atypical ones. We identify a gull as a bird faster than a penguin (which has the added confound of being a confection).

When a person experiences problems with semantic memory, word-finding difficulty is increasingly a problem. Because of this, people start using "thing" to refer to items rather than the word itself. Anomia refers to a profound difficulty finding the right word and is symptomatic of aphasia, an acquired language disorder. It is also present in semantic dementia. Comprehension, too, is affected, starting with less frequently used words. In the case of semantic dementia, another characteristic problem is with naming and classifying objects.

Working memory

Working memory underpins everything we do. It is more than just short-term memory. It refers to our ability to actively manipulate new and old material, attend to many things at a time, and accurately navigate our environment. This is just a few of the activities it is involved in. A large part of my career as a researcher has been dedicated to exploring working memory, specifically the impact of mental health and health conditions on our ability to use working memory. I am talking here about working memory as a single, agreed construct. It is not. But this is not a book on cognitive models of working memory, so for the purpose of this tome, let us assume that it is.

I am finding it very difficult not to go off on an extended digression about the nature of working memory. However, all we really need to say at this stage is that there are different components to working memory. The account I provide here most closely follows that set out by Alan Baddeley. Indeed, he has recently written a book talking about his version of events, one that I heartedly recommend to all who have cognitive leanings (19). There are dedicated systems that enable us to process modality-specific information. By modality, I mean a particular form of sensory input, such as vision, sound, and so on.

Auditory information is processed by the phonological loop. This comprises two elements, one that is a passive time-limited store, the other a subvocal process that keeps the information active. Think about when you need to type in a password that you infrequently use—assuming you do not avail yourself of your browser's capacity to retain this information for you—and you have to seek out a reminder to yourself. This constant repetition of the password up to the point of typing it is what I am referring to here. I could have used the good old example of repeating someone's telephone number, but who does that anymore!

A comparable system called the visuospatial sketch pad processes visual and spatial information. Much like the phonological loop, the sketch pad consists of two separate processes: a transient passive store and a rehearsal process.

As its name would suggest, there is an overarching control process that goes by the name of the central executive. I have already referred to executive functions in previous sections. For the sake of this book, assume executive functions reflect the operation of the central executive. It is not as simple as that. The central executive is a term specific to Baddeley's model, but there are other models, as I have said. So, I shall be referring to executive function in general for most of this book. As I said, I need to resist the urge to write a tract on the topic. There are distinct functions associated with the central executive. These include regulating how information is processed, controlling actions, planning, enabling goal-directed behaviour, and retrieving material from long-term memory (20). The central executive is limited in capacity. In fact, we are only too aware of this in our daily lives. We know we all too often reach and exceed our limits. There are only so many things we can mentally juggle at one time without suffering the costs.

There is a final component of working memory that I have not yet mentioned. I shall now mention it and then move on. The episodic buffer. There. Said it. It is the least well-defined of all Baddeley's components. It is proposed to act as a space wherein multiple streams of information are stored for current operations. It is also the conduit by which material from long-term memory is accessed.

It is important to reinforce that the conceptualization of working memory is a model. As such, it is continually undergoing scrutiny and, when needed, revision.

It is a work in progress that, purely because of that, has led to many advancements in our understanding of memory and how it is affected by different conditions.

When a person experiences deficits in working memory, they are prone to lapses in concentration, such as becoming distracted and then unable to resume a previous thought process again. Problems with working memory occur due to the typical ageing process (4). More specific issues arise as a result of depression and anxiety (21).

Language

In the previous section on semantic memory, we discussed language. A great deal of information can be gleaned about language production and comprehension during the history-taking phase of the consultation. In particular, the clinician will be able to obtain a good understanding of the person's facility for speaking effectively (fluency), their use of stress and changes in pitch (prosody), ability to form and structure sentences (agrammatism), and generate speech sounds (articulation). During such sessions, evidence of word-finding difficulties and incorrect use of words (paraphasia) are easy to detect.

Executive function

After having given myself a good talking to earlier about resisting the urge to digress on the topic of working memory, I need to exercise the same level of constraint here. There are various models of executive function. However, this is not the place to explore this. Instead, I shall present a brief overview of what we mean by executive function in terms of behaviours. It might be summarized as describing a range of cognitive activities that involve the coordination and sequencing of specific actions. Executive function is associated chiefly with the frontal lobes, although the dynamic exchange of information throughout the brain is essential here. Three of the most readily identifiable executive functions reflect our ability to switch from one mode of operation to another (set-shifting), keep track of and revise representations in memory (monitoring and updating), and avoid distraction from irrelevant information (inhibition) (22). When impaired, people find it challenging to plan, make accurate judgements, solve problems, reason, and control their impulses.

Problems carrying out such activities are called executive dysfunction or dysexecutive syndrome (23). Impairments of this nature occur through some damage or malfunctioning of the frontal lobes. Cognitive deficits of the type just described are the result of dorsal damage. In addition to problems coordinating, planning, and initiating behaviour, dysexecutive syndrome also affects verbal fluency and a person's ability to keep on topic during a conversation. In some cases, it may lead to confabulation. This is where memories are added to or elaborated upon. Damage to the ventral regions results in problems controlling emotions (24). I shall come back to this aspect in Chapter 7.

Two classic symptoms of executive dysfunction are perseveration and utilization behaviour. Perseveration refers to the repetition or continuation of a behaviour or response that is no longer appropriate. It can take many forms. When asked to perform a particular movement, many will repeat it even though it is no longer required, a situation referred to as continuous perseveration. In other instances, people find it challenging to switch from one mode of responding to another. This is known as "stuck in set" perseveration. Recurrent perseveration is when a response is repeated after a delay, but the response is no longer appropriate. For example, when asked for the definition of a word, the person responds by providing the definition for a previous word in the list (25).

Utilization behaviour reflects a situation where an object is used correctly but not at an appropriate time or for no apparent reason. The presence of an object compels them to touch and grasp it. They perform the necessary actions, but this is not driven by conscious intention. For example, a water jug is placed on a table in front of someone. Next, a glass is positioned alongside it. The person may pick up the pitcher and pour a glass of water with no intention to drink it. They seem duty-bound to perform the actions without the requisite desire or need.

Impairment of executive function is seen in Alzheimer's disease, among other conditions. Executive dysfunction is a defining feature of frontotemporal dementia. Indeed, the classic "frontal lobe" symptoms of perseveration and utilization behaviour, as described earlier, are clearly evident. Problems with sequencing and coordinating activity are increasingly problematic early on in Alzheimer's disease. These difficulties become more severe as the disease progresses. Perseveration is also seen in Alzheimer's disease (25), primarily continuous perseveration and recurrent perseveration. Utilization behaviour may be seen in those in the latter stages of Alzheimer's disease. Head injury is probably the most common cause (2). Given the frontal lobe is largely subcortical white matter—the conduit for neural connections between cortical and subcortical regions (26)—impairments can occur as the result of genetic disorders that attack the central nervous system (leucodystrophy), loss of myelin insulation around nerve fibres (demyelination), and diseases of the circulatory system (vascular pathology). Damage to the basal ganglia—a region responsible for integrating information and regulating movement and thought—can also lead to such problems. Progressive supranuclear palsy—a rare condition associated with impaired eye movement, muscle rigidity, repetitive actions, slowness, and cognitive impairment—is one example where this is clearly the case.

Before leaving the topic of executive dysfunction, I should point out that earlier texts referred to frontal lobe syndrome. We now know that it is more diverse than that. These problems reflect more than a loss of integrity of the frontal lobes; they also reveal issues with how well other pathways in the brain operate. Adaptive behaviour of the type described in relation to executive function requires the dynamic interplay of all brain areas, all of which are orchestrated by the frontal lobes. We now tend to refer to functional problems rather than specific problems in relation to a particular anatomical structure.

Apraxia

Apraxia describes a person's inability to carry out a voluntary movement with a specific part of the body or to correctly use an object. There is no indication of sensory or motor dysfunction to account for this difficulty (27), nor is there a lack of comprehension. The person is just not able to execute the action. From a clinical perspective, apraxias are best described in relation to the area or a limb affected and the characteristics of the impairment. Problems here are associated with impaired functioning of the left parietal and frontal lobes. Where apraxia is experienced in a single limb, and the symptoms worsen over time, this indicates deterioration in the cortex and basal ganglia, known as corticobasal degeneration.

Visuospatial functioning

The visual cortex is vital for visuospatial functioning. Information from the visual cortex progresses along two routes to reach the temporal and parietal lobes. One way combines visual and spatial data and provides detail about where things occur. This happens in the parietal lobe and is referred to as the dorsal stream. An alternative line of processing brings together visual information and knowledge from semantic memory. This occurs in the temporal lobes and provides details of what is encountered.

Damage to this area and these pathways result in distinct symptoms. For some, visual neglect may occur, manifesting in different ways, such as a person failing to notice and therefore not eating food on one side of their plate. Visual hallucinations occur in several conditions. These are often organic in origin and are linked to diseases such as dementia with Lewy bodies.

Activities of daily living

Activities of daily living (ADLs) refer to the types of tasks we all perform every day. In other words, behaviours that relate to basic care and independence, including washing and dressing, eating, and continence. Assessment here provides the clinician with an index of functional ability (28). This is particularly pertinent when considering a person's ability to live independently (29).

A more comprehensive assessment will include instrumental activities of daily living (IADLs). These reflect a range of physical and cognitive capacities, such as home management, shopping, safety, and the ability to monitor health (30). IADLs reflect a person's ability to be flexible and adaptable. There are also enhanced activities of daily living (EADLs) that focus on this capacity to adapt and change to the demands of the situation. Included here are assessments of a person's ability to perform hobbies, keep in contact with family and friends, and be up to date in their knowledge and use of technology. EADLs reflect activities that are even more cognitively demanding than those described by IADLs (31).

In all cases, a close family member or friend can provide a great deal of helpful information here. The more cognitively demanding ADLs—driving, taking medication, use of appliances—are affected in the earlier stages of dementia. Personal hygiene and continence become affected further down the line.

Behavioural assessment

A reliable indicator of progressive decline is the presence or reporting of behaviours deemed out-of-place or unacceptable in a person who has always upheld rules of etiquette and societal norms. Such transgressions are referred to as inappropriate behaviour. As is the case with assessing activities of daily living, input from a family member or a friend is invaluable here. Indeed, there is often a mismatch between behaviours reported by a significant other and those proffered by the patient. Much can be gleaned about how much insight a person has of their problems by asking direct questions about such contraventions of mores.

A person's ability to consider and act in accordance with the emotional states of others is severely hampered where there is damage to the frontal lobes. There may be evidence of impulsive behaviour that indicates an inability to inhibit actions, a state of affairs associated with impaired functioning of the orbitofrontal cortex.

Disturbed mood

Although there have been long-held debates, many of which are still unresolved, about whether cognitive functioning should be considered separately from emotion processing, it is clear, when looking at clinical conditions, that to do so makes little sense. Cognition and emotion are intimately conjoined. Take, for example, Alzheimer's disease. We know that depression is prevalent in those diagnosed with this dementia. We also know that depression itself results in marked impairments in cognitive functioning. Because of this, it is very difficult to tease out the root cause of impairment in the early stages of dementia: is it dementia, is it depression, or is it both? Clinicians need to keep track of any change in a person's sleep pattern, appetite, and energy levels.

Assessment tools

Screening tests are needed to identify those exhibiting signs of early cognitive decline (32). Sensitive measures will help clinicians ensure appropriate assessments are carried out, and suitable therapies are offered early. Cognitive assessment is still the primary way to detect and diagnose dementia. Biological investigations are used principally to detect and exclude potentially reversible causes of the observed deficits. In this sense, they are adjunctive in nature (33). Several tools are available. Because of this, there is much variability in which measures are used in different clinics (34). The tests used need to be sensitive to deficits in key areas of cognitive functioning to minimize the likelihood that someone will fall through the net and not be offered the treatment and support they need. Such false-negative diagnoses have far-reaching implications for both the person with dementia and their carer (35). The measures used need to be accurate in differentiating patterns of impairment so that it is better able to limit false-positive diagnoses. This is where someone is diagnosed with dementia when, in fact, no disease process is present. The implications here are obvious.

The following is not meant to be comprehensive. There are many more screening tools available. However, the ones presented here are the most widely used and are most familiar to all who work in the field.

General Practitioner Assessment of Cognition

Initial assessments of cognitive function may be carried out by the GP. Many different tests are available, but one commonly used by GPs is the General Practitioner Assessment of Cognition (GPCOG) (36). It comprises two components: an assessment of the patient in the clinic and an appraisal of function carried out by the carer or other relevant person. This second element is only carried out when scores on the first are inconclusive. It consists of standard indicators of cognitive functioning such as immediate and delayed recall, orientation in time, visuospatial processing, and awareness of current affairs. The informant interview requests comment about whether the patient has problems remembering things that had just happened, difficulty recalling recently held conversations, issues finding the right words, and asking about the person's ability to retain independence, such as handling their own medication, managing money, using transport.

Mini-Mental State Examination (MMSE)

The Mini-Mental State Examination, or MMSE, is widely used still (37). This tool allows clinicians to assess a person's orientation in time and space, attention, memory, and language. Often additional tasks are used to compensate for the lack of tests measuring executive function and visuospatial processing (2). The current edition includes the option for a brief screening assessment via tablet or smartphone. There is also a more extended version to be used for a more detailed assessment of conditions such as subcortical dementia.

As seen previously, the MMSE is not without its limitations. It is not particularly sensitive at detecting dementia in its early stages. Some of the assessments are somewhat rudimentary, and there is no examination of verbal fluency. Also, unless suffering from severe aphasia, people tend to perform at ceiling on the language items (37).

Addenbrooke's Cognitive Examination

The Addenbrooke's Cognitive Examination (ACE) was created to tackle the problems identified in the MMSE (38). The revised version, the ACE-R (39), was quick to administer and more convenient for clinicians to use (40). Reliability is good, and it is sensitive to detecting cognitive impairment in the early stages. It can also distinguish different forms of dementia (39). However, the revised version is not without its problems. These include the issue of ceiling effects for several of the items. This is where many of the patients score maximum marks on items, thereby hampering the capacity to differentiate individuals in terms of the severity of their impairment. The ACE-III was developed to address issues relating to the previous incarnation's limitation regarding screening individuals from other cultures (41). The mini-ACE is a shortened version of the ACE-III and was designed to be administered in under five minutes while still retaining sensitivity and specificity (41). There is also a version of this available for tablets, which improves the ease with which it can be administered using resources available in clinics (42). Computerized versions help with standardizing administration, scoring, and reporting, providing greater accuracy overall (43).

Montreal Cognitive Assessment

The Montreal Cognitive Assessment (MoCA) (44) was developed to detect mild cognitive impairment. The MoCA has a short administration time of around ten minutes and is amenable for use in primary care settings, which is important given the need to detect significant cognitive impairment as early as possible. In terms of sensitivity, the MoCA is better than the MMSE for those with mild cognitive impairment or Alzheimer's disease. However, its specificity is lower than the MMSE (45).

Having described the use of neuropsychological testing, we will shortly look at the role of neuroimaging in aiding the assessment process. Neuroimaging has enjoyed a relatively short but productive history. Such technology has expanded considerably since the 1980s. Neuroimaging refers to the use of technology to accurately map different structures and functions within the brain of a living person. Before we do so, we shall take a brief look at other forms of neurological testing that may feed into the assessment process for dementia.

Neurological testing

Aside from cognitive assessment, standard neurological tests should be carried out to examine the integrity of the neurological system. When at rest, patients should be assessed for evidence of involuntary movements. These can include jerky, spasmodic movements (chorea), rhythmic movement (tremor), sustained muscle contractions producing abnormal postures (dystonia), and brief shock-like movements (myoclonus). Such involuntary contractions and twitching—fasciculation—can be extremely helpful in narrowing down a diagnosis. Primitive reflexes should be tested to demonstrate their presence or absence.

Eyes should be scrutinized and include tests of clarity of vision (visual acuity), the response of pupils to changes in lighting, eye movement, focal and peripheral vision (visual fields), and blind spots (optic discs). We have already talked about the importance of assessing language and speech. Swallowing should also be considered alongside speech as there may be evidence of paralysis of the tongue, throat, and larynx, a disorder called bulbar palsy.

The clinician should look for evidence of pyramidal or extrapyramidal symptoms. Where the pyramidal tract has been damaged—nerve fibres from the motor cortex which cross-over at the brainstem—a person will exhibit weakness or paralysis on one side of their body, increased muscle tension on the affected side, jerking movements, and a Babinski reflex—where toes fan out when the sole of the foot is stroked in opposition to the usual curling up. The extrapyramidal system extends from the cortex to the medulla, then pathways involved in voluntary actions progress down the spine. Damage to this pathway is associated with characteristic actions referred to as extrapyramidal symptoms. These include disturbed voluntary movements, often marked by slowness, either an increase or a decrease in muscle tone, as well as involuntary movements such as tremor, jerking, or writhing.

A person's gait should be viewed with an eye to detect possible abnormalities. Evidence of problems coordinating actions, issues with balance, and control of movement may indicate a cause other than Alzheimer's disease or other forms of dementia, such as peripheral neuropathy. Simple activities can quickly highlight if there is a problem here. These include asking patients to copy gestures or perform specific movements alternating from one hand to the other.

Neuroimaging

In some instances, a person with suspected dementia may be referred for a brain scan. Many different forms of neuroimaging exist, each with its own use.

Structural scans

Scans are used to look at structural changes in the brain.

Computed tomography

Computed tomography (CT) scans became available in the 1970s. Until then, it had not been possible to obtain an image of the living brain. Computing power also improved exponentially, enabling further advancements. CT scans are particularly effective at helping clinicians identify conditions that might produce the types of symptoms experienced, conditions that need to be ruled out before entertaining a diagnosis of dementia. These include cerebral haemorrhage, tumour, and hydrocephalus. CT scans can show if there has been a degree of shrinkage of cerebral tissue concomitant with a diagnosis of dementia.

Magnetic resonance imaging

Due partly to the faster processing and storage capacity of computers, techniques other than CT were developed. One of them involved utilizing the principles of nuclear magnetic resonance. Underpinning this is the knowledge that radio frequency waves—RF waves—could be used to detect differences in tissue. This is because atoms inside the molecules that make up the different tissues within the brain resonate at a different rate when a pulsed magnetic field is applied and, as a result, emit RF waves. Differences in reflected RF waves are then used to create an image of the brain. Such magnetic resonance imaging (MRI) provides not only a detailed image of the gross anatomy of the brain, it also allows other aspects to be analysed, such as neural pathways and connectivity (diffusion tensor imaging, DTI), and also the chemical composition of the brain (magnetic resonance spectroscopy, MRS) (46). MRI is used in a similar way to CT scans in that they are used to identify other conditions that may be producing the symptoms a person is experiencing, this time with an emphasis on vascular changes. Changes to blood vessels might indicate stroke or point towards vascular dementia.

Functional scans

In addition to scans that look at changes in the structure of brain tissue, some scans measure changes in brain activity.

Single-photon emission computed tomography

Functional scans developed from nuclear medicine. This is a branch of medicine where radioactive substances aid diagnosis or assist treatment. An early form of functional imaging was the single-photon emission computed tomography (SPECT). This technique made use of radiopharmaceuticals. Following injection into a person's bloodstream, these chemicals can then be tracked. The absorption—referred to as uptake—of these radioactive compounds then measure brain activity. This type of scan provides clinicians with evidence of reduced blood flow or metabolism in specific areas of the brain. As such, SPECT may be used in conjunction with CT and MRI scans to help elucidate more complicated cases.

Positron emission tomography

Similarly to SPECT, positron emission tomography (PET) utilizes radioactive substances that attach themselves to molecules of interest—known as ligands—to again measure how much occurs within the brain. In the case of dementia, it is used to gauge the level of different molecules in the brain, such as the amyloid protein we have already talked about in Chapter 2, high concentrations of which characterizes Alzheimer's disease, and also glucose levels as a way to assess how effectively the brain is using energy.[2]

Functional MRI

We have already talked about MRI as a technique. Functional MRI, or fMRI, allows clinicians to specify which areas of the brain are associated with a particular activity. This is achieved by tracking changes in blood flow and oxygen levels. Differences in the blood oxygen level dependent (BOLD) signal provides a proxy for measuring cognitive activity (47).

Electroencephalography

Electroencephalography (EEG) is a direct way of measuring electrical activity in the brain from the surface of the skull. This is because the brain generates electrical and magnetic fields. EEG detects fluctuations in the electrical activity of the brain. The various traces reflect different forms of activity. EEG can be used to help diagnose and manage a range of medical conditions. Indeed, evidence suggests that it might help discriminate between Alzheimer's pathology and Lewy body dementia (48). EEG accurately tracks changes in functioning over time, but it is less accurate in pinpointing which areas of the brain contribute to that activity; in other words, it has good temporal resolution but poor spatial resolution. The reason for including EEG here is that it is often used in conjunction with neuroimaging methods to provide a more complete picture of functioning.

Magnetoencephalography

Magnetoencephalography (MEG) detects tiny changes in magnetic fields generated by the activity of neurons. This is achieved by using a superconducting quantum interference device, or SQUID, which is incredibly sensitive to minute changes in magnetic flux. Unlike fMRI, MEG directly measures brain activity with excellent temporal and spatial resolution. MEG is often combined with MRI scans, called magnetic source imaging (MSI). MEG has been used to provide evidence of neurocompensation in Alzheimer's disease. This is where the brain, in effect, works harder to offset some of the loss of function due to the disease process (49).

When are scans used?

Much like other forms of assessment, a diagnosis of dementia cannot be made using brain scans alone. Diagnoses are made following a broader range of assessments. Scans are useful nonetheless to identify other problems, such as evidence of stroke or a brain tumour. CT scans are helpful for this. It is important to note that not everyone suspected of having dementia will be referred for a brain scan.

MRI scans provide evidence for the presence of damage to blood vessels that would aid in diagnosing vascular dementia. It also provides the clinicians with evidence of brain shrinkage. This is important for differentiating between the early stages of Alzheimer's disease and frontotemporal dementia. Whereas both are associated with shrinkage in the temporal lobes, only frontotemporal dementia is expected to show such change in the frontal lobes.

SPECT and PET scans provide insight into how the brain operates. In particular, it allows clinicians to identify evidence of abnormalities in blood flow. EEG may be used to rule out epilepsy if it is suspected.

If there is no evidence of structural changes, it does not mean a diagnosis of dementia should be ruled out.

Having just explored neuropsychological assessment and neuroimaging, the final two sections of this chapter will focus on other important issues to examine during the assessment process, namely the behavioural and psychological symptoms of dementia and quality of life.

Behavioural and psychological symptoms of dementia

Behavioural and psychological symptoms of dementia (BPSD) are often the most challenging to someone with dementia and those caring for them. These changes in behaviour can be seen to reflect alterations in that person's sense of self. The essence of the person they once were is changing before their eyes, and before the eyes of family and friends. Such apparent shifts in personality can be devastating and frightening. For instance, people with dementia might become increasingly aggressive, delusional, agitated, and persist in wandering.

The term wandering is loaded with implied meaning. It is generally seen to refer to behaviour rooted in confusion. However, as we shall see in Chapter 6, what first appears as behaviour lacking intent is anything but.

These symptoms are linked to an increased risk of being hospitalized, higher levels of medication, and poorer quality of life (50). A review of existing measures identified those most relevant (51). Measures that provide a more generalized assessment of these symptoms are useful if short, as they can provide the necessary information with minimal fuss. Such measures include the Neuropsychiatric Inventory (NPI) (52), the CERAD (53), and the Geriatric Mental State (GMS) (54), and the BEHAVE-AD (55).

However, more detailed information is often needed about the various behavioural and psychological components. These include the RAS (irritability) (56), the Agitated Behaviour Mapping Instrument (ABMI; agitation) (57), the Apathy Evaluation Scale (AES; apathy) (58), and the Cornell Scale for Depression in Dementia (depression) (59).

Most of the measures developed explicitly for people with dementia are based on either observation or an interview with a carer or someone who knows the person well. It is a notoriously difficult set of behaviours to assess, given that some of the symptoms are less noticeable than others. Another problem is symptoms that appear to overlap.

Quality of life

I mention throughout this book how dementia affects a person's quality of life and what can be done to help improve it. This section is concerned with how quality of life is measured. It is a tricky concept to measure because we have vastly different ideas of what it is and what affects it. The World Health Organization defines quality of life as "an individual's perception of their position in life in the context of the culture and value systems in which they live and in relation to their goals, expectations, standards and concerns."[3] Whichever way you look at it, it is broad and multifaceted. Related to this is well-being, which refers to positivity and life satisfaction.[4] Monitoring quality of life is important not only for people with the diagnosis of dementia, but also for those who care for these same individuals.

Significant predictors of quality of life vary depending on the setting, although common factors include independence, ability to carry out activities of daily living, financial security, and contact with family and friends (60). Although one might expect quality of life to decline with the onset of dementia, evidence shows that it can be maintained or even improved. However, the explanation here is unclear (61). Overall, quality of life ratings tends to be higher when a person continues to live in their own home compared to care home settings (62).

Cognitive impairment is generally associated with a lower rating of quality of life, although it might very well be the case that it is a person's awareness of these problems that drive down these ratings. The more aware a person is that they have problems, the lower their rated quality of life (63). On top of this, cognitive impairment seems to be a stronger predictor of poor quality of life for those in care home settings compared to those living in the community (63). This is more than likely explained by the fact that those in care homes tend to be at a more advanced stage of the disease (64).

Perceptions of what is essential for a person's quality of life clearly depend on the person's perspective filling out the measure. For example, family members of the person with dementia tend to see the person's environment and quality of care as all-important. Caregivers tend to focus on physical aspects. For people with dementia, the emphasis is on the social and psychological aspects of their lives (63).

Although there are generic measures for quality of life, in contexts such as this, disease-specific criteria are generally used; in this case, indices of quality of life designed with dementia in mind. Several measures cover all three domains of functioning, namely psychological, social, and physical (65). These include the Quality of Life in Alzheimer's disease (QOL-AD) scale (66). This is available in versions that can be completed by either the person with dementia or their carer. It has also been modified to be used in care home settings (67). The Psychosocial QoL Domains Questionnaire is a self-report measure. It covers meaningful activities, dignity, and spiritual well-being (68). A recent review rated the QUALIDEM highly as being comprehensive, valid, and reliable, as well as being highly suited for assessing quality of life within a care home setting (65). The QUALIDEM is based on observations (69).

Some measures attempt to capture the quality of life of carers (70). Both the ICECAP (71) and the Adult Social Care Outcomes Toolkit (ASCOT) (72) are seen to be effective measures here (70). The ICECAP measures characteristics of quality of life, not influences. This is because poor quality of life is determined by limitations on what a person can do due to ill health rather than ill-health per se. The ASCOT measures social care-related quality of life and includes items reflecting personal cleanliness, safety, and social participation.

Before concluding this chapter, I would like to briefly describe a questionnaire I developed alongside my colleagues to measure the existential threat associated with dementia.

Threat of Dementia Scale

The Threat of Dementia Scale or ToDS offers the first reliable way to measure the existential threat associated with a diagnosis of dementia (73). Our findings point to a relationship between the threat of dementia and the distancing component of ageism and holding catastrophic attitudes linked to fear of the diagnosis.[5]

Understanding more about the role of dementia threat may facilitate an improved understanding of how emotions impact dementia care. It has been suggested that professionals working in dementia care draw on avoidance strategies when carrying out their duties (74). This results in task-oriented forms of care that minimize emotional engagement with the person they are looking after to the detriment of more person-centred approaches.

Research in this area has been undermined by the absence of a reliable way of measuring the threat. The development of the ToDS will facilitate a future examination of whether psychological mechanisms that protect the self against the threat of dementia impact attitude formation and care practices, widening still further research into social attitudes towards the condition.

Summary

The focus of this chapter has been to provide a glimpse at the various methods used to assess someone who is showing signs of significant cognitive impairment. Not surprisingly, there has been an emphasis on measures that quantify such impairment, aiming to produce a distinct profile of dysfunction that will aid in accurately diagnosing the individual so that the most appropriate form of intervention can be set up. There is a range of behaviour and psychological symptoms to consider alongside cognitive deficits. These are often highly challenging for both those with dementia and their carer. I ended this chapter by considering some measures that aim to assess a person's quality of life. Although infamously difficult to evaluate, by adopting different approaches, several measures perform reasonably well in this most difficult of areas. We know that quality of life depends on many things. In Chapter 10, we shall look at the importance of culture. A person's cultural identity is fundamentally important and will drive in part a person's interests and needs, be it in terms of their preference for music, food, and spiritual or religious belief.

Notes

1 Gull not seagull; family Laridae.
2 www.alzheimers.org.uk/research/take-part-research/pet-scan
3 www.who.int/healthinfo/survey/whoqol-qualityoflife/en/
4 www.healthypeople.gov/2020/about/foundation-health-measures/Health-Related-Quality-of-Life-and-Well-Being
5 As measured by the Fabroni Scale of Ageism and the Fear of Alzheimer's Disease Scale.

References

1 Neary D, Snowden JS. Sorting out the dementias. Pract Neurol. 2002;2(6):328–339.
2 Kipps CM, Hodges JR. Cognitive assessment for clinicians. J Neurol Neurosurg Psychiatry. 2005;76(Suppl 1):i22–i30.
3 Cooper S, Greene JD. The clinical assessment of the patient with early dementia. J Neurol Neurosurg Psychiatry. 2005;76(Suppl 5):v15–v24.
4 Christopher G. The psychology of ageing: From mind to society. Basingstoke, Hampshire: Palgrave Macmillan; 2014.
5 American Psychiatric Association. Diagnostic and statistical manual of mental disorders: DSM-5. 5th ed. Arlington, VA: American Psychiatric Association; 2013.
6 Aleman AA, Mills AT. Our ageing brain: How our mental capacities develop as we grow older. London: Scribe UK; 2014.
7 Sabat SR. Mild cognitive impairment: What's in a name? Philos Psychiatry Psychol. 2006;13(1):13–20.
8 The National Sleep Foundation. Is it ok to sleep in on weekends. The National Sleep Foundation. Available from: www.sleep.org/articles/ok-to-sleep-in-on-weekends/.
9 Geddes L. Late nights and lie-ins at the weekend are bad for your health. New Sci. 2017, 06 June. Available from: https://www.newscientist.com/article/2133761-late-nights-and-lie-ins-at-the-weekend-are-bad-for-your-health/.
10 Moulin C. Episodic memory. In: Davey G, editor. The encyclopaedic dictionary of psychology. London: Hodder Arnold; 2005.
11 Conway M, Smith AD. Autobiographical memory. In: Davey G, editor. The encyclopaedic dictionary of psychology. London: Hodder Arnold; 2005.
12 Conway MA. Sensory-perceptual episodic memory and its context: Autobiographical memory. Philos Trans R Soc B. 2001;356(1413):1375–1384.
13 Moulin C. Recollective experience. In: Davey G, editor. The encyclopaedic dictionary of psychology. London: Hodder Arnold; 2005.
14 Rubin DC, Wetzler SE, Nebes RD. Autobiographical memory across the adult lifespan. In: Rubin DC, editor. Autobiographical memory. Cambridge: Cambridge University Press; 1986.
15 Singer JA, Salovey P. The remembered self: Emotion and memory in personality. New York; London: Free Press; 1993.
16 Milner B, Klein D. Loss of recent memory after bilateral hippocampal lesions: Memory and memories-looking back and looking forward. J Neurol Neurosurg Psychiatry. 2016;87(3):230.
17 Eichenbaum H, Cohen NJ. From conditioning to conscious recollection: Memory systems of the brain. Oxford: Oxford University Press; 2001.
18 Collins AM, Quillian MR. Retrieval time from semantic memory. J Verbal Learn Verbal Behav. 1969;8(2):240–247.

19   Baddeley AD. Working memories: Postmen, divers and the cognitive revolution. 1st ed. London: Routledge; 2018.
20   The encyclopaedic dictionary of psychology. London: Hodder Arnold; 2005.
21   Christopher G, MacDonald J. The impact of clinical depression on working memory. Cogn Neuropsychiatry. 2005;10(5):379–399.
22   Miyake A, Friedman NP, Emerson MJ, Witzki AH, Howerter A, Wager TD. The unity and diversity of executive functions and their contributions to complex "Frontal Lobe" tasks: A latent variable analysis. Cogn Psychol. 2000;41(1):49–100.
23   The encyclopaedic dictionary of psychology. London: Hodder Arnold; 2005.
24   Stuss DT, Levine B. Adult clinical neuropsychology: Lessons from studies of the frontal lobes. Annu Rev Psychol. 2002;53(1):401–433.
25   Ramachandran VS. Encyclopedia of the human brain. San Diego, CA: Academic Press; 2002.
26   Xie S, Zhang Z, Chang F, Wang Y, Zhang Z, Zhou Z, et al. Subcortical white matter changes with normal aging detected by multi-shot high resolution diffusion tensor imaging. PLoS One. 2016;11(6):e0157533.
27   Meredith K, Barisa MT. Apraxia. In: Noggle C, editor. The encyclopedia of neuropsychological disorders. New York: Springer Publishing Company; 2011.
28   Carter S. Activities of daily living. In: Capezuti L, Malone ML, Gardner DS, Khan A, Baumann SL, editors. The encyclopedia of elder care: The comprehensive resource on geriatric health and social care. 4th ed. New York: Springer Publishing Company; 2018/2017.
29   Crabtree JL. Assessing activities of daily living. In: Emlet CA, editor. In-home assessment of older adults: An interdisciplinary approach. Gaithersburg, MD: Aspen; 2007.
30   Roley SS, DeLany JV, Barrows CJ, Brownrigg S, Honaker D, Sava DI, et al. Occupational therapy practice framework: Domain & practice, 2nd edition. Am J Occup Ther. 2008;62(6):625–683.
31   Rogers WA, Meyer B, Walker N, Fisk AD. Functional limitations to daily living tasks in the aged: A focus group analysis. Hum Factors. 1998;40(1):111–125.
32   Prince M, Wimo A, Guerchet M, Ali G, Wu Y, Prina M. The global impact of dementia: An analysis of prevalence, incidence, cost and trends. World Alzheimer Report. 2015. Available from: https://www.alzint.org/resource/world-alzheimer-report-2015/.
33   Panegyres PK, Berry R, Burchell J. Early dementia screening. Diagnostics. 2016;6(1).
34   Cracks in the pathway: People's experiences of dementia care as they move between care homes and hospitals. Care Quality Commission; 2014. Available from: https://www.cqc.org.uk/publications/themed-inspection/cracks-pathway.
35   de Vugt ME, Verhey FR. The impact of early dementia diagnosis and intervention on informal caregivers. Prog Neurobiol. 2013;110:54–62.
36   Brodaty H, Pond D, Kemp NM, Luscombe G, Harding L, Berman K, et al. The GPCOG: A new screening test for dementia designed for general practice. J Am Geriatr Soc. 2002;50(3):530–534.
37   Folstein MF, Folstein SE, McHugh PR. "Mini-mental state". A practical method for grading the cognitive state of patients for the clinician. J Psychiatr Res. 1975;12(3):189–198.
38   Mathuranath PS, Nestor PJ, Berrios GE, Rakowicz W, Hodges JR. A brief cognitive test battery to differentiate Alzheimer's disease and frontotemporal dementia. Neurology. 2000;55(11):1613–1620.
39   Mioshi E, Dawson K, Mitchell J, Arnold R, Hodges JR. The Addenbrooke's Cognitive Examination Revised (ACE-R): A brief cognitive test battery for dementia screening. Int J Geriatr Psychiatry. 2006;21(11):1078–1085.

40 Mathuranath P, Xuereb JH, Bak T, Hodges JR. Corticobasal ganglionic degeneration and/or frontotemporal dementia? A report of two overlap cases and review of literature. J Neurol Neurosurg Psychiatry. 2000;68(3):304–312.

41 Hsieh S, McGrory S, Leslie F, Dawson K, Ahmed S, Butler CR, et al. The mini-Addenbrooke's cognitive examination: A new assessment tool for dementia. Dement Geriatr Cogn Disord. 2015;39(1–2):1–11.

42 ACEmobile. Dementia assessment made easy and free 2013. Available from: www. acemobile.org/index.html.

43 Newman CGJ, Bevins AD, Zajicek JP, Hodges JR, Vuillermoz E, Dickenson JM, et al. Improving the quality of cognitive screening assessments: ACEmobile, an iPad-based version of the Addenbrooke's Cognitive Examination-III. Alzheimers Dement. 2018;10:182–187.

44 Nasreddine ZS, Phillips NA, Bedirian V, Charbonneau S, Whitehead V, Collin I, et al. The Montreal Cognitive Assessment, MoCA: A brief screening tool for mild cognitive impairment. J Am Geriatr Soc. 2005;53(4):695–699.

45 Mast BT, Gerstenecker A. Montreal cognitive assessment. 2nd ed. (ed. Lichtenberg PA). London: Academic; 2010.

46 Bigler ED. Brain imaging and function. In: Ayers S, editor. Cambridge handbook of psychology, health and medicine. 2nd ed. Cambridge: Cambridge University Press; 2007.

47 Papanicolaou AC. Fundamentals of functional brain imaging: A guide to the methods and their applications to psychology and behavioral neuroscience. Lisse: Swets & Zeitlinger; 1998.

48 van der Zande JJ, Gouw AA, van Steenoven I, Scheltens P, Stam CJ, Lemstra AW. EEG characteristics of dementia with Lewy bodies, Alzheimer's disease and mixed pathology. Front Aging Neurosci. 2018;10:190.

49 Song X, Clarke M, Bardouille T, Darvesh S, Fisk J, Beyea S, et al. Changes in prefrontal activation in early Alzheimer's Disease: A magnetoencephalography (Meg) study. Alzheimers Dement. 2014;10(4):P403–P404.

50 Shin I-S, Carter M, Masterman D, Fairbanks L, Cummings JL. Neuropsychiatric symptoms and quality of life in Alzheimer disease. Am J Geriatr Psychiatry. 2005;13(6):469–474.

51 van der Linde RM, Stephan BC, Dening T, Brayne C. Instruments to measure behavioural and psychological symptoms of dementia. Int J Methods Psychiatr Res. 2014;23(1):69–98.

52 Cummings JL, Mega M, Gray K, Rosenberg-Thompson S, Carusi DA, Gornbein J. The Neuropsychiatric Inventory: Comprehensive assessment of psychopathology in dementia. Neurology. 1994;44(12):2308.

53 Tariot PN, Mack JL, Patterson MB, Edland SD, Weiner MF, Fillenbaum G, et al. The behavior rating scale for dementia of the Consortium to Establish a Registry for Alzheimer's Disease. Am J Psychiatry. 1995;152(9):1349–1357.

54 Copeland J, Kelleher M, Kellett J, Gourlay A, Gurland B, Fleiss J, et al. A semistructured clinical interview for the assessment of diagnosis and mental state in the elderly: The Geriatric Mental State Schedule: I. Development and reliability. Psychol Med. 1976;6(3):439–449.

55 Reisberg B, Borenstein J, Salob SP, Ferris SH. Behavioral symptoms in Alzheimer's disease: Phenomenology and treatment. J Clin Psychiatry. 1987;48(5, Suppl):9–15.

56 Ryden MB. Aggressive behavior in persons with dementia who live in the community. Alzheimer Dis Assoc Disord. 1988;2(4):342–355.

57   Cohen-Mansfield J, Marx MS, Rosenthal AS. A description of agitation in a nursing home. J Gerontol. 1989;44(3):M77–M84.

58   Marin RS, Biedrzycki RC, Firinciogullari S. Reliability and validity of the Apathy Evaluation Scale. Psychiatry Res. 1991;38(2):143–162.

59   Alexopoulos GS, Abrams RC, Young RC, Shamoian CA. Cornell Scale for depression in dementia. Biol Psychiatry. 1988;23(3):271–284.

60   Lee DT, Yu DS, Kwong AN. Quality of life of older people in residential care home: A literature review. J Nurs Healthc Chronic Illn. 2009;1(2):116–125.

61   Beerens HC, Zwakhalen SM, Verbeek H, Ruwaard D, Ambergen AW, Leino-Kilpi H, et al. Change in quality of life of people with dementia recently admitted to long-term care facilities. J Adv Nurs. 2015;71(6):1435–1447.

62   Winzelberg GS, Williams CS, Preisser JS, Zimmerman S, Sloane PD. Factors associated with nursing assistant quality-of-life ratings for residents with dementia in long-term care facilities. Gerontologist. 2005;45(suppl_1):106–114.

63   Jing W, Willis R, Feng Z. Factors influencing quality of life of elderly people with dementia and care implications: A systematic review. Arch Gerontol Geriatr. 2016;66:23–41.

64   Nikmat AW, Hawthorne G, Al-Mashoor SH. The comparison of quality of life among people with mild dementia in nursing home and home care—a preliminary report. Dementia. 2015;14(1):114–125.

65   Aspden T, Bradshaw SA, Playford ED, Riazi A. Quality-of-life measures for use within care homes: A systematic review of their measurement properties. Age Ageing. 2014;43(5):596–603.

66   Logsdon RG, Gibbons LE, McCurry SM, Teri L. Quality of life in Alzheimer's disease: Patient and caregiver reports. In: Albert SM, Logsdon RG, editors. Assessing quality of life in Alzheimer's disease. New York: Springer Publishing Company; 2000, pp. 17–30.

67   Edelman P, Fulton BR, Kuhn D, Chang C-H. A comparison of three methods of measuring dementia-specific quality of life: Perspectives of residents, staff, and observers. Gerontologist. 2005;45(suppl_1):27–36.

68   Kane RA, Kling KC, Bershadsky B, Kane RL, Giles K, Degenholtz HB, et al. Quality of life measures for nursing home residents. J Gerontol A Biol Sci Med Sci. 2003;58(3):M240–M248.

69   Ettema TP, Dröes RM, de Lange J, Mellenbergh GJ, Ribbe MW. QUALIDEM: Development and evaluation of a dementia specific quality of life instrument—validation. Int J Geriatr Psychiatry. 2007;22(5):424–430.

70   Jones C, Edwards RT, Hounsome B. Health economics research into supporting carers of people with dementia: A systematic review of outcome measures. Health Qual Life Outcomes. 2012;10(1):142.

71   Coast J, Flynn TN, Natarajan L, Sproston K, Lewis J, Louviere JJ, et al. Valuing the ICECAP capability index for older people. Soc Sci Med. 2008;67(5):874–882.

72   Malley JN, Towers A-M, Netten AP, Brazier JE, Forder JE, Flynn T. An assessment of the construct validity of the ASCOT measure of social care-related quality of life with older people. Health Qual Life Outcomes. 2012;10(1):21.

73   Cheston R, Dodd E, Christopher G, White P, Wildschut T, Sedikides C. The development and validation of the threat of Dementia Scale. Int J Aging Hum Dev. 2022;94(4):496–514.

74   McKenzie EL, Brown PM. Nursing students' death anxiety and fear towards dementia patients. Australas J Ageing. 2017;36(3):E32–E35.

Chapter 5

Diagnosis

How it starts

Increasing problems with memory can have many other causes. When combined with difficulties concentrating, identifying the right word, problems perceiving, and general confusion, it is wise to seek medical advice, especially when a person's everyday existence begins to be affected. As with any change in functioning, be it physical or psychological, we all respond on a basic emotional level. Given the fear surrounding a diagnosis of dementia, it is even more important to consider the impact of a person's emotional responses. This aspect is central to my own research and will be examined in more detail later in this chapter.

In many cases, the concern that a person is experiencing dementia is raised by a family member or friend. Although a person themselves might not notice anything wrong with their behaviour, or they wish not to be aware of it, others do notice even the subtlest of change. This can raise the alarm that something is amiss.

A change in circumstances can often bring to light marked cognitive difficulties. A situation where this all too often occurs is in the wake of a spouse's death. In most long-term relationships, each partner takes on specific roles, roles that reflect individual strengths and predilections. For example, one partner likely monitors finances, the other focuses on their culinary strengths. With time, roles and responsibilities might adapt or change to take account of changes in functioning in one or both partners. The loss of a spouse disrupts all this. On top of bereavement, the person remaining may find themselves entirely out of their depth.

However, as we all know, people are adept at masking their behaviour, covering up shortfalls, by consciously compensating for difficulties faced. Because of this, more severe problems can go undetected for substantial periods. You might argue this is good. Why should someone not do this? It protects their pride. Of course, there is nothing intrinsically wrong with this. As I said, we all do this. The problems lie when such behaviour, such self-protective behaviour, thwarts the early detection of marked cognitive impairment, thereby preventing appropriate treatment from occurring at a time when it would have maximal effect.

DOI:10.4324/9781315681580-5

In previous chapters, I have emphasized how difficult it is to accurately diagnose dementia, especially early on. This is because so many factors confound the situation. We have seen that dementia can strike at an early age. In such cases, a decline in functioning is more noticeable because the person is at the peak of health and actively working. Even the slightest change in how they function will generally be picked up relatively quickly. As we age, however, we all slow down. It is a natural response to the ageing process. Such slowing occurs not just in the physical realm but also mentally. There is considerable literature on cognitive ageing to explore, and it is impossible to do justice here. The issue is that changes in function that might be due to underlying neuropathology can quite easily be masked by age-related decline, especially in other people's eyes. We also know that people are experts in covering their tracks when they realize they are experiencing difficulties. Compensatory strategies are an effective adaptive mechanism. There are, of course, many other factors that make the job of the clinician more difficult. We shall begin by looking at the importance of obtaining detailed accounts of someone's medical history in helping clinicians to start to build a diagnosis.

Medical history

It is essential to obtain a comprehensive medical history for each individual. As already indicated, the GP plays a central role in diagnosing dementia. In many cases, individuals present at their local surgery with a range of concerns about increasingly experiencing problems in their day-to-day lives. On top of this, GPs are increasingly aware of the risk factors associated with the various dementias, and so may enquire about aspects of mental functioning among those with conditions known to be related to the development of dementia, such as those over 60, especially individuals with diabetes and a history of stroke among other things. Alongside the patient, information will be elicited from individuals who know the person very well, usually a spouse or relative.

An accurate list of current medication is crucial. Particular emphasis should be given to drugs that affect the central nervous system. A comprehensive account of what has been prescribed needs to be obtained as specific drugs, either in isolation or in combination with another substance, may account for the symptoms a person is experiencing. Drug interactions are a common problem that increases as a person ages and the number of drugs prescribed grows.

Linked to this is the recent concern with over-the-counter medications that have been linked to the development of dementia. There always seems to be some scare story in the news. Not that long ago, in 2015, newspaper headlines were proclaiming a rising risk of someone developing Alzheimer's disease if they take hay fever tablets. The concern was over anticholinergic drugs; in other words, drugs that had the effect of lowering levels of acetylcholine, a neurotransmitter vital for attention and memory, and one affected by Alzheimer's disease. For more information about this neurotransmitter, see Chapter 11. Such drugs include antihistamines, antidepressants, and medications used to treat urge incontinence (a sudden urge to urinate). Although the headlines were misleading, the authors found that cumulative use of anticholinergic drugs over a long period did appear to increase the likelihood of someone developing dementia. The authors wanted to raise awareness that such prolonged use might be problematic in long term. There were, however, some problems with how the study was conducted that could quite easily limit the generalizability of the findings, such as an incomplete picture of all medications taken and a restricted sample, among other things.

Medication needs to be monitored closely, especially with increasing age. The older we are, the more likely a person experiences problems that require medication. The issue of comorbidity is tricky, in terms of not only what treatment to offer but also how different interventions might affect one another. Drugs interact to produce some rather nasty side effects. Sometimes these effects appear to mimic conditions such as depression or dementia. As a case in point, a person may have undergone a major, invasive operation to reverse or stabilize a life-threatening medical condition. On discharge, strong analgesics are prescribed to ease postoperative pain. However, such medication can result in extreme confusion, mental blunting, and increased sleepiness. The effects on cognitive functioning can be so significant that others start to suspect that there might be a more insidious process at play, namely underlying dementia. It may actually be the case that the person is manifesting symptoms of dementia. It might also be the case that they are receiving too high a painkiller dosage. A review of medications can help alleviate issues such as this.

Process of exclusion

Following history taking, the GP may carry out a range of physical examinations that often include blood tests. Such procedures are required to check for conditions that may explain the current symptoms. The process of diagnosing dementia may be seen as one of increasing exclusion. In other words, clinicians attempt to rule out other potential causes for the symptoms before considering dementia as a possibility. This is because there is a whole host of medical and psychological conditions that produce symptoms similar to those of dementia in the early stages. These include depression, infections, and vitamin deficiencies. How we process sensory information, such as vision and hearing, affects how we function, such that deterioration in any domain can result in increased confusion because we cannot adequately distinguish and make sense of what we are experiencing. In the next chapter, the issue of medication will be discussed. We are all aware that drugs come packaged with a sheet of paper listing a range of side effects. There is the issue also of interactions with other prescribed and over-the-counter medicines. All of which can lead to quite marked symptomology that makes diagnosing dementia problematic.

Delirium

Delirium poses a problem to clinicians when considering a diagnosis of dementia. Both are associated with extreme confusion. However, the main thing that differentiates dementia from delirium is that the confusion is permanent in the former, temporary in the latter. Delirium is often the result of infection.

To further complicate matters, there is a condition referred to as "acute on chronic" confusion (1). This is where there is an acute aggravation of an underlying chronic condition. In this case, a person who has mild dementia contracts an infection. The infection leads to severe confusion. At the time, it would appear the person has rapidly and markedly deteriorated. Once the cause of the delirium subsides, functioning most often returns to normal. In a few cases where the attack was particularly severe, the person may not return to the same level of functioning.

Cognitive testing

Following a physical examination, the GP will administer a short clinical screening tool to test for severe cognitive impairment. For details about assessment, please refer to Chapter 4.

Who makes the diagnosis?

In some instances, GPs can diagnose dementia if they have adequate experience in the area or the symptoms are sufficiently advanced to make it reasonably clear what is going on. However, in many cases, GPs refer patients to a specialized memory clinic or other specialized service for a more comprehensive assessment.

Consultants in specialized memory assessment centres have access to a broader range of equipment. More in-depth cognitive testing may be needed. Also, brain scans may be required to better inform the diagnosis. Referrals may be made to several consultants. For those under the age of 65, referrals may be made to a general psychiatrist, whereas a psychiatrist specializing in older adults will be contacted for those over the age of 65. A geriatrician may be the first port of call for those in poor health as additional testing might be required to rule out physical causes behind a person's symptoms. Where the suspected dementia is a less common type, a neurologist will more than likely be the person the patient is referred to. Demand for these services is high, although most are seen between four and six weeks after initial referral[1] (2).

It might not be a surprise to learn that each type of dementia brings with it its own set of challenges for those attempting to uncover the most appropriate diagnosis. The following section will highlight some of the main issues here.

Which dementia?

In previous sections, I have identified factors that complicate the issue regarding making an accurate diagnosis of dementia. However, there are additional challenges that are specific to individual diagnoses. Making a diagnosis of vascular dementia is particularly problematic. One of the main issues facing clinicians is a lack of clear evidence of stroke. This might be due to the person's general poor state of health due to cardiovascular problems. In a patient who has hypertension (high blood pressure), hypercholesteolaemia (high cholesterol), and diabetes (high blood sugar), the onset of cognitive problems might be less clear-cut than in cases of evident stroke. There is a need on such occasions to supplement clinical examination with a brain scan. However, vascular damage is often seen in the brains of both healthy older adults and in those diagnosed with other forms of dementia. Diagnosis of dementia with Lewy bodies is tricky. Because of the fluctuating nature of the cognitive impairment, a person may seem impaired one minute yet quite lucid the next. This can be an issue when attempting to diagnose dementia. Diagnosing dementia in those with Parkinson's disease is another challenge. The main barriers here are the apparent ennui of Parkinson's patients, as well as the marked slowing down in overall functioning. Progressive supranuclear palsy can often be misdiagnosed as Parkinson's disease. Common presenting symptoms show a great deal of overlap with Parkinson's disease (see Chapter 3).

Mental health issues

Depression

Although not an inevitable part of ageing, the incidence of depression is nonetheless reasonably high among older adults, with 10–16 per cent over 65 experiencing depression. When one considers a person's social environment and general health, specifically those who live either alone or in residential care and those who have a physical illness or disability, this figure rises substantially, with around 40 per cent experiencing depression. I present a more detailed account of depression in my book, *Depression: Current Perspectives in Research and Treatment*, which is also part of this series of publications.

Right at the start of this book, I talked about how specific medical terms have been adopted into everyday language and, in doing so, have lost vital meaning. Dementia was used as one example, and so too was depression. Depression is more than a momentary feeling of sadness and lowered mood. It is a severe and debilitating condition.

Depression can be described as an extremely low mood with feelings of hopelessness and inadequacy. There is an overriding sense of anhedonia, an inability to derive pleasure from life. Depression brings a host of cognitive problems, such as a general slowing down of thought processes and a failure to initiate action. On the other hand, a person may feel restless, thereby exacerbating further problems with concentration. Beck described it as a negative view of the self, the world, and the future (3).

In many instances, depression is triggered by distress associated with growing old, with factors such as social isolation and loneliness, loss of independence, and bereavement accounting for a large number of cases. All of these are seen to increase vulnerability to depression. However, other factors play a role here as well, including neurobiological changes associated with ageing, increased genetic susceptibility as a result of age-related exposure, and also interactions of pre-scribed medications.

For many reasons, depression tends to be under-recognized among older adults. This means that large numbers go untreated. There are serious risks to quality of life here, especially since, if diagnosed, and more importantly, if diagnosed early enough, the outcome can be significantly improved. In the past, depression or depressive-type symptoms were seen as an inevitable part of the normal ageing process. Because of that, there was no real need for any support or treatment. Obviously, things have moved along since then. One of the main challenges fac-ing clinicians is successfully diagnosing depression separately from other ongo-ing physical and/or mental health concerns. For example, depression tends to be present in those who have experienced a stroke, those who have cancer, diabetes, and also dementia. The nature of these conditions makes it very difficult for a separate diagnosis of dementia to be made. On top of that, depression makes it even more difficult for a person to deal with an ongoing condition (4).

To compound this, many older adults do not seek help for depression. It is mainly unreported or underdiagnosed in all too many cases (5). Older adults tend not to report symptoms in a way that the GP would immediately identify as depression, focusing instead on relaying somatic symptoms. Hopefully, this will change with the current and future generations who are more aware of psycho-logical issues and less concerned over talking about such matters. Symptoms may also be seen merely as part of the normal ageing process. Depression is also likely to occur alongside other physical or mental health conditions, further clouding the picture.

Depression and dementia

There is a complicated clinical relationship between depression and dementia. Some of the symptoms of depression are very similar to early-stage symptoms of dementia. This makes accurate diagnosis extremely difficult. In some cases, if the depression is severe enough, a person may be misdiagnosed with dementia. These are cases where poor concentration and memory problems are so extreme that it is referred to as depressive pseudodementia. Besides, someone with dementia is more likely to become depressed. In fact, for many people, a dual diagnosis of depression and dementia is made.

The focus of this final section of the chapter will change slightly. We have so far been looking at how clinicians make a diagnosis, as well as identifying factors that make this a real challenge in many cases. The following section will switch perspectives to view the situation from that of the person receiving the diagnosis of dementia. This is a life-changing situation. The person and their family and friends have to then deal with the emotional consequences of the diagnosis. I will pick up on this in Chapter 7 when I draw heavily from my own research in this area. There are many ways emotion can hinder the resolution of the turmoil individuals face. We will end this chapter by looking at the role of post-diagnostic support for people with dementia.

The emotional impact of diagnosis

Although this is not the place to discuss the pros and cons of diagnosis as a construct, there are clear implications for the individual often experiencing quite disturbing symptoms. One of the main positive aspects of a specific diagnosis is that there is an explanation for the things a person is experiencing. It is a condition known to the medical profession, and so individuals often feel that they are not alone. There have been others who have experienced similar things. Also, there will likely be a cure if there is a name for it. Sadly, this is not really the case for dementia (see Chapter 6).

Once a diagnosis has been received, a person can make the necessary adjustments, both emotionally and in terms of making plans for the future. This is possible only by knowing what is going on and how the condition is likely to progress. As seen with many physical and psychological conditions, acceptance of the diagnosis often leads to improvements in the management and treatment of the condition. The reverse state is where individuals deny the diagnosis or battle against the symptoms. Such behaviour tends to be a major barrier to any therapeutic response (6). From a pragmatic point of view, a diagnosis affords access to the necessary treatments and support.

Receiving a diagnosis

A diagnosis of any kind can be anxiety-inducing at any age. As we grow older, we may be increasingly faced with maladies that reflect that we are not as physically or mentally agile as we once were. We are increasingly likely to be diagnosed with several complaints, each of which interacts with one another to challenge an individual's sense of well-being. However, it is important to note that this is not necessarily the case. We need to move away from seeing age as inherently negative.

In many cases, a confident, positive diagnosis cannot be made until all the test results are available for inspection, so a separate appointment will be required. Given the fear surrounding a diagnosis of dementia, as with other conditions, it is advised that the patient is accompanied by someone they know and trust. Not only will they provide support, but they will also be able to note what the consultant is saying. Some people opt not to receive the diagnosis. If they want to know the outcome, it is crucial to seek clarification on any point where there is uncertainty. To lessen the impact, clinicians may talk about memory problems, but it might be unclear whether they do, in fact, mean dementia. The person must be clear about what form the dementia takes, if it is, in fact, dementia. The doctor may decide not to inform the patient of the outcome as they may feel that the information would be too distressing at that time due to the presence of other major life events which that person is currently trying to come to terms with, such as already being diagnosed with a life-threatening condition.

Issues around how the diagnosis is delivered, be it in terms of phrases used or the actual person making the pronouncement, will be discussed in more detail shortly when talking about my own research in this area around mnemic neglect (see Chapter 7).

When faced with a diagnosis, our ability to regulate emotion determines the extent to which we either respond appropriately to the clinician and take in the relevant information or find ourselves zoning out and not accepting what is being said. Both are reasonable mechanisms by which we can make an emotional experience more manageable. However, in the long term, denial that there is anything wrong is likely to be maladaptive. Chapter 7 will explore the topic of emotion regulation in greater detail.

When faced with a challenging situation that is personally relevant, older adults are often more reactive (7). It might be the case that the way we respond to emotional events in later life is determined to a large extent by how we dealt with similar events in earlier stages of adulthood (8).

The older we are, the more capable we are of dealing with experiencing contrasting emotions that coexist at single points in time (9). We are also better able to distinguish emotional reactions (10, 11). These capacities make it more likely to make better sense of any situation we face and be more effective in communicating how we feel to others (10). This reduces the likelihood of extreme emotional responses (12).

Stability in terms of how we see ourselves is an important factor in determining how well we respond to emotional events. In some instances, a person's sense of self varies depending on the situation they are in. Such self-concept incoherence likely leads to extremes in emotional reactions and may result in psychological problems (13).

Knowing that a diagnosis as life-changing as dementia inevitably brings with it an emotional cost, it is perhaps fundamentally important that appropriate support is provided to the person with dementia and their family immediately after a diagnosis is made. Following the initial period of shock, there will inevitably be a period of assessment and readjustment. The need for additional information and continued help and advice is much needed.

Telling people about the diagnosis

On receiving a diagnosis of dementia, people need to talk to their family and friends about their condition (14). This is because dementia will dramatically change a person's relationship with others in fundamental ways. Changes in relationships occur immediately, although significant alterations in functioning may not happen for months or years further down the line. Behaviours often change as the result of a lack of understanding about dementia. Therefore, it is important to reinforce that, even though a person may have received a diagnosis of dementia, they are the same person they have always been and will continue to be so (14). In other words, they will still enjoy activities that have given them pleasure in the past. Nothing has changed, except it may take longer or require more effort to carry out everyday tasks. However, people cannot be forced into discussing their diagnosis with others. Each individual needs to find the right time for them to begin to open up about their condition. A good place to start is to be honest about which aspects of everyday life a person is finding particularly troublesome. This allows family and friends to discuss how best to support the person with dementia. It also starts the dialogue that, with any luck, will be a permanent fixture in such significant relationships.

As the disease progresses, symptoms become increasingly severe. This means the person with dementia will need more intensive support. If in a long-term relationship, roles and responsibilities will shift. Clear communication at all times is required to help with these transitions. However, the person with dementia will find it increasingly difficult to say how they feel or what they want with time. This can be frustrating for all concerned. Being open about this can help other people provide the person with dementia with necessary prompts and ensure that they do everything possible to ease the process, such as eliminating distracting noise, maintaining eye contact, and so on. Allowing people sufficient time to speak or respond is so important. Understanding can be improved by speaking clearly and using more straightforward sentence construction. Decisions can be eased by avoiding overly complicated options.[2]

Post-diagnostic support

An accurate and, hopefully, early diagnosis is only the start of a long process. On receiving a diagnosis as feared as dementia, the person concerned and their family need to receive an appropriate level of post-diagnostic support to fully prepare for the future that faces them. Such support should be fitted to the needs of the individual and so needs to be sensitive to specific cultural beliefs and expectations.[3]

In 2014, NHS England made available to GPs a Dementia Toolkit (15) that supported them in detecting dementia early on. It also guided them in providing post-diagnostic support. This support may be practical or emotional. Many experience a post-diagnostic dip following a diagnosis of dementia, finding themselves without any form of tangible provision at this difficult time (16).

Many centres offer support following diagnosis, although there is a great deal of regional variation.[4] As already discussed, receiving a diagnosis of dementia is emotionally upsetting for both the patient and the relative or carer. Such sessions are aimed at helping people cope with this. In addition, there are meaningful discussions to be had around treatment compliance, benefits, support agencies, and driving.

Ensuring there is sufficient post-diagnostic support is a challenge. Given increasing pressures on memory services, it becomes increasingly difficult to staff such services (17). It is not enough to merely point people in the direction of third sector organizations, such as the Alzheimer's Society, for information. Some regions offer a single point of contact from diagnosis to end of life, although this is to no extent standard across the country.

This type of support is essential if a person is to make the necessary adjustments to enable them to live well with dementia. The emotional impact of a diagnosis of dementia is enormous. This is something explored in the book I co-wrote. We set out our theory of emotion regulation in dementia (14). There should be a range of support mechanisms on offer because of the variation in response—for some shock, grief, and sometimes relief. The care package presented needs to be specific and individualized. Different forms of dementia require different types and levels of support. Those with learning disabilities need to be provided with adequate care, which can only be achieved if learning disability services receive sufficient backing from specialist dementia services (18). Many still fall between the gaps in care offered. Those who are not prescribed medication are at particular risk because they do not attend regular medication review appointments provided to those receiving drug therapy. As we will see in Chapter 10, many people from other ethnic groups also risk falling through gaps in the care pathway (19). Looking to the future, authorities need to ensure that the needs of other groups do not meet the same ends. Of particular concern are lesbian, gay, bisexual, and transgender individuals receiving a diagnosis of dementia. The person with dementia needs to feel they are understood and that they can talk openly and appropriately about their condition. Only then will truly person-centred care be the service on offer.

A recent briefing, published by the British Psychological Society, recommended that people are not discharged from a memory clinic until they have a detailed care plan in place, one that names a designated key worker who has received the necessary training and has the links to ensure relevant support is provided (20). This should include training for carers and families to provide the basic levels of care. Examples of good practice do exist. These include the models currently in operation in Scotland and the Netherlands.

Summary

There is always much in the news about diagnosing dementia early on. This is because interventions are much more effective before the disease has taken too much of a hold on the individual. This can be a protracted process because so many potential confounds may lead clinicians down the wrong path. There are various avenues to explore to determine which particular form the dementia takes. It is mainly seen as a process of elimination. In a later chapter (Chapter 7), we will return to the emotional toll a diagnosis of dementia entails. Any form of diagnosis generally instils anxiety or fear in the person(s) affected, but none so more than the diagnosis of dementia. As we have already noted, dementia is now the most feared diagnosis, even outstripping cancer in the sense of dread it conjures up. That is why post-diagnostic support is so essential to the whole care package. Much can be done to improve the current level of provision in England and elsewhere to prevent the post-diagnostic cliff many face.

No doubt receiving a diagnosis of dementia changes the lives of the person concerned and their family and friends. This life-changing element is often seen immediately as negative. In one very real sense, it is. Once the disease takes hold, nothing can be done to halt its progress. There is the issue about how far down the line the disease process is. Nonetheless, that person will not suddenly change into the "person with dementia." They will continue being the same person they were a minute before they received the diagnosis. Nothing major will happen in terms of their symptoms. They will not suddenly forget the names of their friends and family. They will not suddenly require 24-hour care. They are the same person with the same capabilities. However, perceptions change immediately. It is difficult for them not to. The person who has received the diagnosis will immediately start to view the situation in a new light. Other people will almost seamlessly begin to treat that person differently. Once these changes start to occur, it is tough to alter them. But do so, we must, or at least try.

I am paraphrasing heavily observations made by the wonderfully erudite Wendy Mitchell, who, in her book, *Somebody I Used to Know*, provides an insightful first-hand account of her dementia (21). I had the pleasure of hearing her speak. She talked about someone actively avoiding her because she was known to have dementia. Her challenge to them was that she was no different from the day before the diagnosis, so why behave differently towards her? It does not make sense, yet it is more common than we might like to believe. People need to be better educated about dementia and what it means to the individual concerned. It is more than a clustering of symptoms. We are talking about a person's life. We should not rob them of their self until it is too late.

Notes

1 www.alzheimers.org.uk/about-dementia/symptoms-and-diagnosis/diagnosis/assessment-process-tests?documentID=260
2 www.nhs.uk/conditions/dementia/relationships-and-dementia/
3 www.gov.uk/government/publications/dementia-post-diagnostic-care-and-support/dementia-post-diagnostic-care-and-support
4 www.gov.uk/government/publications/dementia-post-diagnostic-care-and-support/dementia-post-diagnostic-care-and-support

References

1 Hughes JC. Alzheimer's and other dementias. Oxford: Oxford University Press; 2011.
2 Personal choice programme. Alzheimer's Society; 2017. Available from: www.alzheimers.org.uk/site/scripts/documents_info.php?documentID=260.
3 Beck AT. Cognitive therapy of depression. Chichester: Wiley; 1980.
4 Moussavi S, Chatterji S, Verdes E, Tandon A, Patel V, Ustun B. Depression, chronic diseases, and decrements in health: Results from the World Health Surveys. Lancet. 2007;370(9590):851–858.
5 Lyness JM, Cox C, Curry J, Conwell Y, King DA, Caine ED. Older age and the under-reporting of depressive symptoms. J Am Geriatr Soc. 1995;43(3):216–221.
6 Sturgeon JA. Psychological therapies for the management of chronic pain. Psychol Res Behav Manag. 2014;7:115–124.

7   Kunzmann U, Grun D. Emotional reactions to sad film clips: Evidence for greater reactivity in old age. Annual Meeting of the American Psychological Association; August; Toronto; 2003.

8   Gross JJ. Antecedent- and response-focused emotion regulation: Divergent consequences for experience, expression, and physiology. J Pers Soc Psychol. 1998;74(1): 224–237.

9   Ong AD, Bergeman CS. The complexity of emotions in later life. J Gerontol B Psychol Sci Soc Sci. 2004;59(3):P117–P122.

10   Barrett LF. Feelings or words? Understanding the content in self-report ratings of experienced emotion. J Pers Soc Psychol. 2004;87(2):266–281.

11   Carstensen LL, Pasupathi M, Mayr U, Nesselroade JR. Emotional experience in everyday life across the adult life span. J Pers Soc Psychol. 2000;79(4):644–655.

12   Larsen RJ, Cutler SE. The complexity of individual emotional lives: A within-subject analysis of affect structure. J Soc Clin Psychol. 1996;15:206–230.

13   Diehl M, Hay EL. Contextualized self-representations in adulthood. J Pers. 2007;75(6): 1255–1283.

14   Cheston R, Christopher G. Confronting the existential threat of dementia: An exploration into emotion regulation. Cham: Palgrave Pivot; 2019.

15   Barrett A, Burns A. Dementia revealed what primary care needs to know. Department of Health; 2014. Available from: https://www.england.nhs.uk/wp-content/uploads/2014/09/dementia-revealed-toolkit.pdf.

16   Cheston R, Jones R. A small-scale study comparing the impact of psycho-education and exploratory psychotherapy groups on newcomers to a group for people with dementia. Aging Ment Health. 2009;13(3):420–425.

17   Dodd E, Cheston R, Fear T, Brown E, Fox C, Morley C, et al. An evaluation of primary care led dementia diagnostic services in Bristol. BMC Heal Serv Res. 2014;14(1):592.

18   British Psychological Society, editor. Dementia and people with intellectual disabilities: Guidance on the assessment, diagnosis, interventions and support of people with intellectual disabilities who develop dementia. Leicester: British Psychological Society; 2015.

19   Moriarty J, Sharif N, Robinson J. Black and minority ethnic people with dementia and their access to support and services. London: Social Care Institute for Excellence; 2011.

20   British Psychological Society. Psychological therapies for people with dementia. Leicester: British Psychological Society; 2018.

21   Mitchell W. Somebody I used to know. London: Bloomsbury Publishing; 2018.

Chapter 6

Treatment

Medication

Prescriptions of medication to treat dementia are initially made by the specialist consultant. However, once started, routine prescribing will be made by the GP. As with all conditions, medications must be reviewed regularly, at least on a six-monthly basis. As with all medications, it is essential to consider potential side effects alongside any positive influence of the drug. Cholinesterase inhibitors often result in vomiting and diarrhoea and may interfere with heart functioning.

Pharmacokinetics and pharmacodynamics

Before looking at specific forms of medication, it would be helpful to consider age-related changes that affect how the body deals with drugs. As is generally the case with older adults in terms of all aspects of functioning, there are pronounced individual differences in how drugs operate the older we get (1). Such differences can be described in terms of how the body acts on a drug (pharmacokinetics) and what effect the drug has on the body (pharmacodynamics).

When deciding which medications to prescribe and in what dose, it is essential to consider how they might be absorbed, distributed, metabolized, and excreted (2). Absorption refers to the length of time for the drug to enter the bloodstream and clearly depends on the mode of administration. Distribution concerns the success with which a drug is dispersed throughout the body. Metabolism is the process whereby drugs are broken down and rendered inactive. Finally, excretion is the mechanism where drugs are removed from the body.

Age-related changes at each of the four levels bring potential risks for the individual (3). If absorption of a drug is slow, one may never attain the intended effect within a given time frame; particularly problematic if the condition being treated is severe pain. When looking at distribution, binding of active substances to plasma proteins is not as effective in older adults; the result here being a heightened risk that unbound drugs will reach toxicity. Drugs are metabolized more slowly as we age. This is due to reduced hepatic blood flow (4). In other words, drugs remain in the blood for longer (5). The implication here in terms of severe

DOI:10.4324/9781315681580-6

harm is obvious. Linked to this is a deterioration in kidney function, which limits the excretion of drugs, with a similar risk of toxins accumulating in the older adult's body (2). Renal excretion can drop to up to 50 per cent due to a reduction in glomerular filtration rate, a test of kidney function (4).

Older adults are up to three times more likely to experience adverse drug reactions due to these changes, especially if there is concomitant kidney or liver disease (4). Whether the drug is either fat or water-soluble is important. With age, body fat tends to increase, whereas body water decreases. These changes affect the volume of distribution for both types of drugs. The volume of distribution refers to the calculated dose of medicine needed to enable the necessary blood concentration level; in other words, the dose necessary for the drug to have the desired effect given specific parameters. Hydrophilic drugs—those dissolved by water—are therefore more concentrated as there is less available water in the body of an older adult; in other words, a smaller volume of distribution. Lipophilic drugs—fat-soluble—have available a larger volume of distribution as there is more fat available. This means they have a longer half-life: the time taken for plasma concentration to halve. Because of this, it is vital to check a person's weight and hydration levels before prescribing medication (2).

Given all this, Raik (4) illustrates that the same dose can have quite markedly different effects depending on the person receiving it: opiate medications can have a more significant analgesic effect, benzodiazepines are more sedative, and anticoagulants increase the risk of bleeding.

Having seen how the body affects how drugs work, it is also important to consider what effect drugs have on the body. Of particular relevance to older adults is the dose prescribed. In many cases, a reduced amount can produce the desired result. Linked to this is an increased susceptibility to drug side effects (6). A prime example here would be the prescribing of neuroleptic medications. In older adults, there is the combined effect of fewer dopamine receptors and lower levels of transporters. Drug transporters influence pharmacokinetic processes, particularly how much of a drug reaches its target. Under such conditions, an older adult would be more prone to extrapyramidal side effects if prescribed dopamine antagonists at the standard adult dose (7). There is evidence to suggest that there might be an increased risk of mortality in those with Alzheimer's disease who are prescribed antipsychotic medication in the long term (8), although this is not replicated in all studies that took into account potential confounding factors (9).

Cholinesterase inhibitors

Cholinesterase inhibitors are the main treatments for Alzheimer's disease in the UK. The drugs that are licensed are donepezil (Aricept®), galantamine (Reminyl®), and rivastigmine (Exelon®). I shall talk more about acetylcholine in Chapter 11, but for now, let it suffice to say that this neurotransmitter is essential for attention and memory. Levels are significantly reduced in Alzheimer's disease, hence the severe cognitive impairment associated with this condition.

Cholinesterase inhibitors work by decreasing the activity of enzymes that would otherwise, if unchecked, break down acetylcholine. Because of this, levels of the neurotransmitter are increased. None of these drugs offers a cure, but in around 60 per cent of cases, they help people retain their independence by reducing some of the cognitive and emotional problems associated with Alzheimer's disease. If effective, improvements are seen during the first few months of taking them. If this does not happen, it is unlikely they will be beneficial, so the clinician will stop prescribing it.[1] As with all drugs, there are side effects. Common ones include nausea, a reduction in appetite, feeling tired, and disturbed sleep, among other things.

Glutamate

Some individuals experience problems when taking cholinesterase inhibitors. One alternative in such cases is memantine. Memantine is an N-methyl-D-aspartate (NMDA) receptor antagonist. The drug memantine (Ebixa) is prescribed for those unable to tolerate the cholinesterase inhibitors. Memantine works by reducing levels of glutamate. Glutamate is an excitatory neurotransmitter. Excitatory neurotransmitters increase the likelihood that neurons will fire. In Alzheimer's disease, glutamate is produced in excessive quantities, causing damage to nerve cells. The brain is overstimulated. In such cases, glutamate has a neurotoxic effect. It increases the production of reactive free radicals. Free radicals are the unpaired electrons that result from the metabolism of oxygen. Unpaired electrons wreak havoc throughout the body in their attempt to seek out other electrons so that they can obtain their natural paired state, damaging cells in their wake. This is known as oxidative stress. This reflects a situation where there is an over-abundance of free radicals and insufficient levels of antioxidants—chemicals that stop the oxidation process that leads to the production of free radicals—to correct this imbalance. For some, the reduction in the levels of glutamate as the result of being prescribed memantine is effective for those in the moderate-to-late stages of dementia.[2] Side effects for this drug are similar to those described earlier. Since receiving its license in 2002, no other drugs have been given the status to treat Alzheimer's disease.

Other dementias

So far, I have been talking about drugs used to treat Alzheimer's disease. There is now evidence to suggest that both donepezil and rivastigmine are valuable and safe for those with dementia with Lewy bodies and dementia as the result of Parkinson's disease. Aside from helping with attention and memory, these drugs also help reduce delusions and hallucinations in these conditions. Neither of these is licensed to treat Lewy body dementia, so patients should be aware of the off-label prescribing of these drugs.[3] The same drugs have little effect on people with vascular dementia. However, they are recommended for those diagnosed with mixed dementia where Alzheimer's disease is a recognized contributing factor.[4] Both the cholinesterase inhibitors and memantine exacerbate the symptoms of frontotemporal dementia.

Medicine to treat Parkinson's disease, while effective to treat disease-specific features, can lead to the development of other, troubling symptoms. These include cognitive confusion and hallucinations. The use of cholinesterase inhibitors is particularly effective in treating those diagnosed as having Parkinson's disease dementia.

Behavioural and psychological symptoms

Aside from the characteristic problems with memory, there are a host of other symptoms described as behavioural and psychological. These often cause more distress than cognitive impairments. Such symptoms include strong beliefs not based on fact (delusions), seeing or hearing things that are not present (hallucinations), extreme agitation, and aggression. The latter two are often described as challenging behaviours, a term that no one really likes as it begs one to question, to whom is it challenging. As a result of these symptoms, a person may become hostile, afraid, and defensive. There are many possible reasons for a person with dementia behaving in this way. It is often symptomatic of the disease itself, although, in some cases, such as with agitation, it may be due to underlying yet untreated pain. Infection may also cause a number of these behaviours. Some of these behaviours may be triggered by the environment, which may be too noisy, for example.

Neuroleptic medication

Sometimes antipsychotic medication—referred to as neuroleptics—may be prescribed in dementia. Risperidone is the approved drug to treat aggression and other disturbing behaviours in dementia, although, again, other drugs are used off-label. They are effective for roughly half of those to whom they are given. The course of treatment should be short-lived and medication regularly reviewed. A particular close watch is needed when such drugs are prescribed to those with dementia with Lewy bodies or Parkinson's disease dementia because, although visual hallucinations are more likely, so are adverse reactions to the drugs.

Antidepressant medication

As depression is common among those with dementia, antidepressant medication is often prescribed to help manage symptoms associated with this condition. Given there are reduced levels of acetylcholine as the result of the disease process, tricyclic antidepressants are avoided. Acetylcholine is vital for a range of cognitive functions such as attention and memory. Tricyclics reduce levels of acetylcholine and would, therefore, exacerbate the cognitive deficits already experienced by the individual. Selective serotonin reuptake inhibitors are, on the other hand, effective in the treatment of depressive symptoms. The most widely prescribed antidepressants are sertraline, citalopram, mirtazapine, and trazodone. They may also help reduce agitation.

Anticonvulsants

Although initially developed to prevent seizures in those with epilepsy, anticonvulsants help reduce agitation and aggression in people with dementia. Carbamazepine is most effective at helping with aggression, although side effects include sedation and an increased risk of falls.

Vascular dementia

A great deal of emphasis is placed on treatments for Alzheimer's disease. However, there are higher success rates in treating other forms of dementia. A case in point would be vascular dementia. Like many different conditions, the aim here is to treat early to prevent decline or limit its progression. To a large extent, vascular dementia can be treated in a manner comparable to those with other cardiovascular conditions. Changes in a person's lifestyle can be beneficial, such as improved diet, regular exercise, reducing alcohol, and stopping smoking.

Polypharmacy

Polypharmacy is increasingly an issue with age. It can be defined in two ways: one way is if a person is prescribed four or more medications for ongoing conditions, the other is instances where a person is prescribed more medication than is actually required to treat them (10). Not only are older adults prescribed more medicine, but they also buy more over-the-counter medications than younger generations (11).

We have seen that both the way the body acts on a drug and, in turn, the effect of the drug on the individual is greatly affected by age such that effects may be enhanced or diminished. The consequences can be profound when you start introducing many different drugs into the equation. There have been several well-documented cases where polypharmacy in older adults has led to complications. One of the main problems is that clinicians are often unaware of what medications have been prescribed by colleagues in treating any one patient. This is particularly the case following a stay in hospital (12).

Sometimes drug interactions result in a reduction in the levels of the active substance in a person's system. Two drugs that compete for the same receptor group will affect absorption if they are taken at the same time (4). On the contrary, other interactions lead to more drug being available. We have seen already that metabolism slows, thereby increasing the risk of toxicity as a drug accumulates in the body.

One thing to consider here is the functional capacity of an individual. Poor eyesight is a significant problem, often leading to errors in terms of which medication a person takes at a particular time. Deficit in cognition is clearly another cause for concern. People often forget which drug or drugs they have taken and when. This may lead to erratic behaviour resulting in an overdose (4).

Raik (4) identifies a number of ways to help reduce the issue of polypharmacy. One obvious way is to ask patients to bring all their medications to a consultation, including any over-the-counter items. A regular medication review is essential to ensure only drugs necessary for that person's well-being are taken. When starting a new prescription, it is always advisable to start at a low dose and gradually build up to the suggested level. This is especially pertinent for recently licensed drugs. Another very important suggestion is that, should side-effects manifest, rather than prescribing another medication to counteract such effects, it is better to either lower the dose or find an alternative that does not have these undesirable effects.

It is vital to give close scrutiny here, as some drug combinations may produce symptoms that resemble other conditions (11). A large number of drugs target the cholinergic neurotransmitter system. Included among these are tricyclic antidepressants. A reduction in acetylcholine leads to deficits in cognitive functioning and can manifest as mental confusion. Problematic in a healthy individual, the effect would be incredibly serious for someone who already experiences cognitive impairment (7).

Adherence

To be considered alongside that of polypharmacy is adherence to a medication plan. Compliance increasingly becomes an issue with advancing age for several reasons. Some mental health problems are particularly associated with such matters. Of particular relevance here are cognitive impairments that affect a person's ability to remember whether a specific medication was taken at a particular time and in what dose. Physical problems also play a role here, such as a person's ability to swallow tablets, handle bottles and blister packs (11).

In certain instances, to mitigate problems swallowing tablets, drugs are available in alternative formats, such as in liquid form. To overcome some of the difficulties associated with cognitive impairments, the use of dosette boxes and blister packs that clearly identify days of the week help a person better monitor their drug intake. However, for someone with dementia, there is really no alternative other than careful supervision at the appropriate time to ensure all medications are taken at the correct doses.

Having explored some of the more practical issues of medication adherence, one aspect is yet to be considered, namely that of a patient's attitude to both their condition and their medical care. We have already explored how an individual responds emotionally to a diagnosis of dementia in an earlier chapter. We have also seen how attitudes about dementia may change with time. Given this, medication adherence needs to be considered within this context. If a person denies there is a problem or that the medication that has been prescribed is ineffective, compliance is likely to be poor. The only way to improve adherence here is through discussions concerning both the physical and psychological changes associated with dementia as well as what might be expected in terms of symptom relief from the medication.

Most forms of medication are associated with a range of pros and cons. This is undoubtedly the case with regard to the drugs prescribed to treat dementia. However, for many, such drugs make it easier for a person to remain in their own home for longer (13).

Ethical issues with the use of medication

Current nootropic medication offers greater independence for longer for some individuals. The prospect of disease-modifying drugs that are efficacious in halting, or indeed reversing, the condition is not yet on the horizon, although there is much research being conducted to improve the lot of people with dementia (see Chapter 10). Because of this, at some point, the disease will be so advanced that no medication or surgical technique will be able to improve the situation. It is questionable how the person with dementia or their carer and family will then deal with this reversal of fortune. Having gained respite for a finite period, to be once again faced by the prospect of sudden deterioration is difficult to reconcile.

Although much emphasis is placed on drug treatments, various psychological interventions prove helpful in managing the condition and improving a person's quality of life. Much of the emphasis in the ensuing section is on living well with dementia.

Psychological intervention

There are many forms of psychological intervention. In this section, we shall look at approaches that aim to increase levels of cognitive activation, manage distressing symptoms, inform patients and carers, and engage in emotion regulation strategies. The topic of emotion regulation is something that we will focus on in more detail in Chapter 7.

Cognitive stimulation therapy

Cognitive stimulation therapy (CST) aims to improve a person's daily functioning by focusing on a range of cognitive activities and improving that person's quality of life (14). It is claimed that the degree of improvement across all domains of cognition is similar to that seen with medication. Given the evidence base for the effectiveness of CST, NICE recommended it for those in the mild-to-moderate stages of dementia (15).

CST is generally delivered to a group, although a form of CST administered one-to-one has been developed (iCST). Sessions vary in number, but usually, there are at least 14 sessions, each one with a specific theme. Typically, two sessions are run each week. The reasoning behind this is that not only do individuals actively participate in a range of mental activities, they also benefit from being in a group with the social dynamic that entails. CST can be administered by any trained member of staff and so offers greater flexibility than some other forms of intervention.

CST consists of individually themed sessions. Each session, regardless of theme, begins with the same warm-up activity, a reality orientation (RO) board, and a group theme song. A RO board provides vital information to help a person firmly root themselves in the activities carried out in the group. It displays information such as the name of the group and other relevant information, such as the date, time, and place. There are 14 sessions: physical games, sound, childhood, food, current affairs, faces/scenes, word association, being creative, categorizing objects, orientation, using money, number games, word games, team quiz. Additional sessions can also be incorporated into the programmes and include valuable tips, thinking cards, art discussion, visual clips, and household treasures (16).

The original formulation of CST was tested by conducting a multicentre randomized controlled trial (17). Those in the active arm of the trial showed significant improvements in cognitive functioning. In particular, the biggest gains were seen with language, specifically word-finding and comprehension (18).

There is evidence that, when CST is continued over more extended periods, such as the 26-week Maintenance CST, improvements in quality of life continue over six months (19). There were no longer significant differences between the treatment and control groups in terms of cognitive functioning over this extended period. However, this might, in part, be due to the inevitable decline seen as the disease progresses. Of interest was the finding that improvement was greatest for those receiving a combination of CST and drug therapy.

When looking at the effectiveness of iCST, changes in neither cognitive functioning nor quality of life were significantly different following the programme (20). However, subjective improvement was experienced, as indicated through self-reports from the person with dementia and their carer.

Behaviour management

The aim of behaviour management is to lessen the impact of maladaptive behaviour. This is primarily achieved through positive reinforcement of target behaviours (21, 22).

Aggression is a reasonably typical behaviour exhibited by people in the moderate-to-severe stages of dementia (23). Aggression is one of the various behaviours referred to as "behaviours that challenge." However, various phrases are used to describe these behaviours, none of which are ideal. To some extent, these behaviours are grouped together as they impose a great deal of stress on those in carer roles. Aggression can be either verbal or physical. The carer may be confronted with threats and screamed abuse or be hit or scratched. Indeed, behaviours can be so severe that there is no alternative other than to move the person into formal care.

The flipside is that, while these behaviours are challenging for carers, they are symptomatic of an unmet need in the person with dementia, and so are distressing for them as well (24). Robbed of the usual communication route, exhibiting particular behaviour might be the only way they can express that something is wrong, that they require a specific form of comfort or care—the unmet needs model (25). Agitation may develop because those needs are not being met in a way that fits with the person's liking, habits, and level of incapacity.

Before turning our attention to other forms of challenging behaviour, we should explore some of the causes of aggression in people with dementia. Some potential explanations will hold true for other behaviour explored later in this section. Possible causes may be rooted in the three core domains: biological, social, psychological.

Potential biological causes of aggression include the person experiencing pain or distress, mental confusion resulting from medication, sensory misperceptions, hallucinations, delusions, or a lack of self-control due to the progression of the disease. Social explanations could include isolation, changes to routine, and attempts at hiding their condition from others. Finally, psychological reasons may consist of growing frustration, depression, perceived invasion of privacy, a feeling of being ignored, and an altered sense of reality compared to others.

Advice in these situations is generally to adopt the perspective of the person being cared for. Logical explanations are not likely to produce the desired outcome for many reasons. Certainly, any form of confrontation will be counterproductive. Reassurance is vital here. As is repeated often in dementia care circles, it is essential to focus on the person themselves and not the behaviour they are exhibiting.

In terms of managing such behaviour, a problem-solving approach is generally adopted (26). As is usual with this approach, the initial step is to identify the problem. For example, what is causing the behaviour? Is it the person with dementia, or is it the reactions of others around them? Once the problem has been isolated, the next step is to examine the circumstances. Are there any patterns in the person's behaviour that might help identify likely contributing factors? In terms of the person with dementia, do they look uncomfortable, anxious, embarrassed, and so on. When trying to determine what is wrong and what to do, the carer is ideally suited to consider their own detailed information about the person they are caring for alongside all the situational information. When attempting to address the problem, solutions are often the result of trial-and-error, changing one thing at a time systematically until the situation is resolved.

Another such challenging behaviour is wandering. Many of those who care for someone with dementia report times where the person seems to have a compulsion to walk endlessly. This is often referred to as wandering behaviour. It is seen as being aimless and, therefore, a nuisance in many cases. When linked to the concern that the person may leave a place of safety while carrying out this behaviour, much worry is experienced, with much time being devoted to curtailing this behaviour. The principal concern here is for the person's safety rather than anything else.

As seen earlier with aggression, there are reasons why a person takes to such behaviour (27). The most obvious one is that the person just enjoys walking, and so they are merely continuing something that they have always done. The person might wander around if they are feeling bored and require stimulation. They might feel confused about the time and walk around at night because they think it is daytime. More worryingly, it may be because they feel some form of discomfort, and walking offers a way to alleviate pain.

Again, there are concerns about how to best manage a person who has a tendency to wander. There are safety concerns, as we have already expressed. Still, that person also needs to maintain their independence for as long as possible. Finding the right balance with an acceptable level of risk is a real challenge.

Many question whether someone with dementia should be locked inside their own house as a safety precaution. Aside from the blatant ethical issue here, risks should be considered. What if there is a fire? What happens if the person has a fall? When considering what options are available to minimize harm, one should always err on the least restrictive alternative (27).

Having explored in some detail aggression and wandering, this next section will look at some of the other behavioural changes that might occur with the onset of dementia. These include restlessness, repetition, shouting, problems with sleep, hiding things, accusatory behaviour, constant checking on the carer, losing inhibitions, and sundowning (28).

For some, their bodies seem to be in a constant state of flux; pacing up and down, incessantly fidgeting when seated. There are many reasons for this, similar to those already described. Some may repeat the same action or the same question. In most cases, this is indicative of some underlying anxiety. This type of behaviour is rather wearing for carers. Having discussed aggression already, a related behaviour is shouting and using offensive language. A widespread occurrence in dementia is poor sleep. This might consist of repeated waking throughout the night. Combined with general disorientation, this can lead to behaviours that might make that person more vulnerable, such as getting dressed and leaving the house because they think it is daytime.

We often immediately link dementia with losing things. However, related to this is purposeful hiding of objects and hoarding behaviour. The latter two behaviour might be a manifestation of the person's attempts to control a situation. It might alternatively be symptomatic of paranoia or delusional thinking, believing that others are trying to take the objects from them. Linked to this, then, is an increase in accusatory behaviour. Sometimes such accusations can take on a more bizarre form, with allegations that the carer is, in fact, an imposter. As seen with hiding objects, accusatory behaviour is likely symptomatic of hallucinations or delusions.

Some of the advice offered to carers is to take time out, even a few moments, especially when faced with difficult and challenging behaviours. This is very difficult at the best of times, but it can also be almost impossible when one takes account of another form of behaviour change, what is sometimes referred to as trailing. In other words, the carer may be followed constantly by the person with dementia. If that does not happen, the person they care for might repeatedly call out their name. Although highly invasive, especially if trying to catch moments of calm, it is understandably rooted in feelings of insecurity.

We have talked repeatedly about ensuring as much as possible that the person with dementia retains their dignity. This will be picked up time and again through the remainder of the book. Another typical behaviour in those with this condition is a loss of inhibition. Actions that result as a consequence of this can offer major blows to that person's dignity. Resultant behaviour can be reasonably mild, taking the form of rude comments. However, such behaviours can often be more severe, such as urinating in public or performing sexually uninhibited actions. This type of behaviour is prevalent in frontotemporal dementia.

Some of these behaviours may occur more frequently at the end of the day. This is referred to as sundowning. There are explanations for this, although disturbances in the sleep–wake cycle are a likely cause, as is increased discomfort as medication wears off. The Alzheimer's Society website provides some excellent practical advice for carers who witnesses this type of behaviour (28). It is important to remember not to focus on the behaviour itself but the reason behind it. What is the person with dementia trying to communicate?

As we have seen, pain is often at the root of much challenging behaviour (26). If this is the case, the person might be seen to persistently nurse a specific body part, clench their teeth, rock backwards and forwards, and eat more or eat less, among other things. Common examples of what is causing the pain include constipation, toothache, and arthritic pain.

In a previous section, we talked about the use of antipsychotic medication to treat dementia. One of the reasons why this class of drug is prescribed is to combat aggressive and disruptive behaviour. Many here are concerned that the behaviour is due to a physical complaint and not a psychological one. For example, the antipsychotic drug will lessen or eliminate the perceived problem behaviour but do nothing for the origin of the pain. Because of this, approaches other than medication tend to be preferred in the first instance. Music is often influential here. It can help soothe the individual. Linked to this is reminiscence. Both approaches help improve mood, although it is important to remember that reminiscing about the past, or listening to a familiar tune, might dredge up an unhappy memory if not effectively monitored (29). Increased physical activity is also a good option.

Adapting the environment

As with all forms of intervention, the aim is to help the individual retain independence for as long as possible. A substantial barrier to carrying out daily activities in many cases is the environment the person is living in. Often, simple modifications can result in massive improvements in a person's ability to lead their life. One aim is to reduce the potential risks to safety often inherent in many home environments for someone with dementia. A considerable risk here is falling.

In terms of modifying the home, a relatively simple yet effective strategy is to alter the colour of the flooring such that there is a different colour for each area of the house. Having clear delineations between lounge, kitchen, and bathroom, for example, helps orientate the individual and increases independence. In a similar manner, contrasting colours should be selected for utensils and objects around the home, including crockery, towels, toilet seats, to name but three.

In terms of helping with everyday tasks and activities, simple strategies such as labelling drawers and cupboards using words or pictures improve objects' identification and location. Straightforward, easy to follow instructions on performing certain activities can be placed in crucial areas to encourage independence. These can be visual or audio recordings that can be played at the touch of a button.

Emphasis on predictable routines offers much in terms of reducing uncertainty and confusion for many individuals. This can be augmented with regular reminders. The most obvious example here would be reminders to take specific medications at the appointed time. This could be effectively used in conjunction with automatic pill dispensers. These can be pre-filled by a pharmacist. An alarm sounds, and the necessary compartment will open promptly. If medication has not been taken at the appointed time, the device will notify a carer or friend so that the necessary action can be taken. It is essential to ensure that whatever reminder system is in place, the demands made of the individual are within their limits. The aim is to improve functioning rather than create additional problems.

The resultant effect is that the individual is more aware of their surroundings and what is required. They are more firmly rooted in both space and time. Simple devices such as clocks that indicate whether it is morning or evening help a great deal with this and display the time clearly. Because of that, individuals tend to experience less distress (1).

However, given the progressive nature of many of these conditions, it is important to regularly monitor the home environment to ensure that it maintains a good fit with the individual's capabilities. Loss of this will once again lead to increased levels of distress.

An important point to consider here is that raised by Kitwood and Bredin (30), who argued that it is not just the neuropsychological impairment that one ought only to consider with dementia, but also that person's sense of self, physical health, and social life. All too often, the behavioural symptoms of dementia appear to worsen due to living conditions that act to dehumanize the individual.

Psychoeducation

Educating family and carers is an essential component of managing dementia. This enables people to better understand the disease itself and the individual needs of the person with dementia. Details of support networks can also be provided to attenuate any concern the carer may have.

Doll therapy

We have seen a whole host of symptoms and behaviours linked to dementia on top of the general cognitive decline seen in the condition. These are often quite difficult to manage from a care perspective. Such stress-related behaviours are also very upsetting for the person with dementia, significantly impacting their quality of life (31). There is no intention to be disruptive. That is not what is driving the action. Instead, such activity is an expression of frustration or an indication of suffering from individuals who can no longer adequately express themselves in any other way (31). There are ways to try to address these issues. One current method is to tap into a person's past memories by providing a substitute attachment object in the form of a doll. Utilizing attachment bonds through recall has positive effects (32). This has been achieved through reminiscence therapy (see subsequent section).

Doll therapy is built around Bowlby's work on attachment (33), although, as this work was centred on attachment in childhood, there needs to be appropriate reservations when applying it to older adults (34). However, Miesen's writings brought Bowlby's work into the field of dementia care (35). In particular, this work focused on the often-seen behaviour where someone with dementia searches for their parents. This is termed parent fixation and is seen as expressing a particular need in terms of an attachment figure. An explanation for this seeking behaviour was that the person felt insecure and tried to find solace through their absent parent.

Looking at the evidence from behaviour, there is no reason why attachment theory cannot be relevant to adulthood and later life. Indeed, children increasingly use transitional objects, such as blankets or specific phrases, when moving towards adult-like behaviours (36). There is some evidence of people with dementia using transitional objects. These objects provide stability at a time of doubt (37).

An influential figure in dementia care is Kitwood, with his person-centred care approach (38). Although it has been argued that doll therapy wanders dangerously close to an almost infantilization of people with dementia (34), there might be sufficient resonance with Kitwood's concept that addressing an unmet need is essential if you do not want the person with dementia to retreat into themselves (39). However, there are concerns that doll therapy may inadvertently create a malignant social psychology (39), where the person with dementia is seen as reverting to a state of childhood (40), with all the assumptions about what might be appropriate behaviour in such a case growing out of this situation (41).

In the case of dementia, a person is no longer able, in many cases, to explain what they want due to the progression of the disease, severely limiting their ability to communicate. This means they have various needs that are not being met by their carer. The resultant effect of that is, somewhat understandably, a worsening in mood and behaviour (34).

Early evidence for the effectiveness of doll therapy in dementia claimed that it led to a reduction in agitation, aggression, and wandering (42). Bisiani and

Angus (43) report an interesting single-case study. The patient in this study showed clear improvements in behaviour that appeared to be maintained. In particular, the patient's anxiety was reduced. The doll helped give meaning to their life. Although the doll was not seen as real, the feelings of joy that the patient associated with raising their child were brought to the fore. More generally, the patient was more open to communicating with others during this time. Clearly, this is a study of a single individual. So, we have to ask if this is an isolated incident.

There is evidence to suggest that such an approach does lead to improvements in behaviour that are clinically significant (44). Indeed, comparable findings have been seen in larger, mixed-methods studies (45). There was an overall increase in positive behaviour six months after doll therapy commenced (46). What did become apparent was a concern among care providers that the doll therapy was condescending (47).

There is one important practical question that we have not addressed yet when considering doll therapy. That is, how does the person with dementia perceive the doll? Do they, in fact, see it as a doll, or do they think of it as an actual child? If the person thinks of the doll as a real baby, they should not be challenged (48). The tricky ethical issues around lying to someone with dementia will be addressed later (see Chapter 11). Needless to say, in circumstances such as this, there would be no gain from contradicting someone with dementia over the true identity of the doll. The important thing in this situation is that the person can glean some emotional benefit from the object. That does not make the tricky question go away: Is this the right thing to do? Although doll therapy is increasingly used, there is little real consensus at the moment in terms of whether it is effective, and if it is, what should be done about the ethical issues associated with it (34).

Reminiscence therapy

From very early accounts of memory, it was clear that the age at which a memory was acquired influenced how well it was retained over time. Indeed, Ribot's law (1882) (49) states that more recently acquired memories are more prone to be lost than more distant memories. This is because newer memories require time for the process of consolidation to occur, where synaptic connections are strengthened.

Much weight is given to the notion of the reminiscence bump. This reflects a tendency for older adults to better recall events during adolescence and early adulthood compared to other periods of life. One argument is that events during this period of one's life define who we are as individuals and are, therefore, integral to our life narrative (50). It is not as clear-cut as that. The period of a person's life associated with this bump differs depending on the method used to cue recall, be it the use of pivotal events in a person's life, cue words, or life scripts (51).

The fact that memories associated with one's early life are more efficiently and more accurately recalled go far to explain why reminiscence is so important for so many of us as we age. Simply because the memories are so vivid, they cannot but help instil a feeling of security in the individual. As we get older, we tend to 'live by memory rather than by hope; for what is left to them of life is but little as compared with the long past; and hope is of the future, memory of the past. This, again, is the cause of their loquacity; they are continually talking of the past, because they enjoy remembering it' (Rhetoric Book 2, 13: Aristotle) (52). This is in stark contrast to the feelings associated with trying to remember more recent events, memories of which are vague, or worse still, absent. The person is left feeling that they are a failure and have experienced yet another reminder of their worsening memory (53).

Reminiscence therapy aims to tap into this. It aims to help people remember events that occurred during their life, the people they knew, and places visited. Pictures, objects, and video footage are often used to achieve this. Sharing memories of one's past is seen as a positive activity, where the person with dementia changes role from receiving to giving; a way of engaging with someone interested in what they have to say, rather than being the recipient of care. Such activity lends itself to group work, where similarly aged individuals talk about shared elements of their past. Playing songs associated with a particular period is a typical method to spark discussion. It is believed to improve mood and reduce agitation. Although this technique is used extensively, there is little evidence to suggest it has the intended effect (54). Possible reasons for this will be suggested in Chapter 7 when I talk about my own research on nostalgia. Where there was an effect of reminiscence therapy, it tended to occur in care home settings. It is the case that more studies are needed where the treatment protocol is standardized.

Life story

The British Psychological Society and the Royal College of Psychiatrists emphasized the need to develop methods of support that are personalized to the individual and their support network (55). One way to achieve this is through life story work. This is a way to enable someone to tell their own story. It is a valuable method of self-expression. Importantly, it provides others with an insight into their personal values, likes, and dislikes (56). It gives vent to aspects of that person's life that may have been forgotten. Rather than focusing on the negative, the impairments the person with dementia faces as a result of their learning disability, for example, these accounts concern the person's lived experiences and their interpretation of events that occur around them (57).

Life stories allow individuals to communicate to others defining aspects of their character. Of particular importance is knowing which social groups a person identifies with, their cultural identity and ethnicity, and their sense of self. It allows others to steal valuable glimpses behind that façade that has been erected, or rather imposed, by the diagnosis. Diagnoses often dictate how we see and treat people. They soon become an amalgamation of symptoms rather than the unique individual they are. We can quickly lose sight of the person (58). Life story work is a way to stop this from happening. In fact, the opportunity to do this for someone who may have spent their entire life in care may be the first opportunity they have been given to tell their own story.

Giving people space to do this is empowering (59). It provides a person with a sense of control over their life. It is a time when they feel people are really listening to them. The understanding arising from these stories will help others provide more appropriate care and support by better meeting the needs and expectations of the individual concerned.

Sensory engagement

Sensory engagement emphasizes the often untapped potential of our various senses in enriching the lives of people living with dementia (60). Senses develop early on in. Helping someone connect with these early sensory experiences can be revelatory. A good example is the sensory experiences associated with food. We all have our favourites. Each dish has its own smell, texture, taste, and so on. Tapping into the senses is a great way to communicate with someone who may no longer be able to connect by other means. It can be incredibly reassuring (61).

Being aware of the role the various senses play and noting any change in capacity can reduce distress (61). Engagement with specific activities can be enhanced by better exploring sensory information. Take the example of food again. One of the recommendations around care is that carers should create a sensory environment that nurtures mental well-being.[5]

I am reminded of a conversation I had with an ex-nurse. The exchange turned to food, especially foods of different cultures. One way to ensure a person's environment is rich is to provide food that is stimulating and present it in a way that is accessible to them. This led me to recall this conversation as I was relayed an anecdote describing a person with dementia not really enjoying their food until a new chef was employed by the care home where they lived. The resident was Afro-Caribbean, as was the new chef. Knowing that someone in the home enjoyed Caribbean food, the chef created classic dishes from this cuisine. The impact of this was astonishing. No longer was the resident ambivalent to food. Instead, they relished every bite. This is a true testament to the power of the senses combined with cultural traditions and personal memories.

Having spent most of the chapter talking about the various forms of treatment, I want to end by talking a little about the options available to those with young-onset dementia, before looking at dementia care mapping. I will then end this chapter by expanding on something already mentioned: the notion of unmet needs.

Treating young-onset dementia

I would like to spend some time looking at the issues faced by those diagnosed with young-onset dementia and the types of services available for this group of patients. The pattern of impairment they experience is different to that seen in older people with dementia, with more problems around behaviour, vision, and language rather than memory.[6] From an emotional point of view, the fact that this group has to face the challenges of dementia at a time in their lives when it is least expected exerts an additional toll. They are likely to be otherwise physically fit, work themselves, have a spouse or partner who works, and be weighed down by significant financial obligations. They will probably have children and parents who rely on them. Because of these things, accepting a diagnosis is even more of a problem.

Given the age at which the person is affected by dementia, the support offered must be age-appropriate. This will likely require the involvement of a dementia nurse or adviser who specializes in young-onset dementia. Services can include activity groups and adventure holidays,[7] although they may not be as readily available or practically possible due to distance. This reflects, in part, the fact that young-onset dementia is relatively rare. Most money is allocated to the more prevalent forms that manifest later in life. The upshot is that many diagnosed with young-onset dementia will fall through the gaps in dementia care services.[8]

For many, it will mean explaining what is happening to their children. Although there may be a natural tendency to protect children by not explaining the situation to them, like anyone else, it is important that they know what is going on. Children are very adept at picking up minor fluctuations in behaviour, especially between the people who care for them. Because of that, they need to know the reason for this. In particular, they should be reassured that any behaviour change is not due to them. Although distressing, the element of trust reinforced by appraising children of the situation is extremely important. Not doing so at such a pivotal time may have unintended consequences further down the line, with the child experiencing issues around belief and conviction in significant relationships.

At all times, the child needs to be reassured that they can talk about their feelings and about what is happening around them. They will feel sad and be scared about what the future holds, not only for their parent but also for themselves. They are likely to feel embarrassed by some of the odd behaviours exhibited by their parent in front of other people. Depending on age, their role may change; they may find themselves faced with the situation where they are helping to care for someone whose previous responsibility was to care for them. They may also feel sidelined or rejected, which may instil feelings of resentment and anger. Through all this turmoil, the child needs to know that their parent who has dementia will want to feel still loved and valued.[9]

From a parent's point of view, they need to remain calm when talking about the problems. Making use of simple, concrete examples often help. As mentioned time and again in this book, attempts should be made to emphasize what the person with dementia can still do rather than focusing solely on what is problematic. Importantly, the time spent with their parent who has dementia should be joyful, filled with shared activities, such as listening to music together. As we shall see in Chapter 7, when I talk about my own research, making new shared memories that can be discussed and looked back on fondly is so essential, not only to help deal with the current situation but also to help buffer some of the distress that will be felt later when the person's symptoms are more severe, or they have passed on.

Dementia care mapping

Dementia Care Mapping™ (DCM™) is a technique to help ensure person-centred care for people with dementia developed at the University of Bradford. It grew out of the work of Tom Kitwood (39). The technique allows for continual observation of those with dementia and the type of care they receive. Kitwood argued that well-being is determined by the quality of the relationships the person with dementia has with those around them. It codes for 24 categories of behaviour—behavioural category codes—that include interactions with others (articulation), moving around (coming and going), dozing (nodding), and mental stimulation (intellectual activity). The reporting of these observations help improve the quality of the care provided by identifying things that improve a person's well-being or cause distress, coded as personal enhancers and personal detractions. Because it emphasizes each person's individuality, DCM™ is a way to ensure staff view situations from the perspective of the person they are caring for (62).

End-of-life care

In Chapter 7, I talk about my own work on emotion regulation strategies in dementia, emphasizing dementia as an existential threat. A diagnosis of dementia rips apart a person's sense of who they are. It challenges individuals on all levels. One of the main things a person has to grapple with following a diagnosis is the understanding that there is no cure. There is nothing medically to be done to stop or reverse the effects of the disease once it has taken hold. There are, nonetheless, various strategies to help people live well with dementia. In Chapter 7, I talk about the internal struggle between denying the diagnosis and acknowledging and accepting it. Talking about the condition is incredibly important, and I mention ways to help buffer the emotional turmoil that may otherwise manifest when such discussion takes place. In particular, my work on a nostalgia-based intervention aims to provide an emotional buffer. People must talk about their fears, their expectations, and, increasingly important, issues around end-of-life care. It is to this that I now turn.

The fundamental reason it is so essential to engage in discussions around end-of-life issues is that an individual's particular needs will be met at a point when they will not have the capacity to communicate what they want or how they feel. It is a way to ensure a person is relieved of any discomfort. It is not just about meeting a person's physical needs; it also concerns satisfying their spiritual or religious requirements. Compassion is crucial here.

Advance care planning, then, is essential. A person may, for example, express a wish to refuse certain forms of treatment. This is legalized through an advance decision. A less binding option is to make an advance statement of wishes, but one, nonetheless, that is considered when planning care. The person with dementia may also have a dedicated person who has been granted lasting power of attorney. They are there to ensure the health and social care issues are appropriate concerning the person with dementia's wishes. The senior clinician may direct staff not to resuscitate a person should they stop breathing or their heart stops—a DNR—if they feel it would not be in the person's best interests to do so. This can only be done following a discussion with close family members.

Unless there is another life-limiting illness on top of dementia, the latter stages of the illness will be marked by increased frailty, immobility, difficulty eating, incontinence, and loss of the ability to communicate verbally.[10] Even when the symptoms have reached such severity, death may not be imminent. There is often a great deal of uncertainty at these most distressing times. This is one of the reasons why family and friends need to be clear about how the person desires to be treated.

I should clarify that just because speech may no longer be an option, non-verbal forms of communication are highly effective. Gesture, touch, and facial expressions are effective modes of sending and receiving messages. They can offer much reassurance. How you communicate is so important. Just because the person with dementia may no longer be able to verbalize, it does not mean that family and friends should cease talking to them. The sound of a loved one's voice is essential to retaining a vital connection with others. Familiar sights, sounds, and smells can help calm a person.

The Social Care Institute for Excellence emphasizes "the right care at the right time for the right person."[11] They stress the need to think ahead rather than merely react to any change in the situation.

Issues around end-of-life care are something I will return to in Chapter 8 when looking at the specific challenges of people with intellectual developmental disorders who are also diagnosed with dementia.

Summary

This chapter opened with a summary of the drug therapies available to treat people with dementia. Such drugs not only target the memory problems one immediately associates with dementia, they are also prescribed to help with depression that is often experienced, as well as targeting disturbing symptoms such as hallucinations and delusions. Because multiple drugs are prescribed in many cases, there is the very real issue of drug interactions to deal with, many of which can result in distressing symptoms. We also saw that adherence to a specific drug regimen is an issue for many reasons. However, drugs are not the only solution. Indeed, a range of psychological interventions was highlighted here, from the more ingrained cognitive stimulation and behaviour management approaches to increasing use of doll therapy and reminiscence work in helping to improve the quality of life of those with dementia. Whatever approach is taken, of fundamental importance is a striving to appropriately address the needs of the person with dementia, be it alleviating physical discomfort or the mental anguish of feeling alone. The final section focused on end-of-life care, emphasizing the necessity of person-centred care that meets the needs and wishes of those with dementia.

Notes

1 www.rcpsych.ac.uk/mental-health/treatments-and-wellbeing/alzheimers-drug-treatments
2 www.rcpsych.ac.uk/mental-health/treatments-and-wellbeing/alzheimers-drug-treatments
3 www.alzheimers.org.uk/about-dementia/treatments/drugs/effective-other-types-dementia
4 www.alzheimers.org.uk/about-dementia/treatments/drugs/effective-other-types-dementia
5 www.gov.uk/government/publications/people-with-dementia-and-learning-disabilities-reasonable-adjustments/dementia-and-people-with-learning-disabilities
6 www.alzheimers.org.uk/about-dementia/types-dementia/particular-issues-faced-younger-people-dementia
7 www.alzheimers.org.uk/about-dementia/types-dementia/services-people-young-onset-dementia
8 www.alzheimers.org.uk/about-dementia/types-dementia/services-people-young-onset-dementia
9 www.alzheimers.org.uk/get-support/daily-living/what-you-can-do-help-children
10 www.alzheimers.org.uk/get-support/help-dementia-care/end-life-care-dementia-life-limiting-illness#content-start
11 www.scie.org.uk/dementia/advanced-dementia-and-end-of-life-care/end-of-life-care/introduction.asp

References

1 Boyce N, Walker Z, Rodda J. The old age psychiatry handbook: A practical guide. Chichester: John Wiley & Sons Ltd; 2008.
2 Hacker MP, Messer WS, Bachmann KA. Pharmacology: Principles and practice. Amsterdam: Academic; 2009.
3 Cusack BJ. Pharmacokinetics in older persons. Am J Geriatr Pharmacother. 2004;2(4):274–302.
4 Raik BL. Polypharmacy: Drug—drug interactions. The encyclopedia of elder care: The comprehensive resource on geriatric health and social care. In: Capezuti E, Malone ML, Gardner DS, Khan A, Baumann SL, editors. New York: Springer Publishing Company; 2018.
5 Bond AJ, Lader MH. Understanding drug treatment in mental health care. Chichester: Wiley; 1996.
6 Lövheim H, Karlsson S, Gustafson Y. The use of central nervous system drugs and analgesics among very old people with and without dementia. Pharmacoepidemiol Drug Saf. 2008;17(9):912–918.
7 Routledge PA, O'Mahony MS, Woodhouse KW. Adverse drug reactions in elderly patients. Br J Clin Pharmacol. 2004;57(2):121–126.
8 Ballard C, Hanney ML, Theodoulou M, Douglas S, McShane R, Kossakowski K, et al. The dementia antipsychotic withdrawal trial (DART-AD): Long-term follow-up of a randomised placebo-controlled trial. Lancet Neurol. 2009;8(2):151–157.
9 Brännström J, Boström G, Rosendahl E, Nordström P, Littbrand H, Lövheim H, et al. Psychotropic drug use and mortality in old people with dementia: Investigating sex differences. BMC Pharmacol Toxicol. 2017;18(1):36.

10   Patterson SM, Hughes C, Kerse N, Cardwell CR, Bradley MC. Interventions to improve the appropriate use of polypharmacy for older people. Cochrane Database Syst Rev. 2012;5:CD008165.

11   Christopher G. The psychology of ageing: From mind to society. Basingstoke, Hampshire: Palgrave Macmillan; 2014.

12   Obreli Neto PR, Nobili A, Marusic S, Pilger D, Guidoni CM, Baldoni Ade O, et al. Prevalence and predictors of potential drug-drug interactions in the elderly: A cross-sectional study in the Brazilian primary public health system. J Pharm Sci. 2012;15(2):344–354.

13   Lees A. Alzheimer's: The silent plague. London: Penguin; 2012.

14   University College London. Cognitive stimulation therapy—a new therapy for dementia 2017. Available from: www.ucl.ac.uk/impact/case-study-repository/cognitive-stimulation-therapy-dementia.

15   National Institute for Health and Clinical Excellence. Dementia: Supporting people with dementia and their carers in health and social care (NICE Clinical Guideline 42). National Institute for Health and Clinical Excellence; 2006. Available from: https://www.scie.org.uk/publications/misc/dementia/dementia-understanding.pdf?res=true.

16   Aguirre E, Spector A, Streater A, Hoe J, Woods B, Orrell M. Making a difference 2. London: Hawker Publications; 2012.

17   Spector A, Thorgrimsen L, Woods B, Royan L, Davies S, Butterworth M, et al. Efficacy of an evidence-based cognitive stimulation therapy programme for people with dementia. Br J Psychiatry. 2003;183(3):248–254.

18   Spector A, Orrell M, Woods B. Cognitive Stimulation Therapy (CST): Effects on different areas of cognitive function for people with dementia. Int J Geriatr Psychiatry. 2010;25(12):1253–1258.

19   Aguirre E, Spector A, Hoe J, Russell IT, Knapp M, Woods RT, et al. Maintenance Cognitive Stimulation Therapy (CST) for dementia: A single-blind, multi-centre, randomized controlled trial of Maintenance CST vs. CST for dementia. Trials. 2010;11(1):46.

20   Orgeta V, Leung P, Yates L, Kang S, Hoare Z, Henderson C, et al. Individual cognitive stimulation therapy for dementia: A clinical effectiveness and cost-effectiveness pragmatic, multicentre, randomised controlled trial. Heal Technolgy Assess. 2015;19(64):1–108.

21   O'Connor DW, Ames D, Gardner B, King M. Psychosocial treatments of psychological symptoms in dementia: A systematic review of reports meeting quality standards. Int Psychogeriatr. 2009;21(2):241–251.

22   O'Connor DW, Ames D, Gardner B, King M. Psychosocial treatments of behavior symptoms in dementia: A systematic review of reports meeting quality standards. Int Psychogeriatr. 2009;21(2):225–240.

23   Alzheimer's Society. Aggression 2017. Available from: www.alzheimers.org.uk/site/scripts/documents_info.php?documentID=92.

24   Cohen-Mansfield J. Nonpharmacologic interventions for inappropriate behaviors in dementia: A review, summary, and critique. Focus. 2004;9(2):361–408.

25   Cohen-Mansfield J, Werner P. Environmental influences on agitation: An integrative summary of an observational study. Am J Alzheimers Care Relat Disord Res. 1995;10(1):32–39.

26   Alzheimer's Society. Preventing and managing aggressive behaviour 2017. Available from: www.alzheimers.org.uk/info/20064/symptoms/92/aggression/4.

27 Alzheimer's Society. Moving and walking about. 2013. Available from: https://dementiaroadmap.info/resources/moving-and-walking-about/#.Y9kYNXDP2Uk.

28 Alzheimer's Society. Behaviour changes 2017. Available from: www.alzheimers.org.uk/info/20064/symptoms/87/behaviour_changes.

29 Cheston R, Christopher G. Confronting the existential threat of dementia: An exploration into emotion regulation. Cham: Palgrave Pivot; 2019.

30 Kitwood T, Bredin K. Towards a theory of dementia care: Personhood and well-being. Ageing Soc. 1992;12:269–287.

31 Gruber-Baldini AL, Boustani M, Sloane PD, Zimmerman S. Behavioral symptoms in residential care/assisted living facilities: Prevalence, risk factors, and medication management. J Am Geriatr Soc. 2004;52(10):1610–1617.

32 Kitwood T. Dementia reconsidered: The person comes first. Buckingham: Open University Press; 2007.

33 Bowlby J. Attachment, Vol. 1 of Attachment and loss. New York: Basic Books; 1969.

34 Mitchell G, O'Donnell H. The therapeutic use of doll therapy in dementia. Br J Nurs. 2013;22(6):329–334.

35 Miesen BM. Alzheimer's disease, the phenomenon of parent fixation and Bowlby's attachment theory. Int J Geriatr Psychiatry. 1993;8(2):147–153.

36 Winnicott DW. Transitional objects and transitional phenomena. A study of the first not-me possession. Psyche. 1969;23(9):666–682.

37 Loboprabhu S, Molinari V, Lomax J. The transitional object in dementia: Clinical implications. Int J Appl Psychoanal Stud. 2007;4(2):144–169.

38 Kitwood T. The dialectics of dementia: With particular reference to Alzheimer's disease. Ageing Soc. 1990;10(2):177–196.

39 Kitwood TM. Dementia reconsidered: The person comes first. Buckingham: Open University Press; 1997.

40 Salari SM. Intergenerational partnerships in adult day centers: Importance of age-appropriate environments and behaviors. Gerontologist. 2002;42(3):321–333.

41 Boas I. Why do we have to give the name 'therapy' to companionship and activities that are, or should be, a part of normal relationships. J Dement Care. 1998;6(6):13.

42 Moore D. It's like a gold medal and it's mine'-dolls in dementia care. J Dementia Care. 2001;9(6):20–21.

43 Bisiani L, Angus J. Doll therapy: A therapeutic means to meet past attachment needs and diminish behaviours of concern in a person living with dementia—a case study approach. Dementia. 2013;12(4):447–462.

44 Pezzati R, Molteni V, Bani M, Settanta C, Di Maggio MG, Villa I, et al. Can Doll therapy preserve or promote attachment in people with cognitive, behavioral, and emotional problems? A pilot study in institutionalized patients with dementia. Front Psychol. 2014;5:342.

45 James IA, Mackenzie L, Mukaetova-Ladinska E. Doll use in care homes for people with dementia. Int J Geriatr Psychiatry. 2006;21(11):1093–1098.

46 Ellingford J, James I, Mackenzie L, Marsland L. Using dolls to alter behaviour in patients with dementia. Nurs Time. 2007;103(5):36–37.

47 Mackenzie L, James IA, Morse R, Mukaetova-Ladinska E, Reichelt FK. A pilot study on the use of dolls for people with dementia. Age Ageing. 2006;35(4):441–444.

48 Andrew A. The ethics of using dolls and soft toys in dementia care. Nurs Resident Care. 2006;8(9):419–421.

49 Roeckelein JE. Elsevier's dictionary of psychological theories. Amsterdam; Oxford: Elsevier; 2006.

50 Fitzgerald JM. Vivid memories and the reminiscence phenomenon: The role of a self narrative. Hum Develop. 1988;31(5):261–273.

51 Munawar K, Kuhn SK, Haque S. Understanding the reminiscence bump: A systematic review. PLoS One. 2018;13(12).

52 Aristotle. The art of rhetoric. London: Penguin; 1991.

53 Oyebode F. Sims' symptoms in the mind: An introduction to descriptive psychopathology. 4th ed. Edinburgh: W. B. Saunders; 2008.

54 Woods B, O'Philbin L, Farrell EM, Spector AE, Orrell M. Reminiscence therapy for dementia. Cochrane Database Syst Rev. 2018(3). Available from: https://www.cochranelibrary.com/cdsr/doi/10.1002/14651858.CD001120.pub3/full.

55 British Psychological Society, editor. Dementia and people with intellectual disabilities: Guidance on the assessment, diagnosis, interventions and support of people with intellectual disabilities who develop dementia. Leicester: British Psychological Society; 2015.

56 Talbot P, Astbury G, Mason T. Key concepts in learning disabilities. London: SAGE; 2010.

57 Bogden R, Taylor S. The social meaning of mental retardation. New York: Teacher College Press; 1994.

58 Gray B, Ridden GM. Lifemaps of people with learning disabilities. London: Jessica Kingsley Publishers; 1999.

59 Atkinson D. Research and empowerment: Involving people with learning difficulties in oral and life history research. Disabil Soc. 2004;19(7):691–702.

60 Grace JA. Sharing sensory stories and conversations with people with dementia: A practical guide. London: Jessica Kingsley Publishers; 2018.

61 Grace J. Sensory-being for sensory beings [electronic resource]. London: Taylor and Francis; 2017.

62 Brooker D. Dementia care mapping: A review of the research literature. Gerontologist. 2005;45(suppl_1):11–18.

Chapter 7

Regulating emotions

Social cognition

How we operate socially in our everyday lives is described in the literature on social cognition. Underpinning this is our ability to understand and predict the behaviour of others, as well as our ability to regulate our emotional responses. Such inherent flexibility enables us to react appropriately to whatever situation life throws at us. Various processes can affect this smooth functioning, such as the degeneration associated with dementia.

There are three main stages to developing social cognition (1). We begin by being able to mimic the behaviour of others. This is followed by an understanding that physical posture and expression reflect different emotional states. The final stage is where we impute emotional states to others based on how we would feel if we were in the same situation. Underlying this are schemata that have been built up through experience and act to guide our future behaviour (2).

Theory of mind

Theory of mind is a way of describing how we can infer what other people are thinking and feeling. There is a vast literature on how theory of mind develops in children. The pinnacle of this process is our ability to understand and accept that other people's world view will not be the same as our own. As such, it plays a fundamental role in social cognition (3).

Developing theory of mind

An embryonic form of theory of mind appears around 18 months, as evidenced by children at this age engaging in activities that require shared attention and proto-declarative pointing (4), a pre-linguistic form of communication that results in directing another person's attention to something in the environment or requesting specific objects. Such behaviour is seen as the non-verbal equivalent of "I want" or "Look at that" (5). This is followed by a period where the child can engage in pretend play (6), with such activities often mimicking the roles of adults.

DOI:10.4324/9781315681580-7

However, there is debate whether such activities reflect a burgeoning theory of mind, given the largely imitative nature of the actions. By 24 months, children understand desire as a driving force (7). A further two years down the line, the child can comprehend that another person may hold inaccurate information about a situation and so will be mistaken in their actions (8). Such behaviour is best illustrated in classic "false belief" tasks (9). Advanced metacognitive skills are amassed up to the age of 7 (10). Between the ages of 9 and 11, there are many advancements in understanding social behaviour, such as the ability to recognize instances when a faux pas has occurred.

It is assumed there are two broad aspects to theory of mind: one being cognitive, the other affective. The cognitive component corresponds to our intentions and beliefs about different social situations (11). The affective part primarily deals with how other people feel (12). The *Reading the Mind in the Eyes* test (the Eyes Test) is a good measure here (13). There is a subtle yet distinct difference between affective theory of mind and empathy. When one feels empathy, we feel the emotion of another without necessarily any insight into why the sentiment is expressed. In contrast, with affective theory of mind, we do appreciate the reasons for the emotion but do not manifest the feeling ourselves (14). This distinction between affective theory of mind and empathy is not as clear-cut as that if one accepts that empathy can be subdivided into emotional and cognitive components (15). Affective theory of mind, in this instance, closely resembles cognitive empathy. Regulation of emotional responses depends mainly on the development of executive control. As we have seen, executive function refers to a range of higher-order cognitive processes that underpin much of what we do from one minute to the next. This overarching control mechanism is essential for developing theory of mind (16).

Theory of mind in older adults

Fewer studies have been conducted that explore theory of mind in older adults compared to the extensive literature focusing on childhood and adolescence. On top of that, findings from these studies are somewhat mixed, with some indicating a decline in function (17), whereas others show improvement (18). Studies exploring the different components of theory of mind suggest that the ability to deal effectively with the informational demands imposed by such activity is reduced (19). This is indicative of impairment in executive control, in particular, inhibition (20).

The majority of published studies have tended to emphasize cognitive theory of mind. Studies that have looked at affective theory of mind failed to find any impact of age when the task involved basic emotions, although deficits did start to appear when the task required the processing of more complex emotions (21). This again reflects problems with executive control; more complex emotions make higher demands on attention and require more integration and manipulation (11). This makes sense when considering this in relation to neuroanatomical changes resulting from ageing. Both the amygdala and the basal ganglia are central to any form of emotional response. These structures are relatively spared as we age (22, 23). When looking at the prefrontal cortex, the area implicated in emotion processing, the ventromedial section, undergoes less deterioration. However, regions associated with executive functions are more prone to the ravages of time, thereby making it more difficult to process multiple streams of information.

Theory of mind in dementia

Assessment of social cognition in older adults offers practical benefits in detecting Major Neurocognitive Disorder (DSM-5) (24) in the early stages. One way to do this is by using measures of theory of mind. When looking at a person's ability to recognize subtle emotions, those diagnosed with mild cognitive impairment (MCI) show less accuracy. As MCI can lead to Alzheimer's disease, such an indirect assessment of function might prove helpful in the race to find ways to diagnose conditions in their early stages (25).

Social cognition is particularly affected by Alzheimer's disease. This likely contributes to the loss of independence and reduced quality of life during the middle stages of the disease (26). When looking at the two aspects of theory of mind, Alzheimer's disease appears to impair cognitive theory of mind while having little effect on affective theory of mind (27).

Although there is evidence to indicate affective theory of mind is relatively unaffected by Alzheimer's disease, one's ability to recognize facial expressions in others is worse due to the disease (28). The deficit is compounded when manipulations are made regarding how obvious the facial expression is (29). In addition, positive expressions are assessed more accurately (30), possibly amplifying the finding that negative emotions are generally more challenging to identify as we age anyway (31). When considered together, it is not surprising that there is a reduced empathic response among those with Alzheimer's disease (32).

Emotion regulation

Our ability to control emotion and use it to our advantage contributes to our overall sense of well-being as we grow older. One way that emotion regulation facilitates this is by maintaining positive emotional states while at the same time being aware of physical and mental changes (33). This sense of emotional resilience in the face of anguish helps protect the individual from anxiety and depression and be associated with better physical health. As we shall see in this chapter, our ability to regulate emotion considerably impacts how we can deal with being diagnosed with the condition that threatens our sense of self, the essence of who we are and how we see ourselves.

With age, most of us make a series of adjustments and adaptations such that positive outcomes are more likely while decreasing negative emotions. In doing so, socioemotional selectivity theory argues we are acknowledging that life is finite and that what was once important may no longer be so (34). Our relation-ships with others vary in subtly different ways to how we related to others in childhood and early adulthood, emphasizing friends exerting an emotion regulat-ing effect (35).

Having explored some of the relevant theory of emotion processing, the remainder of this chapter will focus more closely on my own work that has led to the development of a theory of emotion regulation in dementia. I shall begin by looking at work previously carried out in the domain of social psychology. This acted as a springboard for my own work.

Dementia as an existential threat

The central tenet behind my work is that dementia should be seen as an existential threat. With dementia, there are many threats to one's sense of self, covering a loss of autonomy, meaning, identity, feelings of isolation, and, finally, the threat of death. How individuals perceive such threats is variable and depends on many things. One of the key determiners is how much meaning a person finds in the life they lead. Those who feel they have much to contribute tend to face the variform threats with a degree of equanimity.

Having argued this, one direct consequence is the potential to utilize the range of psychological and social strategies that have been shown to be effective in reducing the distress experienced in healthy adults when faced with threats to their existence. One of the central creeds of current care is that it is possible to live well with dementia despite the fears and concerns that the diagnosis brings. Although people with dementia are challenged at all levels, it is necessary to face head-on the genuine fears the diagnosis brings, but in such a way as to protect and enhance a person's sense of purpose in life, their feeling of emotional connection with loved ones; in all, their overall value as a person (36).

The empirical basis of this work consists of a series of connected studies carried out over the past few years. These studies are closely based on research conducted on healthy adults and draw upon several key constructs from social psychology. Although there is much yet to explore, we have amassed sufficient evidence to argue for a model of dementia whereby a person's lived experience can be broken down into a series of discrete threats to self, each processed in specific ways, ways that mirror those seen among healthy adults. Because of this, we propose strate-gies that can be implemented to help people with dementia learn more about their condition without becoming distressed.

More of this shortly. However, to begin with, I need to set the scene describing the theoretical basis for this programme of research. Before doing so, I should draw attention to an important caveat. I shall be referring to threatening and non-threatening stimuli. However, I am not referring to the severe threat associated with traumatic memories. Such memories are beyond the bounds of what I am talking about here and are processed entirely differently from those described subsequently (37).

The mind has evolved in such a way as to have various in-house mechanisms that treat unpleasant memories in an entirely different way to non-distressing ones. In other words, self-threatening information is processed in such a way as to protect the integrity of the individual concerned.

Autobiographical memory

There are, of course, many different types of memory. Broadly speaking, we talk about short-term and long-term memory. The work described here homes in on a particular kind of long-term memory, namely autobiographical memory. By autobiographical memory, I mean our memory for specific episodes in our lives combined with pertinent facts. In other words, autobiographical memory is a combination of episodic memory and knowledge about who we are (38).

There is a long and extensive history of research into all forms of memory. One of the many things to come out of this research is the knowledge that people tend to recall negative memories more accurately than positive ones (39). However, this is not the case for autobiographical memories. Instead, the body of evidence suggests the opposite, with poorer recall for adverse events in a person's life (40). Explanations have been proffered to account for this. One argument is that people generally experience a more significant proportion of positive life events and, as such, there is a more robust and denser associative network associated with such memories, and so it is easier to bring to mind (41). However, the picture was far from clear.

Mnemic neglect

One's sense of self is at the root of the self-protective memory mechanisms mentioned in the previous section. Most of us have a positive and healthy self-concept. We see ourselves as a worthwhile person, competent in various areas of our lives, caring, and morally upstanding (42). There is nothing simple about the self-concept. We like to think of ourselves in this way regardless of the situation we face. There are hidden mental mechanisms at play that achieve continuity of self (43). One of the ways to accomplish this is to protect ourselves against negative feedback from others (44). Think back to a time when your performance was assessed at work. Feedback that is positive and affirms your belief in yourself as a hard-working person fits well with how you view yourself and so is highly consistent with your autobiographical memories. As a result, you integrate this feedback into what you already know about yourself (45). Doing this also helps us recall this same feedback later, should we be asked about it; say, for example, for the purpose of a psychology experiment.

When receiving feedback that is self-threatening—such as being told that you are lacking the expertise for a particular role—we mostly shrug it off, although we don't entirely ignore it. Instead, we provide likely excuses and tell ourselves it will not happen again. Such feedback is not processed at the same level of depth as self-affirming material (46). Due to the relative lack of active processing, such negative feedback is less well remembered later (45).

The mnemic neglect model predicts that people will recall self-affirming feedback better than self-threatening feedback. Because of this mechanism, our sense of who we are is slowly strengthened over time. When this status quo is challenged, the mnemic neglect defence helps maintain continuity of self during times that could potentially threaten how we view ourselves.

Advantages of mnemic neglect

Having explored the mnemic neglect effect, it is perhaps time to consider why this is beneficial. Why did this self-protective mechanism develop? I will soon talk about my own research that extends these findings into the clinical field of dementia, but, for the time being, let us stick with looking at typically ageing adults.

Given what we know about mnemic neglect, it might not be too much of a surprise to find out that such self-protective functions are associated with psychological well-being as indicated by a greater sense of optimism, among other things. Maladaptive feelings and behaviour are accordingly reduced, with people showing lower levels of depression, anxiety, neuroticism, and hostility (47).

However, is it all rosy? Might there be costs to this? The types of negative feedback I am referring to here in this research might be initially upsetting but might also, if acknowledged, lead to personal growth (48). If something we do makes others annoyed or uncomfortable, maybe it is crucial we learn from that feedback and change our ways.

Maybe we could strive for the best of both worlds if we can argue that seeking negative feedback is not an anathema. What I am suggesting, then, is the ability to self-regulate this self-protective function (49). As we have seen, the default is blanket self-protection in the face of negative comments. However, we are living in an age that struggles always to attain higher levels of self-development. Think about the shelf upon shelf of self-help books out there. Turning off or attenuating this self-protective function would allow one to acknowledge negative feedback and use it to improve ourselves (50). Importantly, it matters who provides the opinion, such that a comment provided by a spouse or a friend, for example, will have real implications in terms of the health of that relationship and, as a result, will be processed at a deeper level (51). The feedback would be processed in such a way as to occasion self-improvement, thereby removing all traces of the mnemic neglect effect.

What happens to these memories?

We know that when we are presented with stimuli, if we do not attend to them or engage in some form of active processing, all traces of them will be removed. What then of memories that are not traumatic but are nonetheless threatening? Evidence shows that, given appropriate cues, such memories can be accessed once more (52). Indeed, so far, we have been referring to the conscious recall of memories, whereas there are other ways in which memories can manifest. Our behaviour is constantly influenced by implicit memories of previous events, procedural memories that we have developed, and our recognition of things we have been exposed to previously, all of which control our behaviour without us being aware of them (53, 54).

Recognition memory is better than recall. Given this, recognition memory offers more insight into what information is actually retained by the individual. Just because a person cannot consciously retrieve the details, one cannot conclude that the data is no longer present. There has been too much research into recognition and implicit memory for us to believe that. From the viewpoint of the mnemic neglect model, it has been argued that, although self-threatening material cannot be consciously accessed, it is still there and accessible in other forms. For example, tests of recognition memory for the types of material we have been talking about would not demonstrate the mnemic neglect effect regardless of the threat level. Although most of the research here has focused on recall, the studies of recognition memory that have been conducted so far support these predictions (55). This is evidence for the retention and recoverability of self-threatening memories, at least in typically ageing adults. We keep hold of the material, but we are prevented from consciously accessing it.

Negativity bias versus mnemic neglect

Negativity bias refers to the tendency for unpleasant thoughts or experiences to exert a greater and more lasting effect on the individual compared to both neutral and positive events (56). So, how does this link to what I have just been talking about?

Coming back to mnemic neglect, it can provide an explanation for a lot of what we know about human nature. It can offer a reason why our lives appear more perfect than they actually are when looking back at what we have done; why we tend to remember the successes rather than the failures, why we appear in general (at least to ourselves) such a remarkable individual. The literature on negativity bias has shown us that severely threatening information or events results in the individual challenging them, eliciting a series of outmanoeuvres that generally describe a sense of mobilization (57). On the other hand, where the sense of self-threat is moderate, not life-threatening, for example, the mechanisms we have described as mnemic neglect go into play. We mentally distance ourselves from the material and so not think about it (58, 59). This is described as a process of minimization.

We can see how this can be harnessed for the good. I have shown that mnemic neglect results in a biased sense of self, albeit fuelled by a motivation for self-protection. However, as already intimated, there are times when we need to be brutally honest with ourselves. For this to happen, we need to identify strategies that will allow us to bypass the self-protective bias. Research has identified clues to this. There is empirical evidence to show that the mnemic neglect effect disappears if a person is motivated to improve themselves when negative feedback is provided by someone they feel close to and if they believe the trait to be malleable (60, 61); in other words, they feel supported and have control over the situation.

Parallels with repression

The self-protective function referred to here as mnemic neglect echoes other work carried out in the field of psychology. In particular, the most potent resonance is with theories of repression. Most will automatically think about Freud and his devotees when such a term is used. For the purpose of the argument here, I shall stick to the cognitive literature. Erdelyi refers to avoiding some material that results in a loss of accessibility later on, a situation he calls inhibitory repression (58). From the early days of experimental psychology, we know that information is lost from the mind if we do not actively encode it. In fact, this is an efficient and effective mechanism. We also know that we can purposefully forget information (62). Research has shown this to be more successful for negative memories (63).

One concern that seems ever-present in forced suppression of material is the tendency for the suppressed content to return with even greater force. Wegner showed evidence for such a rebound effect, an effect that appears to be robust (64, 65). Wegner suggested that there are two processes in operation here. The first set out to achieve the desired state of mind, one where you are no longer thinking about the thing you do not want to think about. This is a conscious activity. In other words, you are trying to avoid thinking about something: that tray of biscuits when you are on a diet, for instance. Wegner argues that this suppression activity activates a monitoring process that occurs at a subconscious level. Such monitoring is in place to detect cases of suppressed thought or action breaking through into consciousness. Therein lies the problem. The monitoring process merely acts to increase the activation level of the suppressed material. We are, in effect, thinking about things that we have decided not to think about in order not to think about them. This has the effect of increasing the accessibility of something when we actually want to lower it (66).

Notably, the rebound effect is generally only seen in those with a predilection to engage in the activity they are trying to suppress (67). For example, the rebound effect of trying to stop eating junk food is only seen in habitual dieters. The issue here is that those most at risk from the rebound effect are those most likely to engage in suppression activity. Fortunately, mindfulness techniques offer a way out of this situation as mindfulness emphasizes acceptance, not avoidance (68).

However, the argument here regarding mnemic neglect is that it is not concerned with effortful suppression of material, as is the aforementioned case. Because of this, one might not expect a comparable rebound effect. There is more work needed to verify if this is, in fact, the case. The type of process operating here is something more akin to inhibitory repression rather than active suppression:

avoiding something to reduce its accessibility rather than actively blocking the recall of information (69).

Before moving on to dementia, I need to introduce another facet of my work, namely nostalgia. Having talked about emotion regulation at the start of the chapter, and then about how we respond to information that threatens our sense of self, this next section introduces a technique, nostalgic recall, that has proven useful in helping to alleviate distress and will lead on to my own work around developing an intervention for dementia. I shall introduce the concept of nostalgia before then placing it in the context of how it can be used to reduce distress in dementia. Before doing that, I will also need to introduce the theory of terror management, which forms part of the theoretical basis for this work.

Nostalgia

What then do we mean by nostalgia. It is undoubtedly a term much in use. Right from the start, I wish to draw a distinction between *reminiscence* and *nostalgia*. Often these words are used interchangeably. However, there is a clear difference between the two, which is essential when arguing later for an intervention I have developed with colleagues to be offered to people with dementia. The difference is this. *Reminiscence* is concerned about recalling past events, but there is no specific guidance about what type of event. On the other hand, *Nostalgia* refers to a memory that is intensely personal and positive. Such memories are primarily associated with specific triggers—a piece of music, a particular smell—that can be used to reinstate that memory later. You might say that reminiscence is a shared activity, whereas nostalgia is an individual experience, although I am aware that in making such a generalization, it is not necessarily as clear-cut as this. Nonetheless, it will serve the purpose here. Nostalgia as an activity is widespread. In fact, four-fifths of students report feeling nostalgic at least once a week (70). This is important, especially considering the implications for its use in therapy.

"Nostalgia" is derived from two Greek words, *nostos* (return home) and *algos* (pain). It was first used in the seventeenth century to describe soldiers' disturbed state of mind during a time of war. Many experienced an overwhelming longing to return to their homeland. Initially, it was looked upon as a somewhat negative state to find oneself in. Originally, nostalgia was associated with a maladaptive mindset. Now, however, the opposite is the case, with nostalgia being seen as "absolutely central to human experience."[1] I shall explain why in a moment.

The Oxford English Dictionary defines it as a "Sentimental longing for . . . the past."[2] Synonyms include wistfulness, longing, regret, and sentimentality. As described earlier, a nostalgic memory is meaningful and positive: a specific memory that is of exquisite intrinsic value, one that can be brought vividly back to one's mind by a known trigger, such as a particular smell, taste, location, or myriad other stimuli.

The full dictionary definition adds the qualifier that a nostalgic memory may be a "regretful memory of a period of the past." In other words, nostalgic memories can be bittersweet in nature. The memory you bring to mind may be packed with positive emotions, but there might be a sense of dismay or sorrow that the memory is of a time now past, reflecting a life once lived. A characteristic of nostalgic memories is that, although sadness may be evoked initially, positive emotions win through in the end, leaving the person feeling strengthened. In other words, such memories offer a redemptive quality.

Tchaikovsky's fourth symphony, especially the second movement, fills me with sorrow and joy. It is a melancholy piece; it is true. However, it brings to mind vividly the visceral sensation of holding one of my grandfather's cassettes that I kept after his death. He made a recording from a Radio 3 broadcast many years ago. It was one of his favourite works. I can see the tape box in my mind, re-experience the textural qualities, see his writing on the label, and hear the music in my head. Although I feel sad as he is no longer with us, the overriding feeling is happiness. He greatly influenced me, instilling a love of learning and classical music in me. That is the true power of nostalgic memory.

Sedikides and Wildschut provided evidence that nostalgia serves four main purposes for the individual (70). Nostalgic recall is a reliable source of positive feelings and emotions, thereby bolstering mood. Self-esteem is increased too, such that people feel more positive about themselves after thinking about a nostalgic memory. There is a social element here also, with people reporting feeling a greater sense of connection with others around them. There was evidence of a more secure attachment style in their interactions with others and greater overall confidence. Finally, there is an increased awareness of meaning derived from the life a person leads, an effect that can be harnessed to help a person deal with existential issues (71).

Having now talked about the mnemic neglect effect and the role of nostalgia in typically ageing adults, the following sections focus on how this impacts the lives of people with dementia. To begin with, I need to reintroduce the concept of dementia as an existential threat before providing a brief account of a theory of terror management that underprops this work.

Responding to an existential threat

The concept of living well with dementia is of central importance to the care and treatment of those with the condition (72). In a recent paper, my colleagues and I expressed the view that, for this to occur, we need to see and understand dementia as an existential threat; something that imperils the very essence of who we are as a person (73). Worry about dementia is increasing as a function of the growing public awareness of the condition. Clearly, knowledge and understanding can only be a good thing, but it does also bring with it a spectre of tragedy that threatens a large number of us, be it now or at some future stage in our lives. This fear of dementia grows as we age. It is not the fear of death itself but rather the fear of losing one's command over life (74). Indeed, to many, losing one's faculties is feared more than death.

When looking at how those with dementia lead their lives, there does, on the surface, appear to be a paradox. Dementia is clearly a threat to a person's existence, yet, on the whole, most people seem to be living their life without being emotionally overwhelmed by the knowledge that they have dementia (75). How can that be? It is clearly not the case that dementia poses such an insignificant threat that it is not worth the worry. One argument might be that the condition itself, with the progressive nature of the disease process, renders the person unaware of the real impact of their diagnosis. Indeed, we know there is a lack of self-awareness as the disease develops, a state referred to as anosognosia. However, other factors do seem to be at play here as well. Rather than being biological in origin, these factors are firmly rooted in the person's psychology.

Although conceptual understanding is affected by dementia, studies have shown that people with dementia can offer their own views on death, especially regarding how they would like to be cared for (76). So, they are clearly aware of their own impending mortality. Then, one might argue that awareness is best seen as being on a continuum rather than being either present or absent. In this sense, perception can change over time, and in response to circumstances to which one is confronted. On the face of it, it would seem logical not to dwell on the condition and all it entails. However, people do need to consider not only their own future but also that of their family and friends. Accepting a diagnosis and being aware of what will happen in the future are essential steps in adjusting to any condition. In the case of dementia, such reflection might bring about a period of psychological instability and a concomitant loss of self-control (73, 75, 77, 78). There is, in this sense, a balancing act going on within the individual, incorporating what they know about the condition into their sense of self without being overwhelmed by this knowledge (73). This ongoing struggle has been described as the person experiencing oscillating ambivalence about their condition. In other words, the person flits from a state of awareness to one of denial in a perpetual internal battle.

The psychology literature is replete with accounts of repression of one form or another. This active denial of their condition is one form of this. What is equally clear from the literature, and the basis of many psychotherapeutic approaches, is that repressed material will find its way back to the surface, albeit in a somewhat disguised form (79). One such resurfacing of repressed material is captured in the metaphors people with dementia utilize when telling stories during therapy (80–82). Other manifestations occur through artistic endeavours, such as poetry and painting (83–85). It may also be at the root of some of the challenging behaviours that accompany the condition (86, 87), where the individual seeks to express their distress in the only manner available to them.

As seen, threat-related information is processed differently from neutral material. It is pushed out of conscious awareness. In other words, there is a range of psychological defence mechanisms operating to achieve this. The concept of defence mechanisms at play draws upon research from social psychology, specifically terror management theory.

Nostalgia and terror management

At the root of terror management theory (TMT) is a person's awareness of their own mortality (88). We lead our lives by immersing ourselves in society in such a way that our fear of a finite life does not overwhelm us. We have faith in the beliefs and values of the society we live in. This is described as our cultural world view. In everyday life, we deal effectively with our awareness of our own mortality by upholding these specific world views and, in doing so, flood our lives with a sense of purpose, with meaning, a sense of worthiness, and with belonging and being emotionally connected to others. All these act to protect us from death anxiety. I would highly recommend reading the work of Ernest Becker, Jeff Greenberg, Sheldon Solomon, and Tom Pyszczynski to learn more about this theory. In addition, I encourage you to read *Mortals* by Rachel and Ross Menzies (89).

It is not only knowledge of one's mortality that sets psychological defence mechanisms into play. Reminders of mortality that we all experience every day of our life also invoke these same responses. Two such reminders are illness and ageing (90). Dementia clearly is one such reminder.

We are usually adept at dealing with the types of reminders of our mortality that we encounter in our daily lives. We are not overwhelmed by emotional distress, and, most likely, we may not even notice them. This is because mnemic neglect works in conjunction with other psychological defence mechanisms to make us resilient. Nostalgia can be used to help people defend themselves against reminders of their own mortality. Nostalgic remembrance quells any threat associated with a knowledge of one's impermanence. It achieves it by reinforcing an individual's sense of self-worth (71), helping them feel more connected to other people in their lives, and securing a belief that their lives have meaning (70). Nostalgia builds up these psychological resources and, in doing so, provides a buffer against the anxiety that would otherwise arise from becoming aware of one's mortality. Engaging in nostalgic recall offers a way for people to manage any distress that would otherwise arise from an awareness of their relative ephemerality (71).

Much evidence has been amassed as to the positive psychological effects of nostalgia (71). Nostalgia-prone individuals who were asked to reflect on their own death believed their lives had more value when compared to the group who were not naturally nostalgic. The nostalgia-prone group had the advantage of drawing upon essential psychological resources that helped them deal with thoughts around their own mortality.

The evidence for the benefits of nostalgia is robust. The psychological buffer offered by this technique was not affected by a person's self-esteem or mood or the extent to which they felt connected to influential figures in their social world. The act of reflecting upon their own past was enough to protect them from any distress caused by a sense of their own mortality.

It is now time to bring the focus back to dementia. Having set out the previous research on the mnemic neglect effect and nostalgia, we shall now look at my research driven by a desire to see if these effects could be replicated in people with dementia. The aim was to also develop an intervention that would help people with the diagnosis deal more effectively with the emotional costs of the condition.

Mnemic neglect in dementia

I have argued that dementia should be considered a threat to self. The literature just described is important to help us understand how people with dementia respond to the challenges of their diagnosis. Self-protective mechanisms, such as mnemic neglect, offers insight into how people deal with the emotional turmoil following a diagnosis of dementia.

Using the same methodology as Sedikides and colleagues, this time presenting people with statements about dementia that varied in threat level, we replicated the mnemic neglect effect in a sample of patients with the disease. Information that was highly threatening to the self was less well recalled. Because we also included a test of recognition memory alongside recall, we also showed that the mnemic neglect effect was removed in the recognition memory task. This again reproduced findings seen in healthy adults. This showed that the material had been encoded sufficiently for accurate recognition, but conscious recall was prevented to protect the individual from personal threat (91).

This is consistent with what we know about the behaviour of those with dementia. A person may deny that they have the condition and refuse to acknowledge it, but it is clear they are aware of it from the way they behave. We also know that a common dilemma among patients is whether to accept they have dementia but risk experiencing distress or reject the diagnosis and risk losing control (36).

I have been arguing that it is important to situate the experiences of people with dementia within the paradigm of existential threat outlined by terror management theory. Doing so will enable people to accept the nature of dementia as a terminal condition and encourage a more open and honest viewpoint, emphasizing the importance of the things that really matter in one's existence (73). I shall now present some of my findings concerning nostalgia as an intervention for dementia.

Nostalgia and dementia

Our review paper showed clear evidence that the benefits of nostalgia are substantial in typically ageing adults, with evidence that it improves mood, social connectedness, self-esteem, meaning in life, self-continuity, and optimism (92). The research I have conducted with my colleagues is the first to explore the impact of nostalgia in those with dementia.

Our initial aim was to see if we could replicate the findings in a clinical sample (93). I am pleased to say that we did—otherwise I would not be writing this section!—such that individuals with dementia showed improvements in line with healthy adults, indicating that nostalgia has beneficial psychological effects for individuals with severe cognitive impairment.

Nostalgic conversations

I have already made clear the distinction between "reminiscence" and "nostalgia." Similarly, the nostalgia-based therapy I am developing with colleagues is separate from reminiscence therapy. This is important as the impact of reminiscence therapy on mood and well-being is not clearly understood (94). Indeed, a recent trial offered no evidence for any beneficial therapeutic effect of reminiscence therapy (95).

Current interventions that draw upon a person's past, such as reminiscence therapy and life review therapies, have not discriminated between nostalgic and non-nostalgic recall. The evidence for a nostalgia effect is robust, time and again showing evidence that it

> serves a self-oriented function (by raising self-positivity and facilitating perceptions of a positive future), an existential function (by increasing perceptions of life as meaningful), and a sociality function (by increasing social connectedness, reinforcing socially oriented action tendencies, and promoting prosocial behavior).
>
> (96)

Given the evidence for the overriding importance of nostalgic recall, especially because it buffers against distress from situations that threaten a person's sense of self, we have developed a nostalgia-based intervention for people with dementia, which we call nostalgic conversations.

In addition to replicating the positive effect of nostalgia, we also conducted a study to see if nostalgia improved resilience in someone with dementia when asked to process self-threatening information (93). Participants were presented with statements about dementia that were either high or low in terms of negativity. Those in the nostalgia condition recalled significantly more dementia-related statements. We showed that nostalgia increased positive mood, which then improved recall. We also found that nostalgia increased meaning in life, which led to better recognition memory performance. There was no evidence of any resultant distress. In fact, the evidence pointed to an increase in pleasant mood. In a very real sense, then, nostalgia emboldens individuals through boosting psychological resources, such that they can assimilate self-referent dementia-related information into their self-concept without incurring psychological harm.

Based on our experimental evidence, we have developed a nostalgia intervention for people with a diagnosis of dementia (97). The findings to date have been positive. Participants were able to find time in their daily routine to carry out the activity, and they saw it as beneficial and engaging.

> We are seeing that nostalgia helps people deal with any disconnect between their current experience and what happened in the past.[3]

Our work has shown nostalgic recall buffers someone against the psychological distress associated with dementia. Nostalgic memories improve self-esteem and self-continuity and boost feelings of social connectedness. Overall, people report feeling more optimistic and feel their life has greater meaning.

The benefits of an intervention based on nostalgia are that everyone can participate and gain an advantage. It is truly inclusive. It does not require a great deal of time or effort. Once triggers for a specific nostalgic memory have been identified, individuals can take advantage of the positive effects whenever and wherever they like. People can do it independently, with their spouse or partner, with family, young and old.

Triggers can be wide-ranging. They may include a particular piece of music, an item of clothing, a specific meal, and so on. The role of the senses plays a massive part in all this. Smells are particularly evocative. We are currently working on making such nostalgic triggers readily available, especially for those working in care homes. I would love to be able to develop bespoke bottled scents that can be stored alongside digital music players, photographs, and the like. The smell of fish and chips and the saltiness of the sea air could then permeate the room while a person becomes immersed in a photo from the first time they and their spouse walked arm in arm along the beach carrying freshly fried goodies. How one might make such sprays is another point entirely.

Believing in oneself, knowing we are the same person regardless of our health, being surrounded by people we care about, feeling optimistic, and knowing our life has meaning, is all central to living well with dementia. Therefore, in contrast to current practice in reminiscence therapy, we argue that there is a need to focus on recalling nostalgic memories rather than for people to engage in reminiscence per se. If used on a one-to-one basis, this effect can be produced either by explicitly guiding the individual to remember specific memories or through music selected by the individual (93) as opposed to generic playlists.

This is by no means saying that our approach should replace reminiscence therapy. Instead, they operate differently. Reminiscence therapy suits groups of individuals. Previously, I talked about life story work. This too links with nostalgia but, again, focuses on something else, providing carers with a more in-depth knowledge of the person with dementia. Nostalgia, however, offers a personal, targeted, quick, and cheap way to immediately boost key psychological resources.

I shall labour this point further as I know that we all tend to conflate terms such as reminiscence and nostalgia and that, in everyday conversation, this is fine. However, when trying to convince funders and reviewers that nostalgia and reminiscence are different, the distinctions must be adequately explained. This is because there are reams and reams of papers on reminiscence therapy, whereas the therapeutic effect of nostalgia is new. However, convincing people, including commissioners, that nostalgia is different from reminiscence is challenging.

It is perhaps helpful to think of reminiscence as the process or act of bringing to mind the past, whereas nostalgia is the sensation elicited from this activity. Because of this, not all remembrances from one's past will produce feelings of nostalgia. In the case of reminiscence therapy then, because there is no steer to the type of memories recalled, the likelihood that individuals will recall a deeply personal nostalgic memory is slim. Indeed, the emphasis is on shared memories with the group.

Being someone keen on technology, I am particularly excited by the research that I am about to get underway, developing an augmented reality app to create bespoke nostalgic experiences for older adults with dementia. It will be a way to overlay a person's field of vision with images from a specific moment in their past to recreate a multisensory nostalgic experience that will combine the visuals with sound and the other senses. The beauty of this is that, as opposed to virtual reality, where the experience is in a digital arena, with augmented reality, the individual can interact with the environment and obtain feedback from touch and smell, and so on. An example that springs to mind is a vivid, nostalgic memory of walking in a specific park, on a particular date, with a dear friend, human or animal. The app would then enable the individual to recreate that in any park as the visuals would be overlayed on the actual scene. So, a person would hear and smell a babbling brook and be able to touch and smell the trees. They would be reliving the memory in an authentic sense.

Before I move on to another topic, I want to end this section on nostalgia by including an excerpt penned by the great Classical composer, Joseph Haydn, that I happened upon in the excellent book, *Music and the Mind*, by Anthony Storr.

> Often when I was wrestling with obstacles of every kind, when my physical and mental strength alike were running low and it was hard for me to persevere in the path on which I had set my feet, a secret feeling within me whispered: "There are so few happy and contented people here below, sorrow and anxiety pursue them everywhere; perhaps your work may, some day, become a spring from which the careworn may draw a few moments' rest and refreshment."
>
> (98)

I will now turn to the work of Steven Sabat, an influential writer to whom I shall return in the final chapter. His work of maintaining self-esteem for someone with dementia is essential reading. I knew I wanted to include this aspect of his work, but I was unsure where to slot it. I think this chapter is perhaps the most appropriate place as it links well to my own work on nostalgia and its psychological buffering effect.

Maintaining self-esteem

Self-esteem is talked chiefly of in terms of something tangible and, therefore, measurable. Perhaps this is true in many cases. However, conceptual problems have been identified when referring to self-esteem in people with dementia, among others.

Before looking at these issues, it is important to, first of all, describe what we mean by self-esteem. Intrinsic to this concept is a person's sense of identity. Their sense of self. We are complex beings. We each have a conception of our own selfhood and use this to manage how we appear to others. We are different selves with different people. This is expressed perfectly as a "diversity in unity," or unitas multiplex (99, 100). However, the use of the word "self" can be problematic. Instead, it may be preferable to refer to a "person" whose consciousness is unique (100). The way one presents to others can be described as one's persona. However, in real life, it is a far more complex picture. We may intend to offer our persona in a certain way depending on our situation. Once presented, it is then perceived and interpreted by others. These others will have their own beliefs and expectations about you and your behaviour, further complicating the mix.

Sabat then turns to address what happens in someone with dementia. How is their self-esteem affected? Most obviously, the person with dementia becomes increasingly aware that their ability to function effectively is gradually deteriorating with time. Quite understandably, a person experiencing such loss feels anxious, angry, and starts to grieve for their previous life. The person with dementia must also contend with a malignant psychology, a term coined by Kitwood (101). This can take many forms. Being the recipient of various labels that identify the person as incompetent and impaired can only lead to negative consequences, eventually creating the situation expected by the process of self-fulfilling prophecy. Linked to this is a real or apparent disregard for what the person with dementia is thinking and feeling, a situation described as invalidation.

A problem for many conditions is where someone else takes over responsibilities and actions to help alleviate some of the burdens a person is facing. This can be a good thing if it is appropriate and is agreed upon by the person you are supposedly helping. However, there is a tendency to be overzealous, and, in doing so, the person you are assisting starts to become increasingly dependent on support when, in actual fact, minimal or no aid is needed. This results in disempowerment. In the case of dementia, the person may be quite capable of doing certain things. It might just take them longer, or they are less efficient in their actions. That does not mean that someone should step in to do these things for them. Also, it does not imply support should not be provided. It is a matter of balance, of ensuring you tread the fine line that separates instilling independence from cultivating dependence, a line that is more of a perceptual blur than a distinct gradation to all intents and purposes.

Sabat's point is that dementia as an entity affects the diagnosed person on several discrete yet interacting levels. There are the effects of the disease itself, with its gradual, unrelenting progression. Then there is how the individual responds to the diagnosis and changes in functioning. There is the impact of how other people react to the diagnosis. Also, whether the reactions of others are positive or negative will affect the person with dementia in some way. Such a complex web of intra- and interpersonal dynamics is challenging to gauge and manage.

The self can be split into various elements. One aspect is a person's sense of identity, their beliefs and expectations, their attitudes. This sense of identity can be seen as being pivotal in maintaining a feeling of personal continuity throughout their life. The concept of self-continuity has already been discussed in this chapter, where I talked about the role of nostalgia in improving well-being. This personal sense of identity is firmly rooted in a specific frame of reference, physical and psychological, providing true embodiment. Although there is this continuity, our beliefs about our attributes do change from time to time, referred to as restricted self. Our unrestricted self is our beliefs about our own past, present, and future characteristics. A person may consider attributes they had in the past, although there might be a disconnect with their perception of their characteristics at the present point in time. How we choose to present to others, our persona, is another element. It is this latter manifestation of self that is affected by dementia.

Many conversations are underpinned by a sense of pride and integrity (102). For this to be fully realized, the listener has to buy into what the person is saying. The interlocutor is vital in the construction of the persona. If this does not occur, validation of self is prevented.

From a therapeutic point of view, it is crucial to identify what underlies a person's sense of pride. This would require the therapist to explore their client's past to isolate specific memories. It might be necessary to locate in their past or present which aspect makes them feel incompetent or a liability. Accurately identifying these would help pave the way to improving their overall well-being.

From such accounts, it is clear that self-esteem is, to varying extents, dependent on social exchanges. We need others to validate who we think we are. It is this aspect of the self that is especially vulnerable in dementia. Often with dementia, there is a shutting off from those around us. This might be a personal choice or, in many cases, merely the result of a mismatch between a person's needs and the services available and offered.

An example here would be someone who has been a successful businessperson for much of their life. It was something they held dear, instilling in them a sense of pride and value. These feelings were reflected by those around them. They were treated with the reverence expected of someone who was indeed a success: the much-needed ratification. However, when a person receives a diagnosis of dementia, others begin to treat you differently almost immediately. They respond to you as someone who has dementia. They no longer reflect their deference to you in their actions. Instead, they mirror the increasing impairment that permeates your life. Because of this, retaining that vital sense of self, your projected persona, becomes increasingly difficult; the self becomes fragile. People behave around someone with dementia in a manner that just would not be acceptable in any other condition. The person with dementia is reduced to a set of stereotypical symptoms. They are the dementia. They are no longer Helen or Harry, but rather the manifestation of the disease process that is laying waste to their nervous system.

Although the issue around self-reflection and self-awareness is contentious, the person with dementia is only too acutely mindful that they are no longer able to perform as they once did. This naturally impacts their beliefs about their attributes.

One can see that such inter- and intrapsychic interchanges are a potential tinderbox. Entirely rational behaviour acted out by the person with dementia can easily be misinterpreted as somehow odd, nonsensical. As we have seen, the person with dementia often exists within a malignant social psychology. They will likely rail against this, responding to others in a way entirely in keeping with their sense of being affronted. Rather, that is what they intend. Others may not see it the same way. Indeed, frustration at not accomplishing something can be misinterpreted as anger and not in keeping with the current interaction. In other words, it could be seen as a symptom of the dementia, of irrational rage. Such misattributions reinforce similar explanations in the future while at the same time sounding a death knell for meaningful interactions going forward. No one would be able to maintain their self-esteem under such an unrelenting onslaught.

The final part of this paper by Sabat presents case studies illustrating how people with dementia shape their involvement with others to preserve a belief in their own attributes while at the same time presenting the persona they desire. By no means does this always eventuate in someone withdrawing from others to protect their self-esteem. Indeed, there are accounts here that perfectly capture the insight and creativity of therapists to grasp the meaning behind the extemporizations of those with dementia such that they can engage in essential social activity without embarrassment or frustration. He gives an example of an academic whose outputs throughout their career evidenced a clarity of expression and joy of communication. This jarred with their current situation in which word finding was highly impaired. Through conversations, Sabat, in his role as caregiver, was able to facilitate this client's re-engagement with group activities by giving allowances in terms of time provided that would allow them to better express what they wanted to say without feeling undue pressure. In achieving this, their belief in their own attributes was not eroded, and they were able to contribute considerably to activities, thereby providing the needed verification of their self-worth.

Other accounts showed individuals where there were no such barriers. One example given was of a lady brought up in a theatrical environment. She harnessed her skills as the "life and soul of the party" by telling jokes and encouraging fellow residents to sing along with her. This brought joy to residents and staff alike, supporting her personal beliefs in her attributes and allowing her to project the persona she was happy with.

Sabat summarizes his position as follows. He recognizes that people with dementia can still have pride in a range of attributes that were so important in their past. At the same time, they as individuals are acutely aware of the effects of the disease and the signs of decline in function presented at seemingly every turn. The case studies also showed that the individual with dementia is aware of these competing views. What seems to hold true for all the accounts presented in this paper is that the person with dementia would like others to recognize both that they are experiencing impairment in core areas of their life, but at the same time they do retain key attributes that are essential for their own sense of worth. Sabat notes that this is not something that can be imposed or demanded. Instead, it requires the empathy and combined efforts of others, which leaves the individual with dementia in an extremely exposed position.

Another important insight to develop from this work is that the person with dementia plays an active role here, albeit one that is potentially foreshortened by other people. However, the person with dementia is clear as to which aspects of their unrestricted self are in evidence and accurately identifies which attributes are negatively affected by dementia; in other words, being able to isolate elements that are supportive from those threatening their self-esteem. They are then able to emphasize their positive attributes when interacting with others. As seen, success at being allowed to express the persona they desire is entirely in the hands of those with whom they are interacting.

Before drawing this chapter to a conclusion, there is one final topic that again links well to work outlined so far in this section: existential loneliness.

Existential loneliness

Existential loneliness refers to an acute awareness that one is somehow disconnected from others (103). People also experience a strong grasp of their own mortality. Part of the problem is a lack of someone with whom they can confide their deepest fears. This differs from other conceptions of loneliness in several ways. One can be alone in a spatial sense, such that one might be living somewhere where there is a physical distance from other people. On the other hand, social aloneness indicates that a person does not have many family and friends. Neither of these is intrinsically negative. Subjective loneliness, however, is. It describes a situation where someone has few or no meaningful relationships with others. As a result, people experience negative emotions and a sense of hopelessness. It has been argued that subjective loneliness is distinct from existential loneliness. The former reflects a lack of intimate relationships, whereas existential loneliness is something more; regardless of whether a person has close family and friends, they experience existential loneliness as a sense that they are in some fundamental way separate or detached from the world and the people that inhabit it. In such cases, a person may be surrounded by significant others and, as a result, not experience subjective loneliness, yet still endure existential loneliness.

Existential loneliness tends to be felt when a person confronts their own mortality due to an illness. This is a profound and all-encompassing state. As discussed elsewhere in this chapter and in another book, we are all aware that our lives are limited, that we are mortal. Indeed, R.D. Laing—the famous psychiatrist who had a penchant for existential philosophy—stated that "Life is a sexually transmitted disease and the mortality rate is one hundred percent."[4] However, we do our best not to be aware of this fact in our daily lives. Various subconscious processes operate to protect us from this knowledge. Our lives would be consumed by fear of death were this not the case. Having said that, there are times, such as receiving a poor prognosis, that force us to contemplate our own eventual demise. Although it does not have to be the threat of death in a literal sense. Rather, experiencing a serious mental health problem can also lead to similar thoughts (104). One profound statement, "I am alone wherever I am," perfectly encapsulates this feeling (105). If a person is trying to share their troublesome thoughts about their condition, maybe even their own death, and they feel that they are not being listened to, the person experiences spiritual death. Not being able to talk about their deepest concerns means they risk losing contact with their most profound sense of self (106). Such a situation is described as intrapersonal isolation (107). This state of incongruence—what Rogers would call a less genuine state—leads to internal crisis (106).

In terms of care, the patient must be listened to and their fears respected. To help with existential loneliness, the carer needs to be accepting and allow the person to talk openly about their concerns, to be authentic. Such an environment would help facilitate personal growth and strengthen a person' sense of meaning in life (108).

Nostalgia and existential loneliness

The importance of the link between mental health disorders and existential loneliness speaks for itself. The sense of spiritual death referred to in the previous section resonates with what I talked about concerning dementia. The barriers preventing people from talking about their condition can only feed this sensation. I am exploring this further in my own work on nostalgia, given its ability to help break down such barricades by buffering against distress experienced when talking about their condition. Importantly, nostalgic reverie is something that, as we have seen, lends itself to the inclusion of family members and friends.

Before moving on, another interesting parallel between nostalgia and existential loneliness is around the conception of homelessness (109, 110). Early descriptions of nostalgia centred on feelings of homesickness: a yearning to return. Likewise, people with mental health problems often discuss craving somewhere to call home, where they are acknowledged and belong (111). In terms of mental health, and by extension, loneliness, it could be argued that, as the result of their condition, a person no longer feels life is meaningful. Life no longer seems to make sense. Again, one of the things we see with nostalgia is that it enhances meaning in life and social connectedness.

Reacting to dementia

Dementia is ever-present in our lives, whether we have been diagnosed with the condition, care for someone with it, or see an advertisement on the television. The menace of dementia weighs heavy, yet we manage to find a way of living under its pall without being overwhelmed. Many can maintain an emotional equilibrium in the face of this existential threat. A person may decide to make the most of life today rather than living for tomorrow: as Horace wrote, "*carpe diem, quam minimum credula postero.*"[5] Our understanding of dementia ultimately shapes how we defend ourselves against this knowledge, how we lead our lives.

Our lives are bound by the universal existential truth that we are mortal, yet we do not think about this until we stumble across a reminder. For example, we might have stepped off the curb without paying due attention and narrowly escaped being hit by a car. Knowledge of our own mortality rarely dominates our lives. This duality—of being both aware and not aware of our mortality—is not accidental. The cultural anthropologist, Ernest Becker, argued that our lives are driven by unconscious efforts to deny and transcend death.

> We build character and culture to shield ourselves from the devastating awareness of our underlying helplessness and terror of our inevitable death.
>
> (112)

We devote ourselves to the world we live in, forging relationships that sustain us, and holding up values and systems that will eventually outlive us. This provides us with the crucial psychological resources that protect us from the anxiety and distress that would otherwise come from being reminded of our mortality: in other words, self-esteem, a sense of loving and being loved, a belief that we are the same person we have always been and knowing that life has both meaning and purpose.

The dilemma facing someone with dementia is a graver version of that which meets the rest of us. We should also remember that someone with dementia faces this dilemma from a context of diminishing cognitive ability, thereby making it more difficult for the person to hold onto these psychological resources and maintain an emotional equilibrium.

An explicit existential narrative has been mostly absent in the dementia care literature. Although there is a growing body of research around how best to meet the palliative care needs of people with dementia, the inevitability of gradual deterioration and impending mortality is somewhat the elephant in the room in dementia care. We all know that dementia involves this deterioration, but we struggle to find the words to talk about it, contributing to the feeling of spiritual death that I referred to earlier. A decline in our abilities makes it even more of a challenge to hang onto our self-esteem. We know, too, that people strive to make sense of dementia even though, by doing so, they face being overwhelmed by the very condition with which they are trying to come to terms. This is where nostalgia fits in by offering a buffer allowing people to talk together about fears and concerns without being overwhelmed by distress.

People with dementia fall back on those parts of their life that provide them with a sense of being valued. It is, after all, who they are. It gives their life meaning and purpose. This likely drives them to maintain routines that shape their daily life. Such behaviour may not appear out of place in their own home, but the same behaviour may be deemed aberrant on moving into a nursing home. It is liable to be misunderstood; seen as a symptom of an underlying disease, not a reaction to it.

People often assume that the person with dementia no longer has any awareness of what they are doing or what is happening around them. In fact, peoples' responses to the person with dementia are often predicated on this very belief. However, many behaviours seen in people with dementia are merely a personal response to their comprehension that something is wrong. Their actions are evidence of an internal struggle where the person is trying to make sense of the "wrongness" that is all too evident.

The relationship that a person has with their dementia determines the path their lives take post-diagnosis. If the overwhelming emotion is fear, then denial shapes that person's life and the lives of those around them. If the person acknowledges it, they are more likely to find acceptance and may even achieve a sense of peace. At this point, they can make critical life-changing choices, perhaps the most important of which is the choice to live well with dementia.

Many who live with dementia find a way to assimilate the changes associated with their condition into their lives. In doing so, they allow themselves to be looked after. Over time, they find the strength to gradually let go of even the most precious aspects of their lives, leading a life that is no longer overwhelmed by the disease.

Summary

Emotion regulation has been the focus of this chapter. We began by looking at social cognition and the role of higher-order cognitive processes in helping us deal with the emotional aspects of our everyday life and how this is affected by disease processes. An overriding theme throughout this chapter has been dementia as an existential threat. Having looked at some of the self-protective mechanisms that occur in our minds, I presented my own work on the mnemic neglect effect. Pushing details about dementia that threaten our sense of self out of our conscious minds may be seen as a good thing. However, to fully come to terms with the diagnosis, a person needs to consciously engage with and process such material. This is where my work on nostalgia comes in. My colleagues and I have shown that a nostalgia-based intervention can help protect people with dementia from the distress associated with some of the more serious aspects of their condition. In doing so, it is hoped that people with the disease will be more able to talk about how they feel and accept the changes that will inevitably occur.

Notes

1 www.theguardian.com/society/2014/nov/09/look-back-in-joy-the-power-of-nostalgia
2 www.oed.com/view/Entry/128472?redirectedFrom=nostalgia#eid
3 https://go.uwe.ac.uk/nostalgiablog1218

4 The origin of this quote is unclear, although it would appear the most commonly source cited is that it occurs in footage from the film, "Did You Used to Be R.D. Laing?"
5 Seize the day, put very little trust in tomorrow (Quintus Horatius Flaccus, Carmina, Liber I, Carmen XI).

References

1 Meltzoff AN. Social cognition and the origin of imitation, empathy, and theory of mind. 2010 [cited 05/12/2012]. In: The Wiley-Blackwell handbook of childhood cognitive development [Internet]. Wiley-Blackwell [cited 05/12/2012].
2 Quinn KA, Mcrae CN, Bodenhausen GV. Social cognition. In: Nadel L, editor. Encyclopedia of cognitive science. London: Wiley; 2005.
3 Beer JS, Ochsner KN. Social cognition: A multi level analysis. Brain Res. 2006;1079(1):98–105.
4 Baron-Cohen S. Mindblindness: An essay on autism and theory of mind. Cambridge, MA; London: MIT Press; 1995.
5 Schaffer HR. Proto-language. In: Schaffer HR, editor. Key concepts in developmental psychology. SAGE; 2006.
6 Leslie AM. Pretense and representation in infancy: The origins of "theory of mind". Psychol Rev. 1987;94:412–426.
7 Wellman HM, Woolley JD. From simple desires to ordinary beliefs: The early development of everyday psychology. Cognition. 1990;35(3):245–275.
8 Gopnik A, Astington JW. Children's understanding of representational change and its relation to the understanding of false belief and the appearance-reality distinction. Child Dev. 1988;59(1):26–37.
9 Reber AS, Allen R, Reber ES. The Penguin dictionary of psychology. 4th ed. London: Penguin; 2009.
10 Perner J, Wimmer H. John thinks that Mary thinks that attribution of second-order false beliefs by 5- to 10-year-old children. J Exp Child Psychol. 1985;39:437–447.
11 Coricelli G. Two-levels of mental states attribution: From automaticity to voluntariness. Neuropsychologia. 2005;43(2):294–300.
12 Brothers L, Ring B. A neuroethological framework for the representation of minds. J Cogn Neurosci. 1992;4:107–118.
13 Baron-Cohen S, Ring HA, Wheelwright S, Bullmore ET, Brammer MJ, Simmons A, et al. Social intelligence in the normal and autistic brain: An fMRI study. Eur J Neurosci. 1999;11(6):1891–1898.
14 Baron-Cohen S. Without a theory of mind one cannot participate in a conversation. Cognition. 1988;29(1):83–84.
15 Shamay-Tsoory SG, Tomer R, Berger BD, Goldsher D, Aharon-Peretz J. Impaired "affective theory of mind" is associated with right ventromedial prefrontal damage. Cogn Behav Neurol. 2005;18(1):55–67.
16 Pellicano E. Links between theory of mind and executive function in young children with autism: Clues to developmental primacy. Dev Psychol. 2007;43(4):974–990.
17 Maylor EA, Moulson JM, Muncer AM, Taylor LA. Does performance on theory of mind tasks decline in old age? Br J Psychol. 2002;93(Pt 4):465–485.
18 Happe FG, Winner E, Brownell H. The getting of wisdom: Theory of mind in old age. Dev Psychol. 1998;34(2):358–362.

19   German TP, Hehman JA. Representational and executive selection resources in 'theory of mind': Evidence from compromised belief-desire reasoning in old age. Cognition. 2006;101(1):129–152.

20   Bailey PE, Henry JD. Growing less empathic with age: Disinhibition of the self-perspective. J Gerontol B Psychol Sci Soc Sci. 2008;63(4):P219–P226.

21   Duval C, Piolino P, Bejanin A, Eustache F, Desgranges B. Age effects on different components of theory of mind. Conscious Cogn. 2011;20(3):627–642.

22   Adolphs R. The human amygdala and emotion. Neuroscientist. 1999;5(2):125–137.

23   Lieberman MD, Gaunt R, Gilbert DT, Trope Y. Reflexion and reflection: A social cognitive neuroscience approach to attributional inference. Adv Exp Soc Psychol. 2002;34:199.

24   Diagnostic and statistical manual of mental disorders: DSM-5. 5th ed. American Psychiatric Association; 2013.

25   Spoletini I, Marra C, Di Iulio F, Gianni W, Sancesario G, Giubilei F, et al. Facial emotion recognition deficit in amnestic mild cognitive impairment and Alzheimer disease. Am J Geriatr Psychiatry. 2008;16(5):389–398.

26   Piquard A, Derouesne C, Lacomblez L, Sieroff E. [Planning and activities of daily living in Alzheimer's disease and frontotemporal dementia]. Psychol Neuropsychiatr Vieil. 2004;2(2):147–156.

27   Gregory C, Lough S, Stone V, Erzinclioglu S, Martin L, Baron-Cohen S, et al. Theory of mind in patients with frontal variant frontotemporal dementia and Alzheimer's disease: Theoretical and practical implications. Brain. 2002;125(Pt 4):752–764.

28   Hargrave R, Maddock RJ, Stone V. Impaired recognition of facial expressions of emotion in Alzheimer's disease. J Neuropsychiatry Clin Neurosci. 2002;14(1):64–71.

29   Phillips LH, Scott C, Henry JD, Mowat D, Bell JS. Emotion perception in Alzheimer's disease and mood disorder in old age. Psychol Aging. 2010;25(1):38–47.

30   Guaita A, Malnati M, Vaccaro R, Pezzati R, Marcionetti J, Vitali SF, et al. Impaired facial emotion recognition and preserved reactivity to facial expressions in people with severe dementia. Arch Gerontol Geriatr. 2009;49(Suppl 1):135–146.

31   McDowell CL, Harrison DW, Demaree HA. Is right hemisphere decline in the perception of emotion a function of aging? Int J Neurosci. 1994;79(1–2):1–11.

32   Fernandez-Duque D, Hodges SD, Baird JA, Black SE. Empathy in frontotemporal dementia and Alzheimer's disease. J Clin Exp Neuropsychol. 2010;32(3):289–298.

33   Labouvie-Vief G. The psychology of emotions and ageing. In: The Cambridge handbook of age and ageing. Cambridge University Press; 2005.

34   Carstensen LL, Fung HH, Charles ST. Socioemotional selectivity theory and the regulation of emotion in the second half of life. Motiv Emot. 2003;27:103–123.

35   Coats AH, Blanchard-Fields F. Emotion regulation in interpersonal problems: The role of cognitive-emotional complexity, emotion regulation goals, and expressivity. Psychol Aging. 2008;23(1):39–51.

36   Cheston R, Christopher G. Confronting the existential threat of dementia: An exploration into emotion regulation. Springer; 2019.

37   Dalgleish T, Hauer B, Kuyken W. The mental regulation of autobiographical recollection in the aftermath of trauma. Curr Dir Psychol Sci. 2008;17(4):259–263.

38   Conway MA, Williams HL. Cognitive psychology of memory. In: Byrne JH, editor. Learning and memory: A comprehensive reference. Amsterdam and London: Elsevier; 2008.

39 Baumeister RF, Bratslavsky E, Finkenauer C, Vohs KD. Bad is stronger than good. Rev Gen Psychol. 2001;5(4):323–370.

40 Mather M. Why memories may become more positive as people age. In: Uttl B, Ohta N, Siegenthaler AL, editors. Memory and emotion: Interdisciplinary perspectives. Malden, MA; Oxford: Blackwell; 2006.

41 Unkelbach C, Fiedler K, Bayer M, Stegmüller M, Danner D. Why positive information is processed faster: The density hypothesis. J Pers Soc Psychol. 2008;95(1):36.

42 Sedikides C, Gregg AP. Self-enhancement: Food for thought. Perspect Psychol Sci. 2008;3(2):102–116.

43 Sedikides C, Spencer S. The self: Frontiers in social psychology. New York: Psychology Press; 2007.

44 Campbell WK, Sedikides C. Self-threat magnifies the self-serving bias: A meta-analytic integration. Rev Gen Psychol. 1999;3(1):23.

45 Pinter B, Green J, Sedikides C. How neglect feeds the self: Mechanisms of self-protective memory. Unpublished manuscript, Pennsylvania State University, Altoona; 2008.

46 Brown SC, Craik F. Encoding and retrieval of information. In: Tulving E, Craik FIM, editors. The Oxford handbook of memory. Oxford: Oxford University Press; 2000.

47 Alicke MD, Sedikides C. Self-enhancement and self-protection: What they are and what they do. Eur Rev Soc Psychol. 2009;20(1):1–48.

48 Colvin CR, Griffo R. On the psychological costs of self-enhancement. In: Chang EC, editor. Self-criticism and self-enhancement: Theory, research, and clinical implications. 1st ed. Washington, DC: American Psychological Association; 2008.

49 Sedikides C, Luke M. On when self-enhancement and self-criticism function adaptively and maladaptively. In: Chang EC, editor. Self-criticism and self-enhancement: Theory, research, and clinical implications. 1st ed. Washington, DC: American Psychological Association; 2008.

50 Roese NJ, Olson JM. Better, Stronger, faster: Self-serving judgment, affect regulation, and the optimal vigilance hypothesis. Perspect Psychol Sci. 2007;2(2):124–141.

51 Harvey JH, Omarzu J. Minding the close relationship. Pers Soc Psychol Rev. 1997;1(3):224–240.

52 Payne DG. Hypermnesia and reminiscence in recall: A historical and empirical review. Psychol Bull. 1987;101(1):5.

53 Nobel PA, Shiffrin RM. Retrieval processes in recognition and cued recall. J Exp Psy Learn Mem Cogn. 2001;27(2):384–413.

54 Rovee-Collier C, Hayne H, Colombo M. The development of implicit and explicit memory. Amsterdam: John Benjamins Publishing; 2000.

55 Green JD, Sedikides C, Gregg AP. Forgotten but not gone: The recall and recognition of self-threatening memories. J Exp Soc Psychol. 2008;44(3):547–561.

56 Rozin P, Royzman EB. Negativity bias, negativity dominance, and contagion. Pers Soc Psychol Rev. 2001;5(4):296–320.

57 Ditto PH, Lopez DF. Motivated skepticism: Use of differential decision criteria for preferred and nonpreferred conclusions. J Pers Soc Psychol. 1992;63(4):568.

58 Erdelyi MH. The unified theory of repression. Behav Brain Sci. 2006;29(5):499–511; discussion-51.

59 Simon L, Greenberg J, Brehm J. Trivialization: The forgotten mode of dissonance reduction. J Pers Soc Psychol. 1995;68(2):247.

60　Green JD, Pinter B, Sedikides C. Mnemic neglect and self-threat: Trait modifiability moderates self-protection. Eur J Soc Psychol. 2005;35(2):225–235.

61　Green JD, Sedikides C, Pinter B, Van Tongeren DR. Two sides to self-protection: Self-improvement strivings and feedback from close relationships eliminate mnemic neglect. Self Identity. 2009;8(2–3):233–250.

62　Anderson MC, Green C. Suppressing unwanted memories by executive control. Nature. 2001;410(6826):366–369.

63　Depue BE, Banich MT, Curran T. Suppression of emotional and nonemotional content in memory: Effects of repetition on cognitive control. Psychol Sci. 2006;17(5):441–447.

64　Jacoby LL. Ironic effects of repetition: Measuring age-related differences in memory. J Exp Psy Learn Mem Cogn. 1999;25(1):3–22.

65　Abramowitz JS, Tolin DF, Street GP. Paradoxical effects of thought suppression: A meta-analysis of controlled studies. Clin Psychol Rev. 2001;21(5):683–703.

66　Bargh JA. The automaticity of everyday life. In: Wyer RS, editor. The automaticity of everyday life. Mahwah, NJ: Lawrence Erlbaum; 1997.

67　Erskine JA, Georgiou GJ. Effects of thought suppression on eating behaviour in restrained and non-restrained eaters. Appetite. 2010;54(3):499–503.

68　Bowen S, Witkiewitz K, Dillworth TM, Marlatt GA. The role of thought suppression in the relationship between mindfulness meditation and alcohol use. Addict Behav. 2007;32(10):2324–2328.

69　Sedikides C, Green JD. The mnemic neglect model: Experimental demonstrations of inhibitory repression in normal adults. Behav Brain Sci. 2006;29(5):532–533.

70　Wildschut T, Sedikides C, Arndt J, Routledge C. Nostalgia: Content, triggers, functions. J Pers Soc Psychol. 2006;91(5):975–993.

71　Routledge C, Arndt J, Sedikides C, Wildschut T. A blast from the past: The terror management function of nostalgia. J Exp Soc Psychol. 2008;44(1):132–140.

72　Banerjee S. Living well with dementia—Development of the national dementia strategy for England. Int J Geriatr Psychiatry. 2010;25(9):917–922.

73　Cheston R, Christopher G, Ismail S. Dementia as an existential threat: The importance of self-esteem, social connectedness and meaning in life. Sci Prog. 2015;98(4):416–419.

74　Watkins R, Cheston R, Jones K, Gilliard J. 'Coming out' with Alzheimer's disease: Changes in awareness during a psychotherapy group for people with dementia. Aging Ment Health. 2006;10(2):166–176.

75　Lishman E, Cheston R, Smithson J. The paradox of dementia: Changes in assimilation after receiving a diagnosis of dementia. Dementia. 2016;15(2):181–203.

76　Godwin B, Waters H. 'In solitary confinement': Planning end-of-life well-being with people with advanced dementia, their family and professional carers. Mortality. 2009;14(3):265–285.

77　Robinson L, Clare L, Evans K. Making sense of dementia and adjusting to loss: Psychological reactions to a diagnosis of dementia in couples. Aging Ment Health. 2005;9(4):337–347.

78　Snow K, Cheston R, Smart C. Making sense'of dementia: Exploring the use of the MAPED to understand how couples process a dementia diagnosis. Dementia. 2014.

79　Balfour A. Thinking about the experience of dementia: The importance of the unconscious. J Soc Work Pract. 2006;20(3):329–346.

80　Crisp J. Making sense of the stories that people with Alzheimer's tell: A journey with my mother. Nurs Inq. 1995;2(3):133–140.

81 Cheston R. Stories and metaphors: Talking about the past in a psychotherapy group for people with dementia. Ageing Soc. 1996;16:579.

82 Cheston R, Jones K, Gilliard J. Psychotherapeutic groups for people with dementia: The Dementia Voice group psychotherapy project. Care-giving Dement Res Appl. 2006;4.

83 Burke L. The poetry of dementia: Art, ethics and Alzheimer's disease in Tony Harrison's Black Daisies for the Bride. J Lit Cult Disabil Stud. 2007;1(1):61–73.

84 Gregory H. Using poetry to improve the quality of life and care for people with dementia: A qualitative analysis of the Try to Remember programme. Arts Health. 2011;3(2):160–172.

85 Zeilig H, Killick J, Fox C. The participative arts for people living with a dementia: A critical review. Int J Ageing Later Life. 2014;9(1):7–34.

86 Browne C, Shlosberg E. Attachment behaviours and parent fixation in people with dementia: The role of cognitive functioning and pre-morbid attachment style. Aging Ment Health. 2005;9(2):153–161.

87 Miesen BM. Alzheimer's disease, the phenomenon of parent fixation and Bowlby's attachment theory. Int J Geriatr Psychiatry. 1993;8(2):147–153.

88 Becker E. The birth and death of meaning: An interdisciplinary perspective on the problem of man. 2nd ed. New York: Free Press; 1971.

89 Menzies R, Menzies R. Mortals: How the fear of death shaped human society. Australia, Melbourne: Allen & Unwin; 2021.

90 O'Connor ML, McFadden SH. A terror management perspective on young adults' ageism and attitudes toward dementia. Educ Gerontol. 2012;38(9):627–643.

91 Cheston R, Dodd E, Christopher G, Jones C, Wildschut T, Sedikides C. Selective forgetting of self-threatening statements: Mnemic neglect for dementia information in people with mild dementia. Int J Geriatr Psychiatry. 2018;33(8):1065–1073.

92 Ismail S, Cheston R, Christopher G. A systematic review on the psychosocial functions of nostalgia within the general population using experimental studies. Prospero CRD42014009848.2014. Available from: https://www.crd.york.ac.uk/PROSPERO/display_record.php?RecordID=9848.

93 Ismail S, Christopher G, Dodd E, Wildschut T, Sedikides C, Ingram TA, et al. Psychological and mnemonic benefits of nostalgia for people with dementia. J Alzheimers Dis. 2018;65(4):1327–1344.

94 Woods B, O'Philbin L, Farrell EM, Spector AE, Orrell M. Reminiscence therapy for dementia. Cochrane Database Syst Rev. 2018;3:CD001120.

95 Woods RT, Orrell M, Bruce E, Edwards RT, Hoare Z, Hounsome B, et al. REMCARE: Pragmatic multi-centre randomised trial of reminiscence groups for people with dementia and their family carers: Effectiveness and economic analysis. PLoS One. 2016;11(4):e0152843.

96 Sedikides C, Wildschut T, Routledge C, Arndt J, Hepper EG, Zhou X. Chapter five— To nostalgize: Mixing memory with affect and desire. In: Olson JM, Zanna MP, editors. Advances in experimental social psychology. Vol. 51. London: Academic Press; 2015, pp. 189–273.

97 Dodd E, Ismail S, Christopher G, Wildschut T, Sedikides C, Cheston R. Nostalgic conversations: The co-production of an intervention package for people living with dementia and their spouse. Dementia (London). 2022;21(2):489–502.

98 Storr A. Music and the mind. New York: Free Press and New York and Oxford: Maxwell Macmillan International; 1992.

99 Stern W, Spoerl HD. General psychology from the personalistic standpoint. 1938.

100 Sabat SR, Fath H, Moghaddam FM, Harr¥e R. The maintenance of self-esteem: Lessons from the culture of Alzheimer's sufferers. Cult Psychol. 1999;5(1):5–31.

101 Kitwood T. Brain, mind and dementia: With particular reference to Alzheimer's disease. Ageing Soc. 1989;9(1):1–15.

102 Erikson EH. Childhood and society. 1963.

103 Bolmsjö I, Tengland P-A, Rämgård M. Existential loneliness: An attempt at an analysis of the concept and the phenomenon. Nurs Ethics. 2019;26(5):1310–1325.

104 Erdner A, Nyström M, Severinsson E, Lützén K. Psychosocial disadvantages in the lives of persons with long-term mental illness living in a Swedish community. J Psychiatr Ment Health Nurs. 2002;9(4):457–463.

105 Granerud A, Severinsson E. The struggle for social integration in the community—The experiences of people with mental health problems. J Psychiatr Ment Health Nurs. 2006;13(3):288–293.

106 Rogers CR. On becoming a Person: A therapist's view of psychotherapy. London: Constable & Co; 1961/1995.

107 Yalom ID. Existential psychotherapy. New York: Basic; 1980.

108 Ettema EJ, Derksen LD, van Leeuwen E. Existential loneliness and end-of-life care: A systematic review. Theor Med Bioeth. 2010;31(2):141–169.

109 Svenaeus F. The phenomenology of health and illness. In: Toombs SK, editor. Handbook of phenomenology and medicine. Dordrecht; London: Kluwer Academic; 2001.

110 Heidegger M, Stambaugh J, Schmidt DJ. Being and time: A revised edition of the Stambaugh translation. Albany, NY: Excelsior and Bristol: University Presses Marketing [distributor]; 2010.

111 Avieli H, Mushkin P, Araten-Bergman T, Band-Winterstein T. Aging with schizophrenia: A lifelong experience of multidimensional losses and suffering. Arch Psychiatr Nurs. 2016;30(2):230–236.

112 Becker E. The denial of death. [New]/[with foreword by Sam Keen]. London: Souvenir Press; 2014.

113 Sedikides C, Gregg, AP. Selfenhancement: Food for thought. Persp Psychol Sci. 2007;3(2):102.

Chapter 8

Intellectual developmental disorder and dementia

Intellectual development disorder

This section will examine how intellectual developmental disorders (IDDs) interact with the diagnosis of dementia. IDDs are identified when an individual's mental functioning is severely impaired compared to others in the same age group. The cause is invariably neurological. One condition, in particular, is pertinent here when considering dementia, namely Down's syndrome. Estimated figures of how many live in the UK with IDD vary, although the figure is believed to be over 700,000; for those with Down's syndrome, the figure is around 40,000.[1]

Disease trajectory

The age at which a person typically develops dementia differs from those with an intellectual disability. Those with Down's syndrome, for example, develop dementia at an earlier age, often when in their 50s.[2] The way the symptoms manifest may also differ. The progression of dementia is also generally more rapid. Alongside dementia, people with intellectual disabilities tend to experience poorly managed health-related conditions.[3]

Prevalence

We are continually being told that we live in an ageing society, where people live significantly longer than they did in the past. This change is across the board and includes those with IDDs. These changes are mainly due to advancements in medical science, with more conditions being treated successfully. We tend to view an increase in life expectancy as inherently positive. With improvements in understanding and better treatments, people live longer than in years past. There are inevitable downsides to such advancements. Indeed, we may find treatments or cures to prevent death from certain diseases or conditions. However, this only means we will die from something else where there is no such reprieve.

There is no situation where this is more pertinent than Down's syndrome. In this case, increases in life expectancy have meant people are living into their 60s,

DOI:10.4324/9781315681580-8

whereas in the 1980s, people were only surviving until their mid-20s. However, the consequence is that the risk of developing dementia also rises considerably.

Adults with Down's syndrome tend to develop the disease at an earlier age—neuropathological characteristics often appear by age 40 (1)—and the speed with which the disease progresses results in a steeper rate of decline (2). When looking at the prevalence of AD in other IDDs, there is little difference to that seen in a typically ageing population (3).

Why this should occur in Down's syndrome is in part explained by the gene that controls the expression of the amyloid precursor protein that is located on chromosome 21, the chromosome implicated in Down's syndrome (4). Amyloid precursor protein leads to the formation of beta-amyloid plaque, with such deposits occurring earlier than usual, for example, in Alzheimer's disease. More of this soon.

It has been predicted that the number of individuals with an intellectual disability will double by 2020 due to increased life expectancy. That means a third of this group will be aged 50 and over. With advancing age, the risk of dementia also increases. Estimates of the prevalence of dementia in those with intellectual disabilities vary mainly due to inadequacies in recognizing and diagnosing the condition in this patient group. A recent joint publication by the British Psychological Society and the Royal College of Psychiatrists indicates dementia occurs much earlier for those in this group (5). For those with Down's syndrome, dementia may be diagnosed in a person's 30s. For those aged 60 and above, prevalence is three times higher than in the general population.

At the highest risk of developing Alzheimer's disease are those with Down's syndrome. Of those who reach 70, around 70 per cent will develop dementia.[4] For those aged between 50 and 60, rates of dementia double every five years (6). It is unclear what happens to those over the age of 60. There is some evidence to suggest prevalence increases still further (7, 8), whereas other data suggest a reduction due to death as the result of dementia (6).

The health concerns of those with a range of IDDs are well-known. Due to various factors, including a lack of exercise and poor diet, general health for this group is often poor (9, 10). On top of this, the nature of the condition increases the risk of age-related diseases developing (11). A primary concern here is that a higher proportion of this group who have health concerns fail to receive the appropriate medical care than typically ageing adults (12). In cases such as Down's syndrome, life expectancy has increased to such an extent that many outlive their parents. The impact here is that parents are often the principal conduit between individuals with IDD and the medical profession. Within the current structure, there is usually no clear substitute (13). As a result, medical needs are unmet purely because they are not being identified and communicated to the appropriate healthcare professional, or at least not detected soon enough for timely diagnosis and proper intervention. A clear example of this is cancer, with identification occurring all too often when the disease has progressed to the extent that the prognosis is poor (14). Alternative means of communicating may be the way forward, such as more effective non-verbal behaviour (15).

Similarly, the mental health needs of this group often go undetected. Anxiety and depression are particular concerns (16). It has been suggested that poor quality of life is a crucial factor here, often combined with a series of adverse life events, resulting in mood disturbances (17).

Dementia diagnosis

A recurring theme in this book has been the endemic issues surrounding early detection and diagnosis. There are severe consequences for a person's well-being if this does not occur. Detection early on is particularly poor in those with intellectual disabilities. The fact that dementia may not be detected especially early likely explains to some extent why the progression of the disease is exceptionally rapid in this group. There are also serious issues around how well the person with intellectual disabilities comprehends the diagnosis they have been given. Therefore, the type of post-diagnostic support a person with IDDs receives should to be tailored to their particular needs.

Having provided an overview of intellectual disabilities, I shall now focus on Down's syndrome due to its prevalence and the fact that we just know more about this condition.

Down's syndrome

Based on figures reported by the Alzheimer's Society, for those with Down's syndrome,[5] around 1 in 50 develop dementia while in their 30s. Prevalence is even higher in those over 60, with dementia affecting roughly half. This is significantly higher than expected in those who do not have Down's syndrome. When looking at the prevalence of dementia in other intellectual disabilities, the figure is about 1 in 10 aged between 50 and 65, increasing to roughly 50 per cent in those over the age of 85.[6] Although less than the rates seen in Down's syndrome, they are still higher than those observed in those who do not have an intellectual disability.

The form of dementia most associated with Down's syndrome is Alzheimer's disease. Examination of the brains of those with this condition shows the presence of Alzheimer's pathology in those over the age of 40. However, not all presented clinically with symptoms of dementia (18). The most prominent explanation why this should be the case is associated with the presence of an additional copy of chromosome 21, hence the alternative name for Down's syndrome, Trisomy 21. Chromosome 21 is associated with the production of higher than normal levels of amyloid, deposits of which are characteristic of the pathology associated with Alzheimer's disease.

Symptoms

As might be expected, although there are similarities in the symptoms of dementia experienced by those with and without an intellectual disability, there are also characteristic challenges faced by those in this group.

Looking first at those with Down's syndrome, memory loss—the predominant feature of Alzheimer's disease usually detected in the early stages—is not as distinct as among the general population. The likely explanation is this group's already compromised memory ability. More obvious are changes in personality and behaviour, with an even greater need for support in accomplishing activities of daily living.[7]

Many people with Down's syndrome experience epilepsy. An epileptic seizure is caused by millions of neurons discharging at once, referred to as a paroxysmal discharge (19). A paroxysm describes a sudden intensification of symptoms. If seizures do not occur until later in life, it is almost certainly a sign that additional neurological damage is happening, and so assessment for dementia should be undertaken. More severe seizures presage a faster decline in a person's health.[8]

In the wake of the more advanced stages of Alzheimer's disease, the symptoms experienced by people with Down's syndrome resemble those of the general population. However, as noted earlier, the progression of the disease is often more rapid in this group.

When looking at other intellectual disabilities, the picture is less clear. This is due primarily to other conditions being less well-studied than Down's syndrome. Although the pattern of symptoms of dementia for those with less severe intellectual disabilities is comparable to that seen in the general population, this is not the case for those with more severe problems. Indeed, for this group, detection of dementia is even more challenging as early symptoms are atypical, manifesting chiefly as changes in personality and behaviour.

Detecting dementia

Cognitive impairment and behavioural problems are defining features of intellectual disabilities. However, any marked deterioration in functioning may portend the presence of an underlying disease process. This would be an appropriate time to assess such individuals for dementia. Family and friends often detect such deviation in how a person meets the challenges of everyday life.

One way to ensure such change in functioning is better detected in the future is for every person with Down's syndrome to be formally assessed before 30. Indeed, regular check-ups are recommended.[9] These should include standard health checks, including blood pressure, weight, testing of blood and urine, tests of vision and hearing, and a review of medication. Psychological well-being and functioning should also be considered. This should include an assessment of communication skills, overall functioning, and screening for possible dementia.

Risk factors

As seen in Chapter 2, several known risk factors are associated with dementia. These include obesity, diabetes, depression, and sedentariness.[10]

Assessment

I have already noted that identifying dementia is even more of a challenge when an intellectual disability occurs. Importantly, there is no inevitability here. Nonetheless, clinicians need to be cognizant that symptoms of dementia are not overlooked. The concern is that any worsening impairment is accounted for as part of the intellectual disability and not as a separate, underlying disease process, such as Alzheimer's.

Assessments should only be conducted by those who are IDD specialists. As I have already described the assessment process in Chapter 4, I shall not repeat it here. Instead, I shall focus on elements specific to this patient group.

The major difference is in how psychological and mental functioning is assessed.[11] Standard tools, such as the Mini-Mental State Examination, are not appropriate here. This is because cognitive functioning is already significantly compromised. This makes administering some aspects of the test challenging, among other things. Fortunately, there exist specialist tools for assessing this group.

Using imaging technology can result in extreme distress here. However, these techniques are needed to exclude the presence of a tumour or haemorrhaging.

Diagnosis

We have seen throughout this book the myriad difficulties clinicians face when attempting to make an accurate diagnosis of dementia. The symptoms of dementia may be masked, either intentionally or unintentionally. The picture is even more involved when assessing someone with an intellectual disability.[12] In the case of intellectual disability, some of the early warning signs that foreshadow the onset of dementia may be misinterpreted as another example of the challenging behaviour associated with this group of patients. A person's understanding and insight into any change in functioning may be diminished here, making it less likely that help will be sought unless someone else picks it up. One major indicator that dementia may indeed be developing is the onset of epileptic seizures.[13]

The Dementia Action Alliance reported that it was not uncommon for people with intellectual disabilities not to be told that they have dementia (20). It was emphasized that changes must be made and that it is vital for all concerned to better understand and discuss the condition and the various options for care that are available (20).

Prevention

It has been suggested that around 30 per cent of the current incidence of dementia in the UK is potentially preventable if the various known risk factors—diabetes, elevated blood pressure, obesity, lack of exercise, depression, smoking—are sufficiently addressed.[14] However, blood pressure and smoking are less of a risk for those with intellectual disabilities.[15]

Treatment

In Chapter 6, I talked about the various treatments for dementia. However, there is little evidence to draw upon when one wishes to consider their efficacy for those with intellectual disabilities. There is a paucity of research in this area (21). Even though there are side effects with drugs like donepezil, they can still be prescribed to those with Down's syndrome who are diagnosed with dementia. The exception here is if medical conditions might present a risk, such as cardiovascular disease.[16]

Behaviours that are often deemed challenging already exist in people with Down's syndrome. The main issues are aggression and agitation. Such responses worsen with the onset of dementia. When a person's behaviour changes, the cause is often how others behave towards them, an over-stimulating environment, or unrecognized pain. At the root, all too often, is some unmet need (22).

Support

As is the case for someone without an intellectual disability, post-diagnostic support should be provided for those with dementia and their immediate support network. This should combine psychoeducation and counselling (23). Various simple adaptations—use of colour, labelling, and decluttering—can be made to a person's living environment to prolong the time that they can remain in their own home.

It is essential to plan ahead to reduce the distress experienced further down the line. Although challenging to consider early on, advance care planning helps so many people experience a greater sense of security that they can exercise their choices and retain control even at the final stages of dementia.

Finances and legal issues

Although not always easy, it is generally agreed that planning ahead concerning one's finances and legal matters brings a sense of satisfaction and control. If carried out sufficiently early, a person with an intellectual disability can draw up their own will, arrange for lasting powers of attorney, and make plans for how they wish to be cared for at the latter stages of the illness. There seems to be a lack of confidence among those wishing to obtain such legal advice (24). Among some solicitors, there is evidence of creative ways to help people with IDD better comprehend the options, such as using a combination of pictures and verbal explanations.

End-of-life care

As the disease progresses, there does seem to be an increasing issue with the detection and treatment of pain. Often, during these later stages of the illness, the person can no longer effectively communicate if they are in pain and where the pain occurs. However, because people behave differently when they experience pain, such alterations in behaviour may be picked up by others around them. However, these behavioural changes may be incorrectly attributed to dementia. Therefore, carers need to be especially vigilant for signs that the person may be experiencing physical discomfort or distress due to some underlying and untreated pain condition.

In a guide developed by NHS England in conjunction with the Palliative Care for People with Learning Disabilites Network, there are some crucial tips to help guide those delivering end-of-life care. We should start with a couple of definitions. Palliative care aims to improve the quality of life of those faced with a life-threatening condition. This includes attempts to avert or provide respite from suffering (25). End-of-life care is aimed at those for whom death is imminent or expected within the next few months. [17]

There is good evidence showing that an early death is three times more likely for those with an intellectual disability[18] and that general health is poor, with many health and mental health needs not being met (26). Unfortunately, similar shortcomings are also the case when one looks at palliative and end-of-life care for this group.[19] The explanation given by the Care Quality Commission (CQC) 2016 report is that needs are not met because the care providers do not appreciate what is required for this patient group, and that there is a general lack of confidence in how best to work with this group.[20, 21] It is vital that such shortcomings are tackled as it is the case that people with intellectual disabilities live longer today and that with advancing age, frailty is increasingly likely.

As we have seen in Chapter 10, there are considerable issues to address when looking at the standard of dementia care provided to those from BME communities. This is again mirrored here when one looks at those with intellectual disabilities from these same backgrounds. Culturally sensitive care is essential at all stages, and possibly especially so at the later stages, particularly an approach that is informed by a person's religious or spiritual beliefs.

The NHS England guide identifies six ambitions to inform care at this level. The first is to view each person as an individual. This is something I have addressed previously in this book. In many cases, there is a natural tendency to see the person as an embodiment of their symptoms rather than as an individual. This fails to consider that each person experiences dementia in an entirely unique way. Each person will have their own desires and needs. Much of the subtlety and nuances will be lost if one generalizes about their condition.

In some cases, families may exclude the person with dementia from discussions around end of life issues because they wish not to distress the person concerned. However, a person must be part of the debate and plan around their own death to be better prepared for the end. People should be encouraged to talk about death and to discuss how they feel about it. Central to this is advance care planning. This will allow the person with dementia to specify their preferences for how they wish to be cared for at the end.

The second ambition states that everyone should be able to access the care they need. This is an issue for commissioners to consider when allocating resources. Adequate care and support require people to have experience and knowledge of the specific needs of those with intellectual disabilities diagnosed with dementia.

Ensuring comfort and well-being for all concerned is the third ambition. A good place to start is to ensure the person understands their diagnosis and that they are aware of what will happen. People should be helped to discuss where they would like to be treated to determine whether there is a preference for care in their home or in a hospice. For people with intellectual disabilities, unfamiliar environments can be particularly upsetting. The relatively high rates of mental health issues in this patient group are essential to consider here.[22]

The fourth ambition is coordinated care. A good way to help achieve this is to ensure effective communication between paid carers and the person's family and friends. Also, all information relating to end-of-life care should be available to all relevant parties via the patient's electronic records.

The fifth ambition is to make sure all staff are prepared for the type of care requested. End-of-life care is highly emotional for all concerned. There is an increased risk of "burnout" among carers due to such experiences (27).

The sixth and final ambition concerns the community. It is vital that the person concerned feels they are part of the community in which they live. As part of maintaining links with people, an awareness that speaking openly about death is to be encouraged.

The role of the carer

One of the main issues to contend with here is the impact of the ageing parent, who is the person's primary form of support. Their advocacy on behalf of the person with an intellectual disability helps ensure an appropriate level of care is provided and that the person's needs are addressed. However, since people with intellectual disabilities are living longer, the issue of parents being less able to take on this role needs to be considered. Indeed, in some cases, they lose their parents (28).

The Alzheimer's Society provides some excellent advice for those caring for people with dementia who also have an intellectual disability. Being mindful always of the increasing cognitive difficulties people face is paramount. Ensuring that one uses simple sentences is essential, as is giving the person adequate time to respond. Because language is severely affected by dementia, alternative modes of communication become increasingly important. Non-verbal forms of communication, such as body language and tone of voice, are fundamentally important. Ensuring that social bonds are maintained provides people with the much-needed sense of being connected to others, lessening the likelihood they will feel isolated (29). Developing a routine for each day helps provide a necessary sense of structure. However, we all know that days rarely go as planned, so allowing for change is essential.

In Chapter 7, I talked about my research on nostalgia. The ability to draw on vivid, personal memories is a great way to boost mood and facilitate interactions with others. The use of memory boxes and life story work taps into this fundamental capacity. Harnessing the power of music is so important. Even though a person can no longer talk, they can still hum along to their favourite music.[23]

As we have seen before, a key component of dementia care is supporting someone in their independence for as long as possible, although there will come a time when such activity becomes distressing and increasingly challenging to sustain. There is a need to ensure that independence is not maintained at the cost of the person's dignity or self-esteem.[24]

Guidelines

Here we shall look at guidance aimed at those with intellectual disabilities. This is based on NICE guidelines published in 2016 (30).

When given an annual health check, it is essential to assess the person's mental health, with an eye towards identifying potential signs of the onset of dementia, especially in those with Down's syndrome. Such tests should be carried out by clinicians who specialize in intellectual disabilities. This will ensure tools used and treatments suggested are appropriate for this group.

To help with this process, NICE suggested that people with intellectual disabilities should be tested early to obtain a baseline level of performance that can be compared with subsequent scores on these same measures (31). This will enable clinicians to better detect a significant drop in functioning.

Summary

This chapter looked at more severe forms of impairment, collectively known as intellectual developmental disorders. Specifically, we examined how dementia is also affected by a diagnosis of Down's syndrome. Although previous chapters have covered the topics of diagnosis, assessment, and treatment, the focus here was on how these are affected by the presence of a severe intellectual disability. Although there is a relative lack of literature in this field, it is essential that the individual needs of this subgroup of dementia patients are met through care and that specialist staff are available to provide for them and their families.

Notes

1 www.alzheimers.org.uk/about-dementia/types-dementia/learning-disabilities-dementia#content-start
2 www.alzheimers.org.uk/about-dementia/types-dementia/learning-disability-risk-developing-dementia
3 www.alzheimers.org.uk/about-dementia/types-dementia/dementia-learning-disability-whats-different#content-start
4 www.mentalhealth.org.uk/learning-disabilities/publications/hidden-plain-sight-dementia-and-learning-disability
5 Often the terms Down's syndrome and Down syndrome are interchangeable, the former is more commonly adopted in the UK, whereas the latter is the norm elsewhere.

6 www.alzheimers.org.uk/about-dementia/types-dementia/learning-disability-risk-developing-dementia#content-start
7 www.alzheimers.org.uk/about-dementia/types-dementia/symptoms-dementia-learning-disability
8 www.alzheimers.org.uk/about-dementia/types-dementia/symptoms-dementia-learning-disability
9 www.alzheimers.org.uk/about-dementia/types-dementia/symptoms-dementia-learning-disability
10 www.gov.uk/government/publications/dementia-applying-all-our-health/dementia-applying-all-our-health
11 www.alzheimers.org.uk/about-dementia/types-dementia/symptoms-dementia-learning-disability
12 www.alzheimers.org.uk/about-dementia/types-dementia/learning-disabilities-dementia?msclkid=d1659e2db98b11ec8735fc37055c2bda
13 www.alzheimers.org.uk/about-dementia/types-dementia/learning-disabilities-dementia?msclkid=d1659e2db98b11ec8735fc37055c2bda
14 www.gov.uk/government/publications/dementia-applying-all-our-health/dementia-applying-all-our-health
15 https://digital.nhs.uk/data-and-information/publications/statistical/health-and-care-of-people-with-learning-disabilities/health-and-care-of-people-with-learning-disabilities-experimental-statistics-2014-to-2015
16 www.alzheimers.org.uk/about-dementia/types-dementia/learning-disabilities-dementia-treatments
17 https://assets.publishing.service.gov.uk/government/uploads/system/uploads/attachment_data/file/323188/One_chance_to_get_it_right.pdf
18 www.bris. ac.uk/cipold/
19 www.cqc. org.uk/sites/default/files/20160505%20CQC_EOLC_OVERVIEW_FINAL_3.pdf
20 www.cqc.org. uk/news/stories/different-ending-our-review-looking-end-life-care-published
21 www.england.nhs.uk/improvement-hub/publication/the-route-to-success-in-end-of-life-care-achieving-quality-for-social-work/?msclkid=365e2186b99711eca78483f64247ccde
22 www.gov.uk/government/publications/people-with-learning-disabilities-in-england-2015?msclkid=76ab039ab99711eca35d4ee46d03dec6
23 www.alzheimers.org.uk/about-dementia/types-dementia/learning-disabilities-dementia-treatments
24 www.alzheimers.org.uk/about-dementia/types-dementia/learning-disabilities-dementia-treatments

References

1 Wisniewski KE, Wisniewski HM, Wen GY. Occurrence of neuropathological changes and dementia of Alzheimer's disease in Down's syndrome. Ann Neurol. 1985;17(3):278–282.
2 Wilkinson H, Janicki MP. The Edinburgh principles with accompanying guidelines and recommendations. J Intellect Disabil Res. 2002;46(Pt 3):279–284.
3 World Health Organization. Mental health: New understanding, new hope. Geneva: WHO; 2001.
4 Beyreuther K, Pollwein P, Multhaup G, Monning U, Konig G, Dyrks T, et al. Regulation and expression of the Alzheimer's beta/A4 amyloid protein precursor in health, disease, and Down's syndrome. Ann N Y Acad Sci. 1993;695:91–102.

5 British Psychological Society, editor. Dementia and people with intellectual disabilities: Guidance on the assessment, diagnosis, interventions and support of people with intellectual disabilities who develop dementia. Leicester: British Psychological Society; 2015.

6 Coppus A, Evenhuis H, Verberne GJ, Visser F, Van Gool P, Eikelenboom P, et al. Dementia and mortality in persons with Down's syndrome. J Intellect Disabil Res. 2006;50(10):768–777.

7 Visser F, Aldenkamp A, Van Huffelen A, Kuilman M. Prospective study of the prevalence of Alzheimer-type dementia in institutionalized individuals with Down syndrome. Am J Ment Retard. 1997.

8 Tyrrell J, Cosgrave M, McCarron M, McPherson J, Calvert J, Kelly A, et al. Dementia in people with Down's syndrome. Int J Geriatr Psychiatry. 2001;16(12):1168–1174.

9 Evenhuis H, Henderson CM, Beange H, Lennox N, Chicoine B. Healthy ageing—Adults with intellectual disabilities: Physical health issues. J Appl Res Intellect Disabil. 2001;14(3):175–194.

10 Janicki MP, Davidson PW, Henderson CM, McCallion P, Taets JD, Force LT, et al. Health characteristics and health services utilization in older adults with intellectual disability living in community residences. J Intellect Disabil Res. 2002;46(Pt 4):287–298.

11 Bigby C. Ageing with a lifelong disability: A guide to practice, program, and policy issues for human services professionals. London; New York: Jessica Kingsley; 2004.

12 Beange H, McElduff A, Baker W. Medical disorders of adults with mental retardation: A population study. Am J Ment Retard. 1995;99(6):595–604.

13 Howells G. Are the medical needs of mentally handicapped adults being met? J R Coll Gen Pract. 1986;36(291):449–453.

14 Hogg J, Tuffrey-Wijne I. Cancer and intellectual disability: A review of some key contextual Issues. J Appl Res Intellect Disabil. 2008;21(6):509–518.

15 Read S. The palliative care needs of people with learning disabilities. Br J Community Nurs. 1998;3(7):356–361.

16 Cooper SA. Psychiatry of elderly compared to younger adults with intellectual disabilities. J Appl Res Intellect Disabil. 1997;10(4):303–311.

17 Moss S. Mental health issues of access and quality of life. In: Herr SS, Weber G, editors. Aging, rights, and quality of life: Prospects for older people with developmental disabilities. Baltimore, MD: Paul H. Brookes Publishing; 1999.

18 Lott IT. Down syndrome. In: Nadel L, editor. Encyclopedia of cognitive science. Hoboken, NJ: Wiley; 2005.

19 Scambler G. Epilepsy. In: Ayers S, Baum A, McManus C, Newman S, Wallston K, Weinman J, et al., editors. Cambridge handbook of psychology, health and medicine. Cambridge University Press; 2007.

20 Dementia Action Alliance. Meeting the challenges of dementia for people with learning disabilities: Roundtable discussion briefing paper. London; 2017.

21 Livingstone L, Hanratty J, McShane R, Macdonald G. Pharmacological interventions for cognitive decline in people with Down syndrome. Cochrane Database Syst Rev. 2015;(10):CD011546.

22 Cohen-Mansfield J, Werner P. Environmental influences on agitation: An integrative summary of an observational study. Am J Alzheimers Care Relat Disord Res. 1995;10(1):32–39.

23 Watchman K, Janicki MP. Report of the 2016 International Summit on Intellectual Disability and Dementia. International Summit on Intellectual Disability and Dementia; 2017.

24 Swift P, Johnson K, Mason V, Shiyyab N, Porter S. What happens when people with learning disabilities need advice about the law? Bristol: Norah Fry Research Centre: University of Bristol; 2013;1:2015.

25 Harrison S. Leadership alliance for the care of dying people, one chance to get it right: Improving people's experience of care in the last few days and hours of life. London: LACDP; 2014, 168pp. (Pbk).

26 Emerson E, Hatton C, Robertson J, Roberts H, Baines S, Evison F, et al. People with learning disabilities in England 2011. Durham, NC: Improving Health & Lives: Learning Disabilities Observatory; 2012.

27 Chao SF, McCallion P, Nickle T. Factorial validity and consistency of the Maslach Burnout Inventory among staff working with persons with intellectual disability and dementia. J Intellect Disabil Res. 2011;55(5):529–536.

28 Bailey C. Supporting older people with learning disabilities: A toolkit for health and social care commissioners Sue Turner & Caroline Bernard, 2014, pp. 1–40. British Institute of Learning Disabilities, Birmingham. Br J Learn Dis. 2015;43(4):310–311.

29 Cheston R, Christopher G. Confronting the existential threat of dementia: An exploration into emotion regulation. Cham: Palgrave Pivot; 2019.

30 National Institute for Health and Care Excellence. Mental health problems in people with learning disabilities: Prevention, assessment and management. NICE guideline NG54. London: National Institute for Health and Care Excellence; 2016.

31 National Institute for Health and Care Excellence. Care and support of people growing older with learning disabilities. NICE guideline [NG96]. London: National Institute for Health and Care Excellence; 2018.

Chapter 9

The role of the carer

Early indications of change

Clinicians are adept at picking up the minutest signs in their attempt to formulate an accurate diagnosis. Clinical assessment is not merely about how people verbally respond to questions about their health and well-being; it is about the involuntary, minor gestures or reactions that often serve to support a tentative diagnosis. In mental health, general appearance can indicate much; evidence of self-neglect might signal depression, whereas an odd assortment of clothing might raise alarm bells for a possible diagnosis of mania. Speaking noticeably fast or slow might signpost mania and depression, respectively. Indeed, clinicians find an entire gamut of non-verbal signals incredibly useful.

In the case of dementia, one major indicator that something may be amiss is when individuals increasingly look to the spouse or carer for help rather than respond themselves to questions concerning their behaviour. Carers are so important when one considers the physical and mental well-being of someone with dementia. We shall consider next who takes on this role.

How does it all start?

The role of a carer is challenging for many reasons. The question of who should take on this responsibility is hotly contested. Given the current disease trajectory, the need for care across all levels, formal and informal, rises each year. Clinical care and management of dementia have been discussed in Chapters 6 and 7. Here, the role of informal care will be examined.

There are ongoing concerns that, as a global community, we are underprepared for the needs of an ever-growing older population. As a case in point, the UK has reviewed the retirement age and more-than-likely pension benefits to tackle some of these demands.[1] Aside from the involvement of the NHS, it has been projected that the number of households with older adults with some form of disability will double over the next 20 years, thereby intimating the need for informal care to cover this demand.

DOI:10.4324/9781315681580-9

Due to an ever-increasing reliance on informal care, there is a need to provide an adequate education for those who find themselves in these roles. Informal care refers to work usually carried out by a spouse or other family member that is unpaid. Friends and neighbours also fall under this category (1). At least six million people provide informal care in the UK alone. To provide adequate support, it is essential that the carer has a clear understanding of the particular diagnosis or indeed diagnoses to better meet the needs of the person with dementia. This issue of there being more than one diagnosis does not only reflect that a person may have mixed dementia; for example, it also means that, in all likelihood, the person with dementia will also be experiencing a host of other complaints, in terms of both mental health and physical health. This is something that will be discussed later in this chapter. To be effective as a carer, one must be aware of all potential difficulties a person might be experiencing.

Caring for someone with dementia

One of the many challenges faced by carers is to look after the person with dementia and be mindful of their own physical and mental well-being. A well-balanced diet is essential, as is regular exercise, restorative sleep, and maintaining one's hobbies and interests. If assistance is needed for someone to move about, carers need to be careful that they do not injure their back, so it is advisable for them to undergo training in moving and handling. However, depending on the person and the severity of symptoms, this is not always possible, especially as the disease progresses.[2] Even so, many report that even small breaks help them in their role as a carer. This could be something quick and straightforward as sitting down to listen to a piece of music, taking a coffee break, going out to meet a friend, and taking a small trip.

Changing relationship

It is incredibly challenging to come to terms with the changes that occur over time as the disease takes its toll. From the perspective of the carer, handling these changes is all-important. Although the person with dementia will struggle with activities that were once second nature to them, the carer should keep in mind that there is much they can do to help support the person to identify and focus on activities that they can still do, with a shift away from emphasizing things that are no longer possible.[3]

Impact on the carer

Psychological well-being

By no means is the effect of caring for someone with dementia entirely negative. In fact, many report positive feelings around bringing the family together, of friendship, personal growth and resilience, and feeling good about being able to help someone they care about (2, 3).

For others, the need to care for someone they are close to is exceptionally stressful, impacting as it does all aspects of their lives. This is referred to as "carer burden," although many feel this term is overly negative (4).

Aside from depression, the emotional toil experienced manifests in other ways, with carers reporting feeling guilty, angry, and lacking control over the situation (5). Such reactions may essentially be due to the strain of trying to meet the ever-increasing needs of the person with dementia. However, other factors contribute to carer distress. The carer will likely mourn the loss of their long-term partner and friend and their own freedom, which they have relinquished mainly to better support their spouse. Uncertainty about what each day will bring also adds to the heady mix of stressors and their own feelings of anger (6). Carers may also feel that they are not doing as good a job as they should.

As might be expected, demands become more substantial as the severity of the symptoms increase (7). The presence of what are described as "challenging behaviours"—wandering, aggression, hallucinations, and delusions—also con-tributes significantly to carer stress due to the increased support and monitoring required (8). Carers who live with a person with dementia are clearly at the most significant risk. The majority reported disturbed sleep as a result of their role (9). Carers who are also spouses tend to be older and have their own pre-existing health issues to contend with, many of which are likely to be exacerbated by the stress and strain under which they are placed (10). For carers who are younger, such as the children of the person with dementia, the stressors they have to face are different and include having to hold down a job and maintain a family while providing care (5).

Bereavement reactions

The loss of someone near and dear is a tragedy we all have to face at some stage. How we respond is entirely unique based on a host of psychological and social factors. In the case of dementia, awareness of the loss of a loved one, and the ensuing emotional response, varies in terms of the degree of pathology within the brain. In many cases, the initial reaction to hearing of a loss disappears as the person with dementia no longer recalls the news being broken. The result is that news of a loved one's demise has to be presented time and time again, with the inevitable resurgence of distress.

There is a major ethical and moral debate here about informing someone with dementia of such loss and, more to the point, repeatedly informing them (11). It leads to initial distress and then eventual amnesia. This is also a huge emotional drain on the person relaying the news, especially if it has to be done repeatedly. The impact on the carer is exponentially greater if the person who has died is also a close relative or friend to them. It might be the case that the person with demen-tia has lost their husband, and the person having to relay and reinforce the news has lost a parent or grandparent at the same time. Not only does the person with dementia have to come to terms with the loss, but it is often the case the carer has similar work ahead of them dealing with their own grief. One argument is not to say anything. The question here is, who benefits from this approach? Is it not an individual's right to know if a member of their family or a close friend has passed away? It might be argued that not knowing will lead to even more distress. Honesty between the carer and the cared for is the bedrock of a functional relationship, as it is in any relationship. As with many issues associated with dementia, there can never really be a clear-cut right or wrong answer.

Depression among carers

It has already been shown that there are high levels of depression among those diagnosed with dementia (12). This is clearly a concern when considering how best to manage the person's care. What is worrying is the high rate of depression in those who care for people with dementia, specifically the relatives and spouses providing informal care. Some studies have indicated that around one-fifth of carers show marked symptoms (13). The causes of depression here reflect the incredible demands made upon people who were not trained or even prepared to take on such a challenge. These demands are both physical and mental in nature (14).

The consequences of caring for a loved one with dementia are real, encompassing all aspects of the carer's life, be it psychological, physical, or social (16). In reflection of the true extent of disruption caused by the role, carers have been referred to as "hidden patients" (17).

Physical health

Not only is the mental health of carers adversely affected, but so is their physical health (18). Around a third report feeling tired and lacking in energy (9). Carers experience a compromised immunological response, heightened levels of cortisol (the stress hormone), high blood pressure, and a higher risk of cardiovascular disease (19–22). As with any situation, individual differences in the carer influence how such stress impacts their physical health. Factors include their age, medical history, personality, coping styles, and the level of support received (9).

Isolation

Social isolation is of great concern. This occurs mainly because of the sheer level of demand levied at the carer and the dedication required by the role (23).

One of the chief outcomes of a diagnosis of dementia is increasing social isolation, not only for the person with the condition but also for their carer (8, 22). Carers find it challenging to carve out time with their family, dedicate to hobbies, and take holidays. Maintaining a regular work pattern is also a major issue

(24, 25). Such activity harms a person's well-being (26). With time, the carer's support network diminishes (27). The decline in social support is more considerable for someone caring for a person with dementia when compared to others who look after people with a physical disability (27). In some cases, stigma is the cause of the carer becoming increasingly isolated. Some have felt that others were actively avoiding contact with them and that, in some cases, they were mocked by others (10).

Financial effect

The apparent cost to the carer is the time they offer to the person with dementia. Travel costs are also incurred. On top of this, carers often experience a loss of earnings. In some cases, they need to reduce their hours or opt for early retirement to better fulfil their role as full-time carers (9).

Support

There are various forms of support offered to carers. However, as one might expect, this differs markedly from where a person lives. The aim, in each case, is to help reduce the load and improve the well-being of the carer. A major component of such carer support is education. Carers need to know more about the condition they are facing: its symptoms, its likely progression. Improving the coping strategies of carers is another vital component.

Approaches such as CBT help identify and modify any maladaptive beliefs the carer may have concerning their role. Typical here are feelings of blame or anger at the person with dementia for their behaviour. CBT can be used to help shift the focus away from the person with dementia to a situation where the carer more accurately associates blame with the disease (28).

Social support groups are increasingly seen as being essential for carer well-being. These can be led by professionals, charities, or groups of carers themselves. This enables individuals to share their experiences and concerns with other like-minded individuals faced with a similar situation (29). This form of support improves satisfaction among carers and improves their well-being (29, 30). In all, it acts to empower the carer (31). Evidence that depression and other adverse effects of caring are reduced is less evident from the studies conducted to date (32, 33).

Local authorities can help by providing a range of home adaptations and services. The provision of respite care is an integral part of the overall care package. This is where the informal carer is provided with a break, with substitute care offered for a finite period. This can be in the person's own home, day care centres, or residential care facilities. This affords the much-needed time to re-engage with areas of their life that have previously been on hold (34). Unfortunately, this can come at a cost as the quality of replacement care offered varies substantially (35).

Support mechanisms

Even though caregiver stress is high, utilization of support services is poor on the whole (36). There are several potential explanations for the lack of take-up here, although not being aware support is needed on top of poor understanding of what resources are available probably accounts for much of this.

A range of programs exist to help meet the needs of caregivers. The most effective are ones where the level of support is high and matches the individual requirements of the people involved (37). Also, interventions that identify and muster existing support mechanisms within the family offer the most significant reduction in caregiver stress (38).

Involving the entire family in the process is vital in combatting stress. Eliciting help and delegating responsibility are important weapons in a caregiver's arsenal. Not only does it help improve the caregiver's well-being, but it also helps keep the person with dementia in their own home before full-time nursing home care is required (39).

Educating all involved in the care package about dementia is central to improving understanding and acceptance of the condition. In addition to learning about the specific diagnosis, family members also receive training on dealing effectively with specific issues associated with the disease (40).

Legal and financial matters

It is increasingly common for carers to change their working arrangements to facilitate more flexibility. It is something that businesses are obliged to support. Carer's credit and other benefits can help if it is no longer feasible to work. When looking to the future, it is always worth considering obtaining lasting power of attorney to take control of the finances when the person being cared for loses sufficient mental capacity to make the types of decisions that are necessary themselves. This can be a source of much reassurance for people who have a diagnosis of dementia. It enables them to feel confident that their best interests will be protected.

Many now take advantage of the option to propose a plan for how they wish to be cared for at some future point. This is known as advance care planning. Although this can be a tricky thing to talk about, it does allow the person with dementia to feel confident that their choices will be adhered to. Advance statements enable people to state what their preferred option for care is, as well as whether they wish to deny specific interventions. A person must update their will while they retain the capacity to do so.

Professional caregivers

So far in this chapter, we have been looking at the role of informal carers and the demands and challenges they face. In this section, the focus will be on professional caregivers.

Knowledge and training are essential at all levels, especially in the care of older adults, particularly when caring for older adults diagnosed with dementia. We all hold assumptions and stereotypes about older adults regardless of our age. False stereotypes about older adults are not the sole prerogative of the younger generation; many older adults themselves hold inaccurate beliefs about what it is to be a person of their age. As with all stereotypes, the way we behave towards individuals, and our expectations about how they should act, are informed by how we typecast these individuals.

Many studies have explored stereotypes associated with ageing. Of importance to this chapter is the finding that even those professionally trained in the care of older adults are not immune to false beliefs and assumptions about those they are prepared to care for (41, 42).

Crisis in care

In the past, those with dementia tended to be cared for by their own children. The situation is now different, with more and more siblings having moved away from their home town. On top of that, due to the nature of the ageing population, the children of parents with dementia are now older adults themselves, making it unlikely they will be able to provide the intensity of care required.

A report in 2013 by the Care Quality Commission indicated that a quarter of all home care services fail to meet quality and safety standards.[4] Some of the reasons for this failure included a lack of continuity of care, with carers frequently changing from one visit to the next, incomplete or inaccurate needs assessments, and rushed appointments.

Future availability

There is a genuine concern that, at some point in the future, when the numbers of people living with dementia rise further, the availability of informal carers will not be able to meet demand. There are various explanations for this, although the main ones concern the likelihood that the carer/spouse will also be of advanced years and so have health concerns of their own and a reluctance to provide the care in the first place.[5]

Summary

The role of the carer is multifaceted. From the very beginning, family dynamics change even before a formal diagnosis is made. This is something we have explored in previous chapters. One of the main changes is the increasing demands on the primary caregiving figure. This is often the spouse. Although, in many cases, a natural transition of roles occurs as behaviour changes and needs are met. To begin with, such alterations in the flow of daily interactions are subtle, almost imperceptible to others, but all too quickly, this changes. Taking on the role of carer is not something couples envisage. The person with dementia does not wish to burden their spouse; the spouse did not expect to be placed in such a position. Increased dependency is not something we relish. As with all other forms of care, supporting a person's independence while ensuring their dignity is essential. The role of the carer is both physically and mentally tiring, so it is crucial that appropriate help mechanisms are to hand. Because of increased life expectancy, the carers themselves are of advanced years and often must contend with multiple morbidities. However, we did not only talk about informal care in this chapter. Professional carers are an essential part of the overall package. There is, nonetheless, a growing concern that demand will outstrip availability very shortly if something is not done to rectify the situation. It has been suggested that "Britain is 'woefully' under-prepared for rising numbers" of older adults.[6] We cannot let this continue.

Notes

1 www.theguardian.com/politics/2013/mar/14/britain-unprepared-elderly-people-lords?msclkid=57394d6cbbf011ec9facc837945a5d1f
2 www.alzheimers.org.uk/get-support/help-dementia-care/looking-after-yourself#content-start
3 www.alzheimers.org.uk/get-support/help-dementia-care/caring-for-person-dementia
4 www.bbc.co.uk/news/health-21441893#:~:text=Why%20the%20elderly%20care%20crisis%20is%20here%20to,the%20quality%20and%20safety%20standards%20makes%20depressing%20reading.
5 www.dementia.org.au/publications/access-economics-reports
6 www.theguardian.com/politics/2013/mar/14/britain-unprepared-elderly-people-lords

References

1 Triantafillou J, Naiditch M, Repkova K, Stiehr K, Carretero S, Emilsson T, et al. Informal care in the long-term care system European overview paper (bing.com). 2010.
2 Sanders S. Is the glass half empty or full? Reflections on strain and gain in cargivers of individuals with Alzheimer's disease. Soc Work Health Care. 2005;40(3):57–73.
3 Zarit SH. Positive aspects of caregiving: More than looking on the bright side. Aging Ment Health. 2012;16(6):673–674.
4 Pearlin LI, Mullan JT, Semple SJ, Skaff MM. Caregiving and the stress process: An overview of concepts and their measures. Gerontologist. 1990;30(5):583–594.
5 Cherry MG, Salmon P, Dickson J, Powell D, Sikdar S, Ablett J. Factors influencing the resilience of carers of individuals with dementia. Rev Clin Gerontol. 2013;23(4):251–266.
6 Chan D, Livingston G, Jones L, Sampson EL. Grief reactions in dementia carers: A systematic review. Int J Geriatr Psychiatry. 2013;28(1):1–17.
7 Haro JM, Kahle-Wrobleski K, Bruno G, Belger M, Dell'Agnello G, Dodel R, et al. Analysis of burden in caregivers of people with Alzheimer's disease using self-report and supervision hours. J Nutr Health Aging. 2014;18(7):677–684.
8 Donaldson C, Tarrier N, Burns A. The impact of the symptoms of dementia on caregivers. Br J Psychiatry. 1997;170:62–68.
9 Australian Institute of Health. Australia's health 2012: The thirteenth biennial health report of the Australian Institute of Health and Welfare. AIHW; 2012.

10 Schneider J, Murray J, Banerjee S, Mann A. EUROCARE: A cross-national study of co-resident spouse carers for people with Alzheimer's disease: I—Factors associated with carer burden. Int J Geriatr Psychiatry. 1999;14(8):651–661.

11 Hughes JC. Alzheimer's and other dementias. Oxford: Oxford University Press; 2011.

12 Lyketsos CG, Olin J. Depression in Alzheimer's disease: Overview and treatment. Biol Psychiatry. 2002;52(3):243–252.

13 Molyneux GJ, McCarthy GM, McEniff S, Cryan M, Conroy RM. Prevalence and predictors of carer burden and depression in carers of patients referred to an old age psychiatric service. Int Psychogeriatr. 2008;20:1193–1202.

14 Wills W, Soliman A. Understanding the needs of the family carers of people with dementia. Ment Health Rev. 2001;6:25–28.

15 Alfonso T, Krishnamoorthy ES, Gomez K. Caregiving for dementia: Global perspectives and transcultural issues. In: Krishnamoorthy ES, Prince M, Cummings JL, editors. Dementia: A global approach. Cambridge: Cambridge University Press; 2010.

16 Vitaliano PP, Russo J, Young HM, Teri L, Maiuro RD. Predictors of burden in spouse caregivers of individuals with Alzheimer's disease. Psychol Aging. 1991;6(3):392.

17 Andolsek KM, Clapp-Channing NE, Gehlbach SH, Moore I, Proffitt VS, Sigmon A, et al. Caregivers and elderly relatives: The prevalence of caregiving in a family practice. Arch Intern Med. 1988;148(10):2177–2180.

18 Economics A. Making choices, future dementia care: Projections, problems and preferences. Australia: Access Economics, Report for Alzheimer's Australia; 2009.

19 Fargo KN, Aisen P, Albert M, Au R, Corrada MM, DeKosky S, et al. 2014 report on the milestones for the US national plan to address Alzheimer's disease. Alzheimers Dement. 2014;10(5 Suppl):S430–S452.

20 Burns A, Rabins P. Carer burden in dementia. Int J Geriatr Psychiatry. 2000;15(S1): S9–S13.

21 Brodaty H, Green A. Who cares for the carer? The often forgotten patient. Australian Family Physician. 2002;31(9).

22 Schulz R, Martire LM. Family caregiving of persons with dementia: Prevalence, health effects, and support strategies. Am J Geriatr Psychiatry. 2004;12(3):240–249.

23 Brodaty H, Luscombe G. Psychological morbidity in caregivers is associated with depression in patients with dementia. Alzheimer Dis Assoc Disord. 1998;12(2):62–70.

24 Ory MG, Hoffman RR, Yee JL, Tennstedt S, Schulz R. Prevalence and impact of caregiving: A detailed comparison between dementia and nondementia caregivers. Gerontologist. 1999;39(2):177–185.

25 Prince M, Jackson J. World Alzheimer report 2009. London: Alzheimer's Disease International; 2009.

26 Adams KB, Leibbrandt S, Moon H. A critical review of the literature on social and leisure activity and wellbeing in later life. Ageing Soc. 2011;31(4):683–712.

27 Schofield H, Herrman H, Murphy B, Bloch S. Family caregivers: Disability, illness and ageing. St. Leonards: Allen & Unwin; 1998.

28 Vernooij-Dassen M, Draskovic I, McCleery J, Downs M. Cognitive reframing for carers of people with dementia. Cochrane Database Syst Rev. 2011;(11):CD005318.

29 Hornillos C, Crespo M. Support groups for caregivers of Alzheimer patients: A historical review. Dementia. 2012;11(2):155–169.

30 Pinquart M, Sörensen S. Helping caregivers of persons with dementia: Which interventions work and how large are their effects? Int Psychogeriatr. 2006;18(4):577–595.

31 O'Connor DL. Toward empowerment: ReVisioning family support groups. Soc Work Groups. 2003;25(4):37–56.

32 Lauritzen J, Pedersen PU, Sørensen EE, Bjerrum MB. The meaningfulness of participating in support groups for informal caregivers of older adults with dementia: A systematic review. JBI Database System Rev Implement Rep. 2015;13(6):373–433.

33 Parker D, Mills S, Abbey J. Effectiveness of interventions that assist caregivers to support people with dementia living in the community: A systematic review. Int J Evid Based Healthc. 2008;6(2):137–172.

34 Neville C, Beattie E, Fielding E, MacAndrew M. Literature review: Use of respite by carers of people with dementia. Health Soc Care Community. 2015;23(1):51–53.

35 Singh P, Hussain R, Khan A, Irwin L, Foskey R. Dementia care: Intersecting informal family care and formal care systems. J Aging Res. 2014;2014:486521.

36 Brodaty H, Thomson C, Thompson C, Fine M. Why caregivers of people with dementia and memory loss don't use services. Int J Geriatr Psychiatry. 2005;20(6):537–546.

37 Brodaty H, Green A, Koschera A. Meta-analysis of psychosocial interventions for caregivers of people with dementia. J Am Geriatr Soc. 2003;51(5):657–664.

38 Whitlatch CJ, Zarit SH, von Eye A. Efficacy of interventions with caregivers: A reanalysis. Gerontologist. 1991;31(1):9–14.

39 Mittelman MS, Haley WE, Clay OJ, Roth DL. Improving caregiver well-being delays nursing home placement of patients with Alzheimer disease. Neurology. 2006;67(9):1592–1599.

40 Brodaty H, Gresham M. Effect of a training programme to reduce stress in carers of patients with dementia. BMJ. 1989;299(6712):1375–1379.

41 Rust TB, See SK. Knowledge about aging and Alzheimer disease: A comparison of professional caregivers and noncaregivers. Educ Gerontol. 2007;33(4):349–364.

42 Williams BC, Fitzgerald JT. Brief report: Brief instrument to assess geriatrics knowledge of surgical and medical subspecialty house officers. J Gen Intern Med. 2006;21(5):490–493.

Chapter 10

Cross-cultural issues

Caveat

Let me start with a caveat. The issues discussed in this chapter are essential if we are to offer genuine person-centred care. This is because person-centred care only occurs when it acknowledges the actual individual and all that makes them who they are. A person's beliefs and expectations derive from the culture in which they were raised and still live. Although I aim to highlight some critical issues, I am acutely aware that I am a White, male, middle-aged, middle-class academic. So, it is not without mental trepidation that I write this chapter. I fear that by aiming to raise awareness of cultural issues, I inadvertently distort them. I have consulted with colleagues on this chapter, so I hope it holds true to my intent. Where there are inaccuracies or misrepresentations, I can only apologize in advance.

There is much wrong with using collective terms such as BAME and BME. Although initially adopted to address issues with race inequality, such terms are now part of the problem. This is because they are reductionist and act only to homogenize large swathes of the population. Instead, I refer either to a specific population or to diverse communities more generally. I do this to be inclusive rather than divisive and acknowledge diversity in the UK among White non-British populations.

In writing this chapter, I have drawn heavily on the excellent book by Krishnamoorthy, Prince and Cummings (1), *Dementia: A Global Approach*. This book provides a much-needed account of how dementia affects healthcare in non-Western societies. It brings together experts from several disciplines to offer a cross-cultural perspective on issues in both dementia research and treatment.

An invaluable resource relating to different communities and dementia is the handbook produced by Truswell and Tavera (2). It was written in response to The All-Party Parliamentary Group on Dementia in 2014. This report highlighted the prediction of a higher proportional increase in dementia throughout diverse communities compared to the UK white population. Such documents also brought to light the general lack of research exploring how different communities are affected by dementia, particularly in terms of initial diagnosis and post-diagnostic support.

DOI:10.4324/9781315681580-10

The document by Truswell and Tavera (2) offers healthcare staff a comprehensive resource to help meet the needs of the wider community in this area of healthcare.

Representative research?

Cross-cultural research is an essential aspect of any discipline. Looking back through the archives of psychological research, whole cultures are under-represented in critical areas. A good example is the under-representation of research on dementia until relatively recently in African American populations (3, 4) and various ethnic communities in the UK (5). In some of these studies, there appears to be a higher incidence of Alzheimer's disease in this population (6). However, this is not the case for all studies (7). Such differences generally disappear when educational attainment is factored into the equation (8). The role that education plays in dementia will be discussed shortly.

Levels of education

As seen in Chapter 2, a low level of educational attainment is a risk factor for dementia. This works on several levels, such that education generally pushes people towards healthier behaviours and reduces risk-taking. It is also linked to higher levels of cognitive functioning, among other things. In addition, performance on neuropsychological tests can be influenced by education (8). As one might expect, it is not a simple matter of educational attainment to predict dementia. Instead, lower levels of education are associated with a range of social and environmental variables that pose risk factors for the condition, such as social isolation and exposure to toxins (9).

General health

Diabetes and hypertension are important risk factors for dementia (see Chapter 2). When looking at different cultures, such as African Americans and Black Caribbean, there are higher levels of these conditions (10, 11). It might be argued that higher rates of diabetes and hypertension lead to an increase in the incidence of Alzheimer's disease in such groups. However, this is by no means uncontested (12).

Changing beliefs

An ageing population is a significant issue across the globe. In many Asian countries, this demographic change is due primarily to improved healthcare and low fertility rates (13). Attitudes and expectations about older adults vary hugely across different cultures. Such beliefs are also affected by time. Previous and current populations of older adults mostly hold views based on tradition. This may no longer be the case for the baby boomers who reach older adulthood. Many reasons are proposed for such shifts in perspective, including improvements in education and relative economic prosperity.

In many cultures, such as the Chinese, there are aspirations to lead a long, healthy, and comfortable life. Alongside this is an expectation that children are the enablers, providing both care and support at all levels. However, with the demands of modern urban life, it is becoming more and more of a challenge to uphold these traditions. A significant change here has been a rise in the number of the young moving to areas of industrialization, thereby shattering the once traditional extended family unit so vital to the care of older members.

Satisfaction with life

People rate their overall satisfaction with life by examining their current situation with their goals and ambitions. Satisfaction with life is entirely individualistic. No two people will hold the same views. Although we all talk about quality of life as if it is a knowable entity, it is to some extent easier to conceive than it is to measure. Good quality of life for one person might be abject misery for another. Even though there clearly are issues with trying to assess something that is, to a large extent, intangible, there are many measures available, as we have seen in Chapter 4. Later in this chapter, we shall see how culturally sensitive indices can be used to try to overcome some of these difficulties.

One thing that does appear pertinent here is a link with spirituality. There is certainly evidence to show that older adults who regularly visit places of worship experience lower levels of anxiety and depression (13). A sense of being part of a spiritual community is important here. The beliefs associated with certain faiths promote a healthier lifestyle, among other things. Also, a person's faith may act to mediate stressors experienced in life, thereby reducing potential harmful effects.

Psychological changes

How different cultures deal with psychological disturbances is vital for appreciating what might be deemed appropriate when dealing with such cases. In some instances, a healer may be solicited instead of a clinician. Many traditional cultures maintain intimate links between healthcare and spirituality. Many older adults consult with priests and traditional healers in such societies, often before approaching the healthcare service (14). There is no mention of labels generally associated with the modern psychiatric tradition in these encounters. Symptoms that would usually be associated with depression would be treated because a person was experiencing "weakness of mental energy" (15). As such, there is no hint of the stigma generally associated with these mood states.

Assessment and diagnosis

We have seen in previous chapters that there are various problems with assessment tools that feed into a formal diagnosis of different forms of dementia. To some extent, this is inevitable, given the complex and highly individual nature of these conditions. These problems are compounded when seeing dementia through the eyes of different cultures. Many screening tools are of dubious worth for those with low literacy levels (13). Having said that, short measures that are less reliant on educational attainment have been developed and adopted to address these issues, an example being the Elderly Cognitive Assessment Questionnaire (ECAQ) (16), used increasingly in Singapore and other countries.

As with all forms of assessment, the clinician must have a clear sense of what they want to measure. In terms of dementia, it is likely to be the case that a screening tool is used first. Dependent on this outcome, the clinician will decide who warrants investigation using a more comprehensive battery of neuropsychological measures.

Quality of life

Assessing quality of life is often fraught with problems, as previously mentioned. To begin with, what is meant by quality of life? How does one person's assessment of their life compare to another's? What is clear is that quality of life is multidimensional in nature. It is influenced by various factors, encompassing physical, psychological, and social elements (17). When assessing quality of life, among all other things, it is essential that a person's cultural values are taken into consideration (18). Therefore, it might not be sufficient merely to translate existing measures into the appropriate language (19). There is no point painstakingly translating something into another language when the concepts or underlying beliefs referred to have no meaning in that culture.

Translation of measures is a lengthy process. When translating occurs, alternate processes of forward and back translation are initiated. Forward translation is when the questionnaire is translated into the chosen language. At this point, it is essential to ensure that the actual point of each question is not lost. Once this has been achieved, back translation occurs. This time, the measure is converted back into the original language. It is assessed to ensure the original intention has been maintained. Upon successfully completing these stages, it is crucial to test that the psychometric properties have been preserved, such as their reliability and validity (18).

There are additional barriers to questionnaire-based measures. Even though an accurate translation has been effected, certain cultures may view such tools as intrusive and so do not comply by completing them. It might also be the case that illiteracy might be prevalent in a specific society.

There is a real risk that measures that are not culturally sensitive will overestimate levels of cognitive impairment among those who have received lower levels of formal education or who are less expert in English. There is also evidence that proficiency may be lost as a function of disease progression in cases where English has been learned as a second language (20).

Behavioural and psychological symptoms of dementia

When assessing the behavioural and psychological symptoms of dementia (BPSD), it is again vital to reflect on the culture in which a person is embedded (21). The list of symptoms described in most texts reflects Westernized accounts of dementia based on diagnostic manuals. Although it is vital to remember that no two people will experience dementia in the same way and, as such, the symptoms and behaviours that manifest may differ markedly, there are also cultural differences in terms of the symptoms people generally associate with dementia. For example, apathy is less commonly reported in China (22), whereas wandering is less often reported in Australia (23). However, just because it is less widely reported does not mean such symptoms are less widespread.

For instance, looking at apathy, one reason it is less frequently reported in China is that it is more difficult to detect in Asian populations (24). It might be the case then that there is an under-reporting of apathy here. Experiencing apathy impacts negatively on a person's overall well-being. Apathy significantly affects how well a person can perform everyday activities. Linked to this is clear evidence that executive impairment is more extensive in Alzheimer's disease patients who also experienced depression and apathy (25). Apathy makes it more difficult for people to care for themselves. It also makes them less likely to engage with any form of therapy (25).

Harmonization

To improve the relevance and accuracy of measures in different cultures, items are initially translated into the appropriate language. Native speakers must be included in this process to ensure authenticity. Individual items are then "harmonized" (26). By this, it is meant that questions are consonant with the culture and age group being tested. This is a crucial step as it is an excellent way to ensure none of the items is misleading or unintendedly offensive. For example, slang terms may be appropriate for a younger person but not for an older adult. This can be a lengthy process, with multiple redrafting required before a measure is ready to be piloted (26).

Adaptations

Some measures used in different cultures have been adapted to address culturally specific issues. The questions posed and activities required by the assessment need to be relevant and familiar to the particular culture to which the person belongs (26).

In addition to culturally specific issues, there are also issues related to individual differences. For example, it is possible that the person to whom a dementia screening test is being administered will experience problems with hearing and/ or sight. To offset such difficulties, measures such as the Community Screening Interview for Dementia deviate from the norms of neuropsychological testing.

The Community Screening Interview for Dementia (CSI-D) consists of both test items covering a range of cognitive functions and an interview with a close relative. Interviewing a relative allows the clinician to better gauge the degree of impairment in everyday life. The CSI-D can be administered within 30 minutes. This tool has been adapted for use with various cultures (27), with cross-cultural data showing it to be an effective tool (28).

Many dementia screening tools include items where the individual is required to name an object that is drawn on a sheet. Even though these are usually schematic representations, people with visual impairment will likely struggle with this. One way the CSI-D addresses this is to present actual objects to the patient (e.g., pencil) or touch the part of the body referred to (e.g., knuckle) (26).

Service provision

Earlier in the chapter, the accuracy of assessment tools for screening for dementia was discussed concerning culture-specific attitudes and beliefs. However, it is not just an issue of whether cognitive and behavioural assessments and screening tools are appropriate for other cultures but also whether evaluations in terms of care needs of the individual with dementia are accurate (29). If a person's needs are not accurately gauged, they will not be offered the much-needed level of support warranted by their condition. Inadequate support will likely result in a poorer prognosis for the individual concerned.

This chapter aims to look at how different cultures are affected by dementia. We have seen that underlying beliefs and expectations demand consideration. Indeed, it should be taken as read. This current section explores healthcare provision for dementia. Although it is impossible to fully address all the issues posed by dementia in different communities, I aim to highlight just some of the key challenges that need to be addressed. We shall look specifically at how dementia care is meted out in the UK among diverse communities.

Diverse communities in the UK

We shall now turn our attention to dementia care here in the UK for those in diverse ethnic communities. Of great concern is the fact that it is still the case that large sections of society are falling through the gaps in healthcare in relation to dementia. The number requiring services for dementia is on the rise, as those who moved to the UK since the 1950s are reaching older adulthood (30). Although the healthcare sector is aware of the needs of manifold communities (31), various strategies have failed to fully meet those requirements (32). Communities in most need are those of Black Caribbean and Asian Indian backgrounds (33). With time, the ethnic diversity of older adults with dementia needs in the UK will increase (34), further compounding this effect.

In terms of prevalence for the various forms of dementia, vascular dementia is more of a concern for Asian and Black Caribbean people (11) due to the higher levels of cardiovascular disease, hypertension, and diabetes, all of which are major risk factors for this form of dementia (35). Early-onset dementia is also more common in such communities. In fact, some estimates indicate it is three times as high (36).

As we have seen, and as is clear from the media, early detection and diagnosis are vital in treating and managing the condition. Many communities are at a disadvantage here, as seen by the findings that people of various minority ethnic origins present at clinic much later (37). This means that they do not receive a diagnosis in many cases until the disease is quite advanced. Because of that, they do not receive the care and support that would help them come to terms with their condition and so improve their overall quality of life.

In terms of what can be done, the awareness that high rates of risk factors would suggest the importance of targeted health promotion activities in diverse communities to signpost individuals to make more informed lifestyle choices that would help reduce the risk of vascular dementia (38).

We know that the beliefs and expectations individuals hold about dementia is directly influenced by the culture they grew up in. Rather than trying to ignore, or worse change these ways of thinking, clinical services should accept and embrace such differences, and in doing so, develop ways to work with these beliefs in formulating an appropriate care package (39), something that only be achieved through co-production. When looking at differences in attitudes to people with dementia, those who were White British focused on the importance of maintaining independence, whereas Black Caribbean respondents were concerned about being a burden on their family, and Asian respondents emphasized the pride felt as the result of receiving the support of their family (40).

It was highlighted that general awareness of dementia is relatively poor in many communities (39, 41). Another barrier is that there is no specific word for "dementia" in many South Asian languages (42). What this in effect means is that some of the symptoms indicative of dementia will be likely prescribed to the process of typical ageing (37, 43). In such cases, formal help may only be sought once the disease has progressed extensively (43), with the consequence in terms of fewer appropriate treatment and management options.

Social care

I shall focus here on informal care among diverse communities in the UK. Social care covers many things. It refers in part to services provided by local health authorities and charities to individuals in need living either in their own home or in care. Given the increasing demands on these services, a great deal of the responsibility for the day-to-day support of people with dementia is in the hands of informal carers. Informal carers are defined as family members, friends, and neighbours who provide regular support.

I have been talking throughout this chapter about diverse communities rather than using the entrenched BME or BAME descriptors. Such terms give the impression of a distinct group of individuals. That is clearly not the case. Take for instance South Asian communities. These consist of peoples from India, Pakistan, and Bangladesh. Within these communities, people may be Hindu, Muslim, Sikh, or Christian. They may speak Hindi, Urdu, Punjabi, or Gujarati (44). Within these communities there is a wide range of literacy. In other words, diversity in all sense of the word.

Prevalent within such communities is a belief in the extended family. It is the expectation that all support be provided within this framework. In many cases, this assumption explains why some carers from diverse ethnic backgrounds find it more challenging to ask for help from service providers. In the first instance, due to cultural beliefs and expectations, they may not actually view what they do as being a carer, instead considering their role as the natural part of familial duty (45). In some instances there is the belief that only family can provide the level of care the person with dementia requires (41). Alternatively, in some cases, seeking help from healthcare services might be seen as a failure and so open that family member up to criticism, both from within the family and from those outside the family (46). Given this, families that require outside support face feeling a sense of inadequacy as a result (44). This has significant implications in terms of willingness to seek support even when such help is known to be available.

There appears to be a higher degree of uncertainty among different communities about what services are available to help care for someone with dementia (47). However, various regions have developed initiatives that have met with success. These include using neutral language to describe dementia and the role of the carer, organizing events in community centres, and making use of outreach workers (39).

However, it is not just the case that more lines of communication need to be opened to ensure people know care services exist. The option to seek intervention has to be weighed against potential blame both within and outside the extended family unit.

Even when the need to find support outweighs the social implications, carers in certain communities have the added worry that the help provided will not be appropriate for their family's beliefs. If carers have any concern that support services will not understand their particular cultural norms and expectations, it is likely they will not seek assistance. Providing appropriate care and support for such disparate needs is a real challenge, but one that has to be tackled head-on nonetheless.

Rauf (44) highlights other potential barriers experienced by carers of diverse ethnic origin looking after a relative with dementia. Given the belief that the extended family cares for the person with dementia, the level of understanding of the difficulties faced by someone caring for a person with dementia was rather weak. Because of that, additional support is often not offered by other family members. The taboo of dementia meant that outside help was not solicited. On top of this, support services tend to often lack cultural competency, and so do not match the level and type of support with the beliefs and expectations of particular communities. It is also the case that clinical assessments often fail to take into consideration cultural norms and values. Being aware of family dynamics is an integral part of the assessment process when dealing with diverse communities.

Earlier in the chapter, we explored access issues to services in the UK. We looked at the need in many cases to ensure that assessment tools are in a format that does not harbour any hidden bias. On top of all this, merely accessing the necessary information can be an issue. This is particularly important when it comes to making use of translated material and interpreters. Interpreters, in particular, need to be cognizant of the family dynamics and also have sufficient knowledge about dementia to provide a competent and accurate account. Being mindful of body language is important here too. It is a matter, therefore, of not only portraying precise information, but relaying it in a culturally sensitive way.

Stigma

Stigma has always been an issue for mental health concerns. Even with public awareness initiatives, there is still a stigma surrounding dementia. When looking at different communities, levels of stigma are even more of a concern. This is particularly the case for Asian and Black Caribbean peoples (47, 48) among others. Some of this may be rooted in religious beliefs (49).

One of the effects of stigma is to reduce a person's likelihood to engage with appropriate support services. There is a fear that their diagnosis will become a matter of public knowledge (49). This is compounded further when one also considers seeking outside support is often seen as an admission of failure.

Stigma abounds in terms and phrases that are part of everyday parlance: words that are extracted straight from diagnostic manuals. Dementia is one such example. As a cold, clinical definition, dementia describes a loss of mental ability. However, for many cultures, for example in Japan, the word "dementia" has an altogether more disempowering meaning, one that describes "stupidity" (15). The result of this is an avoidance of any form of medical help.

Carer stress

Chapter 9 explored the role of the carer in some detail. Here we shall be highlighting some of the main differences in this role across cultures. The literature has indicated that, in Western societies, the combination of dementia and depression is highly predictive of carer stress (50). In a study looking at Chinese caregivers, the relationship was not as pronounced (51). What is clear, nonetheless, is that caring for someone becomes increasingly challenging and time consuming.

Carer stress is not just a Western phenomenon, but occurs in many other cultures (52). The role of carer is both physically and mentally challenging. On top of this, many of those in the role of informal carer find themselves forced to reduce the number of hours they work, and in many cases stopping work altogether to dedicate the time needed to the care of their parent. In most societies, the carer role tends to fall on women. However, this is changing due to higher levels of women seeking education and work in some more traditional societies. A problem that exists alongside this is a decrease in the size of the family unit, with the number of children in a family falling in many Asian societies. This means that the potential pool of future carers is decreasing with time while there is a rise in those who will require such care in the future.

The financial cost of all this is massive. For the increasing number who find themselves requiring care, many do not have the bonus of pensions; instead, they find themselves being entirely dependent both physically and financially on their children (13).

It is, again, important to bear in mind that some may not experience caring as stressful. Perception of caregiver stress is often entirely dependent on culture. Distress is perceived to be low in India and China, for example (53). In such cultures, provision of care is not seen as a choice, but instead as an obligation. Older members in these societies enjoy high status. Caregiving in these settings is natural; it is what is expected. This apparent lack of association between any hardship experienced and the person with dementia may, in fact, act to maintain the veracity of the relationship.

Before bringing this chapter to a close, I would like to introduce the concept of bilingualism and the role it plays in dementia. Being a cognitive psychologist, I hope you allow me this indulgence. It is incredibly relevant, as you shall see.

Bilingualism and dementia

We have looked in this chapter at a number of issues faced by peoples from other cultures in relation to dementia care, be it in terms of diagnosis or care provision. We have seen that both require a high degree of cultural sensitivity if it is to work for all concerned. We have looked in particular at how existing measures can be translated so that they are more appropriate to specific cultures. We have also seen that merely translating a measure verbatim into a different language might not always work due to cultural differences in how dementia is understood conceptually.

An area of growing interest is the impact of bilingualism on dementia. In other words, how does being fluent in two languages affect the impact of the disease? Does bilingualism, in fact, offer a level of protection, or more accurately a buffer, against the onslaught of the neurological damage. Other interesting questions exist around different experiences of those who live within a society where two languages are prominent compared to those who learn a second language as the result of migrating to another country. For example, comparing someone who is brought up in Wales, where English is taught alongside the native Welsh language, against someone from India who moved to England later in life, where their native language is Punjabi, with English being learned later on. Will both afford comparable benefits? We also know that, in many cases, people revert back to their native language as the disease progresses (54). For instance, the same person from India, who has spoken English for years, begins to converse only in Punjabi.

Cross-language interference

Problems with language is a major symptom of dementia, in terms of both production and comprehension (55). Fluency in non-native languages tends to decrease as we age (56). On occasion, older adults experience interference between native and second languages, an effect that appears to be accentuated in dementia (57), referred to as cross-language interference. The study by Mendez and colleagues (57) used a sample where English was the second language learned after adolescence. This study described an asymmetrical pattern of language impairment where a person's native language was preserved to the greatest extent (58). This is consistent with what we know about the types of memories best retained in dementia. We know that earlier memories are better preserved than more recent ones (59).

Cognitive reserve

Having just seen that dementia tends to affect a person's non-native language more than the one they were born into, this next section will look at some of the research that has attempted to explore the potential protective effect of a second language. The argument here rests on the concept of cognitive reserve. Cognitive reserve refers to the notion that those of us who keep our minds active will be able to show greater resilience to the effects of ageing and disease (60); in other words, more of a buffer to offset increasing levels of impairment. Because of that, a person would be better able to compensate for a decline in function. When looking at this, it is important to consider the concept of reserve capacity from both a biological perspective and a cognitive perspective, namely neurological brain reserve and behavioural brain reserve (61). Neurological brain reserve refers to cushioning effects of sheer brain volume against pathological change. This form of reserve capacity is believed to be primarily determined at birth. On the other hand, the majority of the literature in this area refers to behavioural brain reserve, or more commonly, cognitive reserve. As already stated, this form of reserve capacity is open to change through various forms of mental exercise.

Although there is a range of proffered activities that are believed to boost cognitive reserve, encompassing not just mental activities, but also physical and social, a controversial argument is that bilingualism offers comparable protection (62). An early paper by Bialystok provided evidence that there was a delay in developing dementia among bilinguals compared to those who do not have a second language (63).

Research since then has highlighted a hidden level of complexity here. It appears the effects are different when one compares Indigenous groups who are bilingual with immigrant groups who learn the language later on (64). When making such comparisons, a number of potential confounding factors come into play, such that the effect may not be due to the presence of another language, but somewhat influenced by lifestyle, diet, levels of education, among other things (62).

In a commentary paper, Fuller-Thomson (65) identifies the main issue with such studies, namely that randomized controlled trials are just not possible. The best available methodology to look at the impact of bilingualism on dementia prognosis is to carry out a prospective cohort study comparing bilingual and monolingual individuals who are not diagnosed with dementia at the start of the study, and then follow them over time to then compare those that do then develop dementia against those that are diagnosis-free. There are only a small number of studies which have followed this methodology, and the evidence is lacking for a significant effect of bilingualism on dementia (66–69). In fact, some of these studies produced findings in the opposite direction (67, 68).

It has been suggested that there is perhaps a Western bias in how we receive this body of evidence. Why should bilingualism be any less important than other form of mental activity that enhances cognitive reserve? Bak and Alladi (62) offer the argument that bilingualism is seen as the exception. Indeed, that would appear to be the case in many Western countries that are English-speaking. In such countries, monolingualism is very much the norm. However, when looking at other countries across the world, this is clearly not the case. Rather than monolingualism being the default state for our brain, evidence would suggest that bilingualism might be the rule (70). The apparent effortlessness with which children acquire different languages might be evidence of this (71).

There is evidence to show that bilingualism has a positive effect on attentional control (72), although the design of many of these experiments does weaken the findings somewhat (65). Being bilingual means that there is a need to control which language is currently being used while at the same time inhibiting any form of interference from the second language (73). Positive effects of this form of control continue into adulthood and older adulthood (74). What is important here is that bilingualism refers to individuals who are fluent in two languages and have spoken both throughout their life. It does not apply to those who can speak two languages, but are fluent in one and less so in the other (63).

There is another reason why the literature on bilingualism is so intriguing. The principal, rather demoralizing, message from many studies that have looked at the impact of brain training on functioning is that, yes, performance might improve as a result, but only on activities that are the same as those on which the person was trained. In other words, there does not seem to be any carry-over effects into other areas of functioning. No generalizability (75). With bilingualism, the argument is quite different. In this case, widespread effects may be possible as the result of a very specific ability, although the jury is still out as to the veracity of the evidence.

What does all this mean?

With each generation, older adults will be increasingly better educated. As such, their skillset will become more highly valued, such that their contribution will likely extend well into retirement. Given the lack of a pension, working through retirement is increasingly probable (13). Those in need of support will not be able to rely on family members to help out as has been the norm in the past. This will be a major challenge for governments across the world.

True equality

The focus of this chapter has been on culture and the fundamental need to provide care and support that is sensitive to the requirements of the individual and delivered in the dialect spoken by them. This can only be achieved by involving Voluntary Community and Social Enterprises (VCSEs) from the very start, beginning with the development of a model of care through to its delivery. At the heart of this are the communities themselves. For this to work, everything must be co-produced.

Summary

The culture into which we are born, the society in which we live, the languages we use, all play a fundamental role in shaping who we are and are a fixed focal point throughout our lives. There is now increasing awareness of the importance of all these factors as we age, and in particular, for those with dementia. Different cultures are associated with different risk factors for various diseases, be it the result of diet and other lifestyle choices, or as the result of inequalities in regard to accessing healthcare or education services. Earlier chapters emphasized the importance of accurate assessment making it possible to detect dementia early on so that appropriate interventions can be started sooner rather than later. We examined various factors that disrupt or make this process more difficult. Such difficulties are even more apparent when one considers people from different cultures. We have seen in this chapter that different cultures have a completely different take on dementia to that adopted by Western societies. We explored too some of the restrictions that occur in various societies with regard to diagnosis and care. When considering the UK and other Western societies, we are increasingly aware that dementia services are just not set up to provide the necessary support and care needed for those who are experiencing cognitive decline; at least, not at the moment. Assessment tools are not on the whole culturally sensitive, and so accurate diagnosis is hampered. Access to support networks may be affected due to cultural values associated with care and who is responsible. On top of all this, there is still the issue of stigma surrounding dementia. The chapter ended on a more positive note, highlighting the importance of research into bilingualism, in particular how those who are fluent in more than one language may be better guarded against the onslaught of dementia, at least to begin with. As with all research where the premise is to demonstrate some form of cognitive protection, there are limitations with current methodologies that need to be addressed before we can make more concrete claims in this area. However, the potential benefits of bilingualism do look promising. I would like to end this chapter by reflecting on the fascinating paper by McKean (56). In it he describes the loss of the second language in bilingual individuals and how this impacts further a person's ability to communicate and to make sense of the world, being as language shapes the way we view ourself and others. McKean identifies the need to tune into silence, as only by doing so will it be possible to appreciate the needs of someone who has become a "linguistic exile." I shall end as the McKean paper began, with a quotation by Audre Lorde (76):

> It is not difference which immobilizes us, but silence. And there are so many silences to be broken.

References

1   Krishnamoorthy ES, Prince M, Cummings JL. Dementia: A global approach. Cambridge: Cambridge University Press; 2010.

2   Truswell D, Tavera Y. An electronic resource handbook for CNWL memory services: Dementia information for Black, Asian and Minority ethnic communities. Chart. 2016;1:13.

3   Hendrie H. Alzheimer's disease: The African American story. In: Krishnamoorthy ES, Prince M, Cummings JL, editors. Dementia: A global approach. Cambridge: Cambridge University Press; 2010. p. 27–31.

4   Allery AJ, Aranda MP, Dilworth-Anderson P, Guerrero M, Haan M, Hendrie H, et al. Alzheimer's disease and communities of color. In: Closing the gap: Improving the health of minority elders in the new millennium. 2004:81–86.

5   Bhattacharyya S, Benbow SM, Kar N. Unmet service needs of ethnic elders with dementia in United Kingdom. Policy. 2012;5(2):202–203.

6   Evans DA, Bennett DA, Wilson RS, Bienias JL, Morris MC, Scherr PA, et al. Incidence of Alzheimer disease in a biracial urban community: Relation to apolipoprotein E allele status. Arch Neurol. 2003;60(2):185–189.

7   Fillenbaum GG, Heyman A, Huber MS, Woodbury MA, Leiss J, Schmader KE, et al. The prevalence and 3-year incidence of dementia in older black and white community residents. J Clin Epidemiol. 1998;51(7):587–595.

8   Fitzpatrick AL, Kuller LH, Ives DG, Lopez OL, Jagust W, Breitner J, et al. Incidence and prevalence of dementia in the Cardiovascular Health Study. J Am Geriatr Soc. 2004;52(2):195–204.

9   Hall KS, Gao S, Unverzagt FW, Hendrie HC. Low education and childhood rural residence Risk for Alzheimer's disease in African Americans. Neurology. 2000;54(1):95.

10 Hendrie HC, Murrell J, Gao S, Unverzagt FW, Ogunniyi A, Hall KS. International studies in dementia with particular emphasis on populations of African origin. Alzheimer Dis Assoc Disord. 2006;20(3 Suppl 2):S42.

11 Richards M, Brayne C, Dening T, Abas M, Carter J, Price M, et al. Cognitive function in UK community-dwelling African Caribbean and white elders: A pilot study. Int J Geriatr Psychiatry. 2000;15(7):621–630.

12 Tang M-X, Cross P, Andrews H, Jacobs D, Small S, Bell K, et al. Incidence of AD in African-Americans, Caribbean Hispanics, and Caucasians in northern Manhattan. Neurology. 2001;56(1):49–56.

13 Ee Heok K. The aging brain and mind: Cultural and anthroplogical perspectives. In: Krishnamoorthy ES, Prince M, Cummings JL, editors. Dementia: A global approach. Cambridge: Cambridge University Press; 2010, pp. 1–7.

14 Kua E, Tan C. Traditional Chinese medicine in psychiatric practice in Singapore. Int Psychiatry. 2005;8:7–9.

15 Kua EH. The depressed elderly Chinese living in the community: A five-year follow up study. Int J Geriatr Psychiatry. 1993;8(5):427–430.

16 Kua E, Ko S. A questionnaire to screen for cognitive impairment among elderly people in developing countries. Acta Psychiatr Scand. 1992;85(2):119–122.

17 Bowling A. Measuring disease: A review of disease specific quality of life measurement scales. Buckingham: Open University Press; 1995.

18 Selai C, Pillas D, Dodds A. Quality of life in dementia: Global perspective and transcultural issues. In: Krishnamoorthy ES, Prince M, Cummings JL, editors. Dementia: A global approach. Cambridge: Cambridge University Press; 2010.

19 Johnson TM. Cultural considerations. In: Spilker B, editor. Quality of life and pharmacoeconomics in clinical trials. 2nd ed. New York: Lippincott-Raven; 1996.

20 Jenkins C. Bridging the divide of culture and language. J Dementia Care. 1998;6(6):22–24.

21 Senanarong V, Cummings JL. Assessing behavior in dementia across cultures. In: Krishnamoorthy ES, Prince M, Cummings JL, editors. Dementia: A global approach. Cambridge: Cambridge University Press; 2010, pp. 73–86.

22 Chow T, Liu C, Fuh J, Leung V, Tai C, Chen LW, et al. Neuropsychiatric symptoms of Alzheimer's disease differ in Chinese and American patients. Int J Geriatr Psychiatry. 2002;17(1):22–28.

23 Chiu M-J, Chen T-F, Yip P-K, Hua M-S, Tang L-Y. Behavioral and psychologic symptoms in different types of dementia. J Formos Med Assoc. 2006;105(7):556–562.

24 Fuh J-L, Lam L, Hirono N, Senanarong V, Cummings JL. Neuropsychiatric inventory workshop: Behavioral and psychologic symptoms of dementia in Asia. Alzheimer Dis Assoc Disord. 2006;20(4):314–317.

25 Nakaaki S, Murata Y, Sato J, Shinagawa Y, Hongo J, Tatsumi H, et al. Association between apathy/depression and executive function in patients with Alzheimer's disease. Int Psychogeriatr. 2008;20(5):964–975.

26 Hall KS. The experience of assessing cognition across cultures. Krishnamoorthy ES, Prince M, Cummings JL, editors. Cambridge: Cambridge University Press; 2010.

27 Hall KS, Ogunniyi AO, Hendrie HC. A cross-cultural community based study of dementias: Methods and performance of the survey instrument. Int J Methods Psychiatr Res. 1996;6:129–142.

28 Hall KS, Gao S, Emsley CL, Ogunniyi AO, Morgan O, Hendrie HC. Community screening interview for dementia (CSI 'D'); performance in five disparate study sites. Int J Geriatr Psychiatry. 2000;15(6):521–531.

29 Rait G, Morley M, Burns A, Baldwin R, Chew-Graham C, St Leger A. Screening for cognitive impairment in older African-Caribbeans. Psychol Med. 2000;30(4):957–963.

30 Health Do. Living well with dementia: A national dementia strategy. Department of Health; 2009. Available from: https://www.gov.uk/government/publications/living-well-with-dementia-a-national-dementia-strategy-good-practice-compendium.

31 Means R, Beattie A, Daker-White G, Gilliard J. Meeting the needs of marginalised groups in dementia care. J Dementia Care. 2003;11(2):37–38.

32 Manthorpe J, Harris J, Lakey S. Strategic approaches for older people from black and minority ethnic groups. London: Better Government for Older People; 2008.

33 White A. Social focus in brief: Ethnicity 2002. London: Office for National Statistics; 2002.

34 Wohland P, Rees P, Norman P, Boden P, Jasinska M. Ethnic population projections for the UK and local areas, 2001–2051. Leeds: University of Leeds; 2010. Available from: http://www geog leeds ac uk/fileadmin/downloads/school/research/projects/migrants/WP_ETH_POP_ PROJECTIONS pdf [accessed 10 April 2011].

35 Oveisgharan S, Hachinski V. Hypertension, executive dysfunction, and progression to dementia: The Canadian study of health and aging. Arch Neurol. 2010;67(2):187–192.

36 Knapp M, Prince M, Albanese E, Banerjee S, Dhanasiri S, Fernandez J, et al. Dementia UK: A report to the Alzheimer's Society on the prevalence and economic cost of dementia in the UK produced by King's College London and London School of Economics. London: Alzheimer's Society; 2007.

37 Mukadam N, Cooper C, Livingston G. A systematic review of ethnicity and pathways to care in dementia. Int J Geriatr Psychiatry. 2011;26(1):12–20.

38 Beattie A, Daker-White G, Gilliard J, Means R. 'They don't quite fit the way we organise our services'—Results from a UK field study of marginalised groups and dementia care. Disabil Soc. 2005;20(1):67–80.

39 Moriarty J, Sharif N, Robinson J. Black and minority ethnic people with dementia and their access to support and services. London: Social Care Institute for Excellence; 2011.

40 Lawrence V, Samsi K, Banerjee S, Morgan C, Murray J. Threat to valued elements of life: The experience of dementia across three ethnic groups. Gerontologist. 2010;51(1):39–50.

41 La Fontaine J, Ahuja J, Bradbury NM, Phillips S, Oyebode JR. Understanding dementia amongst people in minority ethnic and cultural groups. J Adv Nurs. 2007;60(6):605–614.

42 Forbat L. Concepts and understandings of dementia by 'gatekeepers' and minority ethnic 'service users'. J Health Psychol. 2003;8(5):645–655.

43 Purandare N, Luthra V, Swarbrick C, Burns A. Knowledge of dementia among South Asian (Indian) older people in Manchester, UK. Int J Geriatr Psychiatry. 2007;22(8):777–781.

44 Rauf A. Caring for dementia: Exploring good practice on supporting South Asian carers through access to culturally competent service provision. Bradford Council; 2011. Available from: https://www.alzheimer-europe.org/resources/intercultural-support/caring-dementia-exploring-good-practice-supporting-south-asian.

45 Townsend J, Godfrey M. Asian experiences of care-giving for older relatives with dementia: An exploration of barriers to uptake of support services. Leeds: Nuffield Institute for Health; 2001.

46 Adamson J. Carers and dementia among African/Caribbean and South Asian families. Gener Rev. 1999;9:12–13.

47 Mackenzie J. Stigma and dementia: East European and South Asian family carers negotiating stigma in the UK. Dementia. 2006;5(2):233–247.

48 Brownfoot J. The needs of people with dementia and their carers within three ethnic minority groups in Haringey. London: LB Haringey Housing and Social Services/Alzheimer's Disease Society London Region; 1998.

49 Mackenzie J, Coates D, Ashraf F, Gallagher T, Ismail L. Understanding and supporting South Asian and Eastern European family carers of people with dementia. Religion. 2010;37(37):39.

50 Mayer LS, Bay RC, Politis A, Steinberg M, Steele C, Baker AS, et al. Comparison of three rating scales as outcome measures for treatment trials of depression in Alzheimer disease: Findings from DIADS. Int J Geriatr Psychiatry. 2006;21(10):930–936.

51 Pang F, Chow T, Cummings J, Leung V, Chiu H, Lam L, et al. Effect of neuropsychiatric symptoms of Alzheimer's disease on Chinese and American caregivers. Int J Geriatr Psychiatry. 2002;17(1):29–34.

52 Heok KE, Li TS. Stress of caregivers of dementia patients in the Singapore Chinese family. Int J Geriatr Psychiatry. 1997;12(4):466–469.

53 Alfonso T, Krishnamoorthy ES, Gomez K. Caregiving for dementia: Global perspectives and transcultural issues. In: Krishnamoorthy ES, Prince M, Cummings JL, editors. Dementia: A global approach. Cambridge: Cambridge University Press; 2010.

54 McKean TA. The sound of silence—Dementia, language loss, and being heard. Cult Anal. 2021;19(1).

55 Cummings JL, Benson DF, Hill MA, Read S. Aphasia in dementia of the Alzheimer type. Neurology. 1985;35(3):394–397.

56 Hyltenstam K, Obler LK. Bilingualism across the lifespan: Aspects of acquisition, maturity and loss. Cambridge: Cambridge University Press; 1989.

57 Mendez MF, Perryman KM, PontÓn MO, Cummings JL. Bilingualism and dementia. J Neuropsychiatry Clin Neurosci. 1999;11(3):411–412.

58 Paradis M, Libben G. The assessment of bilingual aphasia. New York: Psychology Press; 2014.

59 Schrauf RW, Rubin DC. Bilingual autobiographical memory in older adult immigrants: A test of cognitive explanations of the reminiscence bump and the linguistic encoding of memories. J Mem Lang. 1998;39(3):437–457.

60 Plassman BL, Williams JW, Burke JR, Holsinger T, Benjamin S. Systematic review: Factors associated with risk for and possible prevention of cognitive decline in later life. Ann Intern Med. 2010;153(3):182–193.

61 Valenzuela MJ, Sachdev P. Brain reserve and dementia: A systematic review. Psychol Med. 2006;36(4):441–454.

62 Bak TH, Alladi S. Can being bilingual affect the onset of dementia? Future Neurol. 2014;9(2):101–103.

63 Bialystok E, Craik FI, Freedman M. Bilingualism as a protection against the onset of symptoms of dementia. Neuropsychologia. 2007;45(2):459–464.

64 Chertkow H, Whitehead V, Phillips N, Wolfson C, Atherton J, Bergman H. Multilingualism (but not always bilingualism) delays the onset of Alzheimer disease: Evidence from a bilingual community. Alzheimer Dis Assoc Disord. 2010;24(2):118–125.

65 Fuller-Thomson E. Emerging evidence contradicts the hypothesis that bilingualism delays dementia onset. A commentary on "age of dementia diagnosis in community dwelling bilingual and monolingual Hispanic Americans" by Lawton et al., 2015. Cortex. 2015;66:170.

66 Crane PK, Gibbons LE, Arani K, Nguyen V, Rhoads K, McCurry SM, et al. Midlife use of written Japanese and protection from late life dementia. Epidemiology (Cambridge, Mass). 2009;20(5):766.

67 Lawton DM, Gasquoine PG, Weimer AA. Age of dementia diagnosis in community dwelling bilingual and monolingual Hispanic Americans. Cortex. 2015;66:141–145.

68 Sanders AE, Hall CB, Katz MJ, Lipton RB. Non-native language use and risk of incident dementia in the elderly. J Alzheimers Dis. 2012;29(1):99–108.

69 Zahodne LB, Schofield PW, Farrell MT, Stern Y, Manly JJ. Bilingualism does not alter cognitive decline or dementia risk among Spanish-speaking immigrants. Neuropsychology. 2014;28(2):238.

70 Evans N. Dying words: Endangered languages and what they have to tell us. Oxford: John Wiley & Sons; 2011.

71 Bialystok E. Language processing in bilingual children. Cambridge: Cambridge University Press; 1991.

72 Bialystok E. Bilingualism in development: Language, literacy, and cognition. Cambridge: Cambridge University Press; 2001.

73 Green DW. Mental control of the bilingual lexico-semantic system. Biling Lang Cogn. 1998;1(2):67–81.

74 Bialystok E, Craik FI, Klein R, Viswanathan M. Bilingualism, aging, and cognitive control: Evidence from the Simon task. Psychol Aging. 2004;19(2):290.

75 Owen AM, Hampshire A, Grahn JA, Stenton R, Dajani S, Burns AS, et al. Putting brain training to the test. Nature. 2010;465(7299):775–778.

76 Lorde A. The transformation of silence into language and action. In: Lorde A, editor. Sister outsider: Essays and speeches. London: Penguin; 2019. p. 29–32.

Chapter 11

Future directions

The earlier the better

Research has shown a protracted period of damage before any noticeable symptoms appear. This is referred to as the pre-symptomatic period. The current estimate is between 10 and 15 years (1). The concern then is that it might be too late to slow the progress of the disease as it has already taken hold of the individual. This is why there is a great interest in monitoring pathological changes in vivo; in other words, while the person is still living. This is why much time and money is being invested in finding ways to identify pathology early on to maximise the success of interventions. Of most benefit here has been the identification of CSF markers and the utilization of brain imaging technology to accurately measure levels of amyloid and tau. It is hoped that such techniques will allow intervention to occur before irreversible damage has been meted out.

It is to this we now turn. The initial part of this chapter will focus on biomedical approaches to improve the diagnosis and treatment of dementia. We shall begin by looking at the search for biomarkers that will make it possible to detect the conditions early on, thereby maximizing the efficacy of the various interventions.

Imaging

The use of scanning techniques has led to many advancements in our understanding of the brain. There is much hope that these techniques will be able to help us better diagnose those who will develop dementia in later life. Of great importance is developing a procedure that can now detect levels of protein accumulation in different parts of the brain. To date, it has been thought that there needs to be a certain level of protein accumulating in the brain to warrant a diagnosis of Alzheimer's disease. This was confirmed post mortem. The evidence so far from using this new scanning technique is that even milder levels of protein build-up have a noticeable effect on performance, albeit a less severe one.

It is hoped that techniques such as this will be refined to obtain an even more accurate picture. It has been suggested that a combination of an accurate assessment of protein accumulation, measuring the volume of specific brain structures,

DOI:10.4324/9781315681580-11

neuropsychological testing, as well as a detailed profile of a person's diet, levels of exercise, both physical and mental, may be sufficient to achieve this (2). If this does indeed happen, clinicians will be in a better position to prescribe medication and offer specific advice about how best to change the person's lifestyle to help stop, or at least further reduce the risk of, that person developing dementia.

We have talked previously about compensation. In other words, how we all try to offset impairments by adopting different strategies to aid performance. Leaving notes at strategic locations around the house, activating alarms on our smartphones, and a host of other activities help us compensate for memory lapses.

Evidence from imaging studies shows evidence of compensation at the neuronal level. As we age, we change the way we process information. Our brains alter in size and function. Each hemisphere of our brain specializes in specific functions throughout most of our lives. However, such lateralization is less obvious with age. This is one way that our brains compensate for a decline in function. Each hemisphere supports the activity of the other. This indicates brain plasticity, or neuroplasticity, where changes in brain structure and functioning occur in response to environmental demands (3).

For a long time, it was generally believed that no new cells grow once a person reaches adulthood. However, there is clear evidence of neurogenesis, as shown by the presence of neural stem cells in the adult brain. Stem cells provide the substrate for the development of new neurons. Notably, age does limit the growth potential of these stem cells, thereby imposing restrictions on how much improvement can be made (3).

There is data showing less activity in the hippocampus in those expressing subjective cognitive impairment, although activity in the right prefrontal cortex of this group increases. When comparing the objective performance of this group with a healthy control, there were no differences (4). This appears to support the argument that compensation occurs to offset a decline in function.

Another area of potential importance, given we have the techniques to gauge it, is the ability of different regions of the brain to work in harmony with one another. To be adaptive, various structures in the brain operate simultaneously, with messages being relayed back and forth, with information being assessed, manipulated, and acted upon. We rely on this dynamic interchange. If such activity were disrupted, a whole host of deficits would be experienced. Being able to accurately assess disruptions in connectivity would likely be a most valuable tool in detecting people in the early stages of disease (2).

The search for biomarkers

Biomarkers refer to chemicals whose presence appears to be somehow linked to the development of a disease. They are an essential focus for research as we know that cellular changes occur many years before overt symptoms manifest. In the case of the various dementia diagnoses referred to in this book, disease mechanisms operate below the surface for a long time before people start to experience challenging problems with their memory. This is why detecting these processes early on is so important. Hence, the need to identify and be able to detect biomarkers that are linked to the disease processes that lead to dementia symptoms.

Cerebrospinal fluid—the substance that protects the brain and spinal cord—is also a source of nutrients that ensure the brain's health. Levels of such materials change as the result of disease. A lumbar puncture or spinal tap is carried out to obtain samples of cerebrospinal fluid. This is where a needle is inserted between the bones of the spine to enable a sample to be drawn. Various biomarkers for dementia can be detected in this fluid. Blood tests are also used, although, to date, they are less accurate at helping clinicians diagnose specific forms of dementia.[1]

Abnormal build-up of proteins in the brain in the form of plaques and tangles is a chief characteristic of Alzheimer's disease. When looking at protein expression in the brain, there appear to be differences in which areas protect against such build-up and those that do not. Neurons are less likely to do this, whereas other brain cells—astrocytes and microglia, to name but two—do appear to express genes that protect against protein deposits. Also, neurons are more likely to produce harmful β-amyloid and tau (τ) proteins. The brain regions where this occurs map directly onto those areas associated with the early signs of the disease (5). Findings such as this are likely to be helpful in the development of future treatments. However, the exact mechanisms behind such diseases are far from clear.

There is evidence that drugs can reduce the amount of β-amyloid plaques in the brain (6). However, it is yet unclear whether such plaques play a causal role in the development of Alzheimer's disease.

Insulin

Insulin might play a role in dementia. Insulin is a hormone that regulates blood sugar by controlling how much is taken up by the liver, muscles, and fat cells (7). However, it is also involved in energy consumption in the brain, regulation of certain neurotransmitters central to cognitive operations, and neural plasticity.

Diet rich in fat and sugar results in high insulin levels in the brain. Such levels act to block the enzyme that metabolizes β-amyloid, resulting in toxic levels of the protein building up, thereby causing localized damage to brain tissue. This elevated level of β-amyloid blocks insulin receptors and so makes neurons unresponsive to this hormone. This resistance eventuates in an increase in the production of β-amyloid, thus contributing to the level of toxicity caused by β-amyloid deposits. Over time, insulin production is reduced due to over-exertion of the pancreas, again adding to the overall problem. This is because insulin has been shown to block β-amyloid from causing neuronal damage. If levels of insulin drop, this mechanism no longer occurs, resulting in extensive destruction.

Studies show that cognitive impairment is produced when insulin is blocked and improves when levels increase (7). From an evolutionary perspective, this would appear to make perfect sense. It would suggest that memory for the location of food would be enhanced due to glucose levels rising—and subsequent levels of insulin—following ingestion of food from a rich source.

Although primarily linked to diabetes, some have suggested that Alzheimer's disease may, in fact, be another form of diabetes where the target is not the liver but the brain instead (7).

As we saw in Chapter 2, type 2 diabetes is a significant risk factor for Alzheimer's disease. Among the symptoms of this form of diabetes are mental confusion and memory impairment. Insulin is involved in memory processing within the hippocampus (8). Insulin sensitivity is also markedly reduced in the hippocampus. This means less glucose is available to neurons when required during the performance of cognitive activity.

This would link to growing concerns about diet and how it affects not only general health but dementia also. Highly calorific junk food alters how our bodies respond to insulin. In the case of type 2 diabetes, regular, prolonged ingestion of foodstuffs high in fat and sugar result in elevated levels of insulin. The outcome is that organs and cells in the body no longer respond to insulin. As a result, the blood is saturated with glucose and fat. The body's response is to increase insulin production to try to counteract this, leading to high levels of both insulin and glucose. However, this level of production cannot be sustained, and so the outcome over time is that levels of insulin drop dramatically. It is also thought that those already with insulin insensitivity due to type 2 diabetes may be at even more risk of dementia.

Concerns over diet strengthen advice to both eat more healthily and engage in regular physical exercise. Being overweight is a significant risk factor for developing type 2 diabetes. This is because it seems to affect the action of insulin, resulting in raised levels of blood glucose and potentially insulin resistance.

This then provides a potential link between insulin levels and the development of Alzheimer's disease. The brain is not able to deal with chronically elevated levels of insulin. Again, the possible explanation is the development of insulin resistance, thereby leading to disruptions in cognitive functioning. Although most work so far has been on animals, a recent paper has produced evidence to suggest resistance to insulin in the brain of those with Alzheimer's disease, as indicated by the prevalent theory (9).

It is yet far from clear the various mechanisms at play here. It has been suggested that both β-amyloid and insulin are metabolized by the same enzyme, insulin-degrading enzyme (IDE). When insulin levels rise too high, it cannot deal with both substances, so by focusing on insulin, β-amyloid is not metabolized and instead amasses in cells to form plaque (10). This escalates the problem with insulin by destroying insulin receptors (9).

If insulin is seen as a major player here, it might provide a mechanism for another form of treatment. We have already seen that increased levels of insulin improve cognitive function. A study utilizing a nasal device to deliver insulin to the brain produced some interesting findings (11), although, again, it is early days yet.

Role of microglia

Although it has been a reasonably slow process, there is now general appreciation for the roles played by microglia in our brains. I remember a good friend of mine, who worked at the Institute of Psychiatry, being both excited and proud when unveiling a filmed sequence he had shot of microglia in action, showcasing their seemingly frenetic activity with their processes reaching out and finally engulfing various clumps (12). I seem to recall we were eating a takeaway at the time while all this cellular activity was unfolding. Till then, I had no accurate conception of what microglia were and what they did. Microglia carry out phagocytic action at sites where neural damage or inflammation has occurred, destroying the affected tissue.

Until relatively recently, it was believed that microglia only came to life when such injury or infection occurred. It was roughly a decade ago when the first significant breakthrough came regarding the import of microglia. As happens so often in science, this discovery was partly due to serendipity (13). This paper correctly identified these cells as essential for general housekeeping within the brain. We now know that they are involved in many activities, including being central to removing unnecessary connections and forming new neuronal links as well.

Synaptic pruning is essential for an efficient and healthy brain. In our early years, our brains are in a constant state of flux. Infants and children are voraciously exploring the world to try to make sense of the plethora of stimuli reaching their senses. All this requires the brain to forge new connections in our insatiable drive for understanding. Knowledge is built up, and skills are acquired. However, during adolescence, this mass accrual of knowledge and experience, and as a result, neural connections, has to be assessed. Take the example of learning a new skill. In the early stages, we bumble through using a process of trial-and-error often to achieve our desired goal. This may eventually work, but it is usually less than elegant. With time and practice, we become more efficient at doing things. At the neuronal level, this is achieved by stripping back unnecessary connections so that material can be processed more effectively. Microglia play an active role in this activity.

As already indicated, there is growing evidence to suggest that microglia are involved in the formation of new synapses, thereby playing an active role in neural plasticity (14). The way it does this is to secrete substances such as brain-derived neurotrophic factor (BDNF) and other chemicals that lead to the development of new neural connections. The hippocampus has been identified as a site of high levels of microglial action. As we have seen, the hippocampus is central to memory, specifically the formation of new memories.

All of this activity is vital for a healthy functioning brain and mind. It is unfortunate that, like in so many other cases, the activity of microglia can lead to damage, specifically in relation to among other things, Alzheimer's disease. We know deposits of β-amyloid are linked to Alzheimer's disease. Such deposits interfere with communication between synapses. It has been suggested that the build-up of this transmuted protein occurs because microglia can no longer adequately clear away these secretions. However, a new line of thinking argues that maybe the type of damage seen in Alzheimer's disease is due instead to overactive microglia (15). A recent study has shown an accumulation of C1q—a protein-released microglia—close to synapses in the brain of older adults (16). The thinking here is that drugs could be developed to stop the accumulation of C1q, and in doing so, stop, or at least slowdown, cognitive decline.

Microglia provide an invaluable service to the brain, as we have seen. It has been suggested that the build-up of amyloid protein leads to the activation of microglia, which then attempt to rid the brain of these deposits. However, the rate at which such deposits accumulate exceeds the capacity of microglia to remove them. This results in a permanent state of activation. This heightened level of activity is thought to have an additional negative effect when the body finds itself affected by infection or a chronic condition where there is a pronounced inflammatory response. As part of the response to infection, inflammatory proteins interleukin 34 and colony-stimulating factor-1 signal microglia to action. Microglia then secrete cytokines. Cytokines are immunoregulatory proteins that regulate inflammatory responses. Cytokines induce a distinct behavioural reaction that forms a mechanism that has evolved to deal with sickness—cytokine-induced sickness behaviour (17). This describes a set of adaptive responses to being ill, such as reduced activity levels, general fatigue, and depressed mood.

Because of the elevated level of microglia activity in individuals, it has been suggested that levels of cytokines secreted are excessive. They produce interleukin-1β, which is neurotoxic, and, as a result, neurons are destroyed (18). This effect has led to the hypothesis that an abnormal inflammatory response contributes to the progression of Alzheimer's disease.

In the past, it was generally assumed that inflammation occurring within the brain was a natural response to the build-up of plaque. However, the argument that an abnormal inflammatory response contributes to dementia is gaining more support (19). If this is the case, there might be a future in drugs that exert an anti-inflammatory response (20). Evidence that potentially links microglia activity to the development of dementia may also explain why diabetes is such a risk factor for dementia (21).

Having looked at some of the advancements in biomedical research, we shall turn our attention to psychological and physical efforts to combat mental decline. The literature on cognitive training is notorious for its inconsistent findings, most of which are mainly due to methodological flaws associated with the early studies. There is still a healthy drive to identify approaches that tap into the whole issue of cognitive training. Indeed, there is increasing evidence that multi-modal training offers evidence that improvements can be made. Perhaps a more stable approach is that of physical exercise. There is much evidence showing that physical activity can have many positive effects.

Cognitive training

The concept of keeping mentally active to ward off cognitive decline in older adults has been with us for some time now. Many studies have been conducted to see whether such claims are valid. Some of the earlier studies were far from ideal, with many often including poor control groups and, in some cases, no control group at all. Others had additional design issues, such as using performance measures that were not directly comparable to other studies. In fact, there is a host of problems with early studies in this field. More recent studies have benefitted from much tighter designs, among other things.

Nonetheless, the upshot of all this activity is disappointing (22). The general finding is that, although performance improves after a period of "brain training," the improvement is specific only to the tasks they were trained on. In other words, gains are not generalizable. On top of this, enhancements are not maintained over time, so the effect is relatively transient.

Physical exercise

Much evidence shows that physical exercise offers a tangible way to improve both physical and mental health. It improves cognitive functioning and, as a result, helps people with dementia continue to carry out important everyday activities (23). It does not have to be strenuous workouts in the gym. Instead, walking, gardening, and other forms of exercise improve a person's overall fitness level. There is much consternation over the definitive exercise routine, how frequently one should do it, and how long. No one agrees. The obvious thing here is that it will depend on the individual. The Department of Health indicates 150 minutes of moderate exercise each week.[2] They recommend 30 minutes roughly five times a week. The 30 minutes does not have to be in one go, but they suggest a minimum of 10 minutes for each activity.

Exercise is good for the heart and the vascular system, reducing the risk of a person developing heart disease or experiencing high blood pressure. It also reduces the risk of diabetes, stroke, systemic inflammation (24), and some cancers.[3] Exercise helps with insulin sensitivity and control of glucose levels (25). Maintaining muscle strength and flexibility helps people retain their independence. There are benefits to cognitive functioning, as well as helping to maintain a healthy sleep pattern. There is evidence that exercise offers benefits by protecting the structure of neurons in the brain and helps create new neurons and their interconnection—neurogenesis and synaptogenesis, respectively (26). Physical activity also leads to a rise in brain-derived neurotrophic factor (BDNF) (27). BDNF is crucial for creating new neurons and neuroplasticity within the brain over our lifetime (27). There is evidence too that exercise helps counteract some of the deterioration within the hippocampus by increasing the expression of growth factors, including BDNF (28), thereby leading to increased neurogenesis, angiogenesis—the creation of new blood vessels—and neuroplasticity (29). There is a clear link between the supply and demand of nutrients required by the brain—cerebral perfusion—and a person's physical fitness as well as their cognitive functioning (30).

Aside from the obvious physical benefits of such activity, many forms of exercise incorporate socializing elements. On the whole, physical activity improves a person's mood and boosts self-esteem.[4] There is evidence to suggest that it also benefits caregivers. Carer burden was seen to diminish if the carer oversaw and took part in the exercises carried out by the person with dementia (23). A recent review of the literature found no evidence suggesting that exercise reduced challenging behaviours or reduced depression (23).

It goes without saying that if a person has never exercised or has let it slide, caution is needed when considering what exercises to choose and which intensity. Medical advice is necessary if the person has a history of heart disease, high blood pressure, chest pain, dizziness, problems with joints, problems breathing, and difficulties maintaining balance. Local sports centres generally provide organized classes for tai chi, dance, swimming, and seated exercise, among other things.

During the later stages of the disease, constant supervision is needed. Changing positions from sitting to standing, moving from one room to another, and many other activities are classed as exercise. The most important thing is that the person is encouraged to move around regularly. This will help the individual retain muscle strength and flexibility and, in doing so, hopefully reduce or delay the need for home adaptations such as stairlifts or walk-in baths.

Evidence suggests that physical exercise combined with cognitive training may offer additional benefits (31). Most studies to date have explored the two activities individually. However, the most significant benefits will likely be obtained by simultaneously performing the two forms of activities. We know that the ability to perform two actions at the same time—dual-tasking—is worse as we get older, although it is important to contextualize this by stating that problems tend to arise as the task becomes more complex. So, it is more about the demands imposed by the synchronous activity (32). Such difficulties affect how we perform in our everyday lives. For example, it increases the risk of falls (33) and makes driving more challenging (34). Exergaming combines physical activity and cognitive challenges. Although one could argue that it makes theoretical sense that that would be an effective combination, there is still little evidence to show that the combined activity produces any more of an effect than physical exercise alone (35). Again, we are still faced with a situation where more adequate control groups are needed in order to tease out what is contributing to the overall positive outcomes in such studies.

Volunteering

There has been much research attempting to forge a link between mental and physical activity levels and cognitive decline, often with varying success. Still, one area that maybe warrants more attention is that of continuing work. "Nooooo," I hear you cry. Stay with me here. We shall explore the impact of dementia on the workplace later in this chapter. What I am instead referring to here is examining the potential benefits of keeping active through work, often through volunteering.

Some have argued that older adults should be encouraged to take up voluntary work (36). This is because our expected lifespan is increasing. Many expect to live out their lives in relatively good health. So, what to do with that time? Even though retirement age seems to be ever-shifting, and businesses are being encouraged to re-train older adults to retain their expertise in the active work-force, there will come a time when paid employment will not be an option. How-ever, that does not mean such activity has to cease. Opportunities abound for voluntary work.

Staying active in this way is challenging both mentally and physically. In such situations, there is a constant need to be adaptive. There is some evidence to sug-gest voluntary work can improve cognitive flexibility, opportunities for engage-ment in valuable roles, and productive activity (37, 38). Well-being is seen to also improve, as evidenced by increased satisfaction with life (39), feeling more contented (40), and lower levels of depression (41), among other things. One cru-cial mechanism at play here is increased social contact, which protects individuals from the adverse effects of isolation (42).

Intergenerational care

Although a current buzzword, intergenerational research has been mooted since the mid-1970s. Part of this growing interest includes the concept of intergenera-tional housing, where the younger generations live alongside older residents. Cur-rently, in various locations throughout the UK, nurseries are located near care homes, with much interaction between the two. Indeed, some are even housed on the same premises. The concept here is to eliminate barriers between age groups and, in doing so, eradicate false stereotypes. As we have seen, ageism is a real issue.[5] A local venture at St Monica Trust[6] in Bristol was made into a Channel 4 documentary, "Old People's Homes for 4-Year-Olds." After six weeks of interac-tions with nursery-aged children, some residents showed improved mood, mobil-ity, and memory.

In a review of the literature, Drury, Abrams and Swift (43) highlight some of the problems inherent in this area. Although there are schemes across the world, there is a great deal of variation in what is being carried out and the extent to which it is being evaluated. They draw our attention to the need to draw up guide-lines for good practice to inform policy.

When looking at the various schemes reported in the literature, a distinction between direct and indirect contact must be made. As you would expect, direct contact refers to face-to-face interactions between different generations. Such interaction helps reduce negative attitudes and expectations held by young people towards the older generation. From the evidence base so far, the most effective form of contact is intergenerational friendship. This is where young and old/spend time together regularly and share life stories, experiences, and interests. This type of approach is less common in the UK at the moment (44). With indirect contact, on the other hand, there is no physical interaction; instead, people, for example, are asked to bring to mind an interaction with someone belonging to a differ-ent age group—this is called imagined contact—or where someone has friends who are in other age groups—extended contact. Such forms of contact have been shown to reduce anxiety about ageing and improve attitudes towards older adults.

This report also makes recommendations for practice. The authors argue that intergenerational contact can improve productivity and staff retention, an extension of working lives, and psychological and physical health (43).

When looking at the outcomes of intergenerational programs, Galbraith and colleagues (45) found that, for people with dementia, the findings were generally positive. Sense of self was strengthened, as was confidence, self-esteem, and feeling cared for (46, 47). From behavioural indicators, it appears that people experienced joy and a reduction in anxiety (47, 48). There was a decline in levels of agitation and aggression (49, 50). Socializing behaviour increased, with more smiling and laughter reported (51). Also, engagement with activities improved, with more active participation being observed (52). Effects were not always positive, with one study showing generally negative effects (53).

When examining the outcomes for children, their understanding and views on ageing, and of dementia specifically, improved (50, 54). They were better able to relate to someone with dementia (55). Other studies provided evidence that children became more confident and were more patient, compassionate, and socially responsible due to their interactions (47, 48, 54). For some, joy was reported from helping out (56), although some reported confusion due to the changeability in the person with dementia (53). Some studies showed that the child became more attentive to the needs of the person with dementia (48). In contrast, others indicated that children became more frustrated and less supportive in carrying out activities (53).

From the literature to date, it would appear that the activity itself is less important than the requirement that it be meaningful and conducted in an appropriate setting (45). However, given the wide variation in design, more systematic work is needed before indicators of good practice can be published. Whatever form it takes, there must be sufficient training before such programs are implemented. If this does not happen, there will likely be confusion, especially among the children who participate in the activities (57). There also needs to be agreed outcome measures to monitor the effectiveness of any program that is running (45), as well as randomization of conditions to ensure accurate comparison of effects. The Dementia Care Mapping tool would likely be helpful here (45). On top of this, larger group sizes and more unambiguous inclusion and exclusion criteria are needed to better assess the magnitude of effect and factors relating to class, gender, race, and ethnicity.

In the lead up to considering some of the potential advancements in drug therapy in the future, I shall spend some time on a topic very close to my heart: caffeine. My first postdoc position was a three-year investigation into the behavioural and pharmacological effects of caffeine. I had the pleasure of working with Prof. Andy Smith on this research. I am fortunate to have been taught by or worked with some truly inspirational figures. It is why I have such an undying desire for knowledge. It is perhaps one of those strange foibles of research that apparent disparate strands of research at some stage diverge into a coherent whole. Having dedicated my research career to studying older adults, specifically dementia, I thought I had left the caffeine field far behind. Not so. Let us start by considering the nature of caffeine before exploring its potential use as an intervention.

Psychopharmacology

Caffeine

Caffeine is often mentioned in many different domains of the literature. Claims about the effects of caffeine—be it positive or negative—also often make it into the newspapers. Caffeine, *1,3,7-trimethylxanthine*, a psychoactive stimulant, is contained in many products, including coffee, tea, various carbonated soft drinks, energy drinks, and chocolate, among other things. It also finds its way into multiple medications, such as painkillers and cold and 'flu remedies, as caffeine augments the activity of a drug, a process called potentiation. This is particularly the case with analgesic medications.

Caffeine is undoubtedly mentioned with reasonable regularity in the dementia literature. In such cases, caffeine is talked of in two lights: caffeine, the cognitive enhancer, and caffeine, the neuroprotector.

Neuroprotective effects of caffeine

Epidemiological studies that have examined the protective effects of tea and coffee have, in some instances, shown that lifetime consumption is linked to better performance on a range of cognitive performance measures (58). In this sense, it might be argued that coffee and tea containing caffeine might help reduce some of the age-related declines in cognition. In other words, coffee, tea, and caffeine can be described as having neuroprotective effects. Studies have also been conducted to see whether caffeine consumption in coffee and tea lessens the chances of dementia. The findings from these studies are varied. Some show no effect of consuming coffee and tea over the lifetime and subsequent development of dementia. Other studies indicate that it might be coffee rather than tea that offers some protective effect (59).

Potential explanations for the neuroprotective effects of caffeine have been proposed. Its effect on adenosine is one mechanism. Adenosine is a by-product of neural activity. Throughout the day, levels of adenosine rise and bind to receptors. Adenosine dampens neural activity levels and contributes to feelings of sleepiness. Caffeine predominantly exerts its effect due to its antagonist effect on adenosine receptors, thereby having the converse effect of increasing arousal levels (60). It has been suggested caffeine combats extreme activation of adenosine A2A receptors, specifically in the cortex and hippocampus. This is believed to reduce damage by $A\beta$, enabling normal synaptic transmission (61–63). Studies using mice have shown caffeine to reduce levels of $A\beta$ (64, 65). At the moment, these findings are based solely on animal models.

The findings are far from clear-cut when looking at the lifetime use of caffeinated products in humans. Some studies show positive effects of caffeine intake over the lifespan, but causal mechanisms could not be determined given the cross-sectional nature of the study design (66). Longitudinal studies have shown better performance in women but not in men (67). Again, in a cohort study, there was some indication that lifetime caffeine intake was associated with better overall cognitive function (68). In contrast to other studies, there were no sex differences. Although there is some way to go, there is reasonable evidence that caffeine might find a place as a potential disease modifier for certain dementias, most likely Alzheimer's disease (69), although there is growing evidence that it might be protective against Parkinson's disease as well (70). Caffeine also appears to affect the likelihood of white matter lesions and microvascular ischaemic lesions (71).

Caffeine improved sensitivity to insulin (72). This means the risk of type 2 diabetes is reduced (73). We know that type 2 diabetes is linked to a decline in cognitive functioning and is, in fact, a risk factor for dementia (73). Magnesium, also found in coffee, increases sensitivity to insulin as well (74). Another argument is that coffee reduces neuroinflammation (75) and oxidative stress (76). There are also indirect effects of caffeine that may explain its neuroprotective effects. These include a reduction in depression-like symptoms (77) and so help reduce the extent of cognitive decline (78).

As with most studies, potential confounding factors might contribute to the observed effects. It might be the case that those who drink moderate amounts of coffee and tea—in other words, those where the most significant effect of caffeine is seen in these studies—might be more likely to be healthier in general, thereby contributing to the apparent protective effects of caffeine.

Caffeine as a cognitive enhancer

We shall now explore caffeine as a cognitive enhancer. The biological mechanism behind the caffeine effect is linked to it being an antagonist of adenosine receptors. Adenosine is itself linked to sleep. ATP is the primary source of energy in the body. When broken down, adenosine is formed. The gradual build-up of adenosine throughout the day indicates that the body has used a lot of energy. This build-up triggers the VLPO switch, resulting in sleep. VLPO refers to the ventrolateral preoptic nucleus that is situated in the hypothalamus. It produces gamma-aminobutyric acid—GABA—which acts to reduce levels of arousal.

However, we also know that adenosine receptors are involved in cognitive activity and are located in the hippocampus, cerebral cortex, and the hypothalamus. Caffeine increases adenosine within the noradrenergic, cholinergic, dopaminergic, and serotoninergic neurotransmitter pathways by blocking these receptors. The natural effect of adenosine is to inhibit cortical arousal. By blocking adenosine receptors and thereby preventing their dampening effect, the overall effect increases cortical stimulation.

The main effects of caffeine result from the increase of two significant neurotransmitters. Caffeine increases the synthesis of central noradrenaline. A raised level of noradrenaline is associated with heightened cortical arousal and improved vigilance. Also, it increases levels of acetylcholine. Acetylcholine acts to modulate the level of cortical arousal and leads to more intense attention, with responses being more accurate and faster. In terms of my own research, we found that caffeine boosts performance in those who are fatigued,[7] reflecting the noradrenergic effect of caffeine. The second effect of caffeine is that it improves performance in those already alert[8] (79) and is associated with the cholinergic effect of caffeine.

When looking at working memory, there is little evidence of a positive effect of caffeine. Working memory refers to the active online processing and manipulation of information. One of the main issues with published studies here is that several confounds might contribute to the effects observed (80). It might be the case that caffeine improves working memory performance on mildly challenging tasks but may, in fact, impair performance on more complex tasks (81).

Having looked at the effects of caffeine on attention and short-term memory, we shall now explore the impact on long-term memory. It is important to mention at the start that fewer studies have been conducted on the effects of caffeine on this form of memory. Even though caffeine was shown to have the expected effect on arousal, there tends to be little noticeable effect on long-term memory (82).

Looking specifically at the effects of caffeine in older adults, the aim is to show that caffeine exerts beneficial effects and, as such, might be considered a way to manage some of the symptoms associated with age-related cognitive decline, with the potential also to slow or prevent such deterioration. Caffeine might also be used to manage the symptoms in those who have received a diagnosis of dementia.

A recent study has indicated that tea is associated with improved physical functioning (83). There are several implications to be derived from findings such as this. For one, it might help reduce frailty in older adults.

A combination of green tea and l-theanine has led to improvements in cognitive performance in those with mild cognitive impairment (84). The suggestion here is that some such combination might be used as an intervention to help reduce cognitive deficits.

Having looked at the potential for caffeine to offset the age-related decline in cognitive functioning, we shall turn our attention to dementia. As we have seen, there is little hope for identifying an effective treatment for dementia. The best we can do is identify potential risk factors and intervene to lessen their impact, possibly slowing either onset of symptoms or the rate of decline. Such modifiable risk factors include those linked to the cardiovascular system and a person's metabolism. Related to this is the variety of lifestyle choices a person makes throughout their life (85–88).

Diet is a crucial aspect where lifestyle choices can enormously impact one's health. Caffeine is clearly a principal constituent of many drinks. Studies have demonstrated the acute effects of caffeine (89). However, there has also been research that has examined the effects of caffeine when administered over the long term. Indeed, there is evidence that the chronic administration of caffeine leads to positive outcomes in those with both acute and chronic neurological conditions, including stroke and Parkinson's disease (90–94). There is evidence that caffeine helps with some of the motor problems associated with Parkinson's disease, as well as some of the non-motor problems (95). In a recent study, we found that benefits of caffeine in those with Parkinson's disease was dependent on the demands of the task itself (96).

Much like caffeine, alcohol is continuously in the news, generally proclaiming some new risk. However, emerging evidence shows that this might not necessarily be the case for all situations. Might it be the case that alcohol could offer some protection?

Alcohol

In an earlier chapter, we looked at how alcohol is a significant risk factor for dementia (see Chapter 2). We also saw how there are specific forms of dementia linked to prolonged alcohol abuse (see Chapter 3). However, evidence suggests that alcohol can exert a protective effect. There does seem to be evidence that a regular intake of moderate amounts of alcohol might offer a degree of protection against neurodegeneration in some cases. However, it is equally clear that alcohol does not afford blanket protection for everyone. Any benefit has to be tempered against the harmful effects of this substance.

We will turn our attention now to examining what the future has in store concerning drug therapies for dementia. Can anything be done to improve the effectiveness of drugs in treating the various symptoms of dementia? Is there any hope that the disease can be slowed down, even halted?

Drug treatment

As seen in Chapter 6, current medications can slow the progression of symptoms to some extent in those with mild to moderate dementia. However, there are clear limitations to what these drugs can do. Current research aims to improve drug efficacy, with the ultimate aim of identifying disease-modifying drugs that will alter the progress of the disease itself and maybe even prevent damage from occurring altogether. Several potential alternatives are currently being tested, including antioxidants, stem cell therapy, and vaccination against plaque build-up.

Antioxidants

There has been much written about antioxidants in the treatment of dementia. It is thought antioxidants combat the harmful effects of free radicals (97). Free radicals starve the brain of oxygen. They are produced through interactions of β-amyloid with the lining of blood vessels in the brain. β-Amyloid appears at the centre of neuritic plaques. Levels of β-amyloid are increased due to high levels of low-density lipoprotein, the bad form of cholesterol linked to a range of medical complaints. However, the jury is still out as to whether antioxidants protect against dementia.

Glucose metabolism

Essential to repairing cell damage is amyloid precursor protein (APP). Processes such as this are highly dependent on a steady supply of glucose to provide much-needed energy. However, Alzheimer's disease is associated with a reduction in glucose metabolism. As a result, APP-mediated cell repair is not as effective as it could be, resulting in cell death. Therefore, it has been argued that drugs that enhance glucose metabolism may help slow down the progression of the disease (98).

Stem cell therapy

Stem cell therapy is controversial. Stem cells are the raw material from which specialized cells are produced. Because they can be made to produce specific types of cells, the argument is that they can be harnessed to help repair damaged tissue. This comes under the auspices of regenerative medicine. The ethics of this work is still debated. Although stem cells are found in adults, there is less choice than that offered by embryonic stem cells. Embryonic stem cells are described as pluripotent; they can become any cell type. Therein lies the rub. These stem cells can only be obtained from early-stage embryos. Ethical considerations must direct whether or how such research is used.[9]

Vaccination

As increasing numbers of people live longer with each generation, so too will there be a rise in the prevalence of diseases of older age. In addition, the older one becomes, the more likely that person will suffer from more than one serious medical condition. A rather sobering yet realistic truth is that, although one serious medical condition may be treated successfully, the likelihood is that the same person will die of another condition that cannot be treated.

Inflammation is now implicated in many illnesses, including depression and dementia. As such, treatments that combat inflammation might offer a way to prevent the development, or at least curb the impact, of some conditions (99). Evidence shows chronic activation of microglia and other cells linked to the immune response exacerbates the pathology in people with Alzheimer's disease (100). The immune response is also associated with conditions such as diabetes and cardiovascular disease. Such conditions are identified risk factors for Alzheimer's disease. Because of this, there is a need to explore further the possibility that there is a shared disease pathway between these conditions.

There is much interest at the moment in gum disease bacteria. Ongoing research tests the belief that *Porphyromonas gingivalis* enters the brain and triggers an inflammatory response. This is thought to then activate the build-up of amyloid (101). Should this prove fruitful, one possibility is to stop the bacteria from releasing the toxins that cause the inflammation or even vaccinate against the bacteria in the first instance.[10] One of the problems at the moment is that it is unclear how the bacteria enter the brain in the first place. One potential explanation is that the bacteria cause inflammation in the gums, damaging the mouth's lining. This might then provide the route whereby the bacteria accesses the brain. Usually protected by the blood–brain barrier, *Porphyromonas gingivalis* can enter the cells lining our blood vessels, thereby providing a possible way into the brain.[11]

We are living in an age where huge technological advancements are seemingly made on a daily basis. Indeed, they are in many fields, less so in dementia research. This is not through want of trying. So, what can technology offer those living with dementia now, and what of the future?

Personal genomics

The future promises increasing reliance on personal genomics to identify individual predispositions to a host of medical complaints and, in doing so, open the door to personalized treatment regimens to fend off these conditions. Increasingly, people are showing great interest in receiving genetic screening for various conditions. Of paramount importance is providing adequate counselling to accompany test results. The availability of commercial tests makes this an uphill struggle. At the moment, testing for the presence of ApoE is seen as a way to assess a person's risk of Alzheimer's disease (102).

I will shift the focus now away from drug treatment and instead look at physical aspects of care, be it around mobility or robotic care assistants.

Mobility

How active a person is depending on several factors. Important here is mobility—a person's ability to move—especially when considering a person's participation in events outside their home (103). On the whole, people prefer to stay as long as possible in their own home. The predilection to "age in place" places heavy demands on policymakers to ensure age-friendly environments (104), especially around transportation, to facilitate active engagement in community life (105).

Mobility is determined by various things, including a person's level of cognitive functioning, physical and psychological well-being, and money. On top of that, there are issues around gender, race, and ethnicity, as well as the actual environment itself (106).

Mobility is an essential determinant of quality of life among older adults (107, 108). Mobility is vital for activities that are not only utilitarian in nature but for needs that are linked to the desire for control and independence (affective needs) and enjoyment (aesthetic needs) (108). As already mentioned, the environment in which a person lives is influential here. Factors here include the availability of services, feelings of safety and trust, and being isolated (109).

Although having the independence of one's own car is highly valued (110), driving does exert increasing mental and physical demands on the individual as they age (111). Stopping driving, as a result, restricts a person's out-of-home mobility (112). Adapting to change, such as the need to seek alternative modes of transport, is a challenge, and many barriers exist to exacerbate difficulties, such as low income and declining physical and mental health (113–115). Convenience and accessibility of public transport are central here also (115).

Various approaches have been used to gauge out-of-home mobility. One includes using wearable GPS trackers to measure distances from home travelled. Devices of this nature allow researchers to explore physical activity, locations visited, and patterns of travel (116).

Problems with cognitive functioning and mobility are often linked (117). This is especially the case with dementia. Although Alzheimer's disease is the most prevalent cause, other diseases that lead to dementia symptoms often pose more of a mobility risk for people due to the presence of muscle weakness and motor impairment (118). Indeed, mobility problems occur much earlier in other non-Alzheimer's disease dementias. Vascular dementia is mainly associated with a rapid decline in physical functioning due to white matter lesions occurring in the subcortex that result in general weakness, sensory disturbance, poor balance, and executive dysfunction (119). Also, dependence on others to help with everyday activities due to functional decline is accelerated in those with frontotemporal dementia (120). This is especially so for the behavioural variant. This might be because of the increased apathy that leads to inactivity, a higher risk of motor neuron disease, and impaired motor inhibition and stability (121, 122). This means that interventions can be in place earlier (118) to minimize functional decline. Exercise provides a promising way to offset some of this decline and thus reduce or stave off disability for a while (123). Such activity maintains or improves not only physical strength but also cognitive functioning. There is good evidence that cognitive impairment is implicated in declining physical functioning (118). Helping to keep a person's mobility is fundamental in protecting their quality of life.

Technology

The premise behind gerontechnology is to not only make the lives of older adults easier but its adoption is increasingly seen as being necessary for healthy ageing. We all use technology in our daily lives to improve our well-being, and older adults are no exception here. In many cases, technology is a way for older adults to maintain activities they hold dear and to adjust to life changes (124).

The profusion of telehealth services is a way to meet better the care needs of older adults in their own homes. It is a way to reduce the possible need for them to relocate as, for many, this can be intensely distressing (125).

Technology is increasingly seen as a substantial resource for the care of older adults, including those with a diagnosis of dementia. Indeed, gerontechnology has improved the quality of life in many areas (3). A previous chapter shows that adaptations can be made to the environment to facilitate independence. Such changes can be enhanced by an increasing range of electronic devices that further support the individual. Some of these will be explored in more detail in this chapter.

One crucial point that needs careful consideration before introducing such technology is the extent to which the individual concerned is comfortable with the notion of such devices. Gadgetry is not for everyone. However, the current generation of older adults is increasingly embracing technology in all its forms. Grandparents regularly engage in contests with their grandchildren on the Wii or Xbox. Smartphones and tablets are now commonplace. Skyping relatives and friends is a regular occurrence in many cases. Increasingly technology found in the home facilitates care for physical health conditions. A fuller account is provided in the final chapter of my book, *The Psychology of Ageing: From Mind to Society* (3). For the remainder of this chapter, the focus will be on using technology in dementia care.

Telemedicine

Telemedicine is increasingly seen as a real option in many cases, especially when people live in remote locations or where there is an impediment preventing physical visits to a clinic. In such cases, diagnosis and treatment may occur via the telephone, video conferencing, or robotic assistants in some instances. A variety of monitors and sensors can also feed into this, providing quantitative data about physical health conditions, thereby indicating how well a person is functioning in their home environment. Such tools allow clinicians to regularly monitor progress remotely, thus providing a more efficient service. These devices can also indicate any deviations from the standard behaviour patterns and notify the appropriate services (126).

Technology of this nature lends itself to contributing to the improvement of care and management of individuals diagnosed with dementia. Cameras and sensors situated throughout a person's home can monitor activities day and night. Various failsafe mechanisms can be put in place to ensure the safety of the individual by eradicating, or at the very least minimising, risks that might lead to harm.

There is an emphasis that people should remain in their own homes and lead independent lives for as long as possible. The adoption of in-home technology is in keeping with this drive. In this sense, institutional care will only be sought once impairments become too severe to maintain such levels of independence.

Smart homes

Alarms that alert family, neighbours, or healthcare workers are helpful and provide a valid form of protection for individuals living independently. A warning might be triggered, for example, if sensors detect the front door is open. Auditory prompts might be used to draw a person's attention to the fact that a tap is still running or faucets that automatically turn off to prevent a sink or bath from overflowing.

Motion sensors at critical locations are not only energy-saving but also life-saving. For example, sensors that monitor movement during the night can ensure adequate illumination around potentially hazardous areas like the hallway or bathroom. Motion detected near the front door could be the trigger to play an auditory reminder to lock it.

Pressure-sensitive mats can be used in conjunction with sensors. A clear example where they might be beneficial is by a person's bed. If it registers that a person has risen during the night but failed to return to bed, an alarm would be raised as this might indicate the person has fallen.

Robotic care assistants

There is much current research focusing on developing capable robotic care assistants. The current breed of robots works in communication with an array of smart sensors in the environment to better support the person with dementia. These systems provide passive assistance and are also a source of social interaction for the individual. To provide more naturalistic communication, voice and gesture recognition are being improved upon, as are speech synthesis and sensor feedback.

Although improvements are occurring all the time, interactions with robots are characterized by stilted, superficial bursts of conversation. There is an awkwardness to their movements that further enforce their sense of otherness. Any sense of adaptability to the cultural expectations of the person with whom they are engaging is lacking.[12]

The human interface

When approaching any form of technology, it is vitally important to consider the user. This is particularly the case when considering older adults. Several issues are important here, crucially a person's inherent capabilities and acceptance of the technology. Early pioneering work by Norman (127) indicated how poor design can lead us to make errors and experience fraught encounters when interacting with any product of design, be it kitchen stoves or smartphone apps. Regardless of its intentions to assist you, any form of technology makes demands on one's attentional resources. Where demands imposed are well within a person's capacity, the resultant outcome is positive; any mismatch renders the object unusable.

Gerontechnology is a large business. At its very heart should be the concept of demand-capability fit. A well-designed item will engender a belief in one's competence and, in so doing, boost self-efficacy in that area of a person's life (128). Ease of use is paramount, with unnecessary difficulties or challenges to the user forming a barrier to its ultimate usefulness (129). Aside from making the inevitably indecipherable instruction manual intelligible, the interface between the device and the user needs careful consideration when targeting older adults. Factors such as the level of illumination, font size, colour contrasts, auditory prompts, sensitivity and size of touch zones, among other things, need to be flexible (129). The format should be intuitive. Underpinning all these are the cognitive changes associated with ageing. Speed of information processing is slowed, as is the ability to integrate different streams of information. Such problems are magnified in cases where cognitive impairment is severe.

Having examined some of the ways treatment and care of people with dementia may change in the future, as a direct lead-on from this work, we need also consider some of the not-too-minor ethical concerns that envelop some of these options. It is perhaps inevitable that issues arise with most advancements in practice. It is not the place here to resolve these, as many debates need to take place before we are even in a position to consider what we should do. I wish merely to raise awareness of these concerns.

Ethical issues in treatment and care

Personhood and smart living

Lifestyle monitoring technology is currently being used to help keep an eye on people living with dementia. These systems track a range of activities, particularly identifying and monitoring patterns of behaviour. Their role is not to replace human contact, merely to supplement it. The potential here is to maintain independence and improve well-being. This can be done by early detection of hazards and emerging health problems so that appropriate support mechanisms can be implemented (130–132). There is a concern that the person is reduced to a pattern of code, the self subsumed under an ever-growing sea of data points (133, 134).

Assessing the impact of technology of this nature is complex, especially for a condition such as dementia, where the individual can neither communicate their needs nor provide accurate insight into how they feel about the situation (135, 136).

As seen in Chapter 7, Kitwood (137) argued that others are central in determining our sense of self. In the case of dementia, what happens over time is that the person with the condition becomes increasingly dependent on their carer. He also argued that the tendency is to view the individual as a cluster of symptoms that make up the diagnosis of dementia. He describes a loss of self. This imposed invisibility is referred to as a malignant social psychology (137). The person with dementia then becomes stigmatized, infantilized, and objectified as a result of all this. The more acceptable alternative is a model of care that can be described as positive person work whereby people are seen as individuals who are host to a unique range of abilities. In this sense, their personhood is accepted and supported.

Kontos (136) talks about the embodied self. This talk of an embodied self refers to a self that is situated in a social and material environment. This perspective fits nicely with the use of technology in the home. The development of smart spaces could be argued to be part and parcel of this embodiment. In other words, a home environment of this type is just an extension of the self.

Using technology

As with most things, advancement often comes packaged with concomitant concerns or issues. In the case of the adoption of smart technology, there are concerns about an intrusion of privacy and data protection. Just how much surveillance is needed to ensure the safety of an individual? If the purpose of the technology is to meet the healthcare needs of a particular individual, there is an obligation that the level of monitoring does not overstep the mark (138). In terms of data protection, as most people working in IT will confidently proclaim, except for major businesses and government agencies, no network is really secure if someone has the appropriate equipment and a desire to access certain information (139). With growing adoption and reliance on networked devices monitoring our every move, there is a real need to address these and other weighty ethical issues that directly impact our security and privacy.

In addition to the issue of data protection, such systems should not be seen as a replacement for human interaction. Regardless of advancements, assistive technology can never replace human contact as the primary form of communication, and the aim should not be to try to do so. Technology will also not eradicate risk. However, it can improve safety and enhance a person's quality of life.

Lying to protect

In their excellent paper on doll therapy in the care of people with dementia, Mitchell and O'Donnell (140) highlight some ethical concerns, issues that are by no means confined to this area of care. As we saw in Chapter 6, increasingly, dolls are used to help reduce some of the behavioural and psychological symptoms of dementia. Dolls generally are in the form of a baby, although they can take on other manifestations, such as animals. One explanation for the positive impact of this intervention is that the dolls act as attachment objects. Given the cognitive decline experienced by the person with dementia, combined with the life-like nature of many of the dolls, it is perhaps unsurprising that some people perceive the doll as a real human child in some instances. As in many other similar situations, the general principle here is not to try to correct the person with dementia. Such action would likely lead to a great deal of distress. Minshull (141) talks about seeing the caregiver's response as one of withholding an "unnecessary truth" rather than an outright lie. The question, then, is this an acceptable argument?

The line generally taken is that lying is justified in the case of dementia care as it protects the well-being of the individual (142). Indeed, guidelines have been published to advise carers when lying might be appropriate (143).

It is argued that carers should aim to adopt the person with dementia's perception of reality. This perspective contends that it would be counterproductive, indeed distressing, to attempt to reason with the person about the nature of a doll that is perceived as being real. This is referred to as validation (144). In doing so, one is actively maintaining, not challenging, that person's sense of dignity (144).

Some strongly disagree with any form of lying when caring for someone with dementia. For example, Kitwood (145) argues that any such behaviour undermines the personhood of someone with dementia and affects how others interact with them. A similar position is held by the Nursing and Midwifery Council (146).

Therefore, the entire premise of doll therapy could be seen as undermining and deceptive (147). In fact, the very presence of the doll itself is engineered to misrepresent reality (148).

I would like to end this chapter by reflecting on the politics of dementia. However, before I do so, as a related point, we shall examine the impact that a diagnosis of dementia has on a person's work life. How well, in other words, can our employers accommodate people who may have received such a diagnosis. Again, it is something that we can no longer ignore. With each passing year, increasing numbers of employers will face staff on their payroll who will require a higher level of flexibility to help meet their needs.

Dementia in the workplace

A major challenge facing us all is the growing expectation that we will be working for a lot longer than previous generations. The retirement age is increasing. There have also been changes to the state pension. The upshot of this is that there will be growing numbers of older adults in the workforce. Although not an inevitability of ageing, nonetheless risk of dementia does increase with age. Likely, a person may first become aware that something is going wrong while performing their work (149). That being the case, a lot more needs to be done to ensure that those diagnosed with dementia or prodromal syndromes and who wish to remain working can be supported. One figure estimates 800,000 individuals in the UK with a diagnosis of dementia, 2 per cent of which are under the age of 65 (150). In fact, 18 per cent of people with a diagnosis of dementia continue to work (151). It is perhaps surprising that there is little research looking at this.

With a drive to assess people who express concerns about their memory early on, more and more people will likely receive a diagnosis of either MCI or dementia while still functioning well daily. That is good because an appropriate treatment plan can be devised, but there is added pressure about what to do in terms of their employer. Should they be told and when? Notably, almost half who experience such difficulties do not receive a formal diagnosis of dementia (150). However, one hopes that this will improve with time.

That being the case, steps need to be taken to improve the retention of employees with either MCI or dementia, as early retirement is costly for businesses. The potential economic burden is decidedly higher for those who are diagnosed with early-onset dementia, as they are likely to have more financial obligations than those who are diagnosed later in life. Under the Equality Act of 2010, employers are bound to offer reasonable adjustments to facilitate their continuation within the workforce. This will ensure a more inclusive working environment (151).

As we have seen throughout this book, there is still a great deal of stigma and misunderstanding associated with dementia (152). The workplace is just one area of challenge, but it is a big one. Fearing a less than supportive reaction, many who experience cognitive difficulties, especially when linked to a diagnosis of dementia, refuse to discuss it with their boss (150). In fact, in the case of those who receive a diagnosis of dementia at a younger age, it was found that they were either more likely to be made redundant or dismissed for being inept (153).

There is also the issue of what to do about those working and who are unaware they have dementia (150). In such instances, people cannot explain to themselves or their employer why they are struggling to carry out activities that were once of no concern. Inevitably this will give rise to feelings of inadequacy. The upshot may be that a person feels they can no longer continue working, or poor performance might jeopardise their job. Either way, those in need of support are falling through the net.

In the case of those who have received a positive diagnosis of dementia, there is a clear explanation for why they have been experiencing such difficulty performing their job. A diagnosis will enable that person to reflect on their situation and help them consider what they wish to do; continue working or not. If they keep working, the next constructive step would be to discuss their diagnosis and plans with their employer (150).

Before turning attention to what employers can do to help those who remain working following a diagnosis of dementia, this would be an excellent opportunity to explore how dementia impacts a person's ability to continue working. As one might expect with dementia, problems with memory are usually the first symptoms to be noticed. Also, word-finding difficulties are expressed, a reduced ability to acquire new information, keeping up with changes in technology, problems processing visual-spatial information, and, more generally, issues with motivation (154). As might be expected, a typical reaction to such situations is a drop in a person's confidence in their own abilities (149). In many cases, reported stress levels increased, bringing with it the all too familiar problems with general health.

In some instances, people tried to explain away the problems they were experiencing by designating them as mere consequences of getting old. Our ability to compensate for declines in functioning is quite astounding (3). We are adept at developing ways to deal with almost any hurdle our bodies create. Standards in the arsenal include writing notes and more time set aside for planning what needs to be done and when (149, 155).

Ritchie et al. (154) not only provide a concise overview of the literature in this area—although there is not much, in fact, only six papers—they also present findings from a series of interviews covering various aspects of people's experience of continuing to work with dementia, including how among other things the difficulty dealing with the inconsistency in symptom severity at different points throughout the day, as well as seeking support. The qualitative data presented provides a real insight into the range of issues people face under these conditions.

Another benefit of receiving a diagnosis early on is that it allows the employer to explore what they can do to help enable that individual to remain in their employment for as long as they desire (150). The Alzheimer's Society report that 89 per cent of employers know that dementia poses a growing problem (156). Early retirement of individuals due to dementia exerts a considerable cost on businesses. The figure for the UK alone is £627 million per annum (156).

There are initiatives employers can deploy to help raise awareness of dementia and, at the same time, ameliorate some of the fears the person newly diagnosed with the condition may have. Employers could offer awareness-raising courses for their employees to ensure line managers and senior management are aware of how dementia might affect their staff and generally promote a dementia-friendly environment (150, 157).

Due to the very nature of the condition, at some point, the challenges will be too severe for the person to continue in work. Giving up a job is difficult at the best of times when one considers how big a part of our lives has been dedicated to it (3), but under a cloud of progressive disease, the emotional turmoil surrounding this decision is even greater. To help facilitate a person through this difficult time, people need to feel they can discuss options openly with their employer. It might be the case that there is a mutual decision to reduce the number of hours worked such that it is more of a phase-out rather than an immediate halt to employment (150).

We have been focusing on the person with dementia so far in this section. However, they are not the only people affected by the diagnosis. Indeed, as we have seen throughout this book, the demands and strains placed on family members in a caring role are considerable. In most cases, we have seen that caring occurs on top of a full-time job (158). A recent survey showed that around 17 per cent of carers in employment are forced to either reduce their hours or quit working entirely to continue caring adequately for their relative (158).

A dementia-friendly workplace

In 2015, the Alzheimer's Society published an important document that sets out clearly how employers can help meet the needs of those diagnosed with dementia (156). I shall be relying on this text rather heavily in this section. It is a great resource, with much practical advice for employers. From the very beginning, the document sets out the critical caveat that there is no such thing as a one-size-fits-all strategy to help individuals. We have shown in this book that the way each person experiences dementia is very much individual. No two persons will experience precisely the same things at the same time with the same outcome. I am reminded of a popular quote to describe autism: "If you've met one person with autism, you've met *one* person with autism."[13] Much the same can be said of dementia. In this final section, I shall summarize some of the key propositions.

In tune with the whole concept of dementia-friendly communities, employers could ensure that their workforce understands dementia and how it might affect some colleagues to make them more sensitive to that person's needs should the situation arise. They should also make sure that the rights of the individual with dementia are protected. The aim, then, is to foster an environment that is open and free from prejudice or fear. It is about thinking and acting in a flexible manner (156).

Employers need to be mindful of what early symptoms of dementia might be. These will likely manifest long before a person decides to seek medical advice.

In this sense, run-of-the-mill activities, such as speaking to a worker, can be conducted in an environment with minimal distractors, in an unhurried manner, with prompts to gauge whether or not the person fully understands what is being said to them (156).

Because of the disease's progressive nature, the type and severity of symptoms will change as a matter of course. That makes it vital that employers meet regularly with employees diagnosed with dementia to assess whether the level of support is adequate and that appropriate reasonable adjustments have been made. This will likely involve carrying out risk assessments at various points. A need for honesty is essential here to support achievable goals for both employer and employee. If available, support from occupational health is helpful to better assess situations for individuals working in a particular environment. On top of this, there should be regular contact with the person's care team, including their GP.

Most jobs require input from a team. At some stage, these confidential conversations with one's manager will need to include other team members a person works with. Again, such discussions should be conducted in an open and non-challenging manner. To some extent, the more people are aware of the potential issues that might arise, and the more knowledgeable they are about how to help support that person, the better the working environment will be for all concerned.

Workers with disabilities are protected by law under the Equality Act 2010. This stipulates that employers must make reasonable adjustments to allow a person to continue working without incurring any drawbacks. Such adjustments may consist of straightforward changes to a person's working environment: moving where the person works to a quieter area, changing a person's hours of work, and so on. Needless to say, all of this needs to be carried out in dialogue with the person who has the diagnosis. The barriers they face are likely to be highly idiosyncratic, so it is vital to fully understand what needs that person has before attempts are made to meet them.

There will come a point when the severity of the problems makes it impossible for that person to continue working. As with many situations connected with dementia, the approach should be informed by how best to honour the individual's dignity. Leaving work is difficult at the best of times, but to have to do so because of an illness is even more of a blow to a person's sense of pride. They are also likely to feel abandoned by their employer and society in general. Their retirement plan may no longer be viable (156). In many cases, it might be possible for some contact to be maintained with their place of work and their colleagues.

Politics of dementia

This section is based on the UK government's policy on dementia. Public Health England promotes a message that encourages healthy living. The essence of the argument is, "what is good for your heart is good for your brain" (159).

In 2016, Public Health England set out guidance on what can be done to help people with dementia, covering all aspects of society.[14] At the population level, they emphasized the need to ensure the built environment was appropriate. A healthy lifestyle was promoted. The need for awareness-raising programmes was also identified for the public and healthcare workers alike. At a community level, there needs to be adequate support so that people can adopt a healthier lifestyle and ensure the provision of networks to help reduce isolation and loneliness. In all, they highlighted the need to ensure adequate mechanisms are in place to help people live well with dementia. At the family and individual levels, the report spotlighted a need to improve communication to ensure that people know what advice and support are available. Again, there was an emphasis on improving general health by promoting a healthy lifestyle and thereby reducing risk factors.

British politics are in somewhat of a turmoil at the moment. Many competing demands are vying for the attention of our politicians. Healthcare is up there, but there seems little hope of any positive change in the state of play on the current political horizon. As a nation, we are focused mostly on matters of national identity and security threats. However, concerns over the National Health Service, particularly mental health services, continue to bubble away in the background.

The political response to a burgeoning problem is often woefully slow in manifesting. However, in the UK, the then Prime Minister, David Cameron, set out his Dementia Challenge in 2012. Within this document, Mr Cameron described dementia as the "quiet crisis . . . that steals lives and tears at the hearts of families." Yet, it is a condition that is "hardly acknowledged" by society at large.[15] However, the steadfast work of national and international organizations, such as the Alzheimer's Society in the UK, continue to work to raise awareness and bring this condition into the global political arena (160). In 2009, Alzheimer's Disease International published a Charter to highlight the need to make Alzheimer's disease a worldwide concern (161). This Charter pushed for heightened awareness of the condition, a need to respect the rights of those diagnosed with it, a recognition of the fundamental role played by families and carers, access to appropriate care, fast and effective treatment, and to continue striving to isolate ways to prevent the disease in the first place.

Given the power wielded by politicians across the globe, arguably, one of their principal roles is to protect the vulnerable (160). Included in this are those diagnosed with dementia in all its forms. There is a concern that the widespread assumption that dementia hits only older adults is clearly wrong. It is essential, therefore, that protected under this umbrella of state care are those who may all too often fall through the net. I am referring to those who are diagnosed with young-onset dementia and those who have an intellectual developmental disorder and are diagnosed with dementia (3, 160).

One should also acknowledge and address the impact of culture here. As with all other aspects of living, the requirements of those with dementia differ according to ethnicity, especially when considering access to appropriate care. There is a need to break down barriers imposed by language, cultural diversity, mistrust, and stereotyping in such cases.

Raising awareness and advocating the rights of people with dementia, as well as their families and carers, can be carried out at a more local level through support groups. The advance of the internet combined with the ubiquitous nature of tablets and smartphones has opened up even further the potential to provide such services. In conjunction with larger organizations, these groups do much to raise the voice of those at the sharp end of dementia.

Some memories survive

Although it might at first appear odd, I want to end this book by talking about a form of memory that is intact in someone with dementia. I have decided to leave talking about it until now because it will help us all better understand the people with dementia with whom we interact. I shall focus on the work of Steven Sabat, an influential writer in the field of dementia.

Sabat was spurred on to write a paper on the role of implicit memory in those with Alzheimer's disease primarily due to the popular misconception that people with dementia do not have any memory of recent events (162). Sabat reported anecdotal evidence that there is the assumption that a person with dementia will not retain any memory of an event that they may have found upsetting. For example, someone saying something that resulted in the person with dementia becoming upset is regrettable, but the assumption is that there would be no long-term repercussions as the person with dementia would have no future recollection of the event or the emotions associated with it.

However, this is clearly not true. There is more to memory than consciously recalling events and the feelings experienced, which we refer to as explicit memory. Indeed, there is an entire field dedicated to studying what is referred to as implicit memories. These are memories that affect our behaviour without us being consciously aware that they are doing so. Of relevance here is the knowledge that a person's experience of an event, and the emotions attached to it, often influence our future actions even though we are not actually aware that it is happening. In fact, if asked about the event, a person may not be able to consciously remember anything about it.

Over the years, there have been many ingenious ways to tap into these unconscious memories. A good example is the use of word-stem completion tasks. Here, people are exposed to a list of words they are instructed to study. Later, a person's memory of items in this list can be assessed. For example, they could be asked to recall as many items as possible in any order. This would give an indication of explicit memory. Alternatively, participants could be presented with a series of word stems which they are instructed to complete with the first word that springs to mind. Lo and behold, the proffered word usually belongs to the list presented previously. For example, a person would more than likely complete the word stem COM___ with COMPUTE if "compute" had been among the words in the previous list rather than alternatives such as "compare."

Studies of people with dementia have shown that implicit memory operates in the same way as everyone else, such that they are not able to explicitly recall words, but performance on tests of implicit memory is influenced in the usual way (163–165). In his paper, Sabat sets out a couple of clear examples of how the memory of an event which cannot be explicitly recalled can still determine how that person behaves. He uses the instance where a father treats one of his children differently, apparently showing enmity because of something they had done, even though he cannot specify what it was. In the other example, he refers to a person with dementia bursting into tears. When asked why they are crying by their carer, they cannot say.

In the case just described, where the father appeared suddenly hostile to his son unless one was aware of the previous incident and its influence on behaviour through implicit memory, their actions might be defined as irrational hostility. In other words, on the surface, there was no rational explanation for his changed behaviour. In fact, the father's response could more accurately be described as "righteous indignation" (162). This is because this son had acted in a way that had undermined his father.

Regarding the person who suddenly bursts into tears for no apparent reason, this behaviour could, on the surface, be taken as an example of the emotional lability characteristic of dementia. However, it could just as easily have been triggered by a cue in the environment that is linked to a previous upsetting or traumatic event, an event that the person has no conscious awareness of but where the implicit memory is still in force.

Sabat talks about the relevance of this for people caring for those with dementia. A greater appreciation of the impact of implicit memory in the lives of those with dementia can only help us understand them with greater clarity. We are all too aware of the accuracy, or inaccuracy, of our conscious memory. Indeed, when asked, this is what people generally talk about when referring to memory. Linked to this is the ingrained belief that such memories fail, with the hidden assumption that this includes all we mean by memory. However, this research shows that other forms of memory are, in fact, intact and actively influence the thoughts and actions of those with dementia.

Understanding this, it is easier to appreciate that a person with dementia is behaving in a way that is rational and intrinsically linked to their personal experience. Easy is probably the wrong word. It is by no means easy to do this. We are all quick to pathologize the behaviour of others. This is described as "malignant positioning" in the case of dementia (166). This quickly escalates into a malignant social psychology (167). It is a short step then to view the person with dementia as an escalating set of increasingly severe symptoms and not as an individual. The person with dementia becomes depersonalized (168). Nonetheless, an appreciation of unconscious processes will help us relate to and more successfully understand and interpret the behaviours of those with dementia.

Linking this to my own work on nostalgia, one of the things we need to determine is how the positive effects of nostalgia are sustained in those with dementia. We know there are short-term benefits, but what about medium- and long-term ones? Although the person with dementia may not have an explicit recollection of previous nostalgic conversations, from the point of view of implicit memory, such experience is likely retained, so one could argue that there are longer-term benefits here. Work on this continues.

Summary

Although there is still no real likelihood of a cure for many different forms of dementia, there is no let-up in our determination to continue the quest. There are many exciting and potential fruitful angles that researchers are currently exploring. It might be the case that we become better at differentiating underlying disease pathways. In doing so, we open up opportunities for different classes of drugs to be used to combat the damage. We are certainly making headway in isolating techniques to identify disease processes much earlier on, thereby improving the chance that interventions will be more effective for longer. There is also the ever-present hope that technological advancements will enable clinicians to individually tailor interventions to maximize the likelihood of success. Technology also presents improvements in management and care, offering greater independence for those diagnosed with dementia, although as we saw, there are many ethical concerns to address. Linked to this is a general awakening to securing personal control over end-of-life issues. There is no consensus on this at the moment, but we need to tackle these issues head-on sooner rather than later. There will always be grey areas, but we owe it to individuals and their families to provide more direction. Throughout this book, I have stressed the importance of dignity for those with dementia. There is no more apparent area where dignity holds centre stage than the feelings around end-of-life care. Embroiled in all this are issues concerning ethics of personhood. In exploring such issues, it is clear that there is much to consider here. We then looked at how dementia care and public understanding of this condition is ultimately determined by government policy. There is no need of a lengthy analysis here to come to the conclusion that what is offered is severely lacking on all levels. I brought this chapter to a conclusion by highlighting the importance of focusing on what survives in those with dementia. Memory is multifaceted, and memories in one form or another remain.

Notes

1 www.nia.nih.gov/health/how-biomarkers-help-diagnose-dementia
2 www.alzheimers.org.uk/get-support/daily-living/exercise/early-middle-dementia
3 www.alzheimers.org.uk/get-support/daily-living/exercise/benefits#content-start
4 www.alzheimers.org.uk/get-support/daily-living/exercise
5 www.theguardian.com/social-care-network/2017/sep/06/care-home-toddlers-nursery
6 www.stmonicatrust.org.uk/
7 This effect is evidenced by improved performance on simple reaction time tasks.
8 This is shown by improved performance on vigilance tasks.
9 www.alzheimers.org.uk/about-us/policy-and-influencing/what-we-think/stem-cell-research
10 www.newscientist.com/article/2210245-experimental-alzheimers-drug-targets-gum-disease-bacteria/

11 www.newscientist.com/article/2191814-we-may-finally-know-what-causes-alzheimers-and-how-to-stop-it/
12 www.mdx.ac.uk/news/2020/09/culturally-competent-robots-could-improve-mental-health-and-loneliness-in-older-people
13 Unfortunately, I cannot find the source of this quote. It is perfect, so whoever proclaimed this first, thank you.
14 www.gov.uk/government/publications/health-matters-midlife-approaches-to-reduce-dementia-risk/health-matters-midlife-approaches-to-reduce-dementia-risk
15 www.gov.uk/government/news/dementia-challenge-launched

References

1   Ryan NS, Rossor MN, Fox NC. Alzheimer's disease in the 100 years since Alzheimer's death. Brain. 2015;138(12):3816–3821.
2   Aleman Aa, Mills At. Our ageing brain: How our mental capacities develop as we grow older. London: Scribe UK; 2014.
3   Christopher G. The psychology of ageing: From mind to society. Basingstoke: Palgrave Macmillan; 2014.
4   Erk S, Spottke A, Meisen A, Wagner M, Walter H, Jessen F. Evidence of neuronal compensation during episodic memory in subjective memory impairment. Arch Gen Psychiatry. 2011;68(8):845–852.
5   Freer R, Sormanni P, Vecchi G, Ciryam P, Dobson CM, Vendruscolo M. A protein homeostasis signature in healthy brains recapitulates tissue vulnerability to Alzheimer's disease. Sci Adv. 2016;2(8):e1600947.
6   Sevigny J, Chiao P, Bussière T, Weinreb PH, Williams L, Maier M, et al. The antibody aducanumab reduces Aβ plaques in Alzheimer's disease. Nature. 2016;537(7618): 50–56.
7   Trivedi B. Food for thought: Eat your way to dementia. New Scientist. 2012; 29 August. Available from: https://www.newscientist.com/article/mg21528805-800-food-for-thought-eat-your-way-to-dementia/.
8   McNay EC, Ong CT, McCrimmon RJ, Cresswell J, Bogan JS, Sherwin RS. Hippocampal memory processes are modulated by insulin and high-fat-induced insulin resistance. Neurobiol Learn Mem. 2010;93(4):546–553.
9   Talbot K, Wang H-Y, Kazi H, Han L-Y, Bakshi KP, Stucky A, et al. Demonstrated brain insulin resistance in Alzheimer's disease patients is associated with IGF-1 resistance, IRS-1 dysregulation, and cognitive decline. J Clin Invest. 2012;122(4):1316.
10 Farris W, Mansourian S, Chang Y, Lindsley L, Eckman EA, Frosch MP, et al. Insulin-degrading enzyme regulates the levels of insulin, amyloid β-protein, and the β-amyloid precursor protein intracellular domain in vivo. Proc Natl Acad Sci U S A. 2003;100(7):4162–4167.
11 Craft S, Baker LD, Montine TJ, Minoshima S, Watson GS, Claxton A, et al. Intranasal insulin therapy for Alzheimer disease and amnestic mild cognitive impairment: A pilot clinical trial. Arch Neurol. 2012;69(1):29–38.
12 Rezaie P, Male D. Mesoglia & microglia—A historical review of the concept of mononuclear phagocytes within the central nervous system. J Hist Neurosci. 2002;11(4):325–374.
13 Nimmerjahn A, Kirchhoff F, Helmchen F. Resting microglial cells are highly dynamic surveillants of brain parenchyma in vivo. Science. 2005;308(5726):1314–1318.

14   Kettenmann H, Kirchhoff F, Verkhratsky A. Microglia: New roles for the synaptic stripper. Neuron. 2013;77(1):10–18.

15   Costandi M. The mind minders: Meet our brain's maintenance workers. New Scientist. 2013, October 9. Available from: https://www.newscientist.com/article/mg22029381-000-the-mind-minders-meet-our-brains-maintenance-workers/.

16   Stephan AH, Madison DV, Mateos JM, Fraser DA, Lovelett EA, Coutellier L, et al. A dramatic increase of C1q protein in the CNS during normal aging. J Neurosci. 2013;33(33):13460–13474.

17   Dantzer R. Cytokine-induced sickness behavior: Mechanisms and implications. Ann. N.Y. Acad. Sci. 2001;933(1):222–234.

18   Perry VH, Holmes C. Microglial priming in neurodegenerative disease. Nat Rev Neurol. 2014;10(4):217–224.

19   Guerreiro R, Wojtas A, Bras J, Carrasquillo M, Rogaeva E, Majounie E, et al. TREM2 variants in Alzheimer's disease. N Engl J Med. 2012;368(2):117–127.

20   Griffin ÉW, Skelly DT, Murray CL, Cunningham C. Cyclooxygenase-1-dependent prostaglandins mediate susceptibility to systemic inflammation-induced acute cognitive dysfunction. J Neurosci. 2013;33(38):15248–15258.

21   Griggs J. Eating your way to dementia. Elsevier; 2013. Available from: https://www.sciencedirect.com/science/article/abs/pii/S0262407913627694.

22   Salthouse TA. Mental exercise and mental aging. Curr Dir Psychol Sci. 2006;13:140–144.

23   Forbes D, Forbes SC, Blake CM, Thiessen EJ, Forbes S. Exercise programs for people with dementia. Cochrane Database Syst Rev. 2015;2015(4):CD006489.

24   Lavie CJ, Church TS, Milani RV, Earnest CP. Impact of physical activity, cardiorespiratory fitness, and exercise training on markers of inflammation. J Cardiopulm Rehabil Prev. 2011;31(3):137–145.

25   Ryan M, McInerney D, Owens D, Collins P, Johnson A, Tomkin G. Diabetes and the Mediterranean diet: A beneficial effect of oleic acid on insulin sensitivity, adipocyte glucose transport and endothelium-dependent vasoreactivity. Qjm. 2000;93(2):85–91.

26   Colcombe SJ, Erickson KI, Raz N, Webb AG, Cohen NJ, McAuley E, et al. Aerobic fitness reduces brain tissue loss in aging humans. J Gerontol A Biol Sci Med Sci. 2003;58(2):176–180.

27   Vaynman S, Ying Z, Gomez-Pinilla F. Hippocampal BDNF mediates the efficacy of exercise on synaptic plasticity and cognition. Eur J Neurosci. 2004;20(10):2580–2590.

28   Erickson KI, Miller DL, Roecklein KA. The aging hippocampus: Interactions between exercise, depression, and BDNF. Neuroscientist. 2012;18(1):82–97.

29   Intlekofer KA, Cotman CW. Exercise counteracts declining hippocampal function in aging and Alzheimer's disease. Neurobiol Dis. 2013;57:47–55.

30   Brown AD, McMorris CA, Longman RS, Leigh R, Hill MD, Friedenreich CM, et al. Effects of cardiorespiratory fitness and cerebral blood flow on cognitive outcomes in older women. Neurobiol Aging. 2010;31(12):2047–2057.

31   Tait JL, Duckham RL, Milte CM, Main LC, Daly RM. Influence of sequential vs. simultaneous dual-task exercise training on cognitive function in older adults. Front Aging Neurosci. 2017;9:368.

32   Salthouse T. Major issues in cognitive aging. Oxford: Oxford University Press; 2010.

33   Tinetti ME, Williams CS. Falls, injuries due to falls, and the risk of admission to a nursing home. N Engl J Med. 1997;337(18):1279–1284.

34   Anstey KJ, Wood J, Lord S, Walker JG. Cognitive, sensory and physical factors enabling driving safety in older adults. Clin Psychol Rev. 2005;25(1):45–65.

35   Ogawa EF, You T, Leveille SG. Potential benefits of exergaming for cognition and dual-task function in older adults: A systematic review. J Aging Phys Act. 2016;24(2):332–336.

36   Bradley DB. A reason to rise each morning: The meaning of volunteering in the lives of older adults. Generations: J Am Soc Aging. 1999;23(4):45–50.

37   Rouse SB, Clawson B. Motives and incentives of older adult volunteers. J Ext. 1992;30(3):1–9.

38   Greenfield EA, Marks NF. Formal volunteering as a protective factor for older adults' psychological well-being. J Gerontol B Psychol Sci Soc Sci. 2004;59(5):S258–S264.

39   Van Willigen M. Differential benefits of volunteering across the life course. J Gerontol B Psychol Sci Soc Sci. 2000;55(5):S308–S318.

40   Jirovec RL, Hyduk CA. Type of volunteer experience and health among older adult volunteers. J Gerontol Soc Work. 1999;30(3–4):29–42.

41   Morrow-Howell N, Hinterlong J, Rozario PA, Tang F. Effects of volunteering on the well-being of older adults. J Gerontol B Psychol Sci Soc Sci. 2003;58(3):S137–S145.

42   Musick MA, Herzog AR, House JS. Volunteering and mortality among older adults: Findings from a national sample. J Gerontol B Psychol Sci Soc Sci. 1999;54(3):S173–S180.

43   Drury L, Abrams D, Swift H. Making intergenerational connections—an evidence review: What are they, why do they matter and how to make more of them. London: Age UK; 2017. Available from www.ageuk.org.uk/Documents/EN . . . .

44   Abrams D, Eilola T, Swift H. Attitudes to age in Britain 2004–8. Department for Work and Pensions (Research Report 599). 2009. Available from: https://www.researchgate.net/publication/265031315_Attitudes_to_age_in_Britain_2004-08.

45   Galbraith B, Larkin H, Moorhouse A, Oomen T. Intergenerational programs for persons with dementia: A scoping review. J Gerontol Soc Work. 2015;58(4):357–378.

46   Jarrott SE, Bruno K. Shared site intergenerational programs: A case study. J Appl Gerontol. 2007;26(3):239–257.

47   George D, Whitehouse C, Whitehouse P. A model of intergenerativity: How the intergenerational school is bringing the generations together to foster collective wisdom and community health. J Intergener Relatsh. 2011;9(4):389–404.

48   Waggoner G. Adopt an elder: Linking youth and the elderly. Act Adapt Aging. 1996;20(1):41–52.

49   O'Rourke KA. Intergenerational programming: Yesterday's memories, today's moments, and tomorrow's hopes. 1999. Available at: https://trace.tennessee.edu/utk_graddiss/2642/.

50   Brownell CA. An intergenerational art program as a means to decrease passive behaviors in patients with dementia. Am J Recreat Ther. 2008;7(3):5–12.

51   Xaverius PK, Mathews RM. Evaluating the impact of intergenerational activities on elders' engagement and expressiveness levels in two settings. J Intergener Relatsh. 2004;1(4):53–69.

52   Brenner T, Brenner K. The Montessori method in dementia care. J Dementia Care. 2012;20(4):18–19.

53   Griff M, Lambert D, Dellmann-Jenkins M, Fruit D. Intergenerational activity analysis with three groups of older adults: Frail, community-living, and Alzheimer's Educ Gerontol. 1996;22(6):601–612.

54   Wren DJ. Reaching out, reaching in. Principal Leadersh. 2004;5(1):28–33.

55   Whitehouse PJ, Whitehouse CC. The intergenerational school: Integrating intergenerational approaches in the care of those with age-related cognitive challenges. Australas J Ageing. 2005;24:S57–S58.

56   Camp CJ, Judge KS, Bye CA, Fox KM, Bowden J, Bell M, et al. An intergenerational program for persons with dementia using Montessori methods. Gerontologist. 1997;37(5):688–692.

57   O'Neil B. The effects of intergenerational programs on individuals with Alzheimer's disease or dementia. Doctoral dissertation, Mount Mary College.

58   Panza F, Solfrizzi V, Barulli M, Bonfiglio C, Guerra V, Osella A, et al. Coffee, tea, and caffeine consumption and prevention of late-life cognitive decline and dementia: A systematic review. J Nutr Health Aging. 2015;19(3):313–328.

59   Lindsay J, Laurin D, Verreault R, Hébert R, Helliwell B, Hill GB, et al. Risk factors for Alzheimer's disease: A prospective analysis from the Canadian Study of Health and Aging. Am J Epidemiol. 2002;156(5):445–453.

60   Fredholm BB, Bättig K, Holmén J, Nehlig A, Zvartau EE. Actions of caffeine in the brain with special reference to factors that contribute to its widespread use. Pharmacol Rev. 1999;51(1):83–133.

61   Prediger RD, Batista LC, Takahashi RN. Caffeine reverses age-related deficits in olfactory discrimination and social recognition memory in rats: Involvement of adenosine A1 and A2A receptors. Neurobiol Aging. 2005;26(6):957–964.

62   Dall'Igna OP, Fett P, Gomes MW, Souza DO, Cunha RA, Lara DR. Caffeine and adenosine A 2a receptor antagonists prevent β-amyloid (25–35)-induced cognitive deficits in mice. Exp Neurol. 2007;203(1):241–245.

63   Costenla AR, Cunha RA, De Mendonça A. Caffeine, adenosine receptors, and synaptic plasticity. J Alzheimers Dis. 2010;20(s1):S25–S34.

64   Cao C, Cirrito JR, Lin X, Wang L, Verges DK, Dickson A, et al. Caffeine suppresses amyloid-β levels in plasma and brain of Alzheimer's disease transgenic mice. J Alzheimers Dis. 2009;17(3):681–697.

65   Arendash G, Schleif W, Rezai-Zadeh K, Jackson E, Zacharia L, Cracchiolo J, et al. Caffeine protects Alzheimer's mice against cognitive impairment and reduces brain β-amyloid production. Neurosci. 2006;142(4):941–952.

66   Johnson-Kozlow M, Kritz-Silverstein D, Barrett-Connor E, Morton D. Coffee consumption and cognitive function among older adults. Am J Epidemiol. 2002;156(9):842–850.

67   Ritchie K, Carrière I, De Mendonca A, Portet F, Dartigues J-F, Rouaud O, et al. The neuroprotective effects of caffeine A prospective population study (the Three City Study). Neurology. 2007;69(6):536–545.

68   Corley J, Jia X, Kyle JA, Gow AJ, Brett CE, Starr JM, et al. Caffeine consumption and cognitive function at age 70: The Lothian Birth Cohort 1936 study. Psychosom Med. 2010;72(2):206–214.

69   Cunha R, Mendonça Ad. Special issue: Therapeutic opportunities for caffeine in Alzheimer's disease and other neurodegenerative disorders. J Alzheimers Dis. 2010;20(Suppl. 1):1–252.

70   Mendonça A, Cunha RA. Concluding remarks. J Alzheimers Dis. 2010;20(S1):249–252.

71   Ritchie K, Artero S, Portet F, Brickman A, Muraskin J, Beanino E, et al. Caffeine, cognitive functioning, and white matter lesions in the elderly: Establishing causality from epidemiological evidence. J Alzheimers Dis. 2010;20(S1):161–166.

72 Duarte JM, Agostinho PM, Carvalho RA, Cunha RA. Caffeine consumption prevents diabetes-induced memory impairment and synaptotoxicity in the hippocampus of NONcZNO10/LTJ mice. PLoS one. 2012;7(4):e21899.
73 Biessels GJ. Caffeine, diabetes, cognition, and dementia. J Alzheimers Dis. 2010;20(S1):143–150.
74 de Valk HW. Magnesium in diabetes mellitus. Neth J Med. 1999;54(4):139–146.
75 Kempf K, Herder C, Erlund I, Kolb H, Martin S, Carstensen M, et al. Effects of coffee consumption on subclinical inflammation and other risk factors for type 2 diabetes: A clinical trial. Am J Clin Nutr. 2010;91(4):950–957.
76 Abreu RV, Silva-Oliveira EM, Moraes MFD, Pereira GS, Moraes-Santos T. Chronic coffee and caffeine ingestion effects on the cognitive function and antioxidant system of rat brains. Pharmacol Biochem Behav. 2011;99(4):659–664.
77 Lucas M, Mirzaei F, Pan A, Okereke OI, Willett WC, O'Reilly ÉJ, et al. Coffee, caffeine, and risk of depression among women. Arch Intern Med. 2011;171(17):1571–1578.
78 Beaudreau SA, O'Hara R. The association of anxiety and depressive symptoms with cognitive performance in community-dwelling older adults. Psychol Aging. 2009;24(2):507.
79 Smith A, Sutherland D, Christopher G. Effects of repeated doses of caffeine on mood and performance of alert and fatigued volunteers. J Psychopharmacol. 2005;19(6):620–626.
80 Stafford LD, Rusted J, Yeomans MR. Caffeine, mood and performance: A selective review. In: Caffeine and the activation theory effects on health and behavior. Boca Raton, FL: CRC Press; 2006, pp. 283–309.
81 Nehlig A. Is caffeine a cognitive enhancer? J Alzheimers Dis. 2010;20(S1):85–94.
82 Herz RS. Caffeine effects on mood and memory. Behav Res Ther. 1999;37(9):869–879.
83 Ng TP, Aung KC, Feng L, Nyunt MS, Yap KB. Tea consumption and physical function in older adults: A cross-sectional study. J Nutr Health Aging. 2014;18(2):161–166.
84 Park SK, Jung IC, Lee WK, Lee YS, Park HK, Go HJ, et al. A combination of green tea extract and L-theanine improves memory and attention in subjects with mild cognitive impairment: A double-blind placebo-controlled study. J Med Food. 2011;14(4):334–343.
85 Solfrizzi V, Capurso C, D'Introno A, Colacicco AM, Santamato A, Ranieri M, et al. Lifestyle-related factors in predementia and dementia syndromes. Expert Rev Neurother. 2008;8(1):133–158.
86 Solfrizzi V, Panza F, Frisardi V, Seripa D, Logroscino G, Imbimbo BP, et al. Diet and Alzheimer's disease risk factors or prevention: The current evidence. Expert Rev Neurother. 2011;11(5):677–708.
87 Panza F, Solfrizzi V, Logroscino G, Maggi S, Santamato A, Seripa D, et al. Current epidemiological approaches to the metabolic-cognitive syndrome. J Alzheimers Dis. 2012;30(Suppl 2):S31–S75.
88 Richard E, Moll van Charante EP, van Gool WA. Vascular risk factors as treatment target to prevent cognitive decline. J Alzheimers Dis. 2012;32(3):733–740.
89 Smith AP, Christopher G, Sutherland D. Acute effects of caffeine on attention: A comparison of non-consumers and withdrawn consumers. J Psychopharmacol. 2013;27(1):77–83.
90 Lopez-Garcia E, Rodriguez-Artalejo F, Rexrode KM, Logroscino G, Hu FB, van Dam RM. Coffee consumption and risk of stroke in women. Circulation. 2009;119(8):1116–1123.

91 Ascherio A, Chen H. Caffeinated clues from epidemiology of Parkinson's disease. Neurology. 2003;61(11 Suppl 6):S51–S54.

92 Beghi E, Pupillo E, Messina P, Giussani G, Chiò A, Zoccolella S, et al. Coffee and amyotrophic lateral sclerosis: A possible preventive role. Am J Epidemiol. 2011;174(9):1002–1008.

93 Barranco Quintana JL, Allam MF, Serrano Del Castillo A, Fernández-Crehuet Navajas R. Alzheimer's disease and coffee: A quantitative review. Neurol Res. 2007;29(1):91–95.

94 Santos C, Costa J, Santos J, Vaz-Carneiro A, Lunet N. Caffeine intake and dementia: Systematic review and meta-analysis. J Alzheimers Dis. 2010;20(Suppl 1):S187–S204.

95 Prediger RD. Effects of caffeine in Parkinson's disease: From neuroprotection to the management of motor and non-motor symptoms. J Alzheimers Dis. 2010;20(Suppl 1):S205–S220.

96 Sharma K, Fallon SJ, Davis T, Ankrett S, Munro G, Christopher G, et al. Caffeine and attentional control: Improved and impaired performance in healthy older adults and Parkinson's disease according to task demands. Psychopharmacology. 2022:1–15.

97 Rottkamp CA, Nunomura A, Raina AK, Sayre LM, Perry G, Smith MA. Oxidative stress, antioxidants, and Alzheimer disease. Alzheimer Dis Assoc Disord. 2000;14(1):S62–S66.

98 Kuehn BM. In Alzheimer research, glucose metabolism moves to center stage. JAMA. 2020;323(4):297–299.

99 Mohammadi D. Brain under siege. New Sci. 2015;226(3027):38–41.

100 Kinney JW, Bemiller SM, Murtishaw AS, Leisgang AM, Salazar AM, Lamb BT. Inflammation as a central mechanism in Alzheimer's disease. Alzheimers Dement (N Y). 2018;4:575–590.

101 Dominy SS, Lynch C, Ermini F, Benedyk M, Marczyk A, Konradi A, et al. *Porphyromonas gingivalis* in Alzheimer's disease brains: Evidence for disease causation and treatment with small-molecule inhibitors. Sci Adv. 2019;5(1):eaau3333.

102 Roberts JS, Christensen KD, Green RC. Using Alzheimer's disease as a model for genetic risk disclosure: Implications for personal genomics. Clin Genet. 2011;80(5):407–414.

103 Mollenkopf H, Hieber A, Wahl H-W. Continuity and change in older adults' perceptions of out-of-home mobility over ten years: A qualitative—Quantitative approach. Ageing Soc. 2011;31(5):782–802.

104 Olsberg D, Winters M. Ageing in place: Intergenerational and intrafamilial housing transfers and shifts in later life. AHURI; 2005. Available from: https://www.ahuri. edu.au/research/final-reports/88.

105 World Health Organization. Global age-friendly cities: A guide. World Health Organization; 2007. Available from: https://apps.who.int/iris/handle/10665/43755.

106 Webber SC, Porter MM, Menec VH. Mobility in older adults: A comprehensive framework. Gerontologist. 2010;50(4):443–450.

107 Metz DH. Mobility of older people and their quality of life. Transp Policy. 2000;7(2):149–152.

108 Musselwhite C, Haddad H. Mobility, accessibility and quality of later life. Qual Ageing. 2010;11(1):25.

109 Banister D, Bowling A. Quality of life for the elderly: The transport dimension. Transp Policy. 2004;11(2):105–115.

110   Rosenbloom S. Sustainability and automobility among the elderly: An international assessment. Transportation. 2001;28(4):375–408.

111   Charlton JL, Oxley J, Fildes B, Oxley P, Newstead S, Koppel S, et al. Characteristics of older drivers who adopt self-regulatory driving behaviours. Transp Res Part F Traffic Psychol Behav. 2006;9(5):363–373.

112   Marottoli RA, de Leon CFM, Glass TA, Williams CS, Cooney LM, Berkman LF. Consequences of driving cessation: Decreased out-of-home activity levels. J Gerontol B Psychol Sci Soc Sci. 2000;55(6):S334–S340.

113   Rosenbloom S. Meeting transportation needs in an aging-friendly community. Generations. 2009;33(2):33–43.

114   McCray T, Brais N. Exploring the role of transportation in fostering social exclusion: The use of GIS to support qualitative data. Netw Spat Econ. 2007;7(4): 397–412.

115   Broome K, McKenna K, Fleming J, Worrall L. Bus use and older people: A literature review applying the person-environment-occupation model in macro practice. Scand J Occup Ther. 2009;16(1):3–12.

116   Zeitler E, Buys L. Mobility and out-of-home activities of older people living in suburban environments: 'Because I'm a driver, I don't have a problem'. Ageing Soc. 2015;35(4):785–808.

117   Binder EF, Storandt M, Birge SJ. The relation between psychometric test performance and physical performance in older adults. J Gerontol A Biol Sci Med Sci. 1999;54(8):M428–M432.

118   Tolea MI, Morris JC, Galvin JE. Trajectory of mobility decline by type of dementia. Alzheimer Dis Assoc Disord. 2016;30(1):60–66.

119   Moretti R, Torre P, Antonello RM, Cazzato G. Behavioral alterations and vascular dementia. Neurologist. 2006;12(1):43–47.

120   Rascovsky K, Salmon DP, Lipton AM, Leverenz JB, DeCarli C, Jagust WJ, et al. Rate of progression differs in frontotemporal dementia and Alzheimer disease. Neurology. 2005;65(3):397–403.

121   Scherder E, Eggermont L, Visscher C, Scheltens P, Swaab D. Understanding higher level gait disturbances in mild dementia in order to improve rehabilitation: 'Last in-first out'. Neurosci Biobehav Rev. 2011;35(3):699–714.

122   Perissinotto CM, Stijacic Cenzer I, Covinsky KE. Loneliness in older persons: A predictor of functional decline and death. Arch Intern Med. 2012;172(14):1078–1083.

123   Teri L, Logsdon RG, McCurry SM. Exercise interventions for dementia and cognitive impairment: The Seattle protocols. J Nutr Health Aging. 2008;12(6):391–394.

124   Joyce K, Loe M. A sociological approach to ageing, technology and health. Sociol Health Illn. 2010;32(2):171–180.

125   Lebrón J, Escalante K, Coppola J, Gaur C, editors. Activity tracker technologies for older adults: Successful adoption via intergenerational telehealth. 2015 Long Island Systems, Applications and Technology: IEEE; 2015. Available from: https://www.researchgate.net/publication/283428622_Activity_tracker_technologies_for_older_adults_Successful_adoption_via_intergenerational_telehealth.

126   Hanson J, Osipovič D, Hinew N, Amaral T, Curry R, Barlow J. Lifestyle monitoring as a predictive tool in telecare. J Telemed Telecare. 2007;13(Suppl 1):26–28.

127   Norman DA. The design of everyday things. London: MIT; 1998.

128   Czaja SJ, Charness N, Fisk AD, Hertzog C, Nair SN, Rogers WA, et al. Factors predicting the use of technology: Findings from the Center for Research and

Education on Aging and Technology Enhancement (CREATE). Psychol Aging. 2006;21(2):333–352.

129   Charness N, Champion M, Yordon R. Designing products for older consumers: A human factors perspective. In: The aging consumer [Internet]. London: Routledge; 2010, pp. 249–268.

130   Coronato A. Pervasive and smart technologies for healthcare: Ubiquitous methodologies and tools: Ubiquitous methodologies and tools. Hershey: Medical Information Science Reference; 2010.

131   Scanaill CN, Carew S, Barralon P, Noury N, Lyons D, Lyons GM. A review of approaches to mobility telemonitoring of the elderly in their living environment. Ann Biomed Eng. 2006;34(4):547–563.

132   Price C. Just checking: Lessons three years on. J Dementia Care. 2009;17(3):12–13.

133   Kenner AM. Securing the elderly body: Dementia, surveillance, and the politics of "aging in place". Surveill Soc. 2008;5(3).

134   Brittain K, Corner L, Robinson L, Bond J. Ageing in place and technologies of place: The lived experience of people with dementia in changing social, physical and technological environments. Sociol Health Illn. 2010;32(2):272–287.

135   Hughes JC, Louw SJ, Sabat SR. Dementia: Mind, meaning, and the person. Oxford: Oxford University Press; 2006.

136   Kontos PC. Embodied selfhood in Alzheimer's disease: Rethinking person-centred care. Dementia. 2005;4(4):553–570.

137   Kitwood TM. Dementia reconsidered: The person comes first. Buckingham: Open University Press; 1997.

138   Taipale V. User perspective and the development of gerontechnology. Gerontechnology. 2008;7(2):218.

139   Hoof JV, Kort HSM, Markopoulos P, Soede M. Ambient intelligence, ethics and privacy. Gerontechnology. 2007;6(3):155–163.

140   Mitchell G, O'Donnell H. The therapeutic use of doll therapy in dementia. Br J Nurs. 2013;22(6):329–334.

141   Minshull K. The impact of doll therapy on well-being of people with dementia-interest in doll therapy is growing but it remains controversial. Here Kimberley Minshull describes how she introduced doll therapy to a dementia assessment ward in Edinburgh. J Dement Care. 2009;17(2):35.

142   Schermer M. Nothing but the truth? On truth and deception in dementia care. Bioethics. 2007;21(1):13–22.

143   James IA, Wood-Mitchell AJ, Waterworth AM, Mackenzie LE, Cunningham J. Lying to people with dementia: Developing ethical guidelines for care settings. Int J Geriatr Psychiatry. 2006;21(8):800–801.

144   Feil N, Altman R. Validation theory and the myth of the therapeutic lie. Am J Alzheimers Dis Other Demen. 2003;19(2):77–78.

145   Kitwood T. The dialectics of dementia: With particular reference to Alzheimer's disease. Ageing Soc. 1990;10(2):177–196.

146   Council NM. The code: Standards of conduct, performance and ethics for nurses and midwives. London: NMC; 2008.

147   Brooker D. What is person-centred care in dementia? Rev Clin Gerontol. 2003;13(3):215–222.

148   Mackenzie L, Wood-Mitchell A, James I. Guidelines on using dolls. J Dementia Care. 2007;15(1):26.

149   Öhman A, Nygård L, Borell L. The vocational situation in cases of memory deficits or younger-onset dementia. Scand J Caring Sci. 2001;15(1):34–43.
150   McNamara G. Dementia and the workplace. Occup Health Wellbeing. 2014;66(5):27.
151   ACAS. Dealing with dementia in the workplace 2015. Available from: www.acas. org.uk/index.aspx?articleid=5429.
152   Williamson T. Dementia: Out of the shadows. London: Alzheimer's Society; 2008.
153   Bentham P, La Fontaine J. Services for younger people with dementia. Psychiatry. 2008;7(2):84–87.
154   Ritchie L, Banks P, Danson M, Tolson D, Borrowman F. Dementia in the workplace: A review. J Public Ment Health. 2015;14(1):24–34.
155   Chaplin R, Davidson I. What are the experiences of people with dementia in employment? Dementia. 2016;15(2):147–161.
156   Alzheimer's Society. Creating a dementia-friendly workplace: A practical guide for employers. Alzheimer's Society; 2015. Available from: https://www.alzheimers.org. uk/sites/default/files/migrate/downloads/creating_a_dementia-friendly_workplace. pdf.
157   Alzheimer's Society. Making organisations more dementia-friendly. Available from: www.alzheimers.org.uk/info/20116/making_organisations_more_dementia-friendly.
158   UK C. The state of caring; 2013. Available from: https://www.adass.org.uk/adassme-dia/stories/Carers/State_of_caring_report_PDF_version.pdf.
159   England PH. Dementia: Applying all our health: GOV.UK; 2018. Available from: www.gov.uk/government/publications/dementia-applying-all-our-health/dementia-applying-all-our-health.
160   Hughes JC. Alzheimer's and other dementias. Oxford: Oxford University Press; 2011.
161   Prince M, Jackson J. World Alzheimer report 2009. London: Alzheimer's Disease International; 2009.
162   Sabat SR. Implicit memory and people with Alzheimer's disease: Implication for caregiving. Am J Alzheimers Dis Other Demen. 2006;21(1):11–14.
163   Howard DV. Implicit memory: An expanding picture of cognitive aging. Annu Rev Gerontol Geriatr. 1991;11:1–22.
164   Dick MB, Kean M-L, Sands D. Memory for internally generated words in Alzheimer-type dementia: Breakdown in encoding and semantic memory. Brain Cogn. 1989;9(1):88–108.
165   Randolph C, Tierney MC, Chase TN. Implicit memory in Alzheimer's disease. J Clin Exp Neuropsychol. 1995;17(3):343–351.
166   Sabat SR, Napolitano L, Fath H. Barriers to the construction of a valued social identity: A case study of Alzheimer's disease. Am J Alzheimers Dis Other Demen. 2004;19(3):177–185.
167   Kitwood T. Toward a theory of dementia care: Ethics and interaction. J Clin Ethics. 1998;9(1):23–34.
168   Sabat SR. Excess disability and malignant social psychology: A case study of Alzheimer's disease. J Community Appl Soc Psychol. 1994;4(3):157–166.

Chapter 12

Postlude

COVID-19

It would be remiss of me not to acknowledge the crisis that is enveloping the world as I type. I am referring to the COVID-19 pandemic. Since December 2019, the world has been in the grip of a deadly virus, severe acute respiratory syndrome coronavirus 2 (SARS-CoV-2). There is not one person alive that has gone unscathed by this outbreak. Governments across the world have sanctioned extraordinary restrictions on their people to slow down the spread of the virus and limit its impact. Social distancing has been the norm—although I prefer the phrase physical distancing—where people are required to maintain a distance of 2 m away from one another. Mass quarantining of those exposed to the virus was in operation, as well as self-isolation for those who remained physically healthy. Sanctions were imposed about when it was appropriate for people to leave their homes, restricting movement for all non-essential activities.

It is perhaps not melodramatic to say that we now inhabit a post-COVID world, although this is not entirely accurate as COVID-19 still continues to rampage. I am referring here to the world that has to now take seriously the need to be vigilant to future outbreaks and have the capacity to respond quickly and appropriately. Our pre-COVID assumptions and expectations need revising. Of particular relevance to this book is the impact of the coronavirus on care and research. Healthcare at all levels has been affected. Treatment for non-COVID-related conditions has been delayed due to a lack of resources, not least the over-crowding of hospitals. This resulted in significant numbers of unnecessary deaths. Face-to-face care was restricted and, in many cases, suspended indefinitely. It is a true testament to human ingenuity that the caring professions met these challenges head-on and achieved exemplary solutions. Technology has helped bridge the gap, but more prosaic workarounds were enacted since this was not an option for everyone. For example, music therapy was delivered in the grounds of care homes, with the residents participating behind the windows of such residences during lockdown. Regarding research, many of my colleagues sought alternatives to face-to-face data gathering. For many, however, such a shift was not possible. Many funding calls were suspended, with a great deal of money being set aside

DOI:10.4324/9781315681580-12

for COVID-related research projects. As a researcher, I cannot see a return to my pre-COVID conceptions of how I go about work. Instead, I am trying to forge ahead to ensure that the research I do is achievable in a post-C-19 environment and is, in effect, futureproofed.

I have trawled through some of the literature published since these events shook the world. Much outstanding research is ongoing, so I have selected only a snippet of what is there. Before looking at some of the ongoing research, I would like to start by looking at how this pandemic has affected people with dementia as well as their family and friends. I have primarily focused on what has been happening within the UK. However, I shall start by describing the virus itself.

Neurological symptoms of COVID-19

It became apparent after some time that COVID-19 affected not only the respiratory tract and lungs but also the nervous system and brain (1). It has long been known that coronaviruses can be neuro-invasive and that their presence in the central nervous system can persist (2). Around a third of COVID patients experience cognitive impairment, movement disorder, inflammation of the brain, and stroke (3). It is unclear at this stage whether these effects are the result of a direct impact of the virus on the nervous system or if, instead, they are due to the body's inflammatory responses to the virus (1).

Good practice for dementia

I shall begin by considering some of the difficulties people with dementia faced during this crisis. I have drawn on the Good Practice Guide developed by the British Geriatrics Society.[1] This guide, developed by the National Clinical Director for Dementia at NHS England, Alistair Burns, draws attention to the following. To begin with, someone with dementia is at risk of experiencing delirium if they develop an infection, so healthcare staff must be aware of a person's diagnosis. In the case of COVID-19, a major symptom is a lack of oxygen, called hypoxia. Hypoxia causes delirium (4). Hospital admission should be avoided because of the additional confusion this will cause, especially since many hospitals are overrun with COVID cases, and staff shielded behind personal protective equipment (PPE). When admission is necessary, staff should take extra care and allocate more time to help assuage any concerns the person with dementia is experiencing. Due to the complex and ever-changing advice around what we can do to protect ourselves, it is necessary that this information is presented in an accessible way and repeated regularly. Due to language impairment, a person with dementia often finds it difficult to express how they feel. So, in the case of COVID-19, the need to look at behavioural signs of discomfort is even more vital. Chest infections are also common due to difficulty swallowing. This should be monitored and, where indicated, a swallowing assessment performed.

It has been reported that, in England and Wales, a quarter of all deaths that have been related to COVID-19 consist of those with dementia. This figure is substantially higher for those in care.[2] Of course, these figures are only indicative and are likely to change considerably over the coming months. There is a concern that people with dementia have and will continue to experience even greater hardships during this time. Triaging of COVID-19 patients has often been based on age or medical condition, although how treatment decisions have been made is far from transparent. The result has been that many with dementia have been denied treatment.[3] An insightful and disturbing account of the state of play in Britain during the height of the pandemic is provided by Calvert and Arbuthnott (5).

There have been genuinely worrying statistics reported about the rise in deaths from dementia since the pandemic first hit. People with dementia are a particularly vulnerable group and are at extreme risk of contracting the virus, especially when considering that many people with dementia also have comorbid health conditions, which heightens the risk of contracting the virus.[4] It also appears to be the case that those who carry the ApoEε4/ε4 genotype—the most significant genetic-based risk factor for Alzheimer's disease—are more susceptible to developing complications from COVID-19 (6). Stroke can also occur in those with a severe presentation of the virus. This can then exacerbate cognitive deterioration (7).

On top of that are the emotional effects of being isolated. This has become a real issue for those in care homes during lockdowns: family members were not able to visit, and group activities with other residents halted (4). In some cases, confusion became more pronounced, standard eating patterns disrupted, and communication increasingly restricted.[5] In a recent study, just under a third of people with dementia showed significant deterioration during the first month of lockdown. Around half experienced intensified agitation, increased apathy, and more severe depression (8).

There were urgent calls to introduce regular screening for care home staff and residents so that restrictions on who can visit could be loosened. Under these conditions, care home staff need access to sufficient stocks of PPE, as well as effective training on infection control and prevention. Comprehensive testing procedures need to be in place. Homes need access to appropriate quarantine facilities to prevent the spread of the virus from those infected. When a person with dementia is admitted to the hospital, there should be appropriate stepdown facilities so that care can be provided to those who are sufficiently stable to be discharged from intensive care. Underpinning all levels of care for those with dementia should be compassion and a focus on person-centred approaches. This will help mitigate the psychological impact of isolation and confinement (9). However, this was just not possible given the resources allocated across the sector. For those living with dementia in their own homes, in most cases, their primary carer is a spouse or family member who is potentially at high risk from the virus due to underlying health conditions.

The role of technology

Technology offers several ways to supplement and support care during situations such as the current pandemic. Telecare helped minimize the risk of people being exposed to the virus by providing services in the home. This was especially pertinent for those at significant risk of infection (10).

There is a growing interest in supplying telecare through a person's television rather than through mobile devices. Televisions are a fixture in the majority of homes. One such study offered support that included the latest guidance on COVID-19 on top of content concerning physical and mental health, mental stimulation, and maintaining social connections. This informational content was presented as videos and interactive games. Videocalls with family, friends, and health professionals were also proffered (11). It is perhaps too early to gauge whether such systems worked during a lockdown. Indeed, with interviews restricted to telephone calls, there is only so much a researcher can reasonably ask a person to do under such situations without running the risk of overloading volunteers.

Because future outbreaks of COVID-19 cannot be ruled out, clinicians are increasingly turning to digital technology to ensure a minimum standard of care for various patient groups, including those with cognitive impairment (12). Although digital technology is limited in its scope when considering neurological examination, it can offer an efficient way to evaluate activities of daily living and general cognitive functioning (13). This technology can support carers by making available psycho-educational programmes to improve knowledge, thereby improving competence (14).

Although technology can do many wonderful things, there are several things to consider. With the current COVID situation, most of us are acutely aware of the vagaries of videoconferencing software: the frozen screen, speaking when muted, complete broadband meltdown. Having a state-of-the-art device is all very good if you are in an area with excellent signal coverage. On a more personal level is the individual's familiarity with various technologies. A cognitive assessment requires the individual to be calm and free from distractions. That will not occur if they have a device constantly dropping in and out of connection and confidence in using the device is low. There is also the ethical issue regarding whether the system is GDPR (General Data Protection Regulation) compliant.

The promise of assistive robotic care is much in the news. One recent example was an article in *The Guardian* with the headline, "Robots to be used in UK care homes to help reduce loneliness."[6] The article focuses on the positive effects of robots in reducing loneliness and improving mental health. Although the message is clear that assistive robotic care is there to support and not replace staff, broader issues need resolving. Prominent in our collective minds is the fundamental need to maintain contact with family and friends, especially during this time of crisis. Such human contact is undoubtedly the priority. I would like to be clear about my own position here regarding technology. I am in no sense against the use of technology of all kinds to supplement care—indeed, there is much evidence to support its efficacy—I just feel the emphasis should be on helping family and friends maintain vital connections. Technology can help with this, but it is far from the solution. At the same time, I am mindful that much needs to be done to relieve the increased pressure placed on care home staff who had to work with ever-changing restrictions on what was and what was not acceptable practice during COVID, especially since the virus is still with us, and pandemics are predicted to be a permanent fixture. In this sense, robots could help bridge the gap between interactions with a human carer. So, I am arguing that central to this debate should be the physical and emotional needs of the person. This can only be provided by the excellent staff who work in the caring sector whose emotional and physical needs also need to be met to stem the tide of burnout experienced.

Ageist assumptions

As a gerontologist, I have been concerned with some assumptions underpinning policies rolled out by different governing bodies. On 20 March 2020, in a statement from the President and Members of the National Executive Committee of the British Society of Gerontology—among which I am proud to count myself— we asked that the British Government stop implementing policy based on the simple application of chronological age.[7] By doing so, individual rights and freedoms are unduly restricted. At the time, the concern was that people would be asked to self-isolate based solely on their age. Just because someone is over the age of 70 does not necessarily follow that they are vulnerable. This, to some extent, perpetuates the myth that all older adults are a burden and fails to reflect their many active roles in society.

Emotional toll

The nature of the threat and the restrictions imposed on our movements have adversely affected psychological well-being. All sense of normality was taken away from us in one fell swoop. Instead, we were thrust into a dystopian reality where people wear masks, keep at regimented safe distances from others, avoid physical contact, face food shortages, and inhabit a digitally mediated world. We are consumed by an intoxicating miasma of dread.

> O Death in Life, the days that are no more.
>
> (Tennyson, 1809–1892, The Princess)

Not surprisingly, levels of anxiety and depression increased with the prospect of extended lockdown periods (15, 16). The lockdowns have been especially strict for older adults, and the emotional fallout has been severe (17). As we have seen, depression can exacerbate cognitive decline (18, 19).

During a crisis of this magnitude, all sectors of society need to feel a sense of cohesion, of being connected to others, independent of age and race. Failure to do so can only lead to social isolation and feelings of loneliness. Sadly, this has been borne out in recent surveys (20). Although such states are explicitly linked to older adults, it is crucial to note loneliness and isolation affect all age groups.[8] The risk appears to be highest for those aged between 16 and 24.[9] Loneliness and isolation are not only experienced when a person is apart from others but can occur when a person is surrounded by others. This is a situation I referred to in a previous section when talking about existential loneliness. We know that such beliefs and feelings help bolster people against negative moods. Feeling part of something bigger gives people a sense of purpose, perceiving that their life has meaning. Because of its endemic nature, there is much to be done at all levels of society to improve feelings of connectedness and support for everyone regardless of their age, gender, ethnicity and race, sexual orientation, disability, socioeconomic status, and marital status. In particular, the pivotal work carried out by charities and other Voluntary Community and Social Enterprise (VCSEs) warrant additional support at times such as these.

Underlying many of the policies linked to COVID was the erroneous assumption that people will be living with someone who can advocate on their behalf should they become sick. The reality of the situation do not bear this out. Many live alone, with no one able to immediately act on their behalf should they need it. With COVID restrictions, older adults were encouraged to self-isolate, further shutting them off from society.

The experience for residents in care homes was also scarred by severe restrictions. At the start, the measures in place failed to consider the need for family and friends to maintain contact with residents. In some cases, this led to extreme actions on behalf of relatives.[10] People protested, declaiming an infringement of a person's liberty.[11]

Death is inevitably especially prominent in our minds at this time. Before moving on, we should take time to consider that many during lockdown spent their final hours on their own, without family and friends present to provide comfort. For many, the first wave of this pandemic was harrowing. When facilitated, many bid their final farewells via a video call. The emotional cost to those whose lives sadly came to an end and those who were not able to be present at that time is beyond measure.

Digital divide

We have always looked to technology to facilitate our lives. No more so than during lockdown. Video conferencing has been embraced by the nation. For many, it offers a way to keep in contact with friends and family, albeit in a disembodied manner. However, with this rapid embracing of alternative forms of communication comes a realization of the stark differences in access to the essential. The digital divide has become even more apparent. In April 2020, *The Guardian* reported that just under two million households do not have access to the internet. On top of that, over 20 million rely on pay-as-you-go mobile services.[12] Not everyone can afford Wi-Fi. The most affected were those with disabilities, women, and people over 75. With the growing shift to online healthcare and education during this time, the financial implications for a large proportion of the UK population are dire. Because of this, low-income households and vast swathes of vulnerable individuals found themselves excluded from these benefits and increasingly isolated. Many homes faced the dilemma of buying food or topping-up their pay-as-you-go accounts. Even if someone does have access to an appropriate device, they may not have sufficient privacy to seek online support,[13] such as those who experience domestic abuse.[14]

Digital literacy is another growing concern. With more services being offered online, the assumption is that the service user has sufficient digital savvy to go online and register for services, access resources, and so on and so forth. The norm is to engage with chatbots or live online chats with customer service representatives. Recent figures indicate that over ten million people living in the UK have limited or no digital skills.[15] It is not just digital literacy but literacy, in general, that is problematic for many. One in six adults living in England and Northern Ireland show poor literacy. Just under one million are not able to speak English or not able to do so well.[16,17] Over a million in England find digital content challenging to engage with due to a learning disability.[18]

Some of the most coherent responses came from countries that had been hit previously by SARS. This was because they were aware that this would not be a one-off event and that it was highly probable that they would be faced with something similar in the future. In countries such as Singapore and Taiwan, contact tracing apps were available early on and served to restrict the spread of the virus (21).

We experienced successive waves of COVID-19 and exposure to increasing variants. Such events will continue to occur. A solution to the digital divide is required before this happens again.[19] Although companies donated old technology[20] and digital skills training were on offer,[21] more needs to be done to ensure care providers have an accurate understanding of the needs of different communities and that they can offer an integrated system of care.[22] I urge you to read the excellent briefing published by the *Centre for Ageing Better*.[23]

Final comment

Throughout the ongoing crisis, the desire to provide care that is sensitive to the needs of the person with dementia and complies with COVID restrictions has been one of the biggest challenges. By trying to meet the demands of the COVID situation head-on, many of these needs were not met. We saw the suspension of elective procedures to help hospitals reallocate resources to treat patients with the virus. Many with complex health needs have not received the support they require. At the outset, an already fragile healthcare system has fragmented under stress. Those deemed under the highest risk—frail, older adults with chronic conditions—have had to endure extended periods of self-isolation. Routine care for these individuals, among many others, was disrupted. On top of this was the impact of being socially isolated and confined to a sedentary existence, with the repercussion of this likely to be long-term.

When we consider those with dementia under these conditions, there have been reports of a decline in cognitive and functional capacities. Behavioural and psychological symptoms have worsened, with increased agitation, aggression, depression, and sleep disturbances (4, 22). In many cases, formal care services were unavailable, increasing further the demand for informal carers.

Because those with dementia are particularly affected by this virus, going forward, more needs to be done to protect their physical health and mental well-being (23). Preserving dignity should be at the top of the agenda. We have seen policies that are inherently ageist driving decision-making, with the result that older adults and those with dementia have failed to receive adequate care.

To ensure this, governments need to secure sufficient funds so that those with dementia are adequately supported and that humane mechanisms are in place to guarantee contact with family and friends. The existential threat experienced by those with this condition will only be heightened if they do not receive the level of emotional support they crave and deserve. Policies must be not only driven by scientific discoveries but also individual rights need to be at their core. This is a tall order. Not only do we need to deal with the immediate effects on COVID-19, but many will face long-term challenges that will be part of the lasting legacy of this pandemic. I shall leave the final word to Wordsworth as this single line of poetry sums up what has happened to so many during these times.

A deep distress hath humanised my Soul.
(Wordsworth, 1770–1850, Elegiac Stanzas Suggested by a Picture of Peele
Castle in a Storm, Painted by Sir George Beaumont)

Notes

1 www.bgs.org.uk/resources/covid-19-dementia-and-cognitive-impairment
2 www.theguardian.com/world/2020/sep/01/quarter-covid-victims-england-wales-have-dementia-study
3 www.theguardian.com/world/2020/sep/01/quarter-covid-victims-england-wales-have-dementia-study
4 www.bgs.org.uk/resources/covid-19-dementia-and-cognitive-impairment
5 www.theguardian.com/world/2020/jun/05/covid-19-causing-10000-dementia-deaths-beyond-infections-research-says
6 www.theguardian.com/society/2020/sep/07/robots-used-uk-care-homes-help-reduce-loneliness?CMP=Share_AndroidApp_Other
7 www.britishgerontology.org/publications/bsg-statements-on-covid-19/statement-one
8 www.britishgerontology.org/publications/bsg-statements-on-covid-19/statement-one
9 www.ons.gov.uk/peoplepopulationandcommunity/wellbeing/articles/lonelinesswhatcharacteristicsandcircumstancesareassociatedwithfeelinglonely/2018-04-10#who-is-lonely-more-often
10 www.theguardian.com/commentisfree/2020/may/10/how-did-we-end-up-turning-our-care-homes into jails of enforced loneliness

11 https://theconversation.com/covid-19-stigma-and-the-scandalous-neglect-of-people-living-with-dementia-140817
12 www.theguardian.com/world/2020/apr/28/digital-divide-isolates-and-endangers-millions-of-uk-poorest
13 https://blogs.bmj.com/bmj/2020/09/01/covid-19-is-magnifying-the-digital-divide/
14 www.techvsabuse.info/research-findings
15 www.ons.gov.uk/peoplepopulationandcommunity/householdcharacteristics/homeinternetandsocialmediausage/articles/exploringtheuksdigitaldivide/2019-03-04
16 www.oecd.org/skills/piaac/Country%20note%20-%20United%20Kingdom.pdf
17 www.ons.gov.uk/peoplepopulationandcommunity/culturalidentity/language/articles/detailedanalysisenglishlanguageproficiencyinenglandandwales/2013-08-30#variations-in-general-health-by-english-language-proficiency
18 www.mencap.org.uk/learning-disability-explained/research-and-statistics/how-common-learning-disability
19 www.cam.ac.uk/stories/digitaldivide
20 https://futuredotnow.uk/devicesdotnow/
21 www.onlinecentresnetwork.org/
22 https://blogs.bmj.com/bmj/2020/09/01/covid-19-is-magnifying-the-digital-divide/
23 https://ageing-better.org.uk/sites/default/files/2020-08/landscape-covid-19-digital.pdf

References

1 Tousi B. Dementia care in the time of COVID-19 pandemic. J Alzheimers Dis. 2020;76(2):475–479.
2 Arbour N, Day R, Newcombe J, Talbot PJ. Neuroinvasion by human respiratory coronaviruses. J Virol. 2000;74(19):8913–8921.
3 Mao L, Wang M, Chen S, He Q, Chang J, Hong C, et al. Neurological manifestations of hospitalized patients with COVID-19 in Wuhan, China: A retrospective case series study. MedRxiv; 2020. Available from: https://www.medrxiv.org/content/10.1101/2020.02.22.20026500v1.
4 Wang H, Li T, Barbarino P, Gauthier S, Brodaty H, Molinuevo JL, et al. Dementia care during COVID-19. Lancet. 2020;395(10231):1190–1191.
5 Calvert J, Arbuthnott G. Failures of state: The inside story of Britain's battle with coronavirus. London: HarperCollins Publishers; 2021.
6 Kuo C-L, Pilling LC, Atkins JL, Masoli JA, Delgado J, Kuchel GA, et al. APOE e4 genotype predicts severe COVID-19 in the UK Biobank community cohort. J Gerontol A Biol Sci Med Sci. 2020;75(11):2231–2232.
7 Mao L, Jin H, Wang M, Hu Y, Chen S, He Q, et al. Neurologic manifestations of hospitalized patients with coronavirus disease 2019 in Wuhan, China. JAMA Neurol. 2020;77(6):683–690.
8 Canevelli M, Valletta M, Blasi MT, Remoli G, Sarti G, Nuti F, et al. Facing dementia during the COVID-19 outbreak. J Am Geriatr Soc. 2020;68:1673–1676.
9 Suarez Gonzalez A, Comas-Herrera A, Livingston G. Impact of COVID-19 on people living with dementia: Emerging international evidence. BMJ. 2020;369:m2463.
10 Smith AC, Thomas E, Snoswell CL, Haydon H, Mehrotra A, Clemensen J, et al. Telehealth for global emergencies: Implications for coronavirus disease 2019 (COVID-19). J Telemed Telecare. 2020;26(5):309–313.
11 Goodman-Casanova JM, Dura-Perez E, Guzman-Parra J, Cuesta-Vargas A, Mayoral-Cleries F. Telehealth home support during COVID-19 confinement for

community-dwelling older adults with mild cognitive impairment or mild dementia: Survey study. J Med Internet Res. 2020;22(5):e19434.

12 Cuffaro L, Di Lorenzo F, Bonavita S, Tedeschi G, Leocani L, Lavorgna L. Dementia care and COVID-19 pandemic: A necessary digital revolution. Neurol Sci. 2020;41(8):1977–1979.

13 Kim H, Jhoo JH, Jang J-W. The effect of telemedicine on cognitive decline in patients with dementia. J Telemed Telecare. 2017;23(1):149–154.

14 Godwin KM, Mills WL, Anderson JA, Kunik ME. Technology-driven interventions for caregivers of persons with dementia: A systematic review. Am J Alzheimers Dis Other Demen. 2013;28(3):216–222.

15 Ahmed MZ, Ahmed O, Aibao Z, Hanbin S, Siyu L, Ahmad A. Epidemic of COVID-19 in China and associated psychological problems. Asian J Psychiatr. 2020;51:102092.

16 Meda N, Pardini S, Slongo I, Bodini L, Rigobello P, Visioli F, et al. COVID-19 and depressive symptoms in students before and during lockdown. MedRxiv. 2020. Available from: https://www.medrxiv.org/content/10.1101/2020.04.27.20081695v1.

17 Yang Y, Li W, Zhang Q, Zhang L, Cheung T, Xiang Y-T. Mental health services for older adults in China during the COVID-19 outbreak. Lancet Psychiatry. 2020;7(4):e19.

18 Geerlings MI, Bouter L, Schoevers R, Beekman A, Jonker C, Deeg D, et al. Depression and risk of cognitive decline and Alzheimer's disease: Results of two prospective community-based studies in the Netherlands. Br J Psychiatry. 2000;176(6):568–575.

19 Sachs-Ericsson N, Joiner T, Plant EA, Blazer DG. The influence of depression on cognitive decline in community-dwelling elderly persons. Am J Geriatr Psychiatry. 2005;13(5):402–408.

20 Ganesan B, Al-Jumaily A, Fong KN, Prasad P, Meena SK, Tong RK-Y. Impact of coronavirus disease 2019 (COVID-19) outbreak quarantine, isolation, and lockdown policies on mental health and suicide. Front Psychiatry. 2021;12.

21 Watts G. COVID-19 and the digital divide in the UK. Lancet Digit Health. 2020;2(8):e395–e396.

22 Canevelli M, Bruno G, Cesari M. Providing simultaneous COVID-19—sensitive and dementia-sensitive care as we transition from crisis care to ongoing care. J Am Med Dir Assoc. 2020;21(7):968.

23 Docherty AB, Harrison EM, Green CA, Hardwick H, Pius R, Norman L, et al. Features of 16,749 hospitalised UK patients with COVID-19 using the ISARIC WHO clinical characterisation protocol. MedRxiv. 2020. Available from: https://www.medrxiv.org/content/10.1101/2020.04.23.20076042v1.

Index

For Product Safety Concerns and Information please contact our EU
representative GPSR@taylorandfrancis.com
Taylor & Francis Verlag GmbH, Kaufingerstraße 24, 80331 München, Germany